Artificial Intelligence in Neurobiology and Neurologic Diseases

Artificial Intelligence in Neurobiology and Neurologic Diseases

Editors

Wu Qiu
Hulin Kuang

MDPI Basel • Beijing • Wuhan • Barcelona • Belgrade • Novi Sad • Cluj • Manchester

Editors
Wu Qiu
Huazhong University of Science and Technology
Wuhan
China

Hulin Kuang
Central South University
Changsha
China

Editorial Office
MDPI AG
Grosspeteranlage 5
4052 Basel, Switzerland

This is a reprint of articles from the Special Issue published online in the open access journal *Biomedicines* (ISSN 2227-9059) (available at: https://www.mdpi.com/journal/biomedicines/special_issues/PMS5L2548K).

For citation purposes, cite each article independently as indicated on the article page online and as indicated below:

Lastname, A.A.; Lastname, B.B. Article Title. *Journal Name* **Year**, *Volume Number*, Page Range.

ISBN 978-3-7258-1819-8 (Hbk)
ISBN 978-3-7258-1820-4 (PDF)
doi.org/10.3390/books978-3-7258-1820-4

Contents

About the Editors

Wu Qiu

Wu Qiu is a professor at the School of Life Sciences and Technology and the Department of Biomedical Engineering at Huazhong University of Science and Technology. He received a national high-level young talent award in 2022. He has worked as a research scientist in the Department of Radiology and the Department of Clinical Neuroscience at the University of Calgary in Canada and at Robarts Research Institute, Western University, Canada. He is mainly engaged in medical imaging using machine learning and artificial intelligence, including computer-aided diagnosis, 3D ultrasound imaging, multimodality-imaging-guided intervention, etc. He has published more than 100 peer reviewed papers in top journals and conferences, such as IEEE Trans. Medical Imaging, Medical Image Analysis, Radiology, Nature Communication, Stroke, CVPR, MICCAI, etc.

Hulin Kuang

Dr. Hulin Kuang received his Ph.D. degree from the City University of Hong Kong in 2016 and was a Postdoctoral Fellow with the Department of Clinical Neurosciences, University of Calgary, Canada, from 2017 to 2020. Now, he is a distinguished associate professor with the School of Computer Science and Engineering, Central South University, China. His research interests include medical image analysis, intelligent disease diagnosis and prognosis, deep learning, and intelligent transportation systems.

biomedicines

MDPI

Editorial

A Glimpse into the AI-Driven Advances in Neurobiology and Neurologic Diseases

Wu Qiu [1] and Hulin Kuang [2,*]

[1] School of Life Science and Technology, Huazhong University of Science and Technology, Wuhan 430074, China; wuqiu@hust.edu.cn
[2] Hunan Provincial Key Lab on Bioinformatics, School of Computer Science and Engineering, Central South University, Changsha 410083, China
* Correspondence: hulinkuang@csu.edu.cn

Citation: Qiu, W.; Kuang, H. A Glimpse into the AI-Driven Advances in Neurobiology and Neurologic Diseases. *Biomedicines* **2024**, *12*, 1221. https://doi.org/10.3390/biomedicines12061221

Received: 9 May 2024
Accepted: 24 May 2024
Published: 31 May 2024

Recent developments in AI, especially in machine learning and deep learning, have opened new avenues for research and clinical practice in neurology. These technologies have demonstrated remarkable proficiency in analyzing complex datasets, identifying patterns that elude human observers, and offering insights into the intricate mechanisms of neurologic diseases. From enhancing diagnostic accuracy to personalizing treatment protocols, AI's impact is both profound and far-reaching.

This Special Issue has sought to highlight the significant strides made in the application of AI across various aspects of neurobiology and neurological diseases. It has brought novel methodologies to light, explored the therapeutic potential of AI-driven interventions, and showcased innovative research that leverages AI to tackle longstanding challenges in the field.

The ten papers included in this Special Issue collectively contribute to the rapidly evolving field of AI in neurobiology and neurological diseases, highlighting diverse applications of AI technologies ranging from diagnosis to treatment and prevention strategies. Key themes and findings from the papers include the following:

Advanced Diagnostic Techniques: Several studies present AI-driven methods for enhancing diagnostic accuracy in neurology. For example, novel CNN models are used for the identification of ischemic regions in stroke patients [1] and the prediction of the histologic grades of meningiomas from MRI scans [2]. These approaches significantly improve upon traditional methods by leveraging the subtle patterns in medical imaging data that are often undetectable to human observers.

Enhanced Predictive Models: Some papers introduce machine learning techniques to forecast disease progression, such as the development of dementia and epilepsy [3]. By analyzing large datasets and utilizing sophisticated algorithms like SVMs and deep learning, these studies offer predictive models that potentially enable earlier and more accurate interventions.

Therapeutic Applications and Treatment Planning: AI is shown to support therapeutic planning and intervention strategies. One study, for instance, explores how AI can guide the administration of treatments in real time by accurately scoring collateral circulation in stroke patients using hybrid CNN and transformer networks [4].

Automated Systems for Clinical Efficiency: Several papers discuss the role of AI in automating clinical processes such as activity recognition in epileptic patients and the detection of neurological abnormalities. These automated systems are designed to enhance clinical efficiency and patient monitoring [5,6].

Neurological Mechanisms and Disease Biomarkers: AI's role extends beyond clinical applications into fundamental research, where it helps elucidate underlying disease mechanisms and identify novel biomarkers. This is evident in studies that use AI to analyze EEG patterns and neuroimaging data to gain deeper insights into brain function and disorders [7,8].

This Special Issue marks a significant step forward in our journey toward harnessing the full potential of AI in neurobiology and neurological diseases. There is a need to further refine AI models to increase their accuracy, reliability, and applicability across different populations and disease states. This includes improving the interpretability of AI models to better understand the biological underpinnings of their predictions, integrating multimodal data sources (e.g., imaging, genetic, and clinical data) for comprehensive disease profiling, and exploring the potential of AI in predicting disease onset and progression, as well as response to treatment.

The exploration of AI's capabilities in neurology is just beginning. Future research should focus on refining AI algorithms for broader clinical application, developing interoperable systems that can seamlessly integrate with existing healthcare infrastructure, and exploring the ethical implications of AI in patient care. With these efforts, AI holds the promise of significantly transforming neurobiology and the management of neurological diseases. As we continue to explore this frontier, our collective efforts should be guided by a commitment to improving patient care, advancing scientific understanding, and addressing the ethical considerations that accompany the integration of AI into healthcare. The path ahead is both challenging and promising, beckoning us to continue our exploration with diligence, creativity, and an unwavering focus on the future.

Author Contributions: All authors have read and agreed to the published version of the manuscript.

Conflicts of Interest: The authors declare no conflicts of interest.

References

1. Kuang, H.; Tan, X.; Wang, J.; Qu, Z.; Cai, Y.; Chen, Q.; Kim, B.J.; Qiu, W. Segmenting Ischemic Penumbra and Infarct Core Simultaneously on Non-Contrast CT of Patients with Acute Ischemic Stroke Using Novel Convolutional Neural Network. *Biomedicines* **2024**, *12*, 580. [CrossRef] [PubMed]
2. Santelli, L.; Ramondo, G.; Della Puppa, A.; Ermani, M.; Scienza, R.; d'Avella, D.; Manara, R. Diffusion-weighted imaging does not predict histological grading in meningiomas. *Acta Neurochir.* **2010**, *152*, 1315–1319. [CrossRef] [PubMed]
3. Mirzaei, G.; Adeli, H. Machine learning techniques for diagnosis of alzheimer disease, mild cognitive disorder, and other types of dementia. *Biomed. Signal Process. Control* **2022**, *72*, 103293. [CrossRef]
4. Kuang, H.; Wang, Y.; Liu, J.; Wang, J.; Cao, Q.; Hu, B.; Qiu, W.; Wang, J. Hybrid CNN-Transformer Network with Circular Feature Interaction for Acute Ischemic Stroke Lesion Segmentation on Non-contrast CT Scans. *IEEE Trans. Med. Imaging* **2024**, *in press*. [CrossRef] [PubMed]
5. Yıldırım, Ö.; Baloglu, U.B.; Acharya, U.R. A deep convolutional neural network model for automated identification of abnormal EEG signals. *Neural Comput. Appl.* **2020**, *32*, 15857–15868. [CrossRef]
6. Acharya, U.R.; Oh, S.L.; Hagiwara, Y.; Tan, J.H.; Adeli, H. Deep convolutional neural network for the automated detection and diagnosis of seizure using EEG signals. *Comput. Biol. Med.* **2018**, *100*, 270–278. [CrossRef] [PubMed]
7. Hosseini, M.P.; Tran, T.X.; Pompili, D.; Elisevich, K.; Soltanian-Zadeh, H. Multimodal data analysis of epileptic EEG and rs-fMRI via deep learning and edge computing. *Artif. Intell. Med.* **2020**, *104*, 101813. [CrossRef] [PubMed]
8. Nentwich, M.; Ai, L.; Madsen, J.; Telesford, Q.K.; Haufe, S.; Milham, M.P.; Parra, L.C. Functional connectivity of EEG is subject-specific, associated with phenotype, and different from fMRI. *NeuroImage* **2020**, *218*, 117001. [CrossRef] [PubMed]

biomedicines

MDPI

Article

Segmenting Ischemic Penumbra and Infarct Core Simultaneously on Non-Contrast CT of Patients with Acute Ischemic Stroke Using Novel Convolutional Neural Network

Hulin Kuang [1], Xianzhen Tan [1], Jie Wang [1], Zhe Qu [1], Yuxin Cai [2], Qiong Chen [3], Beom Joon Kim [4,5] and Wu Qiu [2,*]

1 Hunan Provincial Key Lab on Bioinformatics, School of Computer Science and Engineering, Central South University, Changsha 410083, China; hulinkuang@csu.edu.cn (H.K.); 224712155@csu.edu.cn (X.T.); jwang@csu.edu.cn (J.W.); zhe_qu@csu.edu.cn (Z.Q.)
2 School of Life Science and Technology, Huazhong University of Science and Technology, Wuhan 430074, China; m202272350@hust.edu.cn
3 Ultrasound Diagnosis Department, Wuhan No. 1 Hospital, Wuhan 430022, China; qiongchen.wh@gmail.com
4 Department of Neurology, Seoul National University Bundang Hospital, Seongnam-si 13620, Republic of Korea; kim.bj.stroke@gmail.com
5 Gyeonggi Regional Cerebrovascular Center, Seoul National University Bundang Hospital, Seongnam-si 13620, Republic of Korea
* Correspondence: wuqiu@hust.edu.cn

Abstract: Differentiating between a salvageable Ischemic Penumbra (IP) and an irreversibly damaged Infarct Core (IC) is important for therapy decision making for acute ischemic stroke (AIS) patients. Existing methods rely on Computed Tomography Perfusion (CTP) or Diffusion-Weighted Imaging–Fluid Attenuated Inversion Recovery (DWI-FLAIR). We designed a novel Convolutional Neural Network named I^{2}PC-Net, which relies solely on Non-Contrast Computed Tomography (NCCT) for the automatic and simultaneous segmentation of the IP and IC. In the encoder, Multi-Scale Convolution (MSC) blocks were proposed to capture effective features of ischemic lesions, and in the deep levels of the encoder, Symmetry Enhancement (SE) blocks were also designed to enhance anatomical symmetries. In the attention-based decoder, hierarchical deep supervision was introduced to address the challenge of differentiating between the IP and IC. We collected 197 NCCT scans from AIS patients to evaluate the proposed method. On the test set, I^{2}PC-Net achieved Dice Similarity Scores of 42.76 ± 21.84%, 33.54 ± 24.13% and 65.67 ± 12.30% and lesion volume correlation coefficients of 0.95 ($p < 0.001$), 0.61 ($p < 0.001$) and 0.93 ($p < 0.001$) for the IP, IC and IP + IC, respectively. The results indicated that NCCT could potentially be used as a surrogate technique of CTP for the quantitative evaluation of the IP and IC.

Keywords: acute ischemic stroke; ischemic penumbra and ischemic core segmentation; non-contrast CT; multi-scale convolution; symmetry enhancement; hierarchical deep supervision

Citation: Kuang, H.; Tan, X.; Wang, J.; Qu, Z.; Cai, Y.; Chen, Q.; Kim, B.J.; Qiu, W. Segmenting Ischemic Penumbra and Infarct Core Simultaneously on Non-Contrast CT of Patients with Acute Ischemic Stroke Using Novel Convolutional Neural Network. *Biomedicines* **2024**, *12*, 580. https://doi.org/10.3390/biomedicines12030580

Academic Editor: Francesco Piva

Received: 31 January 2024
Revised: 28 February 2024
Accepted: 4 March 2024
Published: 5 March 2024

1. Introduction

Acute ischemic stroke (AIS) is caused by the occlusion or blockage of small or large blood vessels due to a thrombus or embolism event, resulting in reduced blood flow to a portion of the brain tissue. It accounts for 87% of all strokes and has high morbidity and mortality [1,2]. Once an AIS occurs, a portion of the brain tissue may have already suffered irreversible damage (the Infarct Core, IC), and the surrounding brain tissue is also at risk due to reduced blood flow (the Ischemic Penumbra, IP) and may be salvageable [3,4]. Therefore, the goal of AIS treatment is to reperfuse the blood-deprived area before the salvageable IP transforms into the IC. The treatment methods for AIS patients mainly include intravenous thrombolysis and endovascular therapy [5]. Neuroradiologists usually select the appropriate treatment method for patients based on clinical guidelines, e.g., mechanical thrombectomy being more suitable when the IC volume is less than 70 mL, the IP volume is greater than 15 mL and the IP to IC ratio exceeds 1.8 [5–8]. Due to the extremely short 4.5 h treatment window, the rapid and accurate assessment of the volume and location of the IP and IC is important for reperfusion therapy decision making for AIS patients.

In clinical practice, neuroradiologists typically evaluate the IP and IC through manual delineation on multi-modal images, such as by using diffusion imaging to identify the IC and diffusion–perfusion mismatch to identify the IP. However, these manual segmentations are subject to interobserver and intraobserver variability and fatigue-related errors, and they are time consuming. Moreover, invasive imaging modalities are sometimes unavailable. Therefore, a rapid, objective, accurate and widely applicable method for automated IP and IC segmentation is desired in the computer-aided diagnosis of AIS.

Machine learning and deep learning methods have been extensively used in recent years for fully automatic medical image segmentation. Numerous general 3D medical image segmentation methods are available for the segmentation of the IP and IC, such as [9–14], etc. Additionally, some researchers have developed specialized machine learning and deep learning methods for infarct lesion segmentation. Gupta et al. [15] designed a U-shaped encoder–decoder network named MSNet. They utilized a combination of eight modalities of diffusion and perfusion maps to segment the IP and IC, where the diffusion–perfusion mismatch facilitates the differentiation between the IP and IC. Bhurwani et al. [16] utilized U-Net [17] to segment the IC and IP + IC from CTP scans, but they did not differentiate between the IP and IC. Lee et al. [18] and Vupputuri et al. [19] both adopted Diffusion-Weighted Imaging–Perfusion-Weighted Imaging (DWI-PWI) to quantify and differentiate the IP and IC. Werdiger et al. [20] explored XGBoost, followed by 3D neighborhood analysis, for the concurrent segmentation of the IP and IC on CTP scans. Tomasetti et al. [21] implemented a 4D Convolutional Neural Network (CNN) approach to leverage the spatiotemporal data contained within CTP scans, thereby delineating the IP and IC. Sathish et al. [22] deployed an adversarially trained CNN to segment the IP and IC simultaneously from multi-sequence Magnetic Resonance Imaging (MRI) scans. In summary, the specialized methods mentioned here either do not strictly differentiate between the IP and IC or they rely on multiple advanced imaging modalities such as CTP, PWI and DWI to differentiate the IP and IC. However, these advanced imaging techniques are time consuming and sometimes even unavailable, and fast and cheap Non-Contrast CT (NCCT) has seldom been considered in previous studies.

In this study, we propose a neural network named I^2PC-Net, which relies solely on widely available, cheap and fast baseline NCCT scans to simultaneously segment the IP and IC. I^2PC-Net has a seven-level U-shaped encoder–decoder architecture, relying on pure convolution. In the encoder, to model the varying shapes, sizes and locations of the infarct lesions, we designed the Multi-Scale Convolution (MSC) block. To model the anatomical symmetry and capture the difference between the left and right sides of the brain, we propose the Symmetry Enhancement (SE) block. In the attention-based decoder, we utilized hierarchical deep supervision mechanisms for the entire ischemic region (IP + IC) in the three deep levels and for differentiating the IP and IC at the three low levels. Through the effective strategies proposed above, we hypothesized that the I^2PC-Net can segment the IP and IC from NCCT well. Our contributions are summarized as follows: (1) We propose the MSC block to model the high variability of AIS lesions. (2) We introduce the SE block to capture the differences between the bilateral hemispheres of the brain. (3) An attention-based decoder was employed to better integrate high-level and low-level features. (4) Hierarchical deep supervision was designed to more effectively differentiate between the IP and IC on NCCT.

2. Materials and Methods

2.1. Data Acquisition

We collected multi-modal data including DWI, Fluid-Attenuated Inversion Recovery (FLAIR) and NCCT from 197 AIS patients in a prospective stroke registry at a single academic center. The institutional review board of the Seoul National University Bundang Hospital approved the data analysis, image evaluation and modeling process (B-2102/667-106). The included patients or their next of kin provided written consent for the prospective clinical stroke registry to record and collect their data (B-1401/236-007, B-1706/403-303).

All the modalities were coregistered to NCCT. There were two inclusion criteria for the patient samples: (1) each modality's data encompass the entire brain without significant artifacts, and (2) expert annotations of the ischemic tissue region are available. In the dataset, the number of slices in the sagittal view is 512 and the ranges of the number of slices in the coronal and axial views are 512–638 and 28–37, respectively. The range of spacing is 0.326–0.429 mm for both the sagittal and coronal views and 4.999–5.015 mm for the axial view. Groundtruth labels for the IC and IP on NCCT were defined by high signal regions on DWI and DWI-FLAIR mismatch areas, respectively. These labels were first annotated by a neuroradiologist (Qiong Chen) with over 5 years of experience using the software ITK-SNAP version 4.2.0. [23] and were then double checked by another neuroradiologist (Beom Joon Kim) with over 10 years of experience to achieve accurate annotations. Finally, we utilized these 197 annotated NCCT scans and divided them in a ratio of 7:2:1 for training, validation and testing, respectively.

2.2. Image Preprocessing

To eliminate the influence of the skull region, we first removed the skull following the method proposed by Najm et al. [24]. Figure 1 sequentially displays the NCCT after the skull removal, DWI with highlighted infarct signals, FLAIR showing a mismatch with DWI and the category labels for the IP (red) and IC (green).

Considering the robust and powerful performance of nnUNet [9] for medical image segmentation, we followed its preprocessing approach, which depends on the statistical information of a specific dataset (called the dataset fingerprint). Initially, the images were cropped based on the 3D bounding box of the brain tissue to avoid unnecessary computations. Subsequently, all the images were resampled to the dataset's median voxel spacing: 0.3789 mm $\times$ 0.3789 mm $\times$ 5.0 mm. This enhances the performance of CNN networks with inductive bias, enabling them to better learn the typical sizes of brain anatomical structures. Finally, Z-Score normalization was performed based on the mean and variance of the segmentation target (take pixel values within the range of 0.5% to 99.5%). This is equivalent to considering the window width and window level of the target lesion or anatomical structure, which helps the network learn more effective features and accelerates convergence.

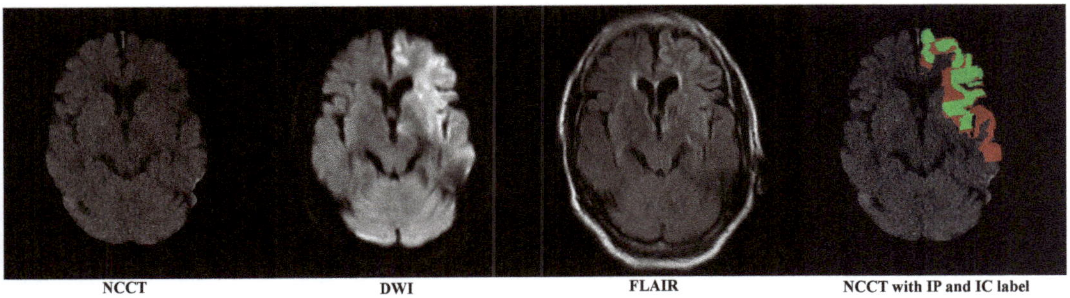

Figure 1. An example of multi-modal image of a patient; DWI and FLAIR are registered to NCCT. The red and green regions represent the manually annotated IP and IC, respectively.

2.3. The Proposed I^{2}PC-Net

As illustrated in Figure 2a, I^{2}PC-Net also adopted a U-shaped structure with a 7-level encoder and a 6-level decoder. The feature channel (i.e., the number of convolution filters) of each encoder level and decoder level are also given in Figure 2a. The three low encoder levels were composed of MSC blocks, and the four deep encoder levels added an SE block after the MSC block. Convolution-based downsampling was interleaved between two adjacent encoder levels. In the six-level decoder, we adopted the attention-based decoder of Oktay et al. [25] to better fuse high-level semantic information with low-level fine-grained image details. Transposed convolution-based upsampling was interleaved between two adjacent decoder levels. Note that for the spatial dimension D, downsampling or upsampling by a convolution of stride 2 was performed twice, i.e., only in the two levels above the bottleneck. Whereas for the H and W dimensions, upsampling or downsampling by a convolution of stride 2 occurred at every level. The input stem and segmentation head were, respectively, responsible for initial feature embedding and output generation. Considering the difficulty in differentiating the IP and IC on NCCT, a hierarchical deep supervision decoding mechanism was used for the decoder levels.

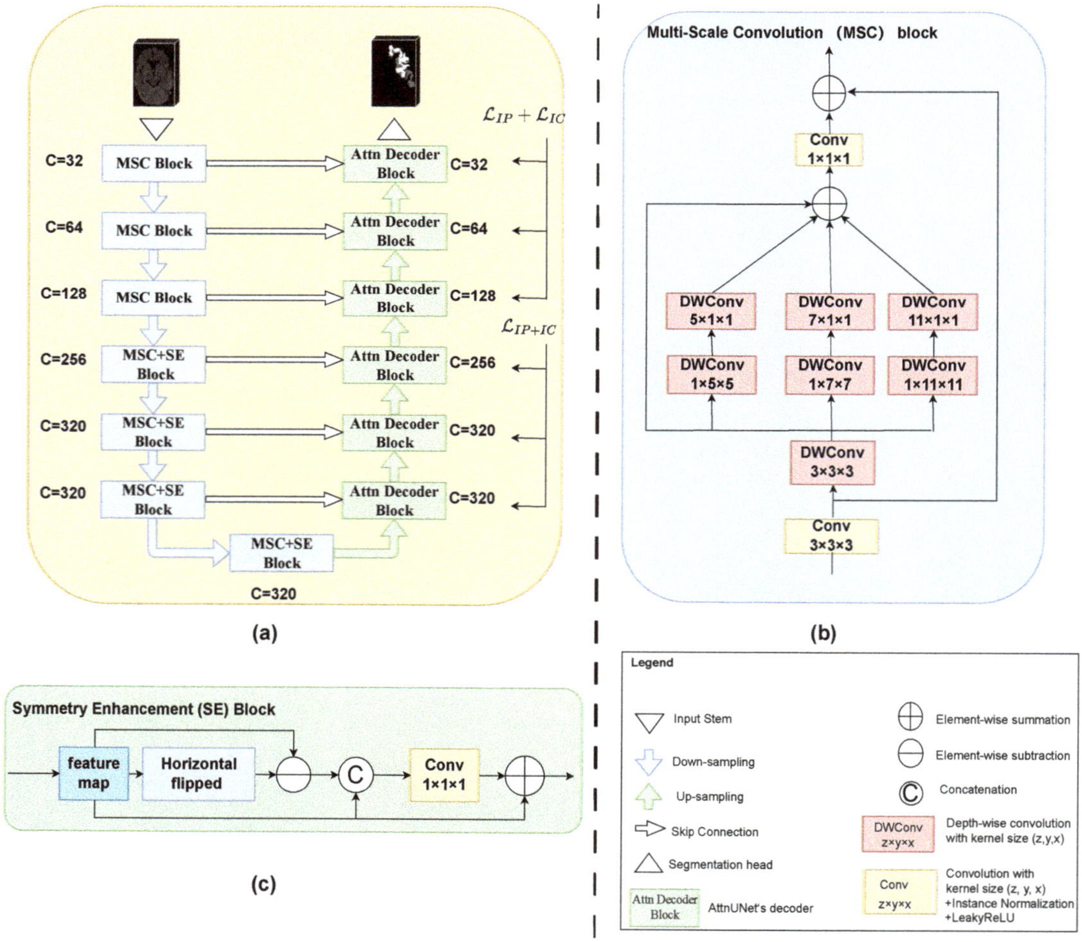

Figure 2. Architecture of the proposed I²PC-Net. (**a**) Overview of the whole architecture. (**b**) Multi-Scale Convolution block. (**c**) Symmetry Enhancement block.

2.3.1. Multi-Scale Convolution Block

Existing general 3D medical image segmentation methods such as those targeting abdominal multi-organ segmentation and the similar shape size and location of the organs determine the feasibility of single-scale modeling. However, high variability in the location, size and shape of the infarct lesions needs multi-scale modeling. Inspired by Guo et al. [26], we propose the MSC block, as shown in Figure 2b. For the sake of simplicity in the diagram, we omitted the activation functions and normalization operations. Taking the MSC block in the first level of the encoder for example, the feature map was firstly passed to a vanilla convolution block (convolution with a kernel size of 3 × 3 × 3 + Instance Normalization + LeakyReLU). The output of this convolution operation was also added to the final output as a residual connection. Then, we designed a parallel depth-wise convolution branch with kernel sizes of 5, 7 and 11 to obtain the multi-scale features (note that here, all depth-wise convolutions were followed neither by normalization nor by activation functions, and to further enlarge the receptive field, a 3 × 3 × 3 depth-wise convolution was positioned before the other three scales). The four outputs of multiple depth-wise convolutional branches were added element-wise and then passed through a fusion convolution block (convolution with a kernel size of 1 × 1 × 1 + Instance Normalization + LeakyReLU). Additionally, to reduce the complexity of the model, depth-wise convolutions with a kernel size of 1 × k × k followed by a kernel size of k × 1 × 1 were employed in place of a kernel size of k × k × k, where $k \in \{5, 7, 11\}$. Given an input feature map $\mathbf{X} \in \mathbb{R}^{B\times C\times D\times H\times W}$, the MSC block's output feature map $\mathbf{Y} \in \mathbb{R}^{B\times C\times D\times H\times W}$ can be formalized as follows:

$$\mathbf{X}' = \sigma(\mathrm{Norm}(\mathrm{Conv}_{3\times3\times3}(\mathbf{X}))) \quad (1)$$

$$\mathbf{Y} = \mathrm{Conv}_{1\times1\times1}\left(\sum_{\mathrm{i}=0}^{3}\mathrm{Scale}_{\mathrm{i}}\left(\mathrm{DWConv}\left(\mathbf{X}'\right)\right)\right) + \mathbf{X}' \quad (2)$$

where $\mathrm{Conv}_{\mathrm{k}\times\mathrm{k}\times\mathrm{k}}$ denotes the convolution with a kernel size of k × k × k, Norm represents Instance Normalization, σ is the LeakyReLU activation function and $\mathrm{DWConv}_{\mathrm{k}\times\mathrm{k}\times\mathrm{k}}$ indicates a depthwise convolution with a kernel of k × k × k. $\mathrm{Scale}_{\mathrm{i}}(\mathrm{DWConv}(\cdot))$ represents the *i*-th depthwise convolutional branch, where $\mathrm{i} = 0$ indicates the identity connection.

2.3.2. Symmetry Enhancement Block

The left and right hemispheres of the brain exhibit axial symmetry along the mid-sagittal line. Typically, the opposite side of a cerebral infarction is normal brain tissue. Previous studies had utilized this prior clinical knowledge to enhance the model's ability to locate suspicious ischemic lesions. However, due to variations in patient positioning during imaging, the mid-sagittal line in the image may not be vertical. Previous strategies include the use of alignment neural networks and direct registration [27–33]. We believe that the influence of slight tilts in brain scans can be mitigated at higher semantic levels, where each pixel represents a larger area of the original image. Therefore, we directly appended an SE block after the MSC block in the 4 high levels of the encoder. The structure of the SE block is shown in Figure 2c. The feature map from the MSC block was first horizontally flipped and then it was element-wise subtracted from the flipped feature maps. The obtained feature map after subtraction was concatenated with the input feature map along the channel dimension. Subsequently, it passed through a convolution block (convolution with a kernel size of 1 × 1 × 1 + Instance Normalization + LeakyReLU) to obtain the fused feature. Finally, the fused feature map was element-wise added to the input feature map to produce the final output. Given the input feature map $\mathbf{H} \in \mathbb{R}^{B\times C\times D\times H\times W}$ from the MSC block, the SE block's output $\mathbf{H}_{\mathrm{SE}} \in \mathbb{R}^{B\times C\times D\times H\times W}$ can be formulated as

$$\mathbf{H}_{\mathrm{SE}} = \mathrm{Conv}_{1\times1\times1}\left(\mathrm{Concat}\left(\mathbf{H}, \mathbf{H} - \mathbf{H}_{\mathrm{flipped}}\right)\right) + \mathbf{H} \quad (3)$$

where $\mathbf{H}_{\mathrm{flipped}}$ represents the feature map after horizontal flipping and Concat denotes concatenation along the channel dimension.

2.3.3. Attention-Based Decoder

The rational fusion of coarse-grained and fine-grained features is important for the final segmentation output. AttnUNet [25] introduced gated attention units in skip connections. It used coarse-grained feature maps as queries to weight fine-grained feature maps from the same level encoder, thereby learning which spatial regions to focus on. Because this structure was designed to address anatomical structures with highly variable shapes, we believed that this design was equally applicable to stroke segmentation. In Figure 2, it was denoted as "Attn Decoder Block". Specifically, for each level of the "Attn Decoder Block", the features from its subsequent level and the features from the corresponding level of the encoder were passed through a $1 \times 1 \times 1$ convolution layer (the number of channels was halved) and then added element-wise. This was followed by a ReLU activation function and then another $1 \times 1 \times 1$ convolution layer (where the number of channels was reduced to 1). The output then went through a Sigmoid activation function to obtain the weight (spatial attention score) at each pixel position. Finally, these weights were used to element-wise multiply with the features from the skip connections, thereby suppressing irrelevant feature responses in the fine-grained feature maps from the encoder. Lastly, the features from the subsequent level and the gated attention-modified features from the encoder at the same level were concatenated along the channel dimension and fused through a convolution layer. For detailed information, please refer to their publication [25]. We believe that, building upon the precise and more powerful encoding blocks like MSC and SA, those multi-scale, symmetry-enhanced features could better suppress irrelevant feature responses transmitted from skip connections, making the final features more effective.

2.3.4. Hierarchical Deep Supervision

Owing to the exceedingly subtle differences between the IP and IC on NCCT, differentiating them directly in the deep layers of the network poses a significant challenge. In clinical practice, neuroradiologists initially approximate the location of the ischemic area and subsequently fine-tune the entire ischemic regions into the IP and IC. Drawing inspiration from this, we incorporated a hierarchical deep supervision strategy. Firstly, we continuously downsampled the ground truth label to match the spatial resolution of each decoder level. For each decoder level, we used a $1 \times 1 \times 1$ convolutional layer to change the number of channels to the number of classification categories to achieve segmentation. That was, for the higher three levels, the number of categories was 2 (the background and IP + IC), and in the lower three levels, the number of categories was three (the background, IP and IC). We then calculated the loss by using the outputs of different levels and the corresponding downsampled ground truth. We used a linear combination of the Dice Similarity Coefficient (DSC) loss and Cross-Entropy (CE) loss as the objective function for each decoder level: $\mathcal{L} = \alpha\mathcal{L}_{DSC} + \beta\mathcal{L}_{CE}$, where α and β are set to 1 in our practice. The total objective function of hierarchical deep supervision can be formalized as

$$\mathcal{L}_{\text{Total}} = \sum_{i=0}^{2} Res_i \times \mathcal{L}_{IP+IC} + \sum_{i=3}^{5} Res_i \times (\mathcal{L}_{IP} + \mathcal{L}_{IC}) \tag{4}$$

where $\mathcal{L}_{IP+IC}$ represents the loss for the total ischemic area, treating the IP and IC as a single category, while $\mathcal{L}_{IP}$ and $\mathcal{L}_{IC}$, respectively, denote the losses for the IP and IC regions and Res_i represents the weights of different decoder level's supervision loss. When i ranges from 0 to 5 (six decoder levels from bottom to top), Res_i takes the respective values of 0.02, 0.08, 0.2, 0.1, 0.2 and 0.4.

2.4. Implementation Details

We randomly sampled 3D patches of size $20 \times 320 \times 256$ from the resampled and normalized data. For each patch, data augmentation includes spatial transformation (random rotation, random scaling and random elastic deformation), mirror transformation, adding white Gaussian noise, Gaussian blurring, low-resolution simulation, Gamma transformation and contrast and brightness adjustments. An initial learning rate of 1×10^{-2} with a polynomial decay schedule and a batch size of 2 were used. The Stochastic Gradient Descent (SGD) optimizer with a Nesterov Momentum of 0.99 and weight decay of 2×10^{-5} was used. The gradient clipping was set during training. We trained for 300 epochs, whereby each epoch consisted of 250 iterations. The code is available at https://github.com/GitHub-TXZ/I2PC-Net/, which is accessible to anyone for free, allowing for the validation and utilization of our method.

We adopted the sliding window strategy and Test Time Augmentation (TTA) strategy [9]. The window size is the same with the training patch size and its stride is 0.5× the patch size. The overlapping regions are weighted by a prepared Gaussian importance map. TTA is implemented via flipping along all axes. We did not perform any post-processing operations.

We compared several existing generic 2D or 3D segmentation methods, including pure CNN models such as nnUNet [9] and AttnUNet [25], pure Transformer models like nnFormer [12] and D-Former [11] as well as hybrid CNN and Transformer models like CoTr [13] and Swin-UNETR [14]. All the comparison methods were subjected to the same data processing and experimental settings to ensure fairness in the comparison. All the experiments were conducted on a ubuntu server (version 18.04) equipped with 5 NVIDIA A6000 48GB GPUs. The primary software dependencies include Pytorch version 2.0, nnU-Net version 2.2 (https://github.com/MIC-DKFZ/nnUNet (accessed on 20 December 2023)), MONAI version 1.3 (https://github.com/Project-MONAI/MONAI (accessed on 20 December 2023)) and Python version 3.10.11 (https://www.python.org/ (accessed on 20 January 2023)).

2.5. Statistical Analysis

In evaluating the segmentation performance for the IP, IC and IC + IP, we computed the metrics DSC, 95th percentile Hausdorff Distance (HD95) and Average Symmetric Surface Distance (ASSD) along with their respective means and standard deviations [31,34]. To assess the volume concordance between the manual segmentation made by neuroradiologists and the I^2PC-Net, we calculated Pearson's correlation coefficients with a 95% confidence interval (CI) and generated regression and Bland–Altman plots. Given a 70 mL cut-off as the volume threshold for binary classification, the volume classification performance was evaluated by using accuracy, Area Under the Curve (AUC), Kappa and their respective 95% CIs. The statistical analyses were conducted by using MedCalc software (version 20.218, MedCalc Software Ltd., Mariakerke, Belgium) and the Python programming language (version 3.10.11, https://www.python.org/, (accessed on 20 January 2023)). *t*-test and proportion tests were used and a two-sided alpha level of less than 0.05 was considered to denote statistical significance.

3. Results

3.1. Study Participants

In the dataset comprising 197 collected cases, the median age of the research participants was 72 [IQR, 63–80], with 72 male subjects (57.36%). The median Onset-to-CT time was 73 [IQR, 41–180] min, and the median baseline NIHSS was 11 [IQR: 6–17]. The details of patient characteristics for all 197 AIS patients collected were listed in Table 1.

Table 1. Patient characteristics for all 197 AIS patients collected.

Characteristics	All 197 Patients
Median age, years (IQR)	72 (63–80)
Gender, male, no. (%)	113 (57.36)
Median Onset-to-CT time (IQR), min	73 (41–180)
Median baseline NIHSS (IQR)	11 (6–17)

IQR: Interquartile Range; NIHSS: National Institutes of Health Stroke Scale.

3.2. Results for IP Segmentation and IC Segmentation

We conducted comparisons with several existing 2D and 3D methods. Table 2 demonstrates the segmentation results for the IP segmentation and IC segmentation. From Table 2, our proposed I^2PC-Net achieved DSCs of 42.76% ± 21.84% and 33.54% ± 24.13%, HD95s of 13.81 ± 10.39 mm and 21.02 ± 14.81 mm and ASSDs of 3.59 ± 2.25 mm and 5.85 ± 4.28 mm for the IP and IC segmentation, respectively, outperforming all the compared 2D and 3D methods. These results show that our I^2PC-Net, benefiting from the effectiveness of the MSC and SA blocks, and the hierarchical deep supervision, achieved the optimal performance across various metrics. Overall, we could find that (1) the 3D methods were not necessarily superior to the 2D methods, which may be attributed to the large slice thickness, resulting in less strong connections between adjacent slices; (2) pure CNN approaches, such as AttnUNet [25] and nnUNet [9], continued to exhibit a robust performance in this task; (3) methods based solely on Transformers showed a weaker performance, possibly due to the challenges that Transformers face in smaller datasets rather than inherent limitations in the model itself; and (4) hybrid CNN–Transformer methods performed intermediately between pure Transformers and pure CNN methods. In other words, CNNs were more suitable for this task.

Table 2. Comparison of IP and IC segmentation performance with some 2D and 3D methods. The best metric is shown in bold, and the second best is underscored. ↑ denotes that higher values are better and ↓ denotes that lower values are better. All metrics are reported as mean ± std.

Methods	IP			IC		
	DSC (%) ↑	**HD95 (mm) ↓**	**ASSD (mm) ↓**	**DSC (%) ↑**	**HD95 (mm) ↓**	**ASSD (mm) ↓**
TransUNet [35]	30.00 ± 19.11	42.22 ± 27.05	10.62 ± 8.19	23.16 ± 16.75	37.27 ± 18.00	9.88 ± 4.06
Swin-UNet [36]	20.99 ± 15.50	39.97 ± 23.35	12.45 ± 8.84	13.97 ± 12.60	53.95 ± 20.15	15.31 ± 7.30
2D nnUNet [9]	31.32 ± 23.73	29.05 ± 24.65	10.34 ± 13.91	25.35 ± 21.11	24.37 ± 15.67	8.64 ± 9.92
UTNet [37]	22.87 ± 15.15	27.13 ± 18.73	7.82 ± 6.65	24.07 ± 21.21	32.36 ± 22.95	9.98 ± 8.71
UNet [38]	28.60 ± 19.98	33.64 ± 25.93	10.16 ± 13.94	13.69 ± 14.79	30.92 ± 19.61	10.14 ± 7.05
V-Net [39]	20.05 ± 18.83	32.93 ± 19.48	10.51 ± 9.11	14.57 ± 15.95	30.19 ± 15.11	10.34 ± 7.26
AttnUNet [25]	34.11 ± 19.93	21.30 ± 14.12	5.91 ± 6.24	27.93 ± 22.26	25.82 ± 19.94	6.92 ± 4.95
UNet++ [40]	33.76 ± 21.32	24.09 ± 19.43	6.13 ± 5.70	27.99 ± 24.49	24.30 ± 18.57	7.11 ± 5.47
3D nnUNet [9]	40.50 ± 21.70	16.50 ± 14.96	4.16 ± 4.08	30.74 ± 23.58	21.17 ± 16.12	6.26 ± 5.65
D-Former [11]	31.46 ± 23.01	23.16 ± 17.24	8.51 ± 9.52	17.89 ± 16.83	25.91 ± 19.09	9.44 ± 13.12
CoTr [13]	36.92 ± 23.93	25.82 ± 21.39	7.23 ± 8.08	17.39 ± 15.51	22.54 ± 11.57	6.77 ± 3.99
TransBTS [41]	26.82 ± 16.47	45.18 ± 22.77	12.06 ± 8.04	19.71 ± 18.33	40.78 ± 21.78	12.61 ± 7.92
UNETR [42]	15.74 ± 10.10	53.37 ± 19.43	15.36 ± 6.23	15.77 ± 19.05	36.66 ± 22.91	13.87 ± 9.07
nnFormer [12]	20.04 ± 15.23	40.71 ± 19.99	12.48 ± 9.86	19.03 ± 22.35	36.00 ± 24.27	13.69 ± 11.03
Swin-UNETR [14]	22.09 ± 14.51	47.61 ± 22.91	13.19 ± 7.72	15.07 ± 15.78	48.29 ± 20.28	16.71 ± 8.62
3D UX-Net [10]	17.78 ± 13.48	41.33 ± 20.91	13.50 ± 10.44	14.82 ± 14.27	32.88 ± 20.19	12.10 ± 7.04
I^2PC-Net	**42.76 ± 21.84**	**13.81 ± 10.39**	**3.59 ± 2.25**	**33.54 ± 24.13**	**21.02 ± 14.81**	**5.85 ± 4.28**

Figure 3 illustrates the visual segmentation results for our method and three representative methods: nnUNet [9], AttnUNet [25] and CoTr [13] for the IP and IC segmentation. In the figure, we could see that our I^2PC-Net could accurately locate the affected regions in the GTs of the IP and IC well, and also match the GT labels (DSC = 47.44% and 74.57% for the IP and IC, respectively) better than the three compared methods, showing its potential to provide affected-region information in clinical applications.

3.3. Results for the Entire Infarct (IP + IC) Segmentation

In clinical practice, the evaluation of the entire ischemic infarct (the IP + IC) is also of paramount importance for diagnosis and prognosis [31,43]. Therefore, we also evaluated the segmentation performance of the entire ischemic infarct. Without any additional training, all the methods' segmentation results and the Groundtruth segmentation results treated the IP and IC labels as one category, without distinguishing between the IP and IC. Subsequently, the segmentation metrics were calculated to obtain Table 3. For the entire ischemic infarcts, our method achieved a DSC of 65.67% ± 12.30%, an HD95 of 12.54 ± 7.96 mm and an ASSD of 2.88 ± 1.27 mm, surpassing all comparative methods. In terms of the DSC, our method outperformed the best 2D method 2D nnUNet [9] (65.67% ± 12.30% vs. 49.44% ± 23.63%), the best pure 3D CNN method 3D nnUNet [9] (65.67% ± 12.30% vs. 62.22% ± 11.74%), the best pure 3D Transformer method D-former [11] (65.67% ± 12.30% vs. 45.18% ± 23.25%) and the best hybrid CNN–Transformer method CoTr [13] (65.67% ± 12.30% vs. 50.09% ± 22.14%).

As shown in the sixth subfigure (denoted by I²PC-Net) in Figure 3, our method could accurately locate the entire ischemic regions and match the GT IP + IC well. Our method shows a similar DSC performance to nnUNet (89.17% vs. 89.77%) for the IP + IC segmentation. However, our method achieved a higher DSC for the IP segmentation and IP segmentation, showing its effectiveness at distinguishing the IP and IC.

Table 3. Comparison of the entire infarct (IP + IC) segmentation performance with some 2D and 3D methods. The best metric is shown in bold, and the second best is underscored. ↑ denotes that higher values are better and ↓ denotes that lower values are better. All metrics are reported as mean ± std.

Methods	IP + IC		
	DSC (%) ↑	**HD95 (mm) ↓**	**ASSD (mm) ↓**
TransUNet [35]	44.54 ± 16.24	43.19 ± 25.19	9.63 ± 6.08
Swin-UNet [36]	31.86 ± 18.55	45.22 ± 21.84	12.08 ± 6.77
2D nnUNet [9]	49.44 ± 23.63	24.70 ± 20.33	6.56 ± 6.60
UTNet [37]	40.12 ± 17.44	26.20 ± 18.80	6.41 ± 3.51
UNet [38]	39.94 ± 22.98	33.47 ± 25.34	10.10 ± 13.71
V-Net [39]	31.90 ± 24.15	32.43 ± 19.38	10.23 ± 9.22
AttnUNet [25]	51.48 ± 22.74	20.74 ± 13.39	5.88 ± 6.27
UNet++[40]	51.56 ± 23.48	24.20 ± 19.08	6.22 ± 5.87
3D nnUNet [9]	<u>62.22 ± 11.74</u>	<u>15.26 ± 12.73</u>	<u>3.67 ± 3.64</u>
D-Former [11]	45.18 ± 23.25	22.53 ± 16.57	7.36 ± 8.04
CoTr [13]	50.09 ± 22.14	25.10 ± 20.22	5.89 ± 4.41
TransBTS [41]	39.77 ± 17.94	45.35 ± 21.83	12.09 ± 7.25
UNETR [42]	25.02 ± 13.68	53.73 ± 18.42	15.38 ± 6.01
nnFormer [12]	32.15 ± 19.93	39.93 ± 19.40	11.92 ± 7.90
Swin-UNETR [14]	32.71 ± 17.92	47.63 ± 21.62	13.46 ± 7.61
3D UX-Net [10]	28.45 ± 18.53	39.00 ± 20.29	12.16 ± 7.84
I² PC-Net	**65.67 ± 12.30**	**12.54 ± 7.96**	**2.88 ± 1.27**

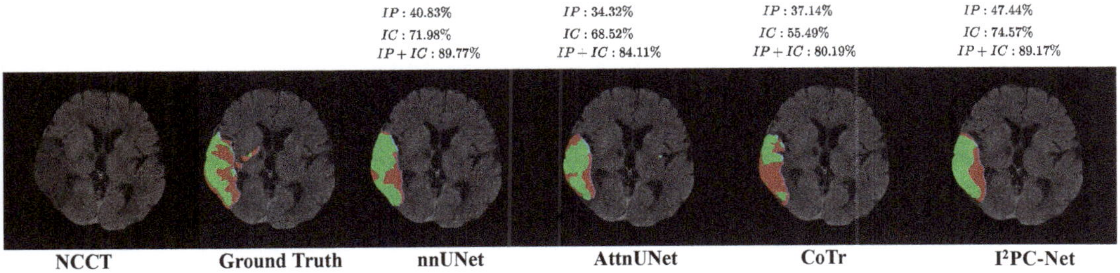

Figure 3. Visual segmentation results of the I²PC-Net and three state-of-the-art methods: nnUNet, AttnUNet and CoTr. The red and green regions in each subfigure represent manual Groundtruth of IP and IC or IP and IC segmented by each compared algorithm, respectively. The numbers above the figure denote the DSC for IP, IC and IP + IC in this slice, respectively.

3.4. Volumetric Analysis of Segmented Infarcts

In clinical practice, the volume correlation as well as the infarct volume (e.g., 70 mL as the cut-off) are crucial for selecting AIS patients who will obtain good outcomes after different treatments [31,44,45]. Therefore, we also conducted a volume analysis on the ischemic infarcts obtained by our method to illustrate the clinical relevance of the proposed method.

Figure 4a–c illustrate the correlation analysis between the I^{2}PC-Net segmented volumes and manual segmented volumes for the IP, IC and IP + IC, respectively. The proposed I^{2}PC-Net achieved Pearson linear correlation coefficients (r) of 0.95 (95% CI: 0.9019–0.9720, $p < 0.001$), 0.61 (95% CI: 0.3637–0.7721, $p < 0.001$) and 0.93 (95% CI: 0.8749–0.9639, $p < 0.001$) for the IP, IC and IP + IC, respectively. These indicate a strong positive volume correlation for the IP and IP + IC, and the more challenging IC also exhibits a moderate volume correlation. Segmenting AIS infarcts in NCCT scans presents significant difficulties. First, compared to other imaging techniques like MRI, NCCT proves harder to analyze because of the lower signal-to-noise and contrast-to-noise ratios in cerebral tissues. Second, distinguishing infarct areas is complicated by normal physiological alterations, with the affected brain regions often exhibiting only slight differences in density and texture [32,33]. In the early stages of stroke, the IC does not appear significantly on NCCT, making it very difficult to distinguish between the IP and IC. Therefore, the correlation of the IC volume is relatively weak.

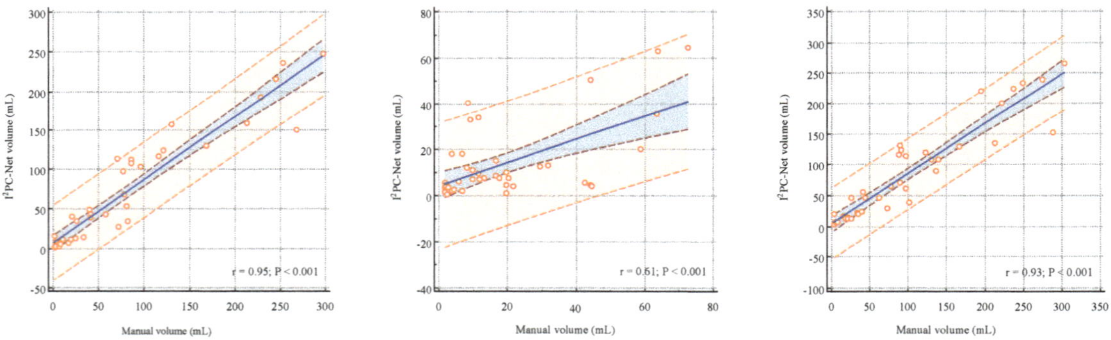

Figure 4. Volume correlation and consistency analysis of the segmented volume by I^{2}PC-Net compared with manual segmentation volumes. (**a**–**c**) represent the linear regression of IP, IC and IP + IC, respectively. The blue straight line represents the regression line, and the pink dotted line and the blue area it contains represent the 95% confidence interval. The dashed orange line and the orange area it contains represent the 95% prediction interval. "r" represents the Pearson correlation coefficient, and "P" denotes the p-value.

We also dichotomized the entire ischemic region (IP + IC) volume by using 70 mL as a cut-off and then evaluated the binary volume classification performance. Our developed I^{2}PC-Net demonstrated the capability to discriminate between patients with lesion volumes of $\leq$70 mL and >70 mL with a Kappa of 0.7536 [95% CI: 0.5579–0.9494], an AUC of 0.886 [95% CI: 0.746–0.965] and an accuracy of 87.50% [95% CI: 73.19%–95.81%], suggesting reasonable dichotomization volume information for therapy decision making.

4. Discussion

In this study, we explored a fully automatic segmentation approach named I^{2}PC-Net to simultaneously segment the IP and IC from NCCT scans. By employing MSC blocks, SA blocks and hierarchical deep supervision mechanisms, the proposed I^{2}PC-Net demonstrated a superior performance compared to some existing methods.

A comparative analysis with other methods revealed that the pure Transformer-based methods exhibited the poorest performance. The hybrid methods showed performance improvements over the pure Transformers, and they did so at the expense of convergence speed and computational cost. Pure convolutional approaches were more suited for this task in terms of convergence speed and final performance. Our method outperformed the powerful nnUNet, attributable to its enhanced capability of muti-scale modeling, suspected ischemic area locating and IP and IC differentiating. The experiment results confirm our hypothesis: employing modules like MSC blocks and SA blocks allow for the better handling of the substantial variability in infarct shape, size and location, while a hierarchical deep supervision decoding mechanism more effectively addresses the challenges in distinguishing between the IP and IC. This study demonstrates the feasibility of using only NCCT for simultaneous quantitative assessments of the IP and IC. I^{2}PC-Net can provide valuable insights for neuroradiologists in making therapeutic decisions, laying the groundwork for future researchers to develop more effective and broadly applicable methods.

From the quantitative segmentation metrics, visual segmentation results and volume analysis results, our approach demonstrated the effective localization of the ischemic region. Moreover, the classification performance using a cut-off volume of 70 mL was also favorable. This implies that in clinical applications, our method, relying solely on NCCT, can furnish valuable information for decision making in AIS treatments. The average time for automatic segmentation using the trained model was 3.49 s per NCCT scan, significantly enhancing the diagnostic efficiency of neuroradiologists for AIS patients.

Furthermore, to explore whether there were relevant clinical factors influencing the volume classification performance using 70 mL as cut-off, we conducted subgroup analyses based on factors such as gender, age, NIHSS score and Onset-to-CT time. As depicted in Table 4, the classification performance for patients aged over 70 was significantly superior to those under 70, and for patients with an Onset-to-CT-time exceeding 180 min, the classification performance was significantly better than for those below 180 min. No significant differences were found in the gender and NIHSS subgroups. A subgroup analysis indicates that age and Onset-to-CT time are two clinical factors closely associated with segmentation and classification performance. The reason why segmentation and lesion volume classification are more effective when the onset-to-CT time $\geq$ 180 min is that the longer the Onset-to-CT time, the more stable the lesion changes become, and lesions become more contrasted against the healthy tissues, making them easier to be segmented. However, given that the golden treatment window for AIS is 4.5 h, it is generally recommended in clinical practice to perform an NCCT scan and decide the appropriate treatment as soon as possible to improve the success rate of the intervention. Therefore, the above results do not imply that we should wait until after 180 min to collect NCCT data for treatment. Future research can incorporate age and Onset-to-CT time into the modeling process to further improve accuracy.

This study also has several limitations. First, the sample size in this paper is limited, and there is no external validation cohort. In the future, we aim to collect more data to train models that are more effective and broadly applicable. Second, from the qualitative results, we can find that even though the model accurately locates the entire ischemic region, the segmentation performance of the IP and IC individually might not be optimal. How to better distinguish the IP and IC while maintaining the accuracy of the entire ischemic IP + IC region remains a topic for future work.

Table 4. Classification performance when IP + IC volume is dichotomized using 70 mL as cut-off (95%CI is shown in square brackets). * denotes that there is significant difference between two subgroups ($p < 0.05$).

Variable	Subgroup	Kappa	AUC	Accuracy (%)
Gender	female	0.7826 [0.4440–1.0000]	0.9286 [0.8214–1.0000]	0.9000 [0.6990–0.9721]
	male	0.6667 [0.3389–1.0000]	0.8125 [0.6429–1.0000]	0.8500 [0.6396–0.9476]
Age (years)	<70	0.5000 [0.1250–0.8623]	0.7500 [0.5625–0.9286]	0.7500 [0.5050–0.8982]
	≥70	0.9155 * [0.7143–1.0000]	0.9643 * [0.8846–1.0000]	0.9583 * [0.7976–0.9926]
Baseline NIHSS	<9	0.7547 [0.4217–1.0000	0.8333 [0.5000–1.0000]	0.9231 [0.6669–0.9863]
	≥9	0.6897 [0.3969–0.9222]	0.8947 [0.7895–0.9750]	0.8519 [0.6752–0.9408]
Onset-to-CT time (min)	<180	0.6316 [0.3331–0.9041]	0.8462 [0.7083–0.9643]	0.8095 [0.6000–0.9233]
	≥180	0.8939 * [0.6587–1.0000]	0.9444 * [0.8125–1.0000]	0.9474 * [0.7536–0.9906]

5. Conclusions

This study proposed a pure CNN-based method, termed I^2PC-Net, which relies solely on NCCT to simultaneously and automatically segment the IP and IC. It mitigates the challenges of significant variations in the size, location and shape of infarct lesions through multi-scale modeling and Symmetry Enhancement blocks. We also employed a hierarchical deep supervision decoding mechanism to address the difficulty in distinguishing between the IP and IC in the deep layer. The results indicate that I^2PC-Net can automatically and quantitatively assess the IP and IC with good localization of the affected regions, strong volume correlation and high dichotomized volume classification performance, potentially providing valuable infarct information for diagnosis and patient selection in clinical applications.

Author Contributions: Conceptualization, H.K., X.T., J.W., Z.Q., Y.C., Q.C., B.J.K. and W.Q.; data curation, H.K., Q.C., B.J.K. and W.Q.; formal analysis, H.K., X.T., J.W., Z.Q., Y.C. and W.Q.; funding acquisition, H.K. and W.Q.; investigation, X.T., J.W., Z.Q., Y.C. and W.Q.; methodology, H.K., X.T., J.W., Z.Q., Y.C. and W.Q.; project administration, W.Q.; resources, H.K., Q.C. and B.J.K.; software, H.K. and X.T.; supervision, H.K.; validation, H.K., X.T. and W.Q.; visualization, H.K. and X.T.; writing—original draft, H.K. and X.T.; writing—review and editing, H.K., X.T., J.W., Z.Q., Y.C., Q.C., B.J.K. and W.Q. All authors have read and agreed to the published version of the manuscript.

Funding: This work was supported in part by the National Natural Science Foundation of China (no. 62102454), the National Key Research and Development Program of China (2021YFF1201200, 2022YFE0209900 and 2023YFC2410802), the Science and Technology Innovation Program of Hunan Province (no. 2022RC1031), the Hubei Provincial Key Research and Development Program (2022BCE042 and 2023BCB007), the High-Performance Computing Center of Central South University, the High-Performance Computing platform of Huazhong University of Science and Technology and computer power at Wuhan Seekmore Intelligent Imaging Inc.

Institutional Review Board Statement: The study was conducted in accordance with the Declaration of Helsinki. The study was approved by the Seoul National University Bundang Hospital, approval code: B-2102/667-10, approval date: 7 February 2021.

Informed Consent Statement: Informed consent was obtained from all subjects involved in this study.

Data Availability Statement: The data presented in this study are available upon request from the corresponding author.

Conflicts of Interest: All authors declare that the research was conducted in the absence of any commercial or financial relationships that could be construed as a potential conflict of interest.

Abbreviations

The following abbreviations are used in this manuscript:

AIS	Acute Ischemic Stroke
IP	Ischemic Penumbra
IC	Ischemic Core
NCCT	Non-Contrast Computed Tomography
MSC	Multi-Scale Convolution
SA	Symmetry Enhancement
DSC	Dice Similarity Coefficient
HD95	95th Hausdorff Distance
ASSD	Average Symmetric Surface Distance
CNN	Convolutional Neural network
I^2PC-Net	IP and IC neural Network
CI	Confidence interval

References

1. Rennert, R.C.; Wali, A.R.; Steinberg, J.A.; Santiago-Dieppa, D.R.; Olson, S.E.; Pannell, J.S.; Khalessi, A.A. Epidemiology, natural history, and clinical presentation of large vessel ischemic stroke. *Neurosurgery* **2019**, *85*, S4. [CrossRef]
2. Smith, W.S.; Lev, M.H.; English, J.D.; Camargo, E.C.; Chou, M.; Johnston, S.C.; Gonzalez, G.; Schaefer, P.W.; Dillon, W.P.; Koroshetz, W.J.; et al. Significance of large vessel intracranial occlusion causing acute ischemic stroke and TIA. *Stroke* **2009**, *40*, 3834–3840. [CrossRef]
3. Ginsberg, M.D. Adventures in the pathophysiology of brain ischemia: Penumbra, gene expression, neuroprotection: The 2002 Thomas Willis Lecture. *Stroke* **2003**, *34*, 214–223. [CrossRef]
4. Paciaroni, M.; Caso, V.; Agnelli, G. The concept of ischemic penumbra in acute stroke and therapeutic opportunities. *Eur. Neurol.* **2009**, *61*, 321–330. [CrossRef]
5. Jauch, E.C.; Saver, J.L.; Adams, H.P., Jr.; Bruno, A.; Connors, J.; Demaerschalk, B.M.; Khatri, P.; McMullan, P.W., Jr.; Qureshi, A.I.; Rosenfield, K.; et al. Guidelines for the early management of patients with acute ischemic stroke: A guideline for healthcare professionals from the American Heart Association/American Stroke Association. *Stroke* **2013**, *44*, 870–947. [CrossRef]
6. Bourcier, R.; Goyal, M.; Liebeskind, D.S.; Muir, K.W.; Desal, H.; Siddiqui, A.H.; Dippel, D.W.; Majoie, C.B.; Van Zwam, W.H.; Jovin, T.G.; et al. Association of time from stroke onset to groin puncture with quality of reperfusion after mechanical thrombectomy: A meta-analysis of individual patient data from 7 randomized clinical trials. *JAMA Neurol.* **2019**, *76*, 405–411. [CrossRef]
7. Evans, M.R.; White, P.; Cowley, P.; Werring, D.J. Revolution in acute ischaemic stroke care: A practical guide to mechanical thrombectomy. *Pract. Neurol.* **2017**, *17*, 252–265. [CrossRef]
8. Powers, W.J.; Rabinstein, A.A.; Ackerson, T.; Adeoye, O.M.; Bambakidis, N.C.; Becker, K.; Biller, J.; Brown, M.; Demaerschalk, B.M.; Hoh, B.; et al. 2018 guidelines for the early management of patients with acute ischemic stroke: A guideline for healthcare professionals from the American Heart Association/American Stroke Association. *Stroke* **2018**, *49*, e46–e99. [CrossRef]
9. Isensee, F.; Jaeger, P.F.; Kohl, S.A.; Petersen, J.; Maier-Hein, K.H. nnU-Net: A self-configuring method for deep learning-based biomedical image segmentation. *Nat. Methods* **2021**, *18*, 203–211. [CrossRef]
10. Lee, H.H.; Bao, S.; Huo, Y.; Landman, B.A. 3d ux-net: A large kernel volumetric convnet modernizing hierarchical transformer for medical image segmentation. *arXiv* **2022**, arXiv:2209.15076.
11. Wu, Y.; Liao, K.; Chen, J.; Wang, J.; Chen, D.Z.; Gao, H.; Wu, J. D-former: A u-shaped dilated transformer for 3D medical image segmentation. *Neural Comput. Appl.* **2023**, *35*, 1931–1944. [CrossRef]
12. Zhou, H.Y.; Guo, J.; Zhang, Y.; Han, X.; Yu, L.; Wang, L.; Yu, Y. nnFormer: Volumetric medical image segmentation via a 3D transformer. *IEEE Trans. Image Process.* **2023**, *32*, 4036–4045. [CrossRef]
13. Xie, Y.; Zhang, J.; Shen, C.; Xia, Y. Cotr: Efficiently bridging cnn and transformer for 3d medical image segmentation. In *Proceedings of the Medical Image Computing and Computer Assisted Intervention–MICCAI 2021: 24th International Conference, Strasbourg, France, 27 September–1 October 2021*; Proceedings, Part III 24; Springer: Berlin/Heidelberg, Germany, 2021; pp. 171–180.
14. Hatamizadeh, A.; Nath, V.; Tang, Y.; Yang, D.; Roth, H.R.; Xu, D. Swin unetr: Swin transformers for semantic segmentation of brain tumors in mri images. In *Proceedings of the International MICCAI Brainlesion Workshop, Virtual, 27 September 2021*; Springer: Berlin/Heidelberg, Germany, 2021; pp. 272–284.
15. Gupta, A.; Vupputuri, A.; Ghosh, N. Delineation of ischemic core and penumbra volumes from mri using msnet architecture. In *Proceedings of the 2019 41st Annual International Conference of the IEEE Engineering in Medicine and Biology Society (EMBC), Berlin, Germany, 23–27 July 2019*; IEEE: Piscataway, NJ, USA, 2019; pp. 6730–6733.
16. Bhurwani, M.M.S.; Boutelier, T.; Davis, A.; Gautier, G.; Swetz, D.; Rava, R.A.; Raguenes, D.; Waqas, M.; Snyder, K.V.; Siddiqui, A.H.; et al. Identification of infarct core and ischemic penumbra using computed tomography perfusion and deep learning. *J. Med. Imaging* **2023**, *10*, 014001. [CrossRef]

17. Ronneberger, O.; Fischer, P.; Brox, T. U-net: Convolutional networks for biomedical image segmentation. In *Proceedings of the Medical Image Computing and Computer-Assisted Intervention–MICCAI 2015: 18th International Conference, Munich, Germany, 5–9 October 2015*; Proceedings, Part III 18; Springer: Berlin/Heidelberg, Germany, 2015; pp. 234–241.
18. Lee, H.; Jung, K.; Kang, D.W.; Kim, N. Fully automated and real-time volumetric measurement of infarct core and penumbra in diffusion-and perfusion-weighted MRI of patients with hyper-acute stroke. *J. Digit. Imaging* **2020**, *33*, 262–272. [CrossRef]
19. Vupputuri, A.; Ashwal, S.; Tsao, B.; Haddad, E.; Ghosh, N. MRI based objective ischemic core-penumbra quantification in adult clinical stroke. In *Proceedings of the 2017 39th Annual International Conference of the IEEE Engineering in Medicine and Biology Society (EMBC), Jeju, Republic of Korea, 11–15 July 2017*; IEEE: Piscataway, NJ, USA, 2017; pp. 3012–3015.
20. Werdiger, F.; Parsons, M.W.; Visser, M.; Levi, C.; Spratt, N.; Kleinig, T.; Lin, L.; Bivard, A. Machine learning segmentation of core and penumbra from acute stroke CT perfusion data. *Front. Neurol.* **2023**, *14*, 1098562. [CrossRef]
21. Tomasetti, L.; Engan, K.; Høllesli, L.J.; Kurz, K.D.; Khanmohammadi, M. CT Perfusion is All We Need: 4D CNN Segmentation of Penumbra and Core in Patients with Suspected Acute Ischemic Stroke. *IEEE Access* **2023**, *11*, 138936–138953. [CrossRef]
22. Sathish, R.; Rajan, R.; Vupputuri, A.; Ghosh, N.; Sheet, D. Adversarially trained convolutional neural networks for semantic segmentation of ischaemic stroke lesion using multisequence magnetic resonance imaging. In *Proceedings of the 2019 41st Annual International Conference of the IEEE Engineering in Medicine and Biology Society (EMBC), Berlin, Germany, 23–27 July 2019*; IEEE: Piscataway, NJ, USA, 2019; pp. 1010–1013.
23. Yushkevich, P.A.; Piven, J.; Cody Hazlett, H.; Gimpel Smith, R.; Ho, S.; Gee, J.C.; Gerig, G. User-Guided 3D Active Contour Segmentation of Anatomical Structures: Significantly Improved Efficiency and Reliability. *Neuroimage* **2006**, *31*, 1116–1128. [CrossRef]
24. Najm, M.; Kuang, H.; Federico, A.; Jogiat, U.; Goyal, M.; Hill, M.D.; Demchuk, A.; Menon, B.K.; Qiu, W. Automated brain extraction from head CT and CTA images using convex optimization with shape propagation. *Comput. Methods Programs Biomed.* **2019**, *176*, 1–8. [CrossRef]
25. Oktay, O.; Schlemper, J.; Folgoc, L.L.; Lee, M.; Heinrich, M.; Misawa, K.; Mori, K.; McDonagh, S.; Hammerla, N.Y.; Kainz, B.; et al. Attention u-net: Learning where to look for the pancreas. *arXiv* **2018**, arXiv:1804.03999.
26. Guo, M.H.; Lu, C.Z.; Hou, Q.; Liu, Z.; Cheng, M.M.; Hu, S.M. Segnext: Rethinking convolutional attention design for semantic segmentation. *Adv. Neural Inf. Process. Syst.* **2022**, *35*, 1140–1156.
27. Barman, A.; Inam, M.E.; Lee, S.; Savitz, S.; Sheth, S.; Giancardo, L. Determining ischemic stroke from CT-angiography imaging using symmetry-sensitive convolutional networks. In *Proceedings of the 2019 IEEE 16th International Symposium on Biomedical Imaging (ISBI 2019), Venice, Italy, 8–11 April 2019*; IEEE: Piscataway, NJ, USA, 2019; pp. 1873–1877.
28. Clèrigues, A.; Valverde, S.; Bernal, J.; Freixenet, J.; Oliver, A.; Lladó, X. Acute and sub-acute stroke lesion segmentation from multimodal MRI. *Comput. Methods Programs Biomed.* **2020**, *194*, 105521. [CrossRef]
29. Cui, L.; Han, S.; Qi, S.; Duan, Y.; Kang, Y.; Luo, Y. Deep symmetric three-dimensional convolutional neural networks for identifying acute ischemic stroke via diffusion-weighted images. *J. X-ray Sci. Technol.* **2021**, *29*, 551–566. [CrossRef]
30. Fuchigami, T.; Akahori, S.; Okatani, T.; Li, Y. A hyperacute stroke segmentation method using 3D U-Net integrated with physicians' knowledge for NCCT. In Proceedings of the Medical Imaging 2020: Computer-Aided Diagnosis, SPIE, Houston, TX, USA, 16–19 February 2020; Volume 11314, pp. 96–101.
31. Kuang, H.; Menon, B.K.; Sohn, S.I.; Qiu, W. EIS-Net: Segmenting early infarct and scoring ASPECTS simultaneously on non-contrast CT of patients with acute ischemic stroke. *Med. Image Anal.* **2021**, *70*, 101984. [CrossRef]
32. Liang, K.; Han, K.; Li, X.; Cheng, X.; Li, Y.; Wang, Y.; Yu, Y. Symmetry-enhanced attention network for acute ischemic infarct segmentation with non-contrast CT images. In *Proceedings of the Medical Image Computing and Computer Assisted Intervention–MICCAI 2021: 24th International Conference, Strasbourg, France, 27 September–1 October 2021*; Proceedings, Part VII 24; Springer: Berlin/Heidelberg, Germany, 2021; pp. 432–441.
33. Ni, H.; Xue, Y.; Wong, K.; Volpi, J.; Wong, S.T.; Wang, J.Z.; Huang, X. Asymmetry Disentanglement Network for Interpretable Acute Ischemic Stroke Infarct Segmentation in Non-contrast CT Scans. In *Proceedings of the International Conference on Medical Image Computing and Computer-Assisted Intervention, Vancouver, BC, Canada, 8–12 September 2022*; Springer: Berlin/Heidelberg, Germany, 2022; pp. 416–426.
34. Kuang, H.; Wang, Y.; Liang, Y.; Liu, J.; Wang, J. BEA-Net: Body and Edge Aware Network With Multi-Scale Short-Term Concatenation for Medical Image Segmentation. *IEEE J. Biomed. Health Inform.* **2023**, *27*, 4828–4839. [CrossRef]
35. Chen, J.; Lu, Y.; Yu, Q.; Luo, X.; Adeli, E.; Wang, Y.; Lu, L.; Yuille, A.L.; Zhou, Y. Transunet: Transformers make strong encoders for medical image segmentation. *arXiv* **2021**, arXiv:2102.04306.
36. Cao, H.; Wang, Y.; Chen, J.; Jiang, D.; Zhang, X.; Tian, Q.; Wang, M. Swin-unet: Unet-like pure transformer for medical image segmentation. In *Proceedings of the European Conference on Computer Vision, Tel Aviv, Israel, 23–27 October 2022*; Springer: Berlin/Heidelberg, Germany, 2022; pp. 205–218.
37. Gao, Y.; Zhou, M.; Metaxas, D.N. UTNet: A hybrid transformer architecture for medical image segmentation. In *Proceedings of the Medical Image Computing and Computer Assisted Intervention–MICCAI 2021: 24th International Conference, Strasbourg, France, 27 September–1 October 2021*; Proceedings, Part III 24; Springer: Berlin/Heidelberg, Germany, 2021; pp. 61–71.
38. Çiçek, Ö.; Abdulkadir, A.; Lienkamp, S.S.; Brox, T.; Ronneberger, O. 3D U-Net: Learning dense volumetric segmentation from sparse annotation. In *Proceedings of the Medical Image Computing and Computer-Assisted Intervention–MICCAI 2016: 19th International Conference, Athens, Greece, 17–21 October 2016*; Proceedings, Part II 19; Springer: Berlin/Heidelberg, Germany, 2016; pp. 424–432.

39. Milletari, F.; Navab, N.; Ahmadi, S.A. V-net: Fully convolutional neural networks for volumetric medical image segmentation. In *Proceedings of the 2016 Fourth International Conference on 3D Vision (3DV), Stanford, CA, USA, 25–28 October 2016*; IEEE: Piscataway, NJ, USA, 2016; pp. 565–571.
40. Zhou, Z.; Rahman Siddiquee, M.M.; Tajbakhsh, N.; Liang, J. Unet++: A nested u-net architecture for medical image segmentation. In *Proceedings of the Deep Learning in Medical Image Analysis and Multimodal Learning for Clinical Decision Support: 4th International Workshop, DLMIA 2018, and 8th International Workshop, ML-CDS 2018, Held in Conjunction with MICCAI 2018, Granada, Spain, 20 September 2018*; Proceedings 4; Springer: Berlin/Heidelberg, Germany, 2018; pp. 3–11.
41. Wang, W.; Chen, C.; Ding, M.; Yu, H.; Zha, S.; Li, J. Transbts: Multimodal brain tumor segmentation using transformer. In *Proceedings of the Medical Image Computing and Computer Assisted Intervention–MICCAI 2021: 24th International Conference, Strasbourg, France, 27 September–1 October 2021*; Proceedings, Part I 24; Springer: Berlin/Heidelberg, Germany, 2021; pp. 109–119.
42. Hatamizadeh, A.; Tang, Y.; Nath, V.; Yang, D.; Myronenko, A.; Landman, B.; Roth, H.R.; Xu, D. Unetr: Transformers for 3D medical image segmentation. In Proceedings of the IEEE/CVF Winter Conference on Applications of Computer Vision, Waikoloa, HI, USA, 3–8 January 2022; pp. 574–584.
43. Qiu, W.; Kuang, H.; Teleg, E.; Ospel, J.M.; Sohn, S.I.; Almekhlafi, M.; Goyal, M.; Hill, M.D.; Demchuk, A.M.; Menon, B.K. Machine learning for detecting early infarction in acute stroke with non–contrast-enhanced CT. *Radiology* **2020**, *294*, 638–644. [CrossRef]
44. Campbell, B.C.; Mitchell, P.J.; Kleinig, T.J.; Dewey, H.M.; Churilov, L.; Yassi, N.; Yan, B.; Dowling, R.J.; Parsons, M.W.; Oxley, T.J.; et al. Endovascular therapy for ischemic stroke with perfusion-imaging selection. *N. Engl. J. Med.* **2015**, *372*, 1009–1018. [CrossRef]
45. Kuang, H.; Wang, Y.; Liu, J.; Wang, J.; Cao, Q.; Hu, B.; Qiu, W.; Wang, J. Hybrid CNN-Transformer Network with Circular Feature Interaction for Acute Ischemic Stroke Lesion Segmentation on Non-contrast CT Scans. *IEEE Trans. Med. Imaging* **2024**. [CrossRef]

biomedicines

Article

Predicting Histologic Grade of Meningiomas Using a Combined Model of Radiomic and Clinical Imaging Features from Preoperative MRI

Jae Hyun Park [1,†], Le Thanh Quang [2,†], Woong Yoon [1,3], Byung Hyun Baek [1,3], Ilwoo Park [1,2,3,4,*] and Seu Kee Kim [3,5,*]

1 Department of Radiology, Chonnam National University Hospital, Gwangju 61469, Republic of Korea; jenny_94@naver.com (J.H.P.); radyoon@jnu.ac.kr (W.Y.)
2 Department of Artificial Intelligence Convergence, Chonnam National University, Gwangju 61469, Republic of Korea; ltquangdigi@gmail.com
3 Department of Radiology, Chonnam National University Medical School, Gwangju 61469, Republic of Korea
4 Department of Data Science, Chonnam National University, Gwangju 61186, Republic of Korea
5 Department of Radiology, Chonnam National University Hwasun Hospital, Hwasun-gun 58128, Republic of Korea
* Correspondence: ipark@jnu.ac.kr (I.P.); kimsk.rad@gmail.com (S.K.K.)
† These authors contributed equally to this work as first authors.

Abstract: Meningiomas are common primary brain tumors, and their accurate preoperative grading is crucial for treatment planning. This study aimed to evaluate the value of radiomics and clinical imaging features in predicting the histologic grade of meningiomas from preoperative MRI. We retrospectively reviewed patients with intracranial meningiomas from two hospitals. Preoperative MRIs were analyzed for tumor and edema volumes, enhancement patterns, margins, and tumor–brain interfaces. Radiomics features were extracted, and machine learning models were employed to predict meningioma grades. A total of 212 patients were included. In the training group (Hospital 1), significant differences were observed between low-grade and high-grade meningiomas in terms of tumor volume ($p = 0.012$), edema volume ($p = 0.004$), enhancement ($p = 0.001$), margin ($p < 0.001$), and tumor–brain interface ($p < 0.001$). Five radiomics features were selected for model development. The prediction model for radiomics features demonstrated an average validation accuracy of 0.74, while the model for clinical imaging features showed an average validation accuracy of 0.69. When applied to external test data (Hospital 2), the radiomics model achieved an area under the receiver operating characteristics curve (AUC) of 0.72 and accuracy of 0.69, while the clinical imaging model achieved an AUC of 0.82 and accuracy of 0.81. An improved performance was obtained from the model constructed by combining radiomics and clinical imaging features. In the combined model, the AUC and accuracy for meningioma grading were 0.86 and 0.73, respectively. In conclusion, this study demonstrates the potential value of radiomics and clinical imaging features in predicting the histologic grade of meningiomas. The combination of both radiomics and clinical imaging features achieved the highest AUC among the models. Therefore, the combined model of radiomics and clinical imaging features may offer a more effective tool for predicting clinical outcomes in meningioma patients.

Keywords: meningioma; radiomic features; machine learning; grading; magnetic resonance imaging

Citation: Park, J.H.; Quang, L.T.; Yoon, W.; Baek, B.H.; Park, I.; Kim, S.K. Predicting Histologic Grade of Meningiomas Using a Combined Model of Radiomic and Clinical Imaging Features from Preoperative MRI. *Biomedicines* **2023**, *11*, 3268. https://doi.org/10.3390/biomedicines11123268

Academic Editor: Wu Qiu

Received: 20 November 2023
Revised: 4 December 2023
Accepted: 9 December 2023
Published: 10 December 2023

1. Introduction

Meningiomas are the most common primary brain tumors, constituting 13–26% of all intracranial tumors [1]. The World Health Organization (WHO) categorizes meningiomas into three histopathologic grades. Approximately 90% are histologically benign (Grade I), 5–7% are atypical (Grade II), and 1–3% are anaplastic (Grade III). High-grade meningiomas

(Grades II and III) are known to have malignant potential and are more likely to recur after complete resection, sometimes requiring adjuvant radiation therapy [2,3]. Also, the survival rate is higher in low-grade meningioma than in high-grade meningioma. Thus, determining preoperative risk factors for higher tumor grades can provide valuable information for both clinicians and patients.

Magnetic resonance imaging (MRI) is the most important imaging technique for the detection and preoperative evaluation of intracranial meningiomas. Previous studies have reported that preoperative MRI is useful for grading meningiomas and evaluating their histopathological characteristics by analyzing imaging findings such as heterogeneous enhancement, marked peritumoral edema, irregular tumor margins, and bone destruction [4–6]. Despite these findings, the image patterns of different grades of meningiomas can often mimic each other, and the usefulness of tumor grading using conventional MRI alone remains controversial [7].

Recently, there has been a rising interest in developing quantitative ways to analyze radiological imaging data. Radiomics is one such way that extracts high-throughput data from medical images using pattern-recognizing mathematical and statistical algorithms to determine pixel intensities. In contrast to the conventional clinical imaging features that are assessed visually by radiologists, which are highly subjective and exhibit inter-observer variability, radiomics analysis can provide a quantitative way to interpret many imaging features. These radiomic features have been shown to reflect underlying pathophysiological characteristics. Furthermore, novel radiomic biomarkers can be developed with prognostic or diagnostic value [8]. As both radiomics and clinical imaging features can serve as prognostic biological factors, machine learning models that combine both radiomics and preoperative clinical imaging features may provide an additional benefit for predicting histologic grade.

The aim of this study is to evaluate the feasibility of using radiomics and clinical imaging features in predicting the histologic grade of meningiomas from preoperative MRI.

2. Materials and Methods

2.1. Patients

We retrospectively reviewed patients who underwent resection for intracranial meningiomas at Chonnam National University Hwasun Hospital (Hospital 1) from April 2016 to September 2021. The inclusion criteria were: (1) histologically confirmed meningioma with a definite grade (according to the 2016 World Health Organization Classification of Tumors of the Central Nervous System) and (2) availability of standard MR scans before any clinical intervention, including biopsy, consisting of T1- and T2-weighted images (T1WI, T2WI), T1-contrast-enhanced (T1-CE) and fluid-attenuated inversion recovery (FLAIR). The exclusion criteria were: (1) ambiguous pathological grade; (2) incomplete MRI sequences and significant motion artifacts on MR scans; (3) irrelevant intracranial disease history; (4) prior history of surgery or treatment before MRI; and (5) an MRI scan that was not performed at our institution. For the external test set, we included patients who underwent preoperative MRI for intracranial meningiomas at Chonnam National University Hospital (Hospital 2) who met the same inclusion criteria in our validation models. Finally, 164 patients from hospital 1 and 48 patients from hospital 2 were included in the study, respectively. The variables were collected from electronic medical records, pathology reports, and radiology reports.

This retrospective study was approved by the Institutional Review Board of Chonnam National University Hospital and was in accordance with the ethical guidelines of the 2008 Declaration of Helsinki. The requirement for written informed consent was waived due to the retrospective nature of the study.

2.2. MRI Protocols

Preoperative MRI studies were performed at two hospitals. At Hospital 1, MR examinations were performed on 3T scanners (Magnetom TimTrio, Skyra, or Vida: Siemens

Healthineers, Erlangen, Germany). The imaging protocols were included T1WI (TR/TE = 2400 − 2540 ms/9.4 ms; matrix = 384 × 269), T2WI (TR/TE = 3500 − 3700 ms/100 − 105 ms; matrix = 448 × 311), FLAIR (TR/TE 7000 ms/80 − 96 ms; matrix = 384 × 230), and T1-CE (TR/TE 149 − 164 ms/3 − 4.4 ms; matrix = 480 × 381). A field of view (FOV) of 230 mm × 230 mm, slice thickness of 4 mm, and no gap were applied to all images. Contrast-enhanced MR scans were acquired after administering a bolus injection of 0.2 mL/kg of contrast agent.

At Hospital 2, MRI examinations were performed using 3T MR scanners (MAGNETOM TimTrio or Vida: Siemens Healthineers, Erlangen, German; Discovery 750; GE Healthcare Chicago, United States; Ingenia CX: Philips, Amsterdam, The Netherlands). The detailed protocols included the following sequences: T1WI (TR/TE = 2000 − 2400 ms/10 − 13 ms; matrix = 320 − 256 × 230 − 287), T2WI (TR/TE = 3000 − 6000 ms/80 − 100 ms; matrix = 400 − 512 × 259 − 400), FLAIR (TR/TE 4800 − 9400 ms/88 − 340 ms; matrix = 256 − 384 × 204 − 264), and T1-CE (TR/TE 287 − 350 ms/2.5 − 4.6 ms; matrix = 320 − 400 × 224 − 321). An FOV of 230 − 240 mm × 230 − 240 mm, a slice thickness of 5 mm, and a gap of 0.5 mm were applied to all images. T1-CE images were acquired after a bolus injection of 0.2 mL/kg of contrast agent.

2.3. Radiologic Evaluation

Two radiologists, with 2 and 20 years of experience, who were blind to the pathological results, reviewed the MR images. Tumor volume, edema volume, and edema-to-tumor volume ratio were measured for all patients included in the study. A semi-automated evaluation of the tumor and peritumoral edema volumes was performed using 3D Slicer software (version 4.11, http://www.slicer.org (accessed on 11 November 2022)). T1-CE images were used to measure the tumor volume, and FLAIR images were used to access the edema volume in all patients. Also, enhancement pattern (homogeneous/heterogeneous), tumor margin (regular/irregular), tumor–brain interface (clear/unclear), and necrosis and dural tail sign (presence or absence) were assessed on MRI. An irregular tumor margin was defined as a tumor that appeared multilobulated or mushroom-shaped. A clear tumor–brain interface was defined as meningiomas with a distinct cerebrospinal fluid (CSF) cleft between the tumor and brain parenchyma. Figure 1a depicts the typical imaging characteristics of a low-grade meningioma, while Figure 1b illustrates those of a high-grade meningioma.

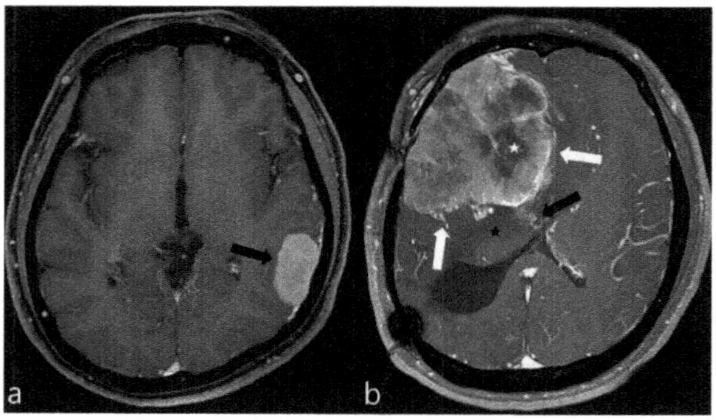

Figure 1. Contrast-enhanced axial MR images of two meningiomas. (**a**) This image exhibits the typical features of a low-grade meningioma, including homogeneous enhancement, smooth margins, absence of peritumoral edema, and no significant mass effect on the surrounding brain parenchyma (black arrow). (**b**) In contrast, this image displays the hallmarks of a high-grade meningioma, characterized by necrotic areas (white asterisk), pronounced mass effect, peritumoral edema (black asterisk), irregular margins (white arrows), and suspicious invasion into the adjacent brain parenchyma (black arrow), indicating a more aggressive tumor behavior.

2.4. Image Preprocessing

A schematic showing the process of image processing and machine learning analysis is shown in Figure 2. Image preprocessing was meticulously designed to standardize radiomic feature extraction from various MRI sequences. The initial step in this process was the application of N4 bias correction, a crucial technique employed to correct for low-frequency-intensity non-uniformities, which are common artifacts in MR imaging. This correction was uniformly applied across T1-CE, T1WI, T2WI, and FLAIR images using the 3D Slicer software. The N4 bias correction, adept at addressing magnetic field inhomogeneities, ensured a homogenous intensity distribution across all images. Subsequently, we engaged in the co-registration of images for each patient, utilizing the General Registration (BRAINS) mode within the 3D Slicer's suite of registration functions. This mode was specifically chosen for its robustness in aligning all MRI sequences to the axial T1-CE sequence, providing a consistent anatomical framework across various imaging modalities. Following co-registration, the next critical step was skull stripping, performed using the SwissSkullStripper extension in 3D Slicer. This tool is particularly effective for accurately removing non-brain tissues from MRI images, thereby significantly enhancing the precision of our analysis by focusing solely on brain tissues and eliminating extraneous confounds. The final phase in our preprocessing workflow was the application of min–max normalization, especially crucial due to the usage of MRI images from three different machines in our study. This normalization process, applied to the region of interest (ROI) in each image, served to standardize pixel intensity values, ensuring a consistent scale for radiomic feature extraction across different scanners. This process, achieved through custom Python scripts, normalized pixel intensity values, ensuring a consistent baseline for feature extraction [9].

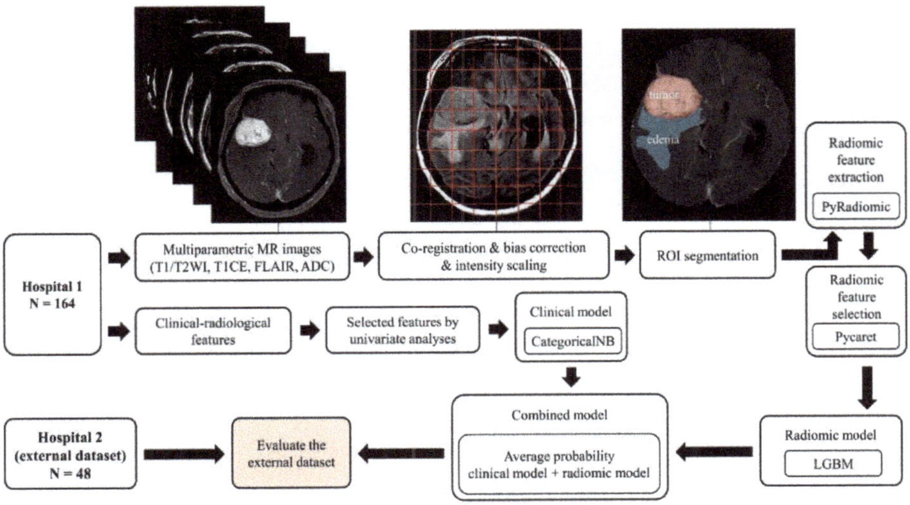

Figure 2. Overview of the image processing and radiomics analysis framework used to develop a machine-learning model.

2.5. Tumor Segmentation and Radiomics Feature Extraction

3D Slicer was used for semi-automated manual segmentation to delineate the region of interest (ROI) associated with meningioma. Tumor boundaries and peritumoral edema were identified from T1WI and FLAIR images, respectively, by employing thresholding and region-growing segmentation algorithms. Radiomics features were extracted utilizing the open-source Python package PyRadiomics, version 3.0.1 [10]. In total, 851 quantitative features were procured, encompassing two categories: original and wavelet-based features.

Prior to their incorporation in the classification model, the values of each feature underwent normalization through the application of the min–max scaler.

2.6. Feature Selection and Classifier Model Training and Testing

We imported all 851 radiomic features into the PyCaret tool, version 2.3.10 [11]. PyCaret is an open-source, low-code machine learning library in Python that streamlines certain workflows, including feature selection. In this study, we relied on PyCaret for feature selection. The feature selection process was iterated 100 times with the random selection of the training data. Eight features were found to be selected by PyCaret in each of the 100 tests. We then removed each of the 8 features one-by-one and checked if the performance increased, which rendered a final 5 features.

Regarding the clinical imaging features, a univariate analysis was conducted to select significantly correlated features for the machine learning model. Features with p-values less than 0.05 were deemed statistically significant in the multivariate analysis and subsequently chosen for inclusion in the model. LightGBM [12] was employed to train the classifier using the top radiomics features, and the categorical Naïve Bayes (CategoricalNB) model [13] was applied for the classification of clinical imaging features. Both models were trained and evaluated on the Hospital 1 data. The data was initially divided into 5 folds with the 4 parts used for training and 1 part for validation. The validation performance was reported as an average of the 5 folds. The radiomics and clinical imaging models that produced the highest performance among the 5 folds were used for the external test set derived from Hospital 2.

To assess the effect of combining the radiomics and clinical imaging models, a fusion model was developed. In the fusion model, the average of the two probabilities from the radiomics and clinical imaging models was taken as the final probability to predict meningioma grade. The performance of the fusion model was evaluated using the Hospital 2 data.

2.7. Statistical Analysis

The clinical imaging features were compared between low-grade and high-grade meningioma groups. Categorical variables were described using percentages, while continuous variables were presented as means. Univariate analysis was performed to select significant radiological characteristics within the low-grade and high-grade groups in the training cohort. Student's t-test and the chi-square test were employed for univariate analysis, with a p-value less than 0.05 deemed statistically significant. Statistical analysis was conducted using IBM SPSS software, version 28.0 (SPSS Inc., Chicago, IL, USA). In order to assess the performance of predictive models for meningioma grading, several metrics, including area under the receiver operating characteristics curve (AUC), accuracy, sensitivity, and specificity, were calculated for both the test and validation sets. The performance of the fusion mode was compared with the clinical imaging and radiomics models using DeLong's test. These evaluations were performed by the in-house-built code using the Python programming language (version 3.7.11).

3. Results

3.1. Patients' Characteristics

The study included a total of 212 patients, divided into two groups for training and testing, with 164 patients in the training group (Hospital 1) and 48 patients in the testing group (Hospital 2). The training group comprised 66 males and 98 females, with a mean age of 60.4 years (age range 25–85 years), while the testing group consisted of 11 males and 37 females, with a mean age of 54.9 years (age range 22–78 years). In Hospital 1, there were 89 patients with low-grade meningioma and 76 with high-grade meningioma, while in Hospital 2, there were 33 with low-grade meningioma and 15 patients with high-grade meningioma. There were no significant differences observed in WHO grade ($p = 0.074$) between the training and testing datasets (Table 1).

Table 1. Characteristics of patients in the training and testing group.

Variables	Training Set (Hospital 1)			Testing Set (Hospital 2)		
	Low Grade	High Grade	*p*-Value	Low Grade	High Grade	*p*-Value
	(*n* = 89)	(*n* = 75)		(*n* = 33)	(*n* = 15)	
Age	59.9	60.88	0.631	55.14	54.66	0.908
Female sex	56	42	0.368	28	9	0.058
Tumor volume (mm^3) (mean)	32.5	49.0	0.012	30.35	38.0	0.461
Edema volume (mm^3) (mean)	24.0	45.1	0.004	41.08	47.25	0.754
Edema/Tumor volume ratio	1.1	1.5	0.433	1.46	1.35	0.859
Enhancement			<0.001			<0.001
Homogeneous	61 (68.5%)	32 (42.7%)		29 (87.9%)	6 (40%)	
Heterogeneous	28 (31.4%)	43 (57.3%)		4 (12.1%)	9 (60%)	
Necrosis			0.046			0.502
Yes	28 (31.4%)	35 (46.7%)		6 (18.2%)	4 (26.7%)	
No	61 (68.5%)	40 (53.3%)		27 (81.8%)	11 (73.3%)	
Dural tail			0.055			0.367
Yes	67 (75.3%)	46 (61.3%)		20 (60.6%)	7 (46.7%)	
No	22 (24.7%)	29 (38.7%)		13 (39.4%)	8 (53.3%)	
Margin			<0.001			0.030
Regular	54 (60.7%)	23 (30.7%)		24 (72.7%)	6 (40%)	
Irregular	35 (39.3%)	52 (69.3%)		9 (27.3%)	9 (60%)	
Tumor-brain interface			<0.001			<0.001
Clear	79 (88.8%)	41 (54.7%)		29 (87.9%)	5 (33.3%)	
Unclear	10 (11.2%)	34 (45.3)		4 (12.1%)	10 (66.7%)	

3.2. Clinical Imaging Features

In the training group (Hospital 1), significant differences were found between low-grade and high-grade meningioma groups for tumor volume ($p = 0.012$), edema volume ($p = 0.004$), enhancement ($p = 0.001$), margin ($p < 0.001$), and tumor–brain interface ($p < 0.001$) (Table 2).

Table 2. Performance of machine learning of models for prediction of tumor grading.

Models	Validation Set (Hospital 1)				Testing Set (Hospital 2)			
	AUC	Accuracy	Sensitivity	Specificity	AUC	Accuracy	Sensitivity	Specificity
Clinical imaging	0.77	0.69	0.67	0.89	0.82	0.81	0.73	0.85
Radiomics	0.83	0.74	0.80	0.72	0.72	0.69	0.67	0.70
Combined					0.86	0.73	0.73	0.73

AUC, area under the receiver operating characteristic curve.

3.3. Radiomics Features

The selectin of radiomics features was executed 100 times, resulting in 100 unique sets of selected features. Eight features were consistently selected across all iterations and, therefore, considered for a further selection. A systematic removal and the evaluation of these eight features yielded a final selection of five radiomics features: original GLSZM small area emphasis, original shape flatness, wavelet-HHL GLSZM gray level non-uniformity, wavelet-HLL first-order mean, and wavelet-LLL first-order interquartile range.

3.4. Diagnostic Performance of the Prediction Model

The LightGBM radiomics model showed an average validation accuracy of 0.74 (range: 0.72–0.75) using 5-fold cross validation (CV). Using the external test data from Hospital 2, this model yielded accuracy, AUC, sensitivity, and specificity of 0.69, 0.72, 0.67, and 0.7, respectively.

The average validation accuracy of clinical imaging features using 5-fold CV was 0.69 (range: 0.63–0.79). Using the external test data from Hospital 2, the clinical imaging model yielded accuracy, AUC, sensitivity, and specificity of 0.81, 0.82, 0.73, and 0.85, respectively. The fusion model that combined the radiomics and clinical imaging models resulted in slightly improved performances, with accuracy, AUC, sensitivity, and specificity of 0.73, 0.86, 0.73, and 0.73, respectively, for the external test data. The results of the radiomics, clinical imaging, and fusion models are shown in Table 2 and Figure 3.

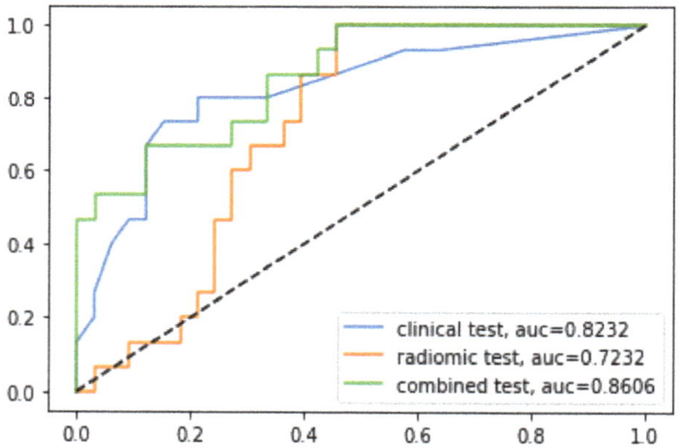

Figure 3. Comparison of receiver operating characteristic curves for the prediction of tumor grading using the external test set from Hospital 2.

The analysis of DeLong's test revealed that the AUC of the combined model was significantly higher than that of the radiomics model (p = 0.0012) but was similar to that of the clinical imaging model (p = 0.31).

4. Discussion

The present study aimed to evaluate the value of radiomics and clinical imaging features in predicting the histologic grade of meningiomas using preoperative MRI. Our results highlight the potential of combining radiomics and clinical imaging features to provide a quantitative way for the preoperative prediction of meningioma grade, which can be crucial for guiding clinical decision-making and patient management.

Generally, meningioma can be easily diagnosed with reasonable confidence using MRI and CT, as they typically appear as well-defined masses with a broad-based dural attachment and show homogeneous enhancement on post-contrast imaging. Beyond this simple diagnosis, researchers have been using non-invasive imaging biomarkers to predict tumor grading, which affects patient treatment decisions and prognosis. In previous studies, several conventional and advanced MRI findings have been identified as suggestive of high-grade meningiomas [4,6,14–20]. The imaging findings associated with high-grade meningiomas include higher degree of peritumoral edema, intratumoral necrosis, lower ADC values, heterogeneous enhancement, dural tail sign, irregular or poorly defined tumor margins, and blurred or irregular tumor–brain interface. In our study, we identified significant differences between low-grade and high-grade meningiomas in terms of tumor volume, edema volume, enhancement, margin, and tumor–brain interface. These findings are consistent with previous literature. However, there are still limitations in the overall predictive accuracy of these findings. To overcome these limitations and improve diagnostic accuracy, machine learning-based predictive models using MRI radiomic features are being developed.

For the selection of radiomic features, we used the PyCaret tool. PyCaret is a high-level, open-source Python library for machine learning that streamlines the process of creating, comparing, and deploying models. It provides a unified interface for several machine learning libraries, enabling the user to implement a wide range of algorithms. In addition, PyCaret includes a variety of preprocessing techniques, feature engineering, and feature selection methods [11]. The feature selection algorithm in PyCaret is based on three main algorithms: random forest, LightGBM, and correlation. One of the most widely used feature selection methods in machine learning is least absolute shrinkage and selection operator (LASSO). LASSO is a linear regression technique that applies regularization to prevent overfitting and perform feature selection [21,22]. While LASSO is a powerful technique for feature selection in linear regression tasks, PyCaret's broader range of tools and features may have provided a more versatile and efficient approach to selecting the optimal features and models compared to using LASSO alone.

Five radiomics features were selected by the PyCaret tool: original GLSZM small area emphasis, original shape flatness, wavelet-HHL GLSZM gray level non-uniformity, wavelet-HLL first-order mean, and wavelet-LLL first-order interquartile range. Original GLSZM small area emphasis is a measure of the distribution of small size zones in the gray level size zone matrix. In the context of meningioma grading, this feature may be relevant as it can help capture differences in tumor cellularity, which can be indicative of the tumor's aggressiveness. Original shape flatness is a shape descriptor that quantifies the elongation of an object in three-dimensional space. It is calculated as the ratio of the smallest to the largest principal axis of the best-fitting ellipsoid. In meningioma grading, this feature may help distinguish between different tumor shapes that could be related to the tumor's invasiveness or growth pattern. Wavelet-HHL GLSZM gray level non-uniformity measures the non-uniformity of gray levels in the texture of an image. High values indicate more heterogeneity in the image, which may be associated with varying cell densities or structural variations within the tumor. Wavelet-HLL first-order mean is the average of the pixel intensity values in an image after applying the wavelet transform. The mean value represents the overall intensity of the image, and changes in this feature may reflect differences in tumor contrast, vascularity, or cell density. These variations could be associated with different meningioma grades and help distinguish between them. Wavelet-LLL first-order interquartile range measures the interquartile range of the pixel intensity values in an image after applying the wavelet transform. The interquartile range can provide information about the distribution and variability of the intensity values in the image. In meningioma grading, this feature may capture variations in tumor heterogeneity or tissue properties. In summary, these five radiomics features presumably reflect different aspects of meningioma characteristics, such as shape, texture, and intensity distribution. They are associated with aggressiveness or growth patterns, which may be predictive of meningioma grading and prognosis.

The LightGBM classifier model demonstrated superior performance among radiomics-based predictive models, with an average validation accuracy of the 5-fold CV of 0.74. When applied to external test data from Hospital 2, the radiomics model achieved an accuracy of 0.69, an AUC of 0.72, a sensitivity of 0.67, and a specificity of 0.7. These findings are consistent with several recently published studies that have investigated the use of radiomics data in the grading of meningiomas [2,7,22–27]. A systematic review and meta-analysis conducted by Ugga reported that the overall pooled AUC for machine learning models in meningioma grading was 0.88 (95% CI = 0.84–0.93) [28].

Although methodological differences among studies, such as variations in patient populations, imaging modalities, feature selection algorithms, classifier models, sample sizes, and external validation, pose significant challenges in making direct comparisons, our study revealed a relatively lower overall predictive value compared to that of the previous research. Several factors might have contributed to these results. First, our training dataset was obtained from multiple MRI machines, whereas most previous studies used data from a single MRI machine. MRIs at Hospital 1, used to obtain radiomics data in this study, were from three different machines. In general, using data from a single MRI machine can yield higher diagnostic accuracy and AUC for machine learning models because the data from a single MRI scanner has less variation than that from multiple MRI scanners. However, the model trained with data from a single MRI scanner may lack generalizability to data from other MRI machines. On the other hand, models trained with radiomics data from multiple MRI machines can lead to a more robust and generalizable machine learning model, as they are trained on a diverse set of imaging data that accounts for variations in imaging parameters, scanner-specific artifacts, and inter-scanner variability. This may result in lower diagnostic accuracy or AUC compared to a model trained on a single MRI machine. The second factor to consider is differences in patient populations. The current study has a higher proportion of high-grade meningioma patients compared to the previously published studies. This is advantageous as it allows us to evaluate the performance of our model in predicting high-grade tumors, which are generally more challenging to diagnose and require more aggressive treatment. In addition, the inclusion of a larger number of high-grade patients provides more robust data for the development of predictive models. The third factor pertains to the disparity in machine learning models. Previous research often employed support vector machine (SVM) or random forest models [22,28]. In contrast, this study utilized LightGBM. This model exhibits exceptional accuracy and speed, making it suitable for handling extensive datasets. Notably, it possesses the ability to handle missing values and outliers, which are frequently encountered in medical datasets. Moreover, its proficiency in managing imbalanced datasets proves advantageous in medical imaging, where certain diseases may have higher prevalence rates. Despite these benefits, LightGBM has several limitations. Overfitting may occur if the model is trained on a small dataset or if too many features are included in the analysis. Additionally, the model's accuracy can be influenced by hyperparameters such as the learning rate and the number of trees [12,29].

One of the significant findings of our study is the novel integration of radiomics and clinical imaging features to develop a robust and effective model for predicting meningioma grades. Most studies in the literature have attempted to predict meningioma grade using either radiomics or clinical imaging features independently. The combination of radiomics and clinical imaging data resulted in a notable improvement in AUC (0.86) compared to either the radiomics (0.72, AUC) or clinical imaging (0.82, AUC) models. Although the AUC of the combined model was statistically higher than that of the radiomics model but similar to that of the clinical imaging model, this finding underscores the importance of integrating multiple features for enhanced performance in meningioma grading. Our findings are consistent with several recently published studies that have investigated the combination of radiomics and non-imaging clinical data in other areas of meningioma studies. For instance, a study by Joo reported that an imaging-based model that combined interface radiomics and peritumoral edema could predict brain invasion by meningioma and improve diagnostic performance [30]. Similarly, a study by Park demonstrated that integrating radiomics with clinicopathological features significantly contributed to predicting recurrence in patients with grade 2 meningiomas [31]. These studies, along with our findings, suggest that combining radiomics and clinical features has the potential to be a powerful tool, providing additional information beyond what is visible on conventional imaging.

Our study has several limitations. First, we only used retrospective data. Second, the sample size of the testing group was relatively small, which may limit the generalizability of our findings. In addition, our study did not include other MR imaging sequences, such as perfusion-weighted imaging or diffusion-weighted imaging, which might offer complementary information for predicting meningioma grade.

5. Conclusions

In conclusion, our study demonstrates the potential of a combined model that incorporates both radiomics and clinical imaging features for predicting the histologic grade of meningiomas using preoperative MRI. By overcoming the limitations of conventional MRI-based grading and reducing subjectivity, our approach can provide valuable information for clinicians and patients in terms of prognosis and management. Future studies could further validate and refine this model using larger, multi-center cohorts and explore the potential of incorporating additional imaging modalities to enhance predictive performance.

Author Contributions: J.H.P., L.T.Q., I.P. and S.K.K. designed the study; J.H.P. and L.T.Q. performed the majority of experiments; J.H.P., L.T.Q., W.Y., B.H.B., I.P. and S.K.K. contributed to the analysis and interpretation of results; J.H.P. and L.T.Q. wrote the first draft of the manuscript; I.P. and S.K.K. approved the final manuscript and completed manuscript. Also, all authors agree with the content of the manuscript. All authors contributed to the article and approved the submitted version. All authors have read and agreed to the published version of the manuscript.

Funding: This study was supported by the Institute of Information & Communications Technology Planning & Evaluation (IITP) under the Artificial Intelligence Convergence Innovation Human Resources Development (IITP-2023-RS-2023-00256629) grant funded by the Korea government (MSIT) and grants from the Ministry of Education, Republic of Korea (NRF-2022R1I1A3072856), and Chonnam National University Hospital Biomedical Research Institute (BCRI22037).

Institutional Review Board Statement: All procedures performed in the study were carried out in accordance with the ethical standards of the institutional research committee and the 1964 Helsinki Declaration and its later amendments. The research proposal was approved by the institutional review board (approval number CNUHH-2022-126).

Informed Consent Statement: Patient consent was waived due to the study's retrospective nature, involving the analysis of existing, anonymized medical images.

Data Availability Statement: The data supporting the conclusions of this study are available from the corresponding authors on reasonable request.

Conflicts of Interest: The authors declare no conflict of interest.

References

1. Marosi, C.; Hassler, M.; Roessler, K.; Reni, M.; Sant, M.; Mazza, E.; Vecht, C. Meningioma. *Crit. Rev. Oncol. Hematol.* **2008**, *67*, 153–171. [CrossRef]
2. Chu, H.; Lin, X.; He, J.; Pang, P.; Fan, B.; Lei, P.; Guo, D.; Ye, C. Value of MRI Radiomics Based on Enhanced T1WI Images in Prediction of Meningiomas Grade. *Acad. Radiol.* **2021**, *28*, 687–693. [CrossRef] [PubMed]
3. Coroller, T.P.; Bi, W.L.; Huynh, E.; Abedalthagafi, M.; Aizer, A.A.; Greenwald, N.F.; Parmar, C.; Narayan, V.; Wu, W.W.; Miranda de Moura, S.; et al. Radiographic prediction of meningioma grade by semantic and radiomic features. *PLoS ONE* **2017**, *12*, e0187908. [CrossRef] [PubMed]
4. Amano, T.; Nakamizo, A.; Murata, H.; Miyamatsu, Y.; Mugita, F.; Yamashita, K.; Noguchi, T.; Nagata, S. Preoperative Prediction of Intracranial Meningioma Grade Using Conventional CT and MRI. *Cureus* **2022**, *14*, e21610. [CrossRef] [PubMed]
5. Shin, C.; Kim, J.M.; Cheong, J.H.; Ryu, J.I.; Won, Y.D.; Ko, Y.; Han, M.-H. Association between tumor size and peritumoral brain edema in patients with convexity and parasagittal meningiomas. *PLoS ONE* **2021**, *16*, e0252945. [CrossRef] [PubMed]
6. Lekhavat, V.; Radeesri, K. The Role of Pre-operative MRI For Prediction of High-Grade Intracranial Meningioma: A Retrospective Study. *Asian Pac. J. Cancer Prev.* **2023**, *24*, 819–825. [CrossRef]
7. Chen, C.; Guo, X.; Wang, J.; Guo, W.; Ma, X.; Xu, J. The Diagnostic Value of Radiomics-Based Machine Learning in Predicting the Grade of Meningiomas Using Conventional Magnetic Resonance Imaging: A Preliminary Study. *Front. Oncol.* **2019**, *9*, 1338. [CrossRef]
8. Tomaszewski, M.R.; Gillies, R.J. The biological meaning of radiomic features. *Radiology* **2021**, *298*, 505–516. [CrossRef]

9. Haga, A.; Takahashi, W.; Aoki, S.; Nawa, K.; Yamashita, H.; Abe, O.; Nakagawa, K. Standardization of imaging features for radiomics analysis. *J. Med. Investig.* **2019**, *66*, 35–37. [CrossRef]
10. van Griethuysen, J.J.M.; Fedorov, A.; Parmar, C.; Hosny, A.; Aucoin, N.; Narayan, V.; Beets-Tan, R.G.H.; Fillion-Robin, J.C.; Pieper, S.; Aerts, H. Computational Radiomics System to Decode the Radiographic Phenotype. *Cancer Res.* **2017**, *77*, e104–e107. [CrossRef] [PubMed]
11. Ali, M. PyCaret: An Open Source, Low-Code Machine Learning Library in Python. Available online: https://www.pycaret.org (accessed on 15 June 2023).
12. Ke, G.; Meng, Q.; Finley, T.; Wang, T.; Chen, W.; Ma, W.; Ye, Q.; Liu, T.-Y. Lightgbm: A highly efficient gradient boosting decision tree. In *Advances in Neural Information Processing Systems 30 (NIPS)*; The MIT Press: Cambridge, MA, USA, 2017.
13. Pedregosa, F.; Varoquaux, G.; Gramfort, A.; Michel, V.; Thirion, B.; Grisel, O.; Blondel, M.; Prettenhofer, P.; Weiss, R.; Dubourg, V. Scikit-learn: Machine learning in Python. *J. Mach. Learn. Res.* **2011**, *12*, 2825–2830.
14. Zhang, S.; Chiang, G.C.; Knapp, J.M.; Zecca, C.M.; He, D.; Ramakrishna, R.; Magge, R.S.; Pisapia, D.J.; Fine, H.A.; Tsiouris, A.J.; et al. Grading meningiomas utilizing multiparametric MRI with inclusion of susceptibility weighted imaging and quantitative susceptibility mapping. *J. Neuroradiol.* **2020**, *47*, 272–277. [CrossRef] [PubMed]
15. Atalay, B.; Ediz, S.S.; Ozbay, N.O. Apparent Diffusion Coefficient in Predicting the Preoperative Grade of Meningiomas. *J. Coll. Physicians Surg. Pak.* **2020**, *30*, 1126–1132. [CrossRef] [PubMed]
16. Salah, F.; Tabbarah, A.; Asmar, K.; Tamim, H.; Makki, M.; Sibahi, A.; Hourani, R. Can CT and MRI features differentiate benign from malignant meningiomas? *Clin. Radiol.* **2019**, *74*, 898.e15–898.e23. [CrossRef]
17. Huang, R.Y.; Bi, W.L.; Griffith, B.; Kaufmann, T.J.; la Fougere, C.; Schmidt, N.O.; Tonn, J.C.; Vogelbaum, M.A.; Wen, P.Y.; Aldape, K.; et al. Imaging and diagnostic advances for intracranial meningiomas. *Neuro Oncol.* **2019**, *21*, i44–i61. [CrossRef]
18. Lin, B.J.; Chou, K.N.; Kao, H.W.; Lin, C.; Tsai, W.C.; Feng, S.W.; Lee, M.S.; Hueng, D.Y. Correlation between magnetic resonance imaging grading and pathological grading in meningioma. *J. Neurosurg.* **2014**, *121*, 1201–1208. [CrossRef] [PubMed]
19. Kawahara, Y.; Nakada, M.; Hayashi, Y.; Kai, Y.; Hayashi, Y.; Uchiyama, N.; Nakamura, H.; Kuratsu, J.-i.; Hamada, J.-i. Prediction of high-grade meningioma by preoperative MRI assessment. *J. Neuro-Oncol.* **2012**, *108*, 147–152. [CrossRef] [PubMed]
20. Nagar, V.A.; Ye, J.R.; Ng, W.H.; Chan, Y.H.; Hui, F.; Lee, C.K.; Lim, C.C. Diffusion-weighted MR imaging: Diagnosing atypical or malignant meningiomas and detecting tumor dedifferentiation. *AJNR Am. J. Neuroradiol.* **2008**, *29*, 1147–1152. [CrossRef]
21. Tibshirani, R. Regression shrinkage and selection via the lasso. *J. R. Stat. Soc. Ser. B (Methodol.)* **1996**, *58*, 267–288. [CrossRef]
22. Brunasso, L.; Ferini, G.; Bonosi, L.; Costanzo, R.; Musso, S.; Benigno, U.E.; Gerardi, R.M.; Giammalva, G.R.; Paolini, F.; Umana, G.E.; et al. A Spotlight on the Role of Radiomics and Machine-Learning Applications in the Management of Intracranial Meningiomas: A New Perspective in Neuro-Oncology: A Review. *Life* **2022**, *12*, 586. [CrossRef]
23. Han, Y.; Wang, T.; Wu, P.; Zhang, H.; Chen, H.; Yang, C. Meningiomas: Preoperative predictive histopathological grading based on radiomics of MRI. *Magn. Reson. Imaging* **2021**, *77*, 36–43. [CrossRef] [PubMed]
24. Zhang, J.; Yao, K.; Liu, P.; Liu, Z.; Han, T.; Zhao, Z.; Cao, Y.; Zhang, G.; Zhang, J.; Tian, J.; et al. A radiomics model for preoperative prediction of brain invasion in meningioma non-invasively based on MRI: A multicentre study. *EBioMedicine* **2020**, *58*, 102933. [CrossRef] [PubMed]
25. Hu, J.; Zhao, Y.; Li, M.; Liu, J.; Wang, F.; Weng, Q.; Wang, X.; Cao, D. Machine learning-based radiomics analysis in predicting the meningioma grade using multiparametric MRI. *Eur. J. Radiol.* **2020**, *131*, 109251. [CrossRef] [PubMed]
26. Hamerla, G.; Meyer, H.J.; Schob, S.; Ginat, D.T.; Altman, A.; Lim, T.; Gihr, G.A.; Horvath-Rizea, D.; Hoffmann, K.T.; Surov, A. Comparison of machine learning classifiers for differentiation of grade 1 from higher gradings in meningioma: A multicenter radiomics study. *Magn. Reson. Imaging* **2019**, *63*, 244–249. [CrossRef]
27. Hale, A.T.; Stonko, D.P.; Wang, L.; Strother, M.K.; Chambless, L.B. Machine learning analyses can differentiate meningioma grade by features on magnetic resonance imaging. *Neurosurg. Focus.* **2018**, *45*, E4. [CrossRef] [PubMed]
28. Ugga, L.; Perillo, T.; Cuocolo, R.; Stanzione, A.; Romeo, V.; Green, R.; Cantoni, V.; Brunetti, A. Meningioma MRI radiomics and machine learning: Systematic review, quality score assessment, and meta-analysis. *Neuroradiology* **2021**, *63*, 1293–1304. [CrossRef]
29. LightGBM. Available online: https://lightgbm.readthedocs.io/en/latest/ (accessed on 22 June 2023).
30. Joo, L.; Park, J.E.; Park, S.Y.; Nam, S.J.; Kim, Y.H.; Kim, J.H.; Kim, H.S. Extensive peritumoral edema and brain-to-tumor interface MRI features enable prediction of brain invasion in meningioma: Development and validation. *Neuro Oncol.* **2021**, *23*, 324–333. [CrossRef]
31. Park, C.J.; Choi, S.H.; Eom, J.; Byun, H.K.; Ahn, S.S.; Chang, J.H.; Kim, S.H.; Lee, S.K.; Park, Y.W.; Yoon, H.I. An interpretable radiomics model to select patients for radiotherapy after surgery for WHO grade 2 meningiomas. *Radiat. Oncol.* **2022**, *17*, 147. [CrossRef]

biomedicines

MDPI

Article

Automated Collateral Scoring on CT Angiography of Patients with Acute Ischemic Stroke Using Hybrid CNN and Transformer Network

Hulin Kuang [1], Wenfang Wan [1], Yahui Wang [1], Jie Wang [1] and Wu Qiu [2,*]

1 Hunan Provincial Key Lab on Bioinformatics, School of Computer Science and Engineering, Central South University, Changsha 410083, China
2 School of Life Science and Technology, Huazhong University of Science and Technology, Wuhan 430074, China
* Correspondence: wuqiu@hust.edu.cn

Abstract: Collateral scoring plays an important role in diagnosis and treatment decisions of acute ischemic stroke (AIS). Most existing automated methods rely on vessel prominence and amount after vessel segmentation. The purpose of this study was to design a vessel-segmentation free method for automating collateral scoring on CT angiography (CTA). We first processed the original CTA via maximum intensity projection (MIP) and middle cerebral artery (MCA) region segmentation. The obtained MIP images were fed into our proposed hybrid CNN and Transformer model (MPViT) to automatically determine the collateral scores. We collected 154 CTA scans of patients with AIS for evaluation using five-folder cross validation. Results show that the proposed MPViT achieved an intraclass correlation coefficient of 0.767 (95% CI: 0.68–0.83) and a Kappa of 0.6184 (95% CI: 0.4954–0.7414) for three-point collateral score classification. For dichotomized classification (good vs. non-good and poor vs. non-poor), it also achieved great performance.

Keywords: acute ischemic stroke; collateral scoring; CT angiography; hybrid CNN and Transformer

Citation: Kuang, H.; Wan, W.; Wang, Y.; Wang, J.; Qiu, W. Automated Collateral Scoring on CT Angiography of Patients with Acute Ischemic Stroke Using Hybrid CNN and Transformer Network. *Biomedicines* **2023**, *11*, 243. https://doi.org/10.3390/biomedicines11020243

Academic Editor: Juan Sahuquillo

Received: 3 December 2022
Revised: 10 January 2023
Accepted: 14 January 2023
Published: 17 January 2023

1. Introduction

Stroke is one of the leading causes of death and disability in adults worldwide, and ischemic stroke accounts for the majority, mainly due to atherosclerosis. Currently, the most effective treatments for acute ischemic stroke (AIS) are intravenous thrombolysis and endovascular therapy (EVT) within a suitable time window [1]. To assess the infract core for AIS patients, there are two classical neuroradiological methods: infarct volume size and location estimation (i.e., infarct segmentation) and the Alberta Stroke Program Early CT Score (ASPECTS). For manual infract segmentation, neuroradiologists often visually quantify and locate the infract core via screening all slices of computed tomography (CT) scans or diffusion weighted imaging (DWI) scans to determine which voxels can be infarcts [2]. ASPECTS is a scale to better quantitatively evaluate the affected status of 10 regions in the middle cerebral artery and is implemented via screening scans to determine whether a region contains infarcts [3]. These two types of methods evaluate the ischemic infarct core from different scales, and they are both used in the diagnosis of AIS and help to select patients who are suitable for endovascular treatment [4–7]. However, the above methods only reflect the infarction core situation and ignore the role of collateral circulation in the treatment of AIS patients. Previous studies have shown that the quality of collateral circulation reflects to a certain extent the amount of brain tissue that can be salvaged [8] and AIS patients with good collateral circulation can receive better clinical outcomes after EVT [9,10]. Therefore, evaluating the collateral circulation status score (i.e., collateral scoring) is necessary and helpful to select patients who may have a good prognosis after EVT.

In the clinical practice, collateral scoring is generally based on visual scoring via screening medical image scans such as CT angiography (CTA) and CT perfusion, which depends on the experience level of the radiologist, resulting in great observer variability [11,12]. Additionally, it is tedious and time-consuming for clinicians to score visual collateral circulation status, which may result in inefficient diagnosis and patient selection. Therefore, an objective and accurate automated collateral scoring method is desired in AIS clinical practice.

In recent years, radiomics and deep neural networks have been widely used in image analysis tasks [13–18]. Several methods that are based on radiomics and deep learning have also been used for automated collateral scoring [19–22]. For example, Su et al. [20] used a convolutional neural network (CNN) to segment blood vessels in the left and right middle cerebral artery (MCA) regions of the brain, and then several quantified features were extracted on the segmented vessels and input into several machine learning approaches to achieve collateral scoring. Some commercial software such as StrokeViewer has also been evaluated for automated collateral scoring in some studies [23,24]. Although these methods can achieve automated scoring of collateral status, most of them are based on the results of vessel segmentation. The performance of vessel segmentation greatly influences the final collateral scoring performance. In this study, we explore vessel-segmentation free methods to potentially improve the collateral scoring performance.

Currently, Transformer [25] has been used in many image analysis tasks due to its excellent ability to capture long-range dependencies. Additionally, how to combine Transformer and CNN to make full use of their advantages has also attracted more and more attention in the field of medical image analysis. For example, Cheng et al. [26] developed a multi-task hybrid CNN–Transformer encoder for isocitrate dehydrogenase prediction and glioma segmentation. Inspired by the fact that CNN is good at learning local representations and Transformer can capture global representations well, we hypothesized that using a hybrid network of Transformer and CNN can score collateral status more accurately and efficiently. We aimed to design a hybrid CNN and Transformer-based vessel-segmentation free method for automating collateral scoring on CTA scans of AIS patients.

2. Materials and Methods

2.1. Data Acquisition

We collected single-phase CTA scans of 154 AIS patients from Xiangya hospital, Changsha, Hunan. The patient inclusion criteria included: (1) The CTA scans of patients covered the whole brain without severe motion artifacts; (2) expert readings of collateral scores were available.

The sizes of the acquired CTA scans were $512 \times 512 \times S$, where S ranged from 124 to 414. The collateral score is a relatively simple three-point scoring system, i.e., good (score = 0), intermediate (score = 1) and poor (score = 2). Good collateral indicated that the degree of collateral filling was 100%, intermediate collateral indicated that the degree of collateral filling was >50% and <100%, and poor collateral indicated that the degree of collateral filling was $\geq$0% and less than 50%. All CTA images were separately assessed by two radiologists with more than 10 years of experience, and images that disagreed between the two radiologists were assessed by a third physician with more than 15 years of experience, and they then came to a consensus score. Of all 154 patients, 69, 52 and 33 patients had collateral scores of 0, 1 and 2, respectively.

2.2. Image Preprocessing

Figure 1 shows the image preprocessing steps used in this study. Skull stripping was first applied, as the high-brightness pixels of the skull had a severe interference in vessel recognition. We used the method in [27] to achieve skull stripping on the acquired CTA images. This method extracts brain within images on a slice-by-slice basis through thresholding combined with convex optimization iterations.

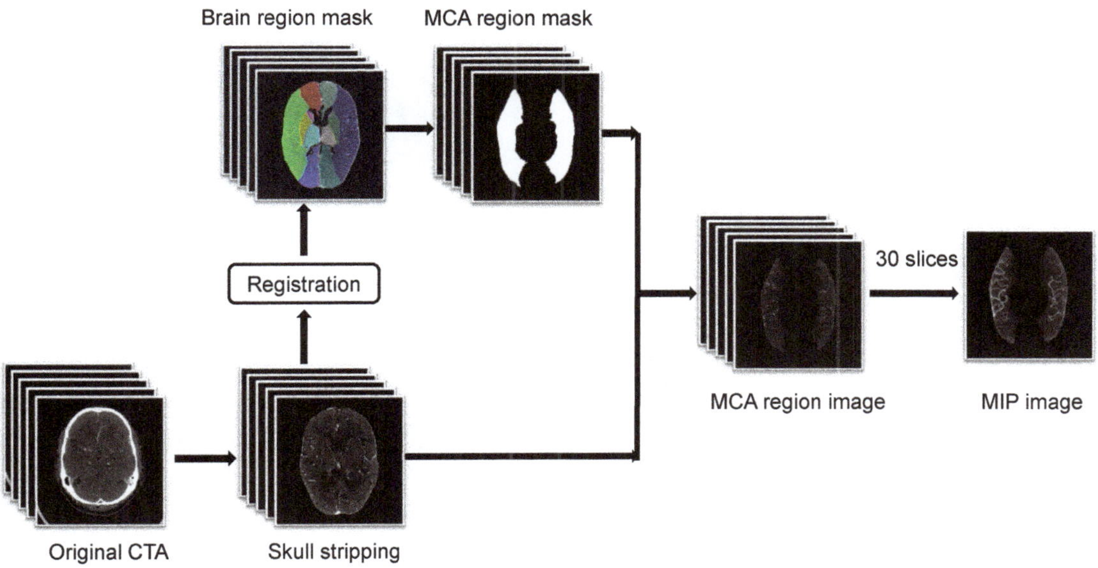

Figure 1. Image preprocessing.

The second preprocessing step was atlas-based registration for MCA region mask generation. We registered the standard brain region atlas onto each CTA scan to obtain the brain region masks of each CTA scan. We generated the MCA region mask from the obtained brain region mask by binarization where voxels that belonged to MCA were set to 1 and the rest were set to 0.

Because the vessel voxels in 3D CTA scans generally had high intensities, maximum intensity projection (MIP) that projected 3D CTA scans to two-dimensional images could well display the degree of stenosis, dilation and filling defect of vessels [21]. Figure 2 shows visualized MIP results of CTA scans with different collateral scores. As shown in Figure 2, after MIP on the whole 3D scans there were significant differences in the degree of collateral filling in patients with different scores, but there existed some interference outside the MCA regions. Additionally, since the vasculature capable of assessing the status of collateral extended from the skull vertex to the circle of Willis, too much irrelevant vasculature would easily interfere with the scoring [28]. Thus, in order to clearly show the vessels in the MCA arterial tree in the left and right hemispheres and reduce the interference from varying numbers of slices, we only took the 30 most-cranial axial slices from the circle of Willis and multiplied the acquired 3D CTA images with the generated MCA masks before performing MIP in the final preprocessing step.

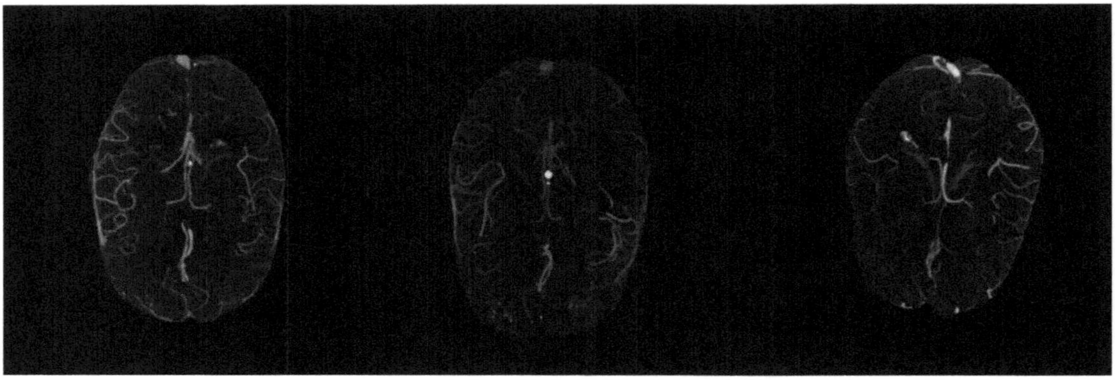

Figure 2. Examples of maximum intensity projection (MIP) images from 3D CTA image with different collateral scores. The left one is good collateral. The middle one is intermediate collateral. The right one is poor collateral.

2.3. Collateral Scoring Based on MIP Images

Due to the class imbalance of the samples, we performed data augmentation to alleviate the imbalance. First, we randomly upsampled the poor and intermediate classes with a smaller sample size to the same size as the good class via copying. However, simply copying a large number of images might lead to an overfitting problem. In order to avoid this problem, we implemented operations such as rotations with small angles and shifts without changing the characteristics of CTA scans to ensure the validity of the augmented samples.

From Figure 2, we found that the vessel regions became more salient in MIP images, making it possible to design a vessel-segmentation free method using MIP images. After performing data augmentation on the obtained MIP images, we used a hybrid deep learning model: the MPViT proposed in [29], which combines Transformer and CNN to capture global and local information at the same time. MPViT first processed the input images through a convolution-based stem module to change the image size to 128 × 128. Then, it utilized four stages to learn effective representations for collateral scoring. Each stage consisted of a multi-scale patch embedding based on convolution with different strides, several Transformer-based blocks (the number of blocks is adjustable) to capture global information, a CNN-based block, and a concatenation layer followed by a 1 × 1 convolution layer to effectively combine features from Transformer and CNN blocks. The classification results were achieved by a global average pooling and a linear layer. For more technical details of MPViT, please refer to [29]. Figure 3 shows the framework of our designed hybrid CNN and Transformer network for collateral scoring.

Additionally, in order to verify the advantages of the MPViT method over other automated scoring methods, we also applied three methods on the same MIP images. The first one was a radiomics-based method where we extracted radiomics features of MCA regions that were fed into support vector machine (SVM) for automated collateral scoring. The extraction of radiomics features was done through the software package Pyradiomics (https://pyradiomics.readthedocs.io/en/latest/, accessed on 1 December 2022). Since the extracted features were not all effective, we used the LASSO method for feature selection to avoid feature redundancy, and selected the optimal feature group as the input of SVM. The second one was a well-known CNN-based method (ResNet [30]) where we directly used the obtained MIP images to train a ResNet model. The third one was a pure Transformer-based method (MViTv2 [31]) whose input was also consistent with MPViT. For fair comparison, all four methods applied the same preprocessing steps and data augmentation.

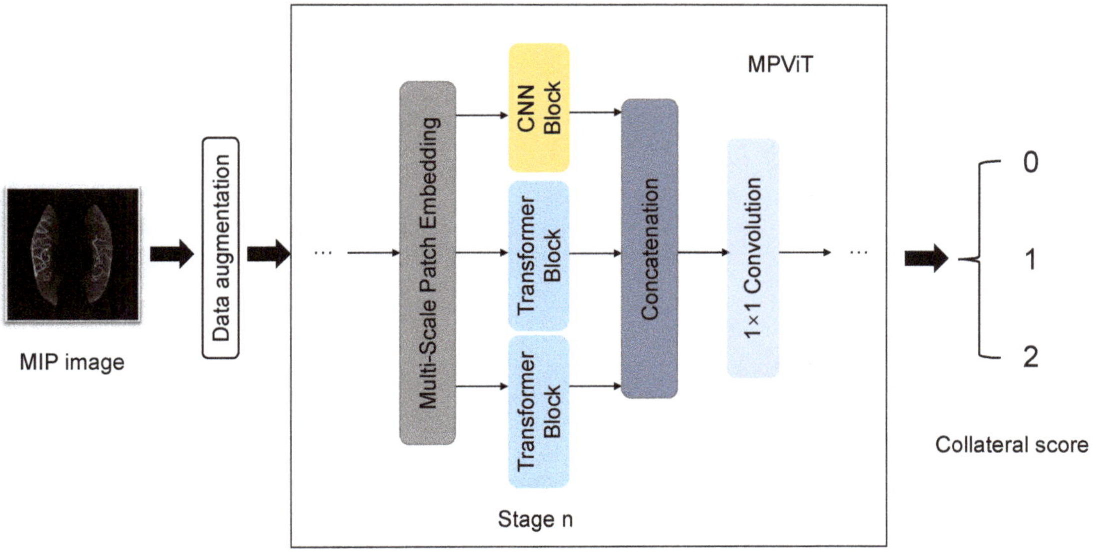

Figure 3. The framework of our designed hybrid CNN and Transformer network for collateral scoring.

To better evaluate the performance for collateral scoring, we used five-fold cross-validation for all four methods. In each cross-validation experiment, all 154 patients were randomly divided into five folds, and then we used four folds for training and parameter tuning, and used the remaining one fold for testing the trained model. After repeating the above operation five times, we obtained the collateral scores of all 154 patients.

2.4. Statistical Analysis

For evaluating the performance of collateral scoring, the agreement between automated collateral scores and expert-reading collateral scores was analyzed by intraclass correlation coefficients (ICC), as well as Kappa and the Pearson correlation coefficient. To further assess the clinical significance of the model, accuracy, sensitivity, area under the receiver operating characteristic curve (AUC) and specificity were used to evaluate the binary-classification performance. We calculated the 95% confidence interval (CI) for each evaluation metric. In the poor vs. non-poor classification, we considered patients with poor collateral and non-poor (good or intermediate) collateral as positive and negative samples, respectively. In the good vs. non-good classification, we considered patients with good collateral and non-good (poor or intermediate) collateral as positive and negative samples, respectively. In addition, subgroup analyses were performed to find the relationship between the collateral scoring performance and some clinical factors including gender, age, Alberta Stroke Program Early CT score (ASPECTS), National Institute of Health Stroke scale (NIHSS) and time from onset to CT imaging.

Accuracy, precision, sensitivity, AUC, specificity and kappa were calculated using SciKit learn toolkit. Pearson coefficient was calculated using the Scipy toolkit, and ICC was calculated using the Pingouin toolkit. The Z-test based on Fisher Z-transformation was used to test whether there were significant differences between the ICC, Kappa and Pearson values of two methods. The N-1 Chi-squared test was used to test whether there were significant differences between the accuracy, sensitivity and specificity of two methods. Statistics tests were performed with software (MedCalc, version 20.0.3, MedCalc

Software, Mariakerke, Belgium). A p-value smaller than 0.05 was considered to represent a significant difference.

3. Results

3.1. Study Participants

Table 1 lists the patient characteristics of the 154 patients involved in this study. The median age was 72 years (interquartile range [IQR], 64–80 years). Out of the 154 patients, 91 patients were male. Median onset-to-CT time was 135 min (IQR, 90–240 min). Median follow-up infarct volume was 4.6 mL (IQR, 0.6–26.0 mL). Median baseline NIHSS, modified Rankin scale (mRS) and ASPECTS were 11.5 (IQR, 4–21), 0 (IQR, 0–1) and 10 (IQR, 9–10), respectively. Median 90 day mRS was 2 (IQR, 1–4).

Table 1. Patient Characteristics for all 154 AIS patients collected.

Characteristics	All 154 Patients
Median age, years (IQR)	72 (64–80)
Gender, male, No. (%)	91 (59)
Median onset-to-CT time (IQR), min	135 (90–240)
Median follow-up infarct volume (IQR), mL	4.6 (0.6–26.0)
Median baseline NIHSS (IQR)	11.5 (4–21)
Median baseline mRS (IQR)	0 (0–1)
Median baseline ASPECTS(IQR)	10 (9–10)
Median 90 days mRS (IQR)	2 (1–4)

3.2. Results for Collateral Scoring

3.2.1. Three-Point Collateral Score Classification

To show the superiority of MPViT (a hybrid CNN and Transformer network), we compared it with three different automated collateral scoring methods: SVM, ResNet and MViTv2. Table 2 details the comparisons of the four automated scoring methods. Figure 4 shows the confusion matrix between the collateral scores obtained by the four methods and the expert consensus scores.

Table 2. Performance for three-point collateral score classification.

Method	ICC	Kappa	Pearson
SVM	0.6774 [0.56, 0.77]	0.5118 [0.3842, 0.6393]	0.5123 [0.3854, 0.6194]
ResNet	0.7358 [0.64, 0.81]	0.5818 [0.4555, 0.7080]	0.5822 [0.4671, 0.6773]
MViTv2	0.6246 [0.48, 0.73]	0.4541 [0.2985, 0.6097]	0.4548 [0.3196, 0.5707]
MPViT	0.767 [0.68, 0.83]	0.6184 [0.4954, 0.7414]	0.6621 [0.5112, 0.7068]

MPViT achieved an ICC of 0.767 (95% CI: 0.68–0.83), a Kappa of 0.6184 (95% CI: 0.4954–0.7414) and a Pearson of 0.6621 (95% CI: 0.5112–0.7068), which were all better than those of the three other types of methods: SVM, ResNet and MViTv2. From Figure 4, we found that MPViT achieved a good tradeoff for the three classes of collateral scores. These results indicate that MPViT had better agreement between the scores obtained by automated methods and the expert scores than traditional machine learning methods, pure convolutional models and pure Transformer models. The reason might be that MPViT combines the advantages of both CNN and Transformer to capture local and global representations for collateral scoring.

	0	1	2
0	46	19	4
1	16	23	13
2	5	9	19

(a)

	0	1	2
0	53	10	6
1	18	27	7
2	3	9	21

(b)

	0	1	2
0	47	15	7
1	10	38	4
2	8	8	17

(c)

	0	1	2
0	57	9	3
1	16	30	6
2	5	8	20

(d)

Figure 4. Confusion matrix between automated scores versus consensus scores. (**a**) SVM; (**b**) ResNet; (**c**) MViTv2; (**d**) MPViT.

3.2.2. Results for Poor vs. Non-Poor and Good vs. Non-Good Classification

In addition to three-point score classification, a dichotomized collateral score might be more useful in decision making.

Tables 3 and 4 show the performance of the four compared methods for poor vs. non-poor and good vs. non-good classification. For poor vs. non-poor classification, MPViT achieved an accuracy of 85.71% (95% CI: 80.18–91.24%), an AUC of 0.766 (95% CI: 0.691–0.83) and a specificity of 92.56% (95% CI: 86.3–96.5%), outperforming the other three methods regarding most metrics. For good vs. non-good classification, MPViT achieved an accuracy of 78.57% (95% CI: 72.09–85.05%), an AUC of 0.79 (95% CI: 0.717–0.851) and a specificity of 82.60% (95% CI: 71.6–90.7%), which is higher than those of the other three methods.

Table 3. Performance for poor vs. non-poor classification.

Method	Accuracy (%)	Sensitivity (%)	AUC	Specificity (%)
SVM	79.87 [73.53, 86.2]	57.57 [39.2, 74.5]	0.718 [0.64, 0.787]	85.95 [78.5, 91.6]
ResNet	83.76 [77.94, 89.59]	63.63 [45.1, 79.6]	0.764 [0.689, 0.829]	89.25 [82.3, 94.2]
MViTv2	82.46 [76.46, 88.47]	51.51 [33.5, 69.2]	0.712 [0.634, 0.782]	90.9 [84.3, 95.4]
MPViT	85.71 [80.18, 91.24]	60.6 [42.1, 77.1]	0.766 [0.691, 0.83]	92.56 [86.3, 96.5]

Table 4. Performance for good vs. non-good classification.

Method	Accuracy (%)	Specificity (%)	AUC	Sensitivity (%)
SVM	71.42 [64.29, 78.56]]	75.29 [64.7, 84.0]	0.71 [0.631, 0.78]	66.66 [54.3, 77.6]
ResNet	75.97 [69.22, 82.72]	75.29 [64.7, 84.0]	0.761 [0.685, 0.826]	76.81 [65.1, 86.1]
MViTv2	74.25 [67.1, 80.95]	78.82 [68.6, 86.9]	0.735 [0.658, 0.803]	68.11 [55.8, 78.8]
MPViT	78.57 [72.09, 85.05]	75.29 [64.7, 84.0]	0.79 [0.717, 0.851]	82.6 [71.6, 90.7]

3.2.3. Subgroup Analysis Based on Patient Characteristics

In this section, we further explore whether there were clinical factors that were related to the performance of collateral scoring via subgroup analysis (Table 5).

We first used gender and age to stratify all 154 patients into subgroups: male patients and female patients, and patients ≥ 70 years old and patients < 70 years old. The results in Table 5 sho that MPViT achieved an ICC of 0.8716 (95% CI: 0.7878–0.9223), a Kappa of 0.7718 (95% CI: 0.6191–0.9245) and a Pearson of 0.7728 (95% CI: 0.6494–0.8552) on female patients, which were significantly better than the performance on male patients (ICC: 0.6549 [95% CI: 0.4771–0.7723], $p = 0.0009$; Kappa: 0.475 [95% CI: 0.2973–0.6527], $p = 0.0024$; Pearson: 0.489 [95% CI: 0.3045–0.6160], $p = 0.0033$), which indicated that the female patients' scoring results had better reliability. The performance of MPViT on patients ≥ 70 years old was non-significantly better than the performance on patients < 70 years old (P values of all metrics >0.05), which shows that the older patients were scored better.

Second, we also stratified patients by clinical scores including baseline ASPECTS (≥7 vs. <7) and NIHSS (≥9 vs. <9) for subgroup analysis according to [32,33]. For the ASPECTS subgroups, the automated scores had non-significantly better agreement with the expert manual scores on patients with ASPECTS ≥ 7. Studies have shown that patients with ASPECTS scores greater than 7 could benefit significantly from mechanical thrombectomy [32]; thus, MPViT has potential to select suitable AIS patients for mechanical thrombectomy. For the NIHSS subgroups, ICC on patients with NIHSS < 9 (0.7308 [95% CI: 0.4165–0.7009]) was significantly better than ICC (0.526 [95% CI: 0.2289–0.7087]) on patients with NIHSS ≥ 9 ($p = 0.0371$) and other metrics on patients with NIHSS < 9 were better but not significantly so (all $p > 0.05$).

According to the onset-to-CT time, we divided all patients into two subgroups of less than 180 min and ≥ 180 min for subgroup analysis. The ICC, Kappa and Pearson on patients with onset-to-CT time < 180 min were all non-significantly higher than those on the other subgroup. This implies that the earlier the CT scans were scanned, the better the collateral scoring performance was.

Table 5. Three-point collateral scoring performance of MPViT of subgroups stratified by gender, age, ASPECTS, NIHSS and onset-to-CT time. * Denotes significant difference ($p < 0.05$).

Variable	Subgroup	ICC	Kappa	Pearson
Gender	male	0.6549 [0.4771, 0.7723]	0.475 [0.2973, 0.6527]	0.489 [0.3045, 0.6160]
	female	0.8716 * [0.7878, 0.9223]	0.7718 * [0.6191, 0.9245]	0.7728 * [0.6494, 0.8552]
Age (years)	≥70	0.7729 [0.6542, 0.8509]	0.6294 [0.4714, 0.7873]	0.6303 [0.4859, 0.7399]
	<70	0.6732 [0.4643, 0.8007]	0.4921 [0.2648, 0.7195]	0.519 [0.2966, 0.6482]
Baseline ASPECTS	≥7	0.7497 [0.6493, 0.8215]	0.5986 [0.4624, 0.7347]	0.5997 [0.4798, 0.6960]
	<7	0.7636 [0.3473, 0.9144]	0.5233 [0.2264, 0.8202]	0.7 [0.2129, 0.7379]
Baseline NIHSS	≥9	0.7308 * [0.4165, 0.7009]	0.5392 [0.3792, 0.6993]	0.5801 [0.3840, 0.6649]
	<9	0.526 [0.2289, 0.7087]	0.3383 [0.0933, 0.5833]	0.3897 [0.1420, 0.5091]
Onset-to-CT time (min)	≥180	0.7245 [0.5408, 0.8347]	0.5592 [0.3349, 0.7835]	0.5699 [0.3638, 0.7075]
	<180	0.7888 [0.6807, 0.8604]	0.6498 [0.5146, 0.7535]	0.6515 [0.5146, 0.7535]

4. Discussion

In this study, we explored several automated collateral scoring methods without vessel segmentation on CTA images that combined the advantages of CNNs and Transformers. Our results show the superiority of hybrid CNN and Transformer models for both three-point collateral scoring and dichotomized scoring, i.e., poor vs. non-poor and good vs. non-good collateral scores.

Comparisons showed that the hybrid CNN and Transformer model—the MPViT based vessel-segmentation free method—achieved better performance than radiomics and traditional machine learning-based, pure CNN-based and pure Transformer-based models for three-point collateral scoring. MPViT also achieved better performance for poor vs. non-poor and good vs. non-good classification. These results also confirm our previous hypothesis that the hybrid CNN and Transformer model could achieve better collateral scoring, showing that combining CNN and Transformer is promising, and showing that the designed MPViT could provide support information for clinical decision-making. Additionally, these results also validate that vessel-segmentation free methods for collateral scoring are feasible. This study could provide future directions for designing good collateral scoring methods.

The average time including preprocessing and classification using the trained model for collateral scoring of a patient was 8.26 s per patient, which is obviously less than the time (more than 5 min) needed for radiologist to score the collateral of a patient. Therefore, the proposed method could reduce the time of collateral scoring and decrease the burden of doctors for diagnosis and prognosis of AIS, and then has potential to reduce the economic cost of AIS patients. Additionally, it can be seen from the results that the proposed automated collateral scoring model had a high enough consistency with total scores read by experts and especially achieved better performance for the binary classification tasks such as good and non-good classification, which makes the proposed method helpful for selecting patients who could achieve good prognosis. In summary, due to the efficiency and the effectiveness of the proposed method for collateral scoring, it is feasible to be applied in the AIS clinical context to diagnose AIS and make treatment decisions.

When stratifying the patients based on clinical characteristics, we found that the clinical factors of gender, age, baseline ASPECTS, baseline NIHSS and onset-to-CT time were all related to collateral scoring, and gender was the most significant related factor to collateral scoring. These findings imply that incorporating these clinical factors into the automated collateral scoring models might potentially further improve the performance.

This study has several limitations. The sample size in this paper was limited, and there was no external validation cohort. More patients will be collected to obtain more effective models and test the generalizability of the designed models. Second, the timing of CTA acquisition is not accounted for in our model. However, around 10–20% of CTA scans were not acquired at the peak artery phase, which might bias the evaluation results. Multi-phase CTA scans can provide temporal information, and have potential to achieve more reliable collateral scoring across different observers. Extending our current models on multi-phase CTA scans should be explored in the future.

5. Conclusions

This study explored a vessel segmentation free collateral scoring method, i.e., hybrid CNN and Transformer model—MPViT—on single-phase CTA scans of AIS patients. The results show that the hybrid CNN and Transformer model, MPViT, could achieve accurately automated three-point collateral scoring and dichotomized collateral scoring. Subgroup analysis revealed that clinical factors, such as gender, age, baseline ASPECTS, baseline NIHSS and onset-to-CT time, were associated with collateral scoring. This study provides evidence that artificial intelligence is helpful to objectively assess collateral status based on imaging, therefore assisting decision making.

Author Contributions: H.K. and W.Q.: conceptualization, funding acquisition, resources, supervision, project administration, visualization, writing—review and editing; W.W.: conceptualization, data curation, formal analysis, investigation, methodology, writing—original draft; Y.W. and J.W.: formal analysis, investigation, visualization, writing—review and editing. All authors have read and agreed to the published version of the manuscript.

Funding: This work was supported in part by the National Natural Science Foundation of China (No. 62102454, No. 61877059), the science and technology innovation Program of Hunan Province (No. 2022RC1031), the National Natural Science Foundation for Excellent Young Scholars of China (Oversea), the Natural Science Foundation of Changsha (No. kq2202108), the Natural Science Foundation of Hunan Province (No. 2022JJ40636, No. 2021JJ30082), the Fundamental Research Funds for the Central Universities of Central South University (No. 1053320213221) and the High Performance Computing Center of Central South University.

Informed Consent Statement: Informed consent was obtained from all subjects involved in the study.

Data Availability Statement: The data presented in this study are available upon request from the corresponding author.

Conflicts of Interest: The authors declare no conflict of interest.

Abbreviations

The following abbreviations are used in this manuscript:

AIS	Acute ischemic stroke
ASPECTS	Alberta Stroke Program Early CT score
CTA	Computed tomography angiography
CNN	Convolutional neural network
ICC	Intraclass correlation coefficient
MIP	Maximum intensity projection
AUC	Area under the receiver operating characteristic curve
NIHSS	National Institute of Health Stroke scale
IQR	interquartile range
mRS	modified Rankin scale

References

1. Jauch, E.C.; Saver, J.L.; Adams, H.P.; Bruno, A.; Connors, J.B.; Demaerschalk, B.M.; Khatri, P.; McMullan, P.W.; Qureshi, A.I.; Rosenfield, K.; et al. Guidelines for the Early Management of Patients With Acute Ischemic Stroke: A Guideline for Healthcare Professionals From the American Heart Association/American Stroke Association. *Stroke* **2013**, *44*, 870–947. [CrossRef] [PubMed]
2. Na, D.G.; Thijs, V.N.; Albers, G.W.; Moseley, M.E.; Marks, M.P. Diffusion-Weighted MR Imaging in Acute Ischemia: Value of Apparent Diffusion Coefficient and Signal Intensity Thresholds in Predicting Tissue at Risk and Final Infarct Size. *AJNR Am. J. Neuroradiol.* **2004**, *25*, 1331.
3. Barber, P.A.; Demchuk, A.M.; Zhang, J.; Buchan, A.M. Validity and reliability of a quantitative computed tomography score in predicting outcome of hyperacute stroke before thrombolytic therapy. *Lancet* **2000**, *355*, 1670–1674. [CrossRef]
4. Saver, J.L.; Johnston, K.C.; Homer, D.; Wityk, R.; Koroshetz, W.; Truskowski, L.L.; Haley, E.C. Infarct Volume as a Surrogate or Auxiliary Outcome Measure in Ischemic Stroke Clinical Trials. *Stroke* **1999**, *30*, 293–298. [CrossRef] [PubMed]
5. Pexman, J.H.W.; Barber, P.A.; Hill, M.D.; Sevick, R.J.; Demchuk, A.M.; Hudon, M.E.; Hu, W.Y.; Buchan, A.M. Use of the Alberta Stroke Program Early CT Score (ASPECTS) for Assessing CT Scans in Patients with Acute Stroke. *Am. J. Neuroradiol.* **2001**, *22*, 1534. [PubMed]
6. Yoo, A.J.; Chaudhry, Z.A.; Nogueira, R.G.; Lev, M.H.; Schaefer, P.W.; Schwamm, L.H.; Hirsch, J.A.; González, R.G. Infarct Volume Is a Pivotal Biomarker After Intra-Arterial Stroke Therapy. *Stroke* **2012**, *43*, 1323–1330. [CrossRef] [PubMed]
7. Huisa, B.N.; Raman, R.; Ernstrom, K.; Tafreshi, G.; Stemer, A.; Meyer, B.C.; Hemmen, T. Alberta Stroke Program Early CT Score (ASPECTS) in Patients with Wake-Up Stroke. *J. Stroke Cerebrovasc. Dis.* **2010**, *19*, 475–479. [CrossRef]
8. Bang, O.Y.; Saver, J.L.; Buck, B.H.; Alger, J.R.; Starkman, S.; Ovbiagele, B.; Kim, D.; Jahan, R.; Duckwiler, G.R.; Yoon, S.R.; et al. Impact of collateral flow on tissue fate in acute ischaemic stroke. *J. Neurol. Neurosurg. Psychiatry* **2008**, *79*, 625. [CrossRef]
9. Goyal, M.; Menon, B.K.; van Zwam, W.H.; Dippel, D.W.J.; Mitchell, P.J.; Demchuk, A.M.; Dávalos, A.; Majoie, C.B.L.M.; van der Lugt, A.; de Miquel, M.A.; et al. Endovascular thrombectomy after large-vessel ischaemic stroke: A meta-analysis of individual patient data from five randomised trials. *Lancet* **2016**, *387*, 1723–1731. [CrossRef]
10. Kucinski, T.; Koch, C.; Eckert, B.; Becker, V.; Krömer, H.; Heesen, C.; Grzyska, U.; Freitag, H.; Röther, J.; Zeumer, H. Collateral circulation is an independent radiological predictor of outcome after thrombolysis in acute ischaemic stroke. *Neuroradiology* **2003**, *45*, 11–18. [CrossRef]
11. Berkhemer, O.A.; Jansen, I.G.; Beumer, D.; Fransen, P.S.; van den Berg, L.A.; Yoo, A.J.; Lingsma, H.F.; Sprengers, M.E.; Jenniskens, S.F.; Lycklama à Nijeholt, G.J.; et al. Collateral Status on Baseline Computed Tomographic Angiography and Intra-Arterial Treatment Effect in Patients With Proximal Anterior Circulation Stroke. *Stroke* **2016**, *47*, 768–776. [CrossRef] [PubMed]
12. Tan, J.C.; Dillon, W.P.; Liu, S.; Adler, F.; Smith, W.S.; Wintermark, M. Systematic comparison of perfusion-CT and CT-angiography in acute stroke patients: Comparison of CT Modalities for Stroke Imaging. *Ann. Neurol.* **2007**, *61*, 533–543. [CrossRef] [PubMed]
13. Kuang, H.; Najm, M.; Chakraborty, D.; Maraj, N.; Sohn, S.; Goyal, M.; Hill, M.; Demchuk, A.; Menon, B.; Qiu, W. Automated ASPECTS on Noncontrast CT Scans in Patients with Acute Ischemic Stroke Using Machine Learning. *Am. J. Neuroradiol.* **2019**, *40*, 33–38. [CrossRef]
14. Cheng, J.; Liu, J.; Yue, H.; Bai, H.; Pan, Y.; Wang, J. Prediction of Glioma Grade using Intratumoral and Peritumoral Radiomic Features from Multiparametric MRI Images. *IEEE/ACM Trans. Comput. Biol. Bioinform.* **2020**. [CrossRef] [PubMed]
15. Yi, P.; Jin, L.; Xu, T.; Wei, L.; Rui, G. Hippocampal Segmentation in Brain MRI Images Using Machine Learning Methods: A Survey. *Chin. J. Electron.* **2021**, *30*, 793–814. [CrossRef]
16. Shen, C.; Wang, X.; Yin, Y.; Song, J.; Luo, S.; Song, M. Progressive Network Grafting for Few-Shot Knowledge Distillation. In Proceedings of the AAAI Conference on Artificial Intelligence (AAAI), Virtually, 2–9 February 2021; Volume 35, pp. 2541–2549.

17. Liu, J.; Du, H.; Guo, R.; Bai, H.X.; Kuang, H.; Wang, J. MMGK: Multimodality Multiview Graph Representations and Knowledge Embedding for Mild Cognitive Impairment Diagnosis. *IEEE Trans. Comput. Soc. Syst.* **2022**, 1–10. [CrossRef]
18. Qiu, W.; Kuang, H.; Teleg, E.; Ospel, J.M.; Sohn, S.I.; Almekhlafi, M.; Goyal, M.; Hill, M.D.; Demchuk, A.M.; Menon, B.K. Machine Learning for Detecting Early Infarction in Acute Stroke with Non-Contrast-enhanced CT. *Radiology* **2020**, *294*, 638–644. [CrossRef]
19. Boers, A.; Sales Barros, R.; Jansen, I.; Berkhemer, O.; Beenen, L.; Menon, B.; Dippel, D.; van der Lugt, A.; van Zwam, W.; Roos, Y.; et al. Value of Quantitative Collateral Scoring on CT Angiography in Patients with Acute Ischemic Stroke. *Am. J. Neuroradiol.* **2018**, *39*, 1074–1082. [CrossRef]
20. Su, J.; Wolff, L.; van Es, A.C.G.M.; van Zwam, W.; Majoie, C.; Dippel, W.J.D.; van der Lugt, A.; Niessen, W.J.; Van Walsum, T. Automatic Collateral Scoring From 3D CTA Images. *IEEE Trans. Med. Imaging* **2020**, *39*, 2190–2200. [CrossRef]
21. Rava, R.A.; Seymour, S.E.; Snyder, K.V.; Waqas, M.; Davies, J.M.; Levy, E.I.; Siddiqui, A.H.; Ionita, C.N. Automated Collateral Flow Assessment in Patients with Acute Ischemic Stroke Using Computed Tomography with Artificial Intelligence Algorithms. *World Neurosurg.* **2021**, *155*, e748–e760. [CrossRef]
22. Kim, Y.C.; Chung, J.W.; Bang, O.Y.; Hong, M.; Seo, W.K.; Kim, G.M.; Yeop Kim, E.; Lee, J.S.; Hong, J.M.; Liebeskind, D.S.; et al. A Deep Learning-Based Automatic Collateral Assessment in Patients with Acute Ischemic Stroke. *Transl. Stroke Res.* **2022**. [CrossRef] [PubMed]
23. Wolff, L.; Uniken Venema, S.M.; Luijten, S.P.R.; Hofmeijer, J.; Martens, J.M.; Bernsen, M.L.E.; van Es, A.C.G.M.; van Doormaal, P.J.; Dippel, D.W.J.; van Zwam, W.; et al. Diagnostic performance of an algorithm for automated collateral scoring on computed tomography angiography. *Eur. Radiol.* **2022**, *32*, 5711–5718. [CrossRef] [PubMed]
24. Yang, W.; Soomro, J.; Jansen, I.G.H.; Venkatesh, A.; Yoo, A.J.; Lopes, D.; Beenen, L.F.M.; Emmer, B.J.; Majoie, C.B.L.M.; Marquering, H.A. Collateral Capacity Assessment: Robustness and Interobserver Agreement of Two Grading Scales and Agreement with Quantitative Scoring. *Clin. Neuroradiol.* **2022**. [CrossRef] [PubMed]
25. Vaswani, A.; Shazeer, N.; Parmar, N.; Uszkoreit, J.; Jones, L.; Gomez, A.N.; Kaiser, L.; Polosukhin, I. Attention Is All You Need. *arXiv* **2017**, arXiv:1706.03762.
26. Cheng, J.; Liu, J.; Kuang, H.; Wang, J. A Fully Automated Multimodal MRI-Based Multi-Task Learning for Glioma Segmentation and IDH Genotyping. *IEEE Trans. Med. Imaging* **2022**, *41*, 1520–1532. [CrossRef] [PubMed]
27. Najm, M.; Kuang, H.; Federico, A.; Jogiat, U.; Goyal, M.; Hill, M.D.; Demchuk, A.; Menon, B.K.; Qiu, W. Automated brain extraction from head CT and CTA images using convex optimization with shape propagation. *Comput. Methods Programs Biomed.* **2019**, *176*, 1–8. [CrossRef]
28. Stib, M.T.; Vasquez, J.; Dong, M.P.; Kim, Y.H.; Subzwari, S.S.; Triedman, H.J.; Wang, A.; Wang, H.L.C.; Yao, A.D.; Jayaraman, M.; et al. Detecting Large Vessel Occlusion at Multiphase CT Angiography by Using a Deep Convolutional Neural Network. *Radiology* **2020**, *297*, 640–649. [CrossRef]
29. Lee, Y.; Kim, J.; Willette, J.; Hwang, S.J. MPViT: Multi-Path Vision Transformer for Dense Prediction. *arXiv* **2021**, arXiv:2112.11010.
30. He, K.; Zhang, X.; Ren, S.; Sun, J. Deep Residual Learning for Image Recognition. *arXiv* **2015**, arXiv:1512.03385.
31. Li, Y.; Wu, C.Y.; Fan, H.; Mangalam, K.; Xiong, B.; Malik, J.; Feichtenhofer, C. MViTv2: Improved Multiscale Vision Transformers for Classification and Detection. *arXiv* **2022**, arXiv:2112.01526.
32. Lees, K.R.; Bluhmki, E.; von Kummer, R.; Brott, T.G.; Toni, D.; Grotta, J.C.; Albers, G.W.; Kaste, M.; Marler, J.R.; Hamilton, S.A.; et al. Time to treatment with intravenous alteplase and outcome in stroke: An updated pooled analysis of ECASS, ATLANTIS, NINDS, and EPITHET trials. *Lancet* **2010**, *375*, 1695–1703. [CrossRef] [PubMed]
33. Aoki, J.; Suzuki, K.; Kanamaru, T.; Kutsuna, A.; Katano, T.; Takayama, Y.; Nishi, Y.; Takeshi, Y.; Nakagami, T.; Numao, S.; et al. Association between initial NIHSS score and recanalization rate after endovascular thrombectomy. *J. Neurol. Sci.* **2019**, *403*, 127–132. [CrossRef] [PubMed]

biomedicines

Article

Classification of First-Episode Psychosis with EEG Signals: ciSSA and Machine Learning Approach

Şerife Gengeç Benli

Department of Biomedical Engineering, Faculty of Engineering, Erciyes University, Kayseri 38280, Turkey; serifegengec@erciyes.edu.tr

Abstract: First-episode psychosis (FEP) typically marks the onset of severe psychiatric disorders and represents a critical period in the field of mental health. The early diagnosis of this condition is essential for timely intervention and improved clinical outcomes. In this study, the classification of FEP was investigated using the analysis of electroencephalography (EEG) signals and circulant spectrum analysis (ciSSA) sub-band signals. FEP poses a significant diagnostic challenge in the realm of mental health, and it is aimed at introducing a novel and effective approach for early diagnosis. To achieve this, the LASSO method was utilized to select the most significant features derived from entropy, frequency, and statistical-based characteristics obtained from ciSSA sub-band signals, as well as their hybrid combinations. Subsequently, a high-performance classification model has been developed using machine learning techniques, including ensemble, support vector machine (SVM), and artificial neural network (ANN) methods. The results of this study demonstrated that the hybrid features extracted from EEG signals' ciSSA sub-bands, in combination with the SVM method, achieved a high level of performance, with an area under curve (AUC) of 0.9893, an accuracy of 96.23%, a sensitivity of 0.966, a specificity of 0.956, a precision of 0.9667, and an F1 score of 0.9666. This has revealed the effectiveness of the ciSSA-based method for classifying FEP from EEG signals.

Keywords: first-episode psychosis; electroencephalography; circulant spectrum analysis; machine learning

Citation: Gengeç Benli, Ş. Classification of First-Episode Psychosis with EEG Signals: ciSSA and Machine Learning Approach. *Biomedicines* **2023**, *11*, 3223. https://doi.org/10.3390/biomedicines11123223

Academic Editors: Wu Qiu and Hulin Kuang

Received: 6 October 2023
Revised: 21 November 2023
Accepted: 23 November 2023
Published: 5 December 2023

1. Introduction

Psychotic disorders include a set of fundamental characteristics, including delusions, hallucinations, disordered thinking and speech, and negative symptoms, as outlined in the Diagnostic and Statistical Manual of Mental Disorders, Fifth Edition (DSM-5) [1]. The prognosis for individuals who undergo their initial episode of psychosis (FEP) shows considerable diversity. Whereas some patients may encounter only one psychotic episode, others may contend with recurring episodes or endure chronic symptoms associated with schizophrenia spectrum disorders. The use of early intervention strategies has the potential to significantly impact long-term results [2]. Diagnosing FEP involves a comprehensive psychiatric evaluation to assess symptoms, history, and any potential underlying medical or substance-related causes. Given the variability and complexity of psychotic disorders, an accurate diagnosis is essential for providing appropriate treatment and support to individuals experiencing FEP. Early intervention and treatment are crucial for improving outcomes and preventing potential relapses or chronicity of symptoms. In recent times, there has been a growing trend in utilizing computational methods to analyze neuroimaging data acquired from techniques like electroencephalography (EEG) and various magnetic resonance imaging modalities. These methods have become increasingly popular, as they offer valuable insights into the neurobiological underpinnings of psychiatric disorders due to the analysis of the whole brain.

There is an increasing interest in utilizing the features obtained from MR images for classification in distinguishing neuropsychiatric disorders [3–7]. In the study proposed by Squarcina et al., classification based on the measurement results of cortical thicknesses from different brain regions was performed, including 127 healthy controls and 127 individuals with FEP. When individuals were evaluated to classify, up to more than 80% for frontal and temporal areas was achieved in covariate multiple kernel learning, indicating that fronto-temporal cortical thickness could be used as a potential biomarker for classifying psychotic patients [8]. Faria et al. utilized different analysis methods to brain images from various MRI modalities belonging to 87 individuals of FEP and 62 healthy participants. These multiple approach methods have been more successful in distinguishing between healthy control and FEP subgroups using two-sample *t*-tests. Furthermore, the study highlights that the thalamus is significantly different in FEP [9]. In the study conducted by Nadal et al. involving 27 healthy individuals and 31 individuals with FEP, comparisons of brain volumes and nucleus accumbens volumes were performed based on structural MR images. In this study, where linear regression was applied, FEP exhibited an increased nucleus accumbens volume compared to controls [10].

When reviewing the studies in the literature, it is clear that there is a significant concentration of analyses focusing on artificial intelligence techniques involving EEG signals in healthy individuals, especially through multi-task-based approaches, for the development of brain–computer interface systems. On the other hand, there is a growing effort to develop patterns using multi-channel EEG data gathered from individuals, aiming to distinguish individuals with psychiatric disorders from healthy ones. There are only a few resting-state EEG studies aimed at finding patterns of EEG signals belonging to FEP. For instance, the study by Missonnier et al. was performed with eighteen healthy individuals and 15 individuals with FEP using 20-channel EEG signals. For these two groups, event-related gamma (35–45 Hz) and delta (0.5–4 Hz) oscillatory responses were evaluated in a visual n-back working memory task. Oscillation periodicity analyses were calculated to investigate the relationship between the psychiatric condition reflected by each frequency range and the working memory load. Statistical differences were obtained in sub-band oscillations between these two groups [11]. Focused on the delta frequency band of resting-state EEG signals, a study proposed by Renaldi et al. was conducted with 24 individuals with FEP and 24 healthy controls. Individuals with FEP had a significant increase in delta absolute power in both the frontal and posterior areas when compared to healthy controls. Furthermore, it was shown that the fluctuating influence of the delta frequency band had a crucial role in predicting the improvement of symptoms and functionality in those who underwent conventional therapy over the span of one year [12]. Lee et al. aimed to investigate the spatiotemporal neural correlations of cognitive function impairment in schizophrenia by focusing on resting-state EEG signals involving the default mode network regions. In this context, they conducted a study with 59 individuals with FEP and 50 healthy controls. In their study, they found that FEP patients exhibited a greater theta phase-gamma amplitude connectivity in the left posterior cingulate cortex compared to healthy controls [13]. In addition to the summarized FEP studies, researchers have focused on studies examining EEG frequency sub-bands in other psychiatric disorders [14,15].

Due to its nonlinear and non-stationary nature, EEG requires the application of certain signal processing techniques to reveal its intrinsic features. Specifically, examining the characteristics of EEG sub-bands obtained using techniques like empirical mode decompositions (EMD), variational mode decomposition (VMD), wavelet transform (WT), and singular spectrum analysis (SSA), or investigating the characteristic frequency sub-bands of EEG, are important approaches. Particularly, these approaches enhance success in resting-state or task-based EEG studies on psychiatric disorders or healthy controls. For instance, Aslan and Akin have proposed a deep learning study using two different datasets to differentiate between individuals with psychotic disorders and healthy controls. They employed the EMD approach to obtain four intrinsic functions, and the Hilbert spectrum images of the first intrinsic function were used as inputs for classification with the VGG16 model. They achieved accuracies of 98.2% and 96.02% for the first and second datasets, respectively, in the classification of these images, distinguishing between the two groups, thus demonstrating a remarkable ability to discern between the two cohorts [16]. In the study proposed by Khare and Bajaj, a robust VMD method was applied to multi-channel EEG signals in a cohort involving 49 individuals with schizophrenia and 32 healthy controls. In the classification using features extracted from intrinsic mode functions, an accuracy of 92.93% was achieved [17].

A novel approach has been proposed in the conducted study to achieve a high-performance classification of healthy individuals and those with first-episode psychosis (FEP) using EEG signals.

In pursuit of this objective, a new method called ciSSA was employed to uncover hidden patterns within the EEG signals and to reveal their dynamic behavior by decomposing them into sub-bands. Entropy, frequency, and statistical features were extracted from these sub-band signals, and machine learning techniques were applied to the obtained models to analyze their classification performance.

The contributions of this study to the literature are summarized as follows:

- EEG signals from the datasets used for FEP classification were analyzed for the first time in this study.
- The ciSSA method was applied for the first time within the scope of this study, specifically for the stated purpose, and its performance was analyzed.
- The classification performance of features obtained from both non-decomposed EEG signals and ciSSA-decomposed sub-band EEG signals was demonstrated.
- The novel entropy, statistical, and frequency features, combined with the ciSSA sub-bands of EEG signals for FEP classification, were analyzed for their performance.
- The classification performance of machine learning algorithms such as SVM, ANN, and ensemble methods in FEP classification using the new ciSSA-based model was examined.

2. Materials and Methods

In this study, new approaches have been proposed in terms of the methods and utilized dataset in the literature for the classification of FEP, resulting in the development of a high-performance classification model.

In this section, the dataset from which EEG signals were obtained, the preprocessing steps applied to the dataset, the sub-band decomposition procedures, the feature extraction and selection processes, and the classification algorithms are discussed. The framework of this study is presented in Figure 1.

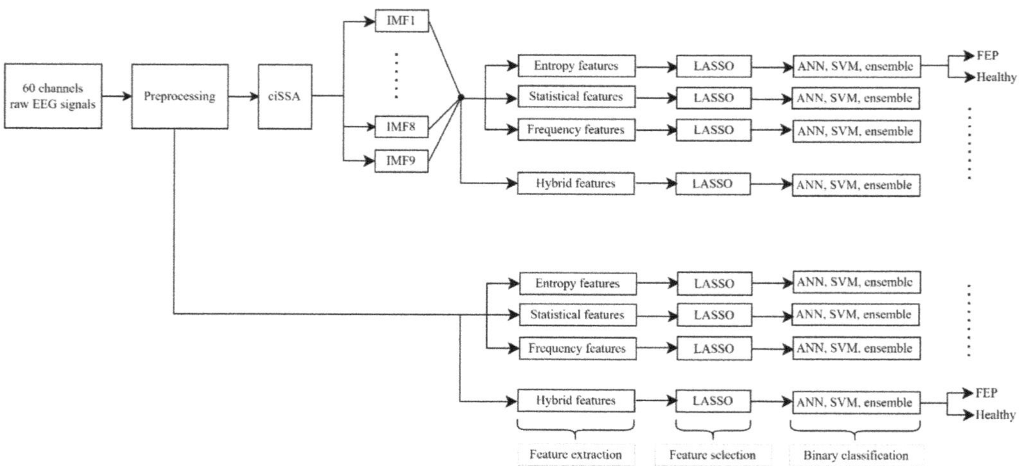

Figure 1. The entire framework of the proposed approach for the automated classification via EEG raw and ciSSA sub-band signals.

2.1. Datasets

Two publicly available datasets [18,19] were used to classify FEP in this study. The study was conducted with two groups, a total of 78 individuals with FEP (23 females, 55 males) and 60 healthy controls (26 females, 34 males) across both datasets. The FEP group consisted of participants aged between approximately 12 and 36 (mean 22.83), whereas the control group ranged from 12 to 38 (mean 22.89). Forty-seven individuals with FEP and thirty healthy control individuals from the first dataset were included. From the second dataset, 31 individuals with FEP and 30 healthy controls were included. Demographic information about the individuals included in this study is presented in Supplementary Material S1. The EEG physiological signals of each individual were recorded during a resting state for a duration of 5 min with a 64-channel system using an Elekta Neuromag Vectorview system. The first 60 channels, containing only EEG signals, were used. Furthermore, the phenotype directory containing clinical assessment results and the data divided by type for all participants is detailed extensively in the relevant section of the datasets [18,19].

2.2. Preprocessing

This study uses the down-sampled data at 250 Hz, where the original sampling rate is 500 Hz. All included raw EEG records were preprocessed using the open-source software package EEGLAB [20] in MATLAB 2022a. These psychological signals were filtered with a 0.5–45 Hz bandpass filter. Furthermore, to remove noises from the records such as muscle, eye, heart, and line noise, among others, independent component analysis was performed. The first 3 min of the data consisting of EEG signals lasting for 5 min have been utilized in this study. The EEG signals before and after preprocessing are seen in Figures 2 and 3.

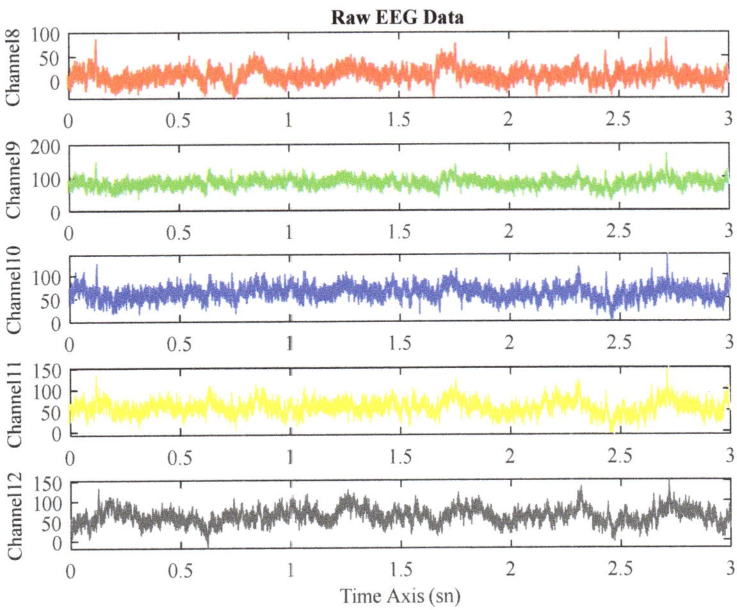

Figure 2. Multi-channel EEG signals before preprocessing.

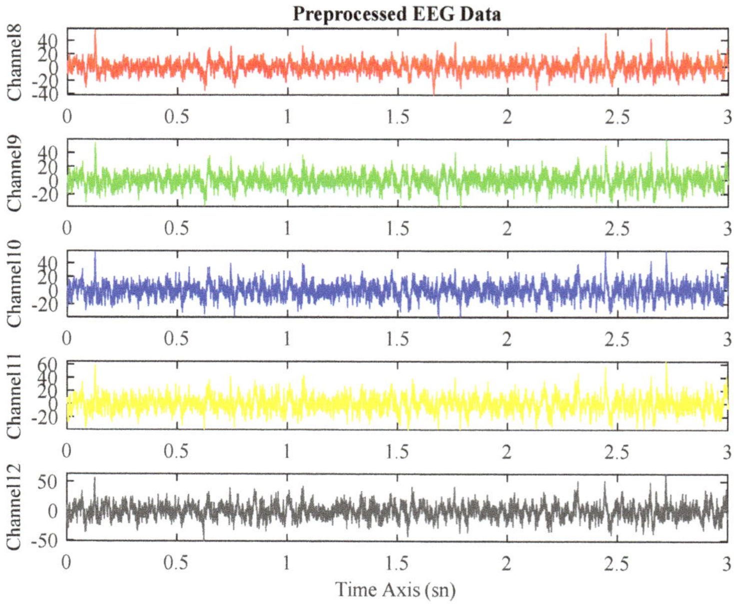

Figure 3. Multi-channel EEG signals after preprocessing.

2.3. Circulant Singular Spectrum Analysis

SSA, EMD, and RLMD, as nonparametric procedures, perform time series decomposition using distinct approaches and they come with advantages and disadvantages that can be chosen based on the characteristics of the data. The selection of which method to use depends on the nature of the data, the purpose, and the requirements. On the other hand, whereas SSA is commonly employed for general time series analysis, ciSSA is often preferred for the analysis of irregular time series such as biomedical data. The ciSSA method's key benefit is that users may combine the extracted components according to their requirements, since the components are specified accurately by frequency. The circulant SSA approach comprises the embedding, decomposition, grouping, and reconstruction processes [21].

Embedding step: In the first step, the time series of each EEG channel is transformed into a multidimensional trajectory matrix by sliding it over a specific window length. This matrix organizes time series data in a space that represents different dimensions.

The trajectory matrix is defined according to Equation (1):

$$X = \begin{bmatrix} x_1 & x_2 & \cdots & x_N \\ x_2 & x_3 & \cdots & x_{N+1} \\ \vdots & \vdots & \vdots & \vdots \\ x_L & x_{L+1} & \cdots & x_T \end{bmatrix} \tag{1}$$

In this context, T represents the length of the time series x_t, whereas L denotes the window length.

Decomposition step: The trajectory matrix is decomposed into components at different frequencies. In this step, matrix cross-correlations are used, leveraging second-order moments to obtain circulant matrix Sc. This allows the separation of components at different frequencies. Components of Sc are characterized by the following equations:

$$s_m = \frac{1}{T-m} \sum_{t=1}^{T-m} x_t x_{t-m}, \quad m = 0,\ 1,\ \ldots,\ L-1 \tag{2}$$

The first-row components and eigenvectors of S_C are obtained by Equations (3) and (4), respectively:

$$\alpha_m = \frac{L-m}{L} s_m + \frac{m}{L} s_{L-m}, \quad m = 0,\, 1,\, \ldots L-1 \tag{3}$$

$$diag(\lambda_1, \lambda_2, \ldots \lambda_L) = U * S_C U \tag{4}$$

in which U represents the Fourier matrix. In order to get a more in-depth explanation, Refs. [22,23] should be consulted. The k-th eigenvalue (Equation (6)) and accompanying eigenvector are associated with the following frequencies, as given in Equation (5):

$$f_k = \frac{k-1}{L} f_s \tag{5}$$

in which fs is the EEG signal sampling frequency.

$$\lambda_K \cong f\left(\frac{k-1}{L}\right) = \sum_{m=-\infty}^{\infty} s_m exp\left(i2\pi m\frac{k-1}{L}\right) \tag{6}$$

This allows us to define Equation (7), which states that the X trajectory matrix may be divided into X_k elementary matrices:

$$X = \sum_{k=1}^{L} x_k = \sum_{k=1}^{L} U_k U_k^* X \tag{7}$$

Diagonal Averaging: The decomposed components are further processed by performing diagonal averaging among those with similar frequencies. This process leads to obtaining higher-level components.

Grouping: Finally, the higher-level components are grouped, with each group representing a signal at a specific frequency.

The main goal of ciSSA is to separate complex and high-dimensional time series data into lower-dimensional components, revealing meaningful structures. This method can be particularly useful for analyzing time series data like brain activity, where the separation and analysis of signals at different frequencies are important.

In this study, EEG signals were decomposed into sub-bands ranging from 4 to 15. Since the classification performance was optimal at 9, EEG signals were decomposed into 9 sub-bands using the ciSSA method. As an example, Figure 4 presents 9 ciSSA sub-bands of the eighth-channel EEG signal of an individual.

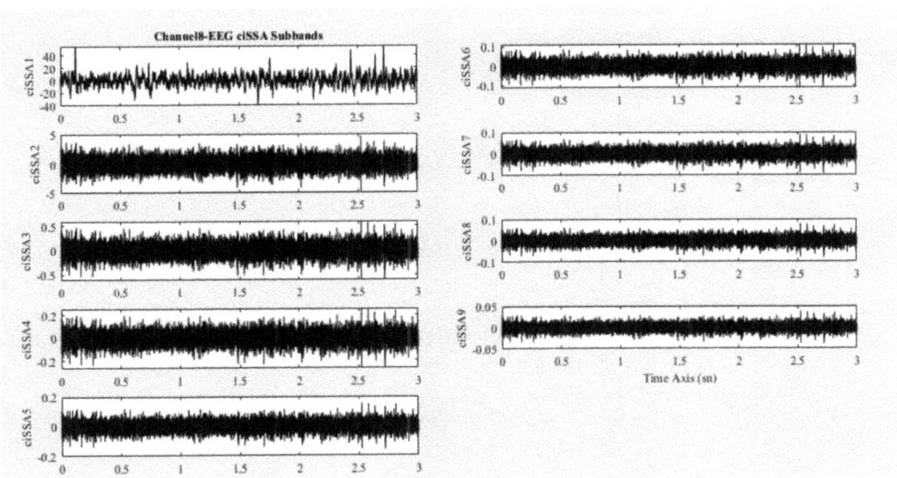

Figure 4. ciSSA sub-band signals belonging to channel 8 of an individual.

2.4. Feature Extraction

This work involves the extraction of three distinct kinds of feature datasets from EEG signals, including entropy, statistical, and frequency. These features are briefly mentioned below. Additionally, equations belonging to the features have been given in Supplementary Material S2.

2.4.1. Entropy Features

Entropy is a method for quantifying the unpredictability of non-linear time series data. There are several derived variants of information entropy that are used in the processing of electroencephalography (EEG) data. Tsallis entropy [24,25], Tsallis entropy with different options, Shannon entropy [25], logenergy entropy [26], Renyi entropy [27], and Renyi entropy with different options were used to extract significant information from the EEG data. In total, 6 statistical features were included in the classification problem.

2.4.2. Statistical Features

To perform tasks like feature extraction, classification, and pattern recognition, many different EEG applications rely on the data provided by statistical features. Thus, in this study, both basic and advanced statistical features have been used together in the classification problem. The arithmetic mean, median value, standard deviation, skewness, kurtosis, maximum, minimum, first difference, normalized first difference, second difference, normalized second difference, mean energy, mean teager energy, and log root sum of sequential variation were calculated for each channel signal. In addition to the other features, Hjorth parameters, including activity, mobility, and complexity, based on the variance of the derivatives of the EEG signal, have also been calculated. Thus, a total of 17 statistical features have been utilized.

2.4.3. Frequency Features

Autoregressive (AR) models offer a wide range of applications in EEG signal processing, from estimating spectral properties and temporal dynamics to discriminating stationary signals. The AR model is very effective at representing and modeling the features and information contained in a signal. This model helps uncover patterns and relationships within brain activity [28]. In this study, an AR model was utilized to extract power spectral features from cortical EEG recordings. Furthermore, the order of the AR model was identified as 10, indicating that the AR-derived feature vector had 10 dimensions in any signal. In addition to the AR features, the power of the alpha, beta, delta, and theta bands and the ratio of band power alpha to theta were used as frequency features. In total, 15 features were included in this fiction.

2.5. Feature Selection

The high-dimensional nature of the EEG feature space makes feature selection inevitable. The advantage of feature selection in EEG signals lies in its ability to enhance the efficiency and effectiveness of analyzing and processing, e.g., increasing classification performance. In this study, the least absolute shrinkage and selection operator (LASSO) was performed for the purpose of feature selection. The LASSO, a statistical method introduced by Tibshirani [29], is used in regression analysis to perform parameter estimates and variable selection. LASSO may provide both an analytical solution and a low-variance estimate that is highly interpretable in the context of linear regression.

In this study, during the feature selection process using the LASSO method from the feature set obtained from the EEG signals, different lambda (λ) parameters were tested. Considering the computational load dependent on the number of features and the classification performance, the lambda value that provides the optimal solution has been determined as 0.005. The numbers of the features used in this study are given in the table below (Table 1).

Table 1. Numbers of features used in the study.

	EEG Signals Not Decomposed into Subbands			
	Entropy	**Statictical**	**Frequency**	**Hybrid**
Number of feature set	60 × 6 = 360	60 × 17 = 1020	60 × 15 = 900	60 × 38 = 2280
Number of selected features	70	104	106	128
	EEG Signals Secomposed into ciSSA Subbands			
	Entropy	**Statistical**	**Frequency**	**Hybrid**
Number of feature set	60 × 6 × 9 = 3240	60 × 17 × 9 = 9180	60 × 15 × 9 = 8100	60 × 38 × 9 = 20,520
Number of selected features	164	153	141	181

2.6. Classification

In this study, after extracting the features and selecting the important ones, the binary classification of the EEG signals was performed using three supervised machine learning classifiers, such as SVM, ANN, and ensemble methods, via automated hyperparameter tuning. These classifiers are often used in several applications that include biological signals, such as EEG, as given in the [30,31] survey papers.

In the conducted study, the size of the dataset, the evaluation of desired outcomes, and factors such as the performance of algorithms in similar studies were taken into account when selecting these algorithms for the classification of the obtained features. Additionally, the ability of the chosen machine learning solution to effectively process the current data volume while maintaining accuracy and generalization capabilities has been assessed.

Cross-validation and testing on representative subsets of the used data were integral to my decision-making process. In summary, supporting the inclusion of ensemble models, SVM, and ANN while classifying them separately involves recognizing the individual strengths of each model, tailoring the evaluation process, and aiming for a comprehensive understanding of the research problem. This approach allows for a nuanced analysis, considering the diverse aspects captured by each model.

The next subsections provide concise explanations of the classifiers.

2.6.1. Support Vector Machines

Support vector machines (SVMs) are a class of supervised machine learning algorithms used for classification and regression tasks. They are particularly effective for problems where the data are not linearly separable. SVMs work by finding a hyperplane that best separates different classes of data points in a high-dimensional space [32]. SVMs have been used to assist in diagnosing psychiatric disorders by analyzing EEG data for patterns indicative of conditions like attention deficit hyperactivity disorders [33], schizophrenia [34], and more.

2.6.2. Artificial Neural Network

An artificial neural network (ANN) is a computational model that establishes a non-linear relationship between input vectors and output vectors by the use of a network of linked neurons. Each node in the current layer is linked to every node in the subsequent and preceding layers. The output of a neuron is multiplied by the connecting weight and then sent forward to serve as an input, which is then processed by a nonlinear activation function for the neurons in the subsequent layer of the network. The use of nonlinear sigmoid activation functions is seen in both the hidden-layer neurons and the output-layer neurons inside a multilayer ANN [35]. ANN has been widely applied in various EEG-based studies [31,36,37].

2.6.3. Ensemble Methods

Ensemble approaches involve the combination of multiple models aiming to address a common problem. The fundamental principle of this approach is that by bringing together these models, a more robust and accurate overall model can be created, thereby offering more reliable predictions and options compared to any individual model. The importance of aggregating the outcomes of many classifiers to reduce generalization errors has been emphasized [38,39]. Ensemble techniques have been shown to be particularly effective due to the existence of different inductive biases among various classifier types. These ensemble techniques have the potential to effectively harness the diversity present in a dataset to decrease variance error while minimizing bias error [40].

In this study, the classifier parameters for all classifiers were determined using the Bayesian optimization algorithm. The input feature vector was normalized to have a mean of 0 and a standard deviation of 1, and then applied to the classifier.

3. Results

This study was conducted using the signals of 60-channel EEG recordings taken from 60 healthy individuals and 78 individuals with first-episode psychosis. The preprocessed data were decomposed into nine sub-bands using the methods of ciSSA. In the feature extraction stage, features based on entropy, statistics, and the frequency of the original signal and its corresponding nine sub-bands obtained from each decomposition method were acquired for each channel.

In addition, among these obtained features, the most important ones have been identified for classification using the LASSO method in two approaches, i.e., both raw and ciSSA data.

The success of ciSSA sub-bands and the original signal in distinguishing FEP and healthy individuals has been examined using different approaches, including SVM, ensemble, and multilayer perception classifiers. The classification performance measures such as area under the curve (AUC), accuracy (Acc), sensitivity, specificity, and F1 score obtained from the binary classification have been evaluated. tables 2 and 3 show the mean classification performance as binary for all subjects through different feature types of datasets and hybrid datasets as raw signals and ciSSA sub-band signals, respectively. Upon examining these tables, the classification performance using features derived from the original data and ciSSA sub-band signals can be observed. During the classification study, the 10-fold cross-validation method was used to determine the training and testing data. Each classification process was repeated 10 times, and the given tables provide the mean performance achieved in the classification results.

Table 2. Classification results with various features obtained from the original EEG signals.

Features	Classification Methods	AUC	Accuracy	Sensitivity	Specificity	Precision	F-Score
Entropy	Ensemble	0.5477	0.5731	0.7333	0.365	0.606	0.6552
	SVM	0.6470	0.6050	0.6410	0.5583	0.6617	0.6429
	ANN	0.5893	0.5862	0.6346	0.5233	0.6407	0.6302
Statistical	Ensemble	0.6123	0.5920	0.7038	0.4466	0.6230	0.6604
	SVM	0.9074	0.8492	0.8448	0.855	0.883	0.8636
	ANN	0.9250	0.85	0.8410	0.8616	0.8878	0.8634
Frequency	Ensemble	0.5166	0.5471	0.8076	0.2083	0.5724	0.6605
	SVM	0.7501	0.7050	0.7128	0.695	0.7540	0.7324
	ANN	0.7549	0.6985	0.7217	0.6683	0.7385	0.7298
Hybrid	Ensemble	0.5747	0.5623	0.6589	0.4366	0.6034	0.6278
	SVM	0.9555	0.9036	0.9076	0.8983	0.9207	0.9140
	ANN	0.9549	0.9057	0.9038	0.9083	0.9280	0.9156

Table 3. Classification results with various features obtained from the ciSSA sub-bands of EEG signals.

Features	Classification Methods	AUC	Accuracy	Sensitivity	Specificity	Precision	F-Score
Entropy	Ensemble	0.5945	0.5862	0.6846	0.4583	0.6222	0.6513
	SVM	0.8941	0.8644	0.9025	0.815	0.8641	0.8827
	ANN	0.9043	0.8666	0.9115	0.8083	0.8609	0.8852
Statistical	Ensemble	0.6336	0.5971	0.7128	0.4466	0.6268	0.5439
	SVM	0.9454	0.9050	0.9307	0.8716	0.9039	0.9170
	ANN	0.9675	0.9253	0.9320	0.9166	0.9359	0.9337
Frequency	Ensemble	0.5391	0.5485	0.6615	0.4016	0.5925	0.6161
	SVM	0.9492	0.9159	0.9256	0.9033	0.9257	0.9255
	ANN	0.9592	0.9202	0.9179	0.9233	0.9389	0.9279
Hybrid	Ensemble	0.6327	0.6079	0.7269	0.4533	0.6340	0.6763
	SVM	0.9893	0.9623	0.9666	0.9566	0.9667	0.9666
	ANN	0.9880	0.9601	0.9564	0.965	0.9725	0.9643

In this study, the classification performance results of 10 different trials using 10-fold cross validation are presented with box plots. This visual analysis demonstrates the stability of the proposed classification models and the consistency of the results, as seen in Figure 5. Box plots clearly illustrate the central tendencies, distributions, and potential outliers of the outcomes from various trials.

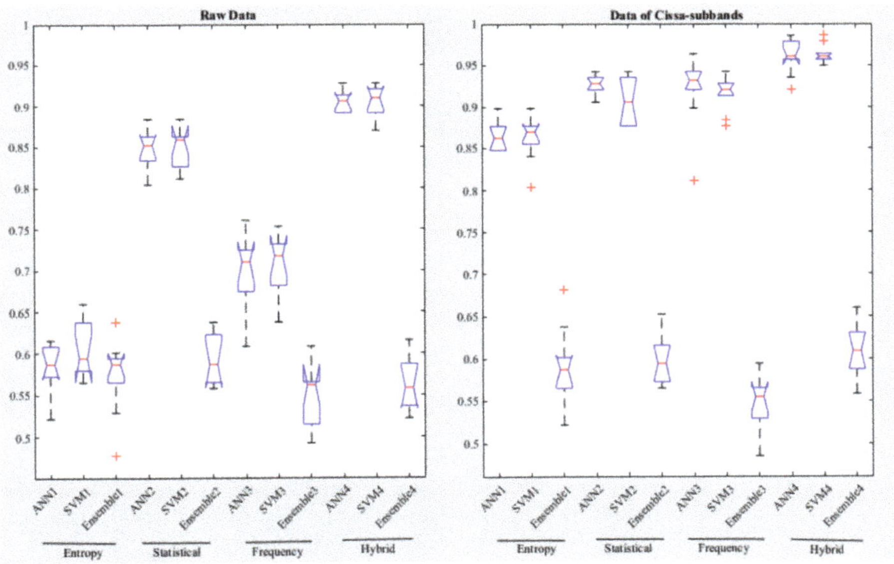

Figure 5. Box plots of classification accuracy obtained from various feature domains.

4. Discussion and Conclusions

The detection of first-episode psychosis is a crucial healthcare issue for both individuals and society, and accurate and early detection provides an opportunity for early intervention and treatment. Early treatment is important in reducing the severity of symptoms, slowing the progression of the illness, and improving the individual's quality of life.

In the literature, many studies have been conducted to detect FEP using EEG signals. These studies have utilized various features extracted from EEG signals obtained from different datasets, including spectral power, phase-based and amplitude-based functional connectivity, macroscale network characteristics, density, power spectral density/spectral features, etc. [11–15]. Also, machine learning and statistical methods, either individually or together, have been utilized for classification purposes in the literature. Taking this into consideration, it would be appropriate to mention here that in this proposed study, only the machine learning approach has been applied. However, due to the limited number of studies incorporating a machine learning approach and the prevalence of literature reviews that predominantly focus on statistical evaluations, studies emphasizing statistical assessments have also been added to the comparative table.

An overview of the literature on studies using EEG signals for FEP detection can be seen in Table 4. These studies have shown classification performance ranging from 50.2% to 88.06%.

In this proposed study, a new approach was employed by decomposing EEG signals into ciSSA sub-band signals to obtain their different domain-specific features. This approach allowed for the extraction of important features from EEG signals for FEP detection from multiple perspectives. Using ensemble methods, as well as ANN and SVM machine learning techniques, this study presented a new method in the literature based on the feature and classifier combination that achieved the best classification performance.

As shown in Table 3, the classification results based on entropy features calculated from ciSSA sub-bands using ANN averaged 86.66% over 10 trials, whereas the statistical features and ANN yielded 92.53%, the frequency-based features and ANN achieved 92.02%, and all features with SVM resulted in a 96.23% classification success rate. As indicated in Table 2, in the approach that employed EEG signals without decomposing them into sub-bands and utilized entropy, statistical, frequency-based, and hybrid features with machine learning methods, a lower classification performance was obtained compared to the ciSSA feature machine learning approach.

Based on these results, a high-performance classification model for FEP detection from EEG signals was proposed, utilizing ciSSA sub-band signals and hybrid features consisting of entropy, statistical, and frequency features, along with an SVM model.

Upon analyzing literature reviews and the obtained results, it has been observed that significant advantages are achieved in this study compared to other studies utilizing statistical approaches, particularly in utilizing signal processing and machine learning models to achieve high accuracy and precision. Furthermore, the proposed combined model has demonstrated a substantial improvement in performance compared to other models employing machine learning approaches. In these regards, the suggested model provides a significant advantage by generating high-performance classification results. One of the most notable advantages of this study is the capability to classify the disease with high performance at its earliest stage. This contributes significantly to the accurate guidance of disease progression and treatment through early diagnosis. Additionally, in this study, 3-min EEG data were used. Revealing this system with recordings of such a short duration holds high potential for speed and performance in developing expert systems for this purpose. However, in the implementation stage of the model, the decomposition of data into sub-bands and the feature extraction from these sub-bands may introduce processing overhead. In this regard, the proposed model may have higher processing complexity compared to models directly analyzing the data.

In future studies, this method can be applied to the diagnosis of various neurological disorders, aiming to establish a ciSSA feature extraction machine learning model for the high-performance classification of neurological disorders.

Table 4. Summary of the classification performance of various scenarios with EEG signals from different datasets belonging to FEP.

Refs.	Dataset	Ch Size	FEP/Ctrl	Tasks/Duration	Signal Processing Methods/Features	Machine Learning Techniques/Statistics	Accuracy
[41]	Collected data	64 Ch	62/106	Resting state/45 min	Several features (60) of four fequency subbands (spectral power, phase-based and amplitude-based functional connectivity, and macroscale network characteristics were analyzed)	a random forest (RF) classifier/Mann–Whitney U test and RF regression were used for statistical analysis	50.2%
[42]	Collected data	19 Ch	29/25	Resting state	Microstate analysis/EEG microstate dynamics	ANOVAs	Between-group comparisons at baseline indicated significant differences
[43]	Collected data	19 Ch	17/30 mFEP/uFEP	Several tasks during 20 min	Microstate analysis/EEG microstates dynamics	ANOVA and *t*-test	Statistically significant differences were found
[44]	Collected data	64 Ch	20/33	Mismatch negativity (MMN) paradigm	Various measures from alpha, delta, and theta	k-means	Not presented
[45]	Collected data	64 Ch	26/17	Resting state/eyes open (EO) and eyes close (EC): EO (3 min), EC (3 min), EO (3 min), EC (3 min)	Power spectral density (PSD)/PSD vaues of EEG frequency subbands	channel-wise permutation-based statistics (paired Student's *t*-tests and two-tailed were used; 1000 permutations)	There was no significant difference in EEG power between FEP and healthy controls in the following bands and conditions: AM/EC delta, theta, and higher alpha bands; PM/EC delta and alpha bands; AM/EO delta, theta, and alpha bands; PM/EO delta, theta, and lower alpha bands
[46]	Collected data	192 Ch	29/30	Resting state/10 min	Spectral power analysis/gamma spectral power	MANOVA and one-way ANOVA	The gamma spectral power in 31–50 Hz and 51–70 Hz frequency bands was found to be significantly higher in patients in most brain regions.
[47]	Collected data	64 Ch	16/11	After transcranial magnetic stimulation/na		not given detail	found no differences
[48]	Collected data	16 Ch	10/10	Emotional state (pleasant, unpleasant, neutral)	Wavelet coherence	Least-squares support-vector machine/ANOVA	83.89%, 86.39%, 88.06%, respectively/statistically significant differences were found
This proposed study	FEP1 [19] and FEP2 [18]	60 Ch	78/60	Resting state/3 min	ciSSA/Entropy, statistical, and frequency features	SVM, Ensemble classifier, Multi-layer perceptron-ANN	Given binary classifier results at Tables 2 and 3

Ch: channels, Ctrl: healthy controls.

Supplementary Materials: The following supporting information can be downloaded at: https://www.mdpi.com/article/10.3390/biomedicines11123223/s1, Supplementary Materials S1: Demographic Informations of Participants; Supplementary Materials S2: Features Descriptions.

Funding: This research received no external funding.

Institutional Review Board Statement: Not applicable.

Informed Consent Statement: Not applicable.

Data Availability Statement: The datasets used are publicly available at the given links below: https://openneuro.org/datasets/ds003944/versions/1.0.1 (accessed on 10 February 2023) and https://openneuro.org/datasets/ds003947/versions/1.0.1 (accessed on 10 February 2023).

Conflicts of Interest: The author declares no conflict of interest.

References

1. American Psychiatric Publishing. *Diagnostic and Statistical Manual of Mental Disorders: DSM-5TM*, 5th ed.; American Psychiatric Publishing, Inc.: Arlington, VA, USA, 2013. [CrossRef]
2. Farooq, S.; Green, D.J.; Singh, S.P. Sharing information about diagnosis and outcome of first-episode psychosis in patients presenting to early intervention services. *Early Interv. Psychiatry* **2019**, *13*, 657–666. [CrossRef] [PubMed]
3. Benli, Ş.G.; Andaç, M. Constructing the Schizophrenia Recognition Method Employing GLCM Features from Multiple Brain Regions and Machine Learning Techniques. *Diagnostics* **2023**, *13*, 2140. [CrossRef] [PubMed]
4. Hu, M.; Qian, X.; Liu, S.; Koh, A.J.; Sim, K.; Jiang, X.; Guan, C.; Zhou, J.H. Structural and diffusion MRI based schizophrenia classification using 2D pretrained and 3D naive Convolutional Neural Networks. *Schizophr. Res.* **2022**, *243*, 330–341. [CrossRef] [PubMed]
5. Chilla, G.S.; Yeow, L.Y.; Chew, Q.H.; Sim, K.; Prakash, K.N.B. Machine learning classification of schizophrenia patients and healthy controls using diverse neuroanatomical markers and Ensemble methods. *Sci. Rep.* **2022**, *12*, 2755. [CrossRef] [PubMed]
6. Guo, Y.; Qiu, J.; Lu, W. Support Vector Machine-Based Schizophrenia Classification Using Morphological Information from Amygdaloid and Hippocampal Subregions. *Brain Sci.* **2020**, *10*, 562. [CrossRef]
7. Vyškovský, R.; Schwarz, D.; Churová, V.; Kašpárek, T. Structural MRI-Based Schizophrenia Classification Using Autoencoders and 3D Convolutional Neural Networks in Combination with Various Pre-Processing Techniques. *Brain Sci.* **2022**, *12*, 615. [CrossRef] [PubMed]
8. Squarcina, L.; Castellani, U.; Bellani, M.; Perlini, C.; Lasalvia, A.; Dusi, N.; Bonetto, C.; Cristofalo, D.; Tosato, S.; Rambaldelli, G.; et al. Classification of first-episode psychosis in a large cohort of patients using support vector machine and multiple kernel learning techniques. *Neuroimage* **2017**, *145*, 238–245. [CrossRef]
9. Faria, A.V.; Zhao, Y.; Ye, C.; Hsu, J.; Yang, K.; Cifuentes, E.; Wang, L.; Mori, S.; Miller, M.; Caffo, B.; et al. Multimodal MRI assessment for first episode psychosis: A major change in the thalamus and an efficient stratification of a subgroup. *Hum. Brain Mapp.* **2021**, *42*, 1034–1053. [CrossRef]
10. Forns-Nadal, M.; Bergé, D.; Sem, F.; Mané, A.; Igual, L.; Guinart, D.; Vilarroya, O. Increased nucleus accumbens volume in first-episode psychosis. *Psychiatry Res. Neuroimaging* **2017**, *263*, 57–60. [CrossRef]
11. Missonnier, P.; Prévot, A.; Herrmann, F.R.; Ventura, J.; Padée, A.; Merlo, M.C.G. Disruption of gamma-delta relationship related to working memory deficits in first-episode psychosis. *J. Neural Transm.* **2020**, *127*, 103–115. [CrossRef]
12. Renaldi, R.; Kim, M.; Lee, T.H.; Kwak, Y.B.; Tanra, A.J.; Kwon, J.S. Predicting Symptomatic and Functional Improvements over 1 Year in Patients with First-Episode Psychosis Using Resting-State Electroencephalography. *Psychiatry Investig.* **2019**, *16*, 695–703. [CrossRef] [PubMed]
13. Lee, T.H.; Kim, M.; Hwang, W.J.; Kim, T.; Kwak, Y.B.; Kwon, J.S. Relationship between resting-state theta phase-gamma amplitude coupling and neurocognitive functioning in patients with first-episode psychosis. *Schizophr. Res.* **2020**, *216*, 154–160. [CrossRef] [PubMed]
14. Garakh, Z.; Zaytseva, Y.; Kapranova, A.; Fiala, O.; Horacek, J.; Shmukler, A.; Gurovich, I.Y.; Strelets, V.B. EEG correlates of a mental arithmetic task in patients with first episode schizophrenia and schizoaffective disorder. *Clin. Neurophysiol.* **2015**, *126*, 2090–2098. [CrossRef] [PubMed]
15. Newson, J.J.; Thiagarajan, T.C. EEG Frequency Bands in Psychiatric Disorders: A Review of Resting State Studies. *Front. Hum. Neurosci.* **2018**, *12*, 521. [CrossRef] [PubMed]
16. Zülfikar, A.; Mehmet, A. Empirical mode decomposition and convolutional neural network-based approach for diagnosing psychotic disorders from eeg signals. *Appl. Intell.* **2022**, *52*, 12103–12115. [CrossRef]
17. Khare, S.K.; Bajaj, V. A hybrid decision support system for automatic detection of Schizophrenia using EEG signals. *Comput. Biol. Med.* **2022**, *141*, 105028. [CrossRef] [PubMed]
18. Salisbury, D.; Seebold, D.; Coffman, B. *EEG: First Episode Psychosis vs. Control Resting Task 2*; Dataset; OpenNeuro: Stanford, CA, USA, 2022. [CrossRef]
19. Salisbury, D.; Seebold, D.; Coffman, B. *EEG: First Episode Psychosis vs. Control Resting Task 1*; Dataset; OpenNeuro: Stanford, CA, USA, 2022. [CrossRef]
20. Delorme, A.; Makeig, S. EEGLAB: An open source toolbox for analysis of single-trial EEG dynamics including independent component analysis. *J. Neurosci. Methods* **2004**, *134*, 9–21. [CrossRef] [PubMed]

21. Bógalo, J.; Poncela, P.; Senra, E. Circulant singular spectrum analysis: A new automated procedure for signal extraction. *Signal Process.* **2021**, *179*, 107824. [CrossRef]
22. Hu, H.; Pu, Z.; Wang, P. A flexible and accurate method for electroencephalography rhythms extraction based on circulant singular spectrum analysis. *PeerJ* **2022**, *10*, e13096. [CrossRef]
23. Chaitanya, M.K.; Sharma, L.D. Electrocardiogram signal filtering using circulant singular spectrum analysis and cascaded Savitzky-Golay filter. *Biomed. Signal Process. Control* **2022**, *75*, 103583. [CrossRef]
24. Tsallis, C. Possible generalization of Boltzmann-Gibbs statistics. *J. Stat. Phys.* **1988**, *52*, 479–487. [CrossRef]
25. Sneddon, R. The Tsallis entropy of natural information. *Phys. A Stat. Mech. Its Appl.* **2007**, *386*, 101–118. [CrossRef]
26. Aydin, S.; Saraoğlu, H.M.; Kara, S. Log energy entropy-based EEG classification with multilayer neural networks in seizure. *Ann. Biomed. Eng.* **2009**, *37*, 2626–2630. [CrossRef] [PubMed]
27. Baraniuk, R.G.; Flandrin, P.; Janssen, A.J.E.M.; Michel, O.J.J. Measuring time-frequency information content using the Renyi entropies. *IEEE Trans. Inf. Theory* **2001**, *47*, 1391–1409. [CrossRef]
28. Atyabi, A.; Shic, F.; Naples, A. Mixture of autoregressive modeling orders and its implication on single trial EEG classification. *Expert Syst. Appl.* **2016**, *65*, 164–180. [CrossRef] [PubMed]
29. Tibshirani, R. Regression Shrinkage and Selection via the Lasso. *J. R. Stat. Soc. Ser. B* **1996**, *58*, 267–288. Available online: http://www.jstor.org/stable/2346178 (accessed on 19 November 2023). [CrossRef]
30. Lanillos, P.; Oliva, D.; Philippsen, A.; Yamashita, Y.; Nagai, Y.; Cheng, G. A review on neural network models of schizophrenia and autism spectrum disorder. *Neural Netw.* **2020**, *122*, 338–363. [CrossRef] [PubMed]
31. Hosseini, M.-P.; Hosseini, A.; Ahi, K. A Review on Machine Learning for EEG Signal Processing in Bioengineering. *IEEE Rev. Biomed. Eng.* **2021**, *14*, 204–218. [CrossRef]
32. Cortes, C.; Vapnik, V. Support-vector networks. *Mach. Learn.* **1995**, *20*, 273–297. [CrossRef]
33. Altınkaynak, M.; Dolu, N.; Güven, A.; Pektaş, F.; Özmen, S.; Demirci, E.; İzzetoğlu, M. Diagnosis of Attention Deficit Hyperactivity Disorder with combined time and frequency features. *Biocybern. Biomed. Eng.* **2020**, *40*, 927–937. [CrossRef]
34. Miras, R.; Molina, A.J.; Soriano, M.F.; Parro, S.I. Schizophrenia classification using machine learning on resting state EEG signal. *Biomed. Signal Proces. Control* **2023**, *79*, 104233. [CrossRef]
35. Zhang, G.; Hu, M.Y.; Patuwo, B.E.; Indro, D.C. Artificial neural networks in bankruptcy prediction: General framework and cross-validation analysis. *Eur. J. Oper. Res.* **1999**, *116*, 16–32. [CrossRef]
36. Gu, Y.; Liang, Z.; Hagihira, S. Use of Multiple EEG Features and Artificial Neural Network to Monitor the Depth of Anesthesia. *Sensors* **2019**, *19*, 2499. [CrossRef] [PubMed]
37. Li, R.C.; George, S.T.; Rajan, A.A.; Subathra, M.S.P. Detection of ADHD from EEG Signals Using Different Entropy Measures and ANN. *Clin. EEG Neurosci.* **2022**, *53*, 12–23. [CrossRef]
38. Ju, C.; Bibaut, A.; van der Laan, M. The relative performance of ensemble methods with deep convolutional neural networks for image classification. *J. Appl. Stat.* **2018**, *45*, 2800–2818. [CrossRef] [PubMed]
39. Kim, C.-L.; Kim, B.-G. Few-shot learning for facial expression recognition: A comprehensive survey. *J. Real-Time Image Process.* **2023**, *20*, 52. [CrossRef]
40. Brown, G. Ensemble Learning. In *Encyclopedia of Machine Learning*; Sammut, C., Webb, G.I., Eds.; Springer: Boston, MA, USA, 2010; pp. 312–320. [CrossRef]
41. Dominicus, L.S.; Oranje, B.; Otte, W.M.; Ambrosen, K.S.; Düring, S.; Scheepers, F.E.; Stam, C.J.; Glenthøj, B.Y.; Ebdrup, B.H.; van Dellen, E. Macroscale EEG characteristics in antipsychotic-naïve patients with first-episode psychosis and healthy controls. *Schizophrenia* **2023**, *9*, 5. [CrossRef]
42. de Bock, R.; Mackintosh, A.J.; Maier, F.; Borgwardt, S.; Riecher-Rössler, A.; Andreou, C. EEG microstates as biomarker for psychosis in ultra-high-risk patients. *Transl. Psychiatry* **2020**, *10*, 300. [CrossRef]
43. Mackintosh, A.J.; Borgwardt, S.; Studerus, E.; Riecher-Rössler, A.; de Bock, R.; Andreou, C. EEG Microstate Differences in Medicated vs. Medication-Naïve First-Episode Psychosis Patients. *Front. Psychiatry* **2020**, *11*, 600606. [CrossRef]
44. Qu, X.; Liukasemsarn, S.; Tu, J.; Higgins, A.; Hickey, T.J.; Hall, M.-H. Identifying Clinically and Functionally Distinct Groups Among Healthy Controls and First Episode Psychosis Patients by Clustering on EEG Patterns. *Front. Psychiatry* **2020**, *11*, 541659. [CrossRef]
45. Zhang, Y.; Geyfman, A.; Coffman, B.; Gill, K.; Ferrarelli, F. Distinct alterations in resting-state electroencephalogram during eyes closed and eyes open and between morning and evening are present in first-episode psychosis patients. *Schizophr. Res.* **2021**, *228*, 36–42. [CrossRef]
46. Yadav, S.; Nizamie, S.H.; Das, B.; Das, J.; Tikka, S.K. Resting state quantitative electroencephalogram gamma power spectra in patients with first episode psychosis: An observational study. *Asian J. Psychiatry* **2021**, *57*, 102550. [CrossRef]
47. Ferrarelli, F.; Kaskie, R.E.; Graziano, B.; Reis, C.C.; Casali, A.G. Abnormalities in the evoked frontal oscillatory activity of first-episode psychosis: A TMS/EEG study. *Schizophr. Res.* **2019**, *206*, 436–439. [CrossRef]
48. Aydın, S.; Demirtaş, S.; Yetkin, S. Cortical correlations in wavelet domain for estimation of emotional dysfunctions. *Neural Comput. Appl.* **2018**, *30*, 1085–1094. [CrossRef]

biomedicines

Article

Analyzing Facial Asymmetry in Alzheimer's Dementia Using Image-Based Technology

Ching-Fang Chien [1,2], Jia-Li Sung [3], Chung-Pang Wang [3], Chen-Wen Yen [3,4,5,*] and Yuan-Han Yang [1,2,4,5,*]

1 Department of Neurology, Kaohsiung Municipal Ta-Tung Hospital, Kaohsiung Medical University Hospital, Kaohsiung Medical University, Kaohsiung 80756, Taiwan
2 Department of Neurology, Kaohsiung Medical University Hospital, Kaohsiung Medical University, Kaohsiung 80756, Taiwan
3 Department of Mechanical and Electromechanical Engineering, National Sun Yat-sen University, Kaohsiung 80424, Taiwan
4 Department of and Master's Program in Neurology, Faculty of Medicine, College of Medicine, Kaohsiung Medical University, Kaohsiung 80708, Taiwan
5 Neuroscience Research Center, Kaohsiung Medical University, Kaohsiung 80708, Taiwan
* Correspondence: cmurobot@gmail.com (C.-W.Y.); endlessyhy@gmail.com (Y.-H.Y.)

Abstract: Several studies have demonstrated accelerated brain aging in Alzheimer's dementia (AD). Previous studies have also reported that facial asymmetry increases with age. Because obtaining facial images is much easier than obtaining brain images, the aim of this work was to investigate whether AD exhibits accelerated aging patterns in facial asymmetry. We developed new facial asymmetry measures to compare Alzheimer's patients with healthy controls. A three-dimensional camera was used to capture facial images, and 68 facial landmarks were identified using an open-source machine-learning algorithm called OpenFace. A standard image registration method was used to align the three-dimensional original and mirrored facial images. This study used the registration error, representing landmark superimposition asymmetry distances, to examine 29 pairs of landmarks to characterize facial asymmetry. After comparing the facial images of 150 patients with AD with those of 150 age- and sex-matched non-demented controls, we found that the asymmetry of 20 landmarks was significantly different in AD than in the controls ($p < 0.05$). The AD-linked asymmetry was concentrated in the face edge, eyebrows, eyes, nostrils, and mouth. Facial asymmetry evaluation may thus serve as a tool for the detection of AD.

Keywords: Alzheimer's dementia; facial asymmetry; facial landmarks; accelerated aging; Procrustes method

Citation: Chien, C.-F.; Sung, J.-L.; Wang, C.-P.; Yen, C.-W.; Yang, Y.-H. Analyzing Facial Asymmetry in Alzheimer's Dementia Using Image-Based Technology. *Biomedicines* **2023**, *11*, 2802. https://doi.org/10.3390/biomedicines11102802

Academic Editors: Wu Qiu and Hulin Kuang

Received: 1 September 2023
Revised: 12 October 2023
Accepted: 13 October 2023
Published: 16 October 2023

1. Introduction

Alzheimer's dementia (AD) is characterized by a gradual decline in cognitive functions, particularly memory, impacting spatial awareness, judgment, and causing neuropsychiatric symptoms, and thus significantly affecting daily life. The prevailing understanding of AD pathology involves the accumulation of β-amyloid plaques outside nerve cells and tau protein tangles inside nerve cells, leading to neuronal damage and death [1]. However, these pathological changes are considered late-stage manifestations, and there are few hypotheses regarding the events preceding AD onset. In AD, synaptic degeneration can be detected in the early stages of pathological progression before neuronal degeneration. Synapses are where β-amyloid peptides are generated and serve as targets for toxic β-amyloid oligomers [2]. Neuroinflammation, which has been confirmed to play a pivotal role in AD, involves various inflammatory processes within the central nervous system [3]. Activated immune cells release inflammatory molecules in the brain, potentially causing neuronal damage. This inflammation may be a consequence of neuronal damage and abnormal protein metabolism, contributing to the progression of the disease. Among innate immune cells, microglial cells are central participants in neuroinflammation. Activated microglial cells exhibit diverse cellular profiles and interact with β-amyloid and tau proteins, as well as neuronal circuits in various ways. In later AD stages, excessive neuroinflammation leads to neuronal and glial cell death. Aβ clearance is impaired, and microglial cells release high levels of pro-inflammatory molecules, causing neurodegeneration. This creates a vicious cycle, and the release of ROS and NOS by microglial cells accelerates neuronal loss [3,4]. Vascular dysregulation may also be associated with AD. In post-mortem studies, 60–90% of clinical diagnosed AD patients exhibit brain vascular abnormalities, with 30% showing signs of cerebral infarctions [5]. About one-third of clinical diagnosed vascular dementia patients present AD-related pathological features, including amyloid plaques and neurofibrillary tangles [6]. Genetic factors play a role, particularly in early-onset AD with mutations in genes like APP, PSEN1, and PSEN2. However, most AD cases are late-onset and involve complex interactions between multiple genetic and environmental factors. From a macroscopic perspective, AD primarily affects brain regions such as the cerebral cortex and the hippocampus, resulting in atrophy and volume loss. Owing to the limited treatability of AD currently, earlier detection of AD and earlier use of medications such as acetylcholinesterase inhibitors is important as this may postpone disease progression and preserve patients' activities of daily living.

The developmental processes of the brain and facial morphology are highly interconnected [7,8]. During early embryonic development, the neuroepithelial cells located within the neural folds gives rise to facial precursor cells known as Cranial Neural Crest Cells (CNCC) [9]. These CNCCs undergo a transformation from an epithelial to a mesenchymal state and migrate ventrally, playing a significant role in the development of a majority of craniofacial bones and connective tissues. Early brain growth impacts facial prominence positioning and growth. In proximity to the CNCCs is the forebrain, which encompasses the cerebral cortex. The CNCC-secreted paracrine factors also regulate brain development. These interactions are well-documented in animal embryo studies and align with the co-occurrence of neurodevelopmental and craniofacial abnormalities in humans [8].

Many studies have demonstrated a pattern of accelerated brain aging in patients with AD. Based on MRI imaging, the BrainAGE algorithm linked AD to accelerated brain aging compared with a cognitively normal group and a group with mild cognitive impairment (MCI) [10–13]. Huang et al. utilized MRI and a machine learning model to predict brain age based on gray matter volume, revealing an accelerated brain aging trajectory in patients with MCI compared with healthy individuals [14]. Linden et al. found that facial asymmetry increases with age [15], and normal face development is highly contingent on normal brain development [8,16,17]. Facial malformation was also observed to be related to underlying brain disease [18]. Face–brain asymmetry has been identified in autism spectrum disorders [19] and in patients with focal epilepsy [20]. The etiology of facial asymmetry is multifactorial, including functional, neuromuscular, stomatognathic, environmental, congenital, traumatic, and neoplastic factors, as well as the effects of chronic skin diseases and aging. The face reveals clues to sex, age, and genetics. One study reported that AD patients have an "older-appearing face" based on the estimation of an independent panel of eight human raters [21]. Penke et al. also found that facial asymmetry was an important predictor of cognitive decline in older persons [22].

Most diagnostic procedures for AD are invasive or time consuming. For example, psychological assessment is time consuming, cerebrospinal fluid examination is invasive, and amyloid positron emission tomography is costly [23]. Beyond the conventional chemical and imaging biomarkers, other markers for AD detection are being developed [24,25]. As far as we know, there are no facial presentations that are typical of AD.

Review articles have appeared that cover many single-face image-based methods for estimating age [26–28]. However, these articles do not focus on the relationship between face aging and neurodegenerative diseases such as AD. In an initial investigation of the impact of AD on the human face, the above-cited literature points to facial symmetry as an interesting feature to focus on.

Considering that obtaining facial images is much easier than obtaining brain images, the aim of this study was to investigate whether facial asymmetry is potentially a marker for differentiating patients with AD from age- and sex-matched, healthy control subjects.

2. Materials and Methods

2.1. Participants

A total of 300 Taiwanese participants, including 150 AD patients and 150 controls without dementia, were recruited at Kaohsiung Municipal Ta-Tung Hospital in southern Taiwan. Participants had no previous facial trauma or disease. The diagnosis of AD was based on the NINCDS-ADRDA criteria [29] with reference to a series of comprehensive neuropsychological tests, including the Mini-Mental State Examination (MMSE) [30] derived from the Cognitive Abilities Screening Instrument (CASI) [31], Neuropsychiatric Inventory (NPI) [32], and Clinical Dementia Rating (CDR) scale [33]. The neuroimaging and blood check to exclude other conditions possibly contributing to the diagnosis of dementia were conducted simultaneously. The control group without dementia was recruited by a senior neurologist to exclude dementia and other systemic diseases.

This study was approved by the institutional review board of the Kaohsiung Medical University Chung-Ho Memorial Hospital (KMUHIRB-SV(I)-20210067). All patients gave written consent for the use of their images for research purposes before the image was taken.

2.2. Data Collection

2.2.1. Image Retraction

The images of patients were recorded with a stereo camera (Intel RealSense D435) to capture three-dimensional (3D) facial images. With a 30 Hz frame rate, every participant took thirty images. The resolution of the infrared camera is 1280 × 720. The resolution of the RGB camera is 1920 × 1080. Under standardized lighting conditions and against a constant background, test subjects were guided by a clinician to a natural head position at a distance of about 40 to 60 cm from the 3D camera. While keeping the Frankfort horizontal (FH) plane parallel to the floor subjects were asked to maintain a neutral facial expression with both eyes looking forward. The experiments were carried out in a quiet room of Kaohsiung Municipal Ta-Tung Hospital and subjects were required to stay seated during the test. Subjects were instructed to show a natural and relaxed facial expression while the images were taken. After removing images with closed-eyes or other inappropriate expressions, we included those with adequate quality for further analysis.

2.2.2. Face Landmark Detection and Pre-Processing

For each of the 3D face images analyzed in this study, we used OpenFace [34], a facial behavior analysis toolkit, to detect 68 facial landmarks. OpenFace's open-source availability, robust facial landmark detection, and strong performance make it a preferred choice for research and development in the field of facial analysis. As shown in Figures 1 and 2, as a machine learning algorithm, OpenFace detects 29 hemiface landmarks for each side of the face and 10 midface landmarks. Each landmark is represented by its 3-dimension x (horizontal), y (vertical), and z (depth) coordinates. Since OpenFace also provides the yaw angle for the human face, we took the face with the smallest yaw angle as the frame for subsequent calculation (Figure 3).

In measuring the position of the facial landmarks, inaccurate results were frequently encountered in estimating the depth of facial contour landmarks since these landmarks are located in the boundary between face and background regions. To remedy this problem, by processing the depth measurements provided by the camera system, we used K-means clustering algorithm [35] to automatically classify image pixels into a foreground (face) cluster and a background cluster. For each of the facial landmarks that were incorrectly assigned into the background cluster, we used the following rules to replace its depth measurement. First, with such a landmark as the center, we set up a 7 × 7 pixel window. Next, we examined how many pixels within this window were clustered into the facial cluster and used the average depth of these pixels as the depth of the landmark. When pixels of this 7 × 7 window were all assigned into the background cluster, the landmark depth was chosen as the median value of the depth of all 68 landmarks.

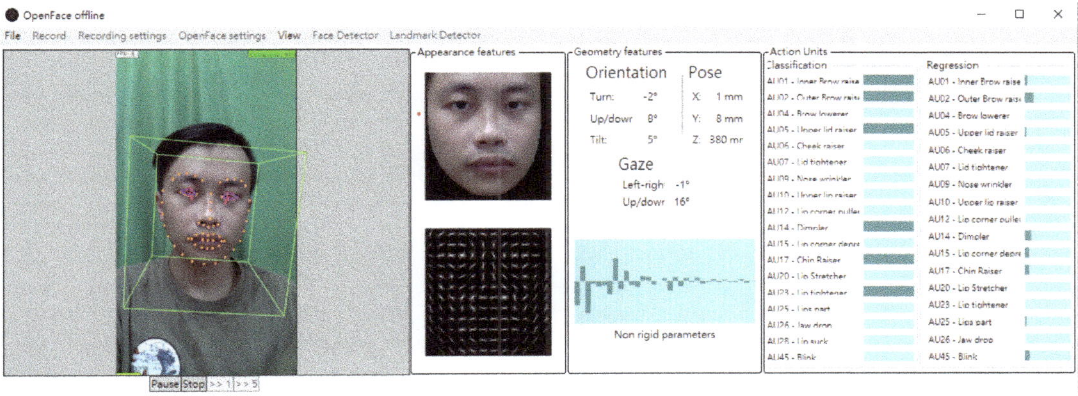

Figure 1. The image registration process example of OpenFace.

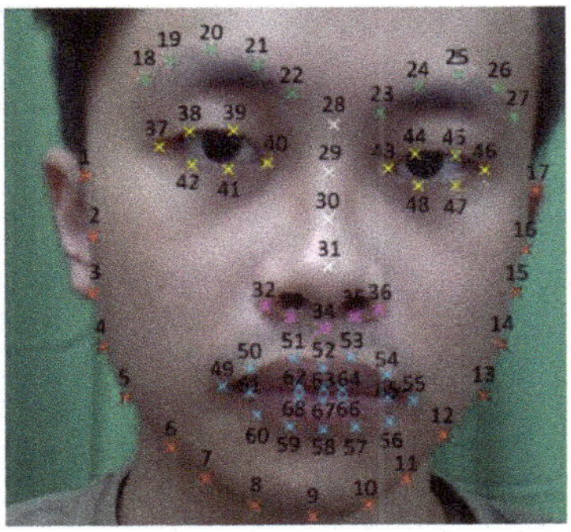

Face part	number
Face edge	1-17
Eyebrows	18-27
Nose	28-31
Nostrils	32-36
Eyes	37-48
Mouth	49-68

Figure 2. Facial feature points distribution map by OpenFace.

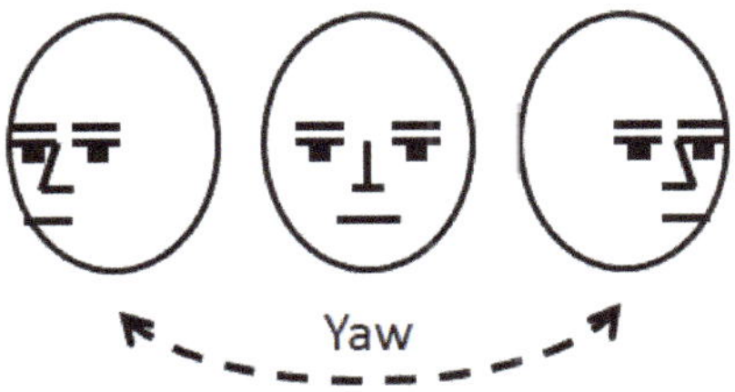

Figure 3. Yaw angle.

The size of a face image varies with the actual face size and the distance between the subject and the camera. To develop asymmetry measures that are invariant to these variations, we first calculated the centroid of all facial landmarks and denoted its coordinates as $(\overline{x}, \overline{y})$. Next, we used Equation (1a) to determine the horizontal normalized coefficient d_x which is the average of all the horizontal distances between the landmark centroid and landmarks. Similarly, this work used Equation (1b) to determine the vertical normalized coefficient d_y. Note that in the xy plane, distances are measured in pixels whereas distances in the z direction are measured in mm. This unit inconsistency problem will be addressed in the following section.

$$\sum_{i=1}^{68} \frac{|x_i - \overline{x}|}{68} = d_x \tag{1a}$$

$$\sum_{i=1}^{68} \frac{|y_i - \overline{y}|}{68} = d_y \tag{1b}$$

Note that the above normalization procedure was not employed in the depth direction. There are two reasons for such an arrangement. The first is that, in the depth direction, the differences between the landmarks are invariant to the distance between the subject and the camera. The second reason is that, as shown in the next section, the proposed asymmetry measure does not account for depth direction differences.

2.3. Normalization and Procrustes Analysis of the Facial Coordinates

This work characterizes facial asymmetry by comparing the location of each of the 29 right hemiface landmarks to the location of the corresponding left hemiface landmarks. To achieve this goal, the basic idea of the proposed approach is first to create a mirror face image by horizontally flipping the original image and then uses the Procrustes method [36,37] to align the mirror and original images. The Procrustes method, used in shape analysis and image alignment, aligns objects like facial images by translation, rotation, scaling, and reflection to minimize differences. It places facial landmarks in a shared coordinate system and orientation. This is employed to create a mirrored right-face image for LSAD calculations with the left face. Note that since the right hemiface of the mirror image is essentially the left hemiface of the original image, the Procrustes method only needs to align the right hemiface of the original and mirror images. This alignment procedure is critical for accurate asymmetry assessment since it is very difficult to perfectly orient the test subjects toward the camera.

To implement the proposed approach, we first denoted the coordinates of the *i*th right hemiface landmarks of the original image and mirror image as (x_i, y_i, z_i) and $(\alpha_i, \beta_i, \gamma_i)$, respectively. The coordinates of the centroids of the right hemiface landmarks of the original and mirror images are denoted as $(\overline{x}, \overline{y}, \overline{z})$ and $(\overline{\alpha}, \overline{\beta}, \overline{\gamma})$, respectively. Based on the normalization concept introduced in the previous section, we used Equation (2a) to calculate the normalized horizontal coordinate of the *i*th right hemiface landmarks of the original image. In an identical manner, we used Equation (2b) to determine the normalized vertical coordinate of the *i*th right hemiface landmarks of the original image. Similarly, for the mirror image, Equation (3a,b) were used to determine the normalized horizontal and vertical coordinates of *i*th right hemiface landmarks of the mirror image. For the depth direction, this work used Equations (2c) and (3c) to determine the normalized depth coordinates of the right hemiface landmarks of the original image and mirror image, respectively. Note that the depth coefficient c of Equations (2c) and (3c) was introduced to adjust the relative weighting between the alignment errors of the xy plane and the depth direction in applying the Procrustes method and at the same time resolving the unit inconsistency problem of the xy plane and the z direction.

$$X_i = (x_i - \overline{x})/d_x \tag{2a}$$

$$Y_i = (y_i - \overline{y})/d_y \tag{2b}$$

$$Z_i = c * (z_i - \overline{z}) \tag{2c}$$

$$A_i = (\alpha_i - \overline{\alpha})/d_x \tag{3a}$$

$$B_i = (\beta_i - \overline{\beta})/d_y \tag{3b}$$

$$C_i = c * (\gamma_i - \overline{\gamma}) \tag{3c}$$

Once the depth coefficient c was determined, with the alignment error of the *i*th right hemiface quantified as $(X_i - A_i)^2 + (Y_i - B_i)^2 + (Z_i - C_i)^2$, we used the Procrustes method to translate and rotate the original image so that the sum of squares of the alignment error of all right hemiface landmarks could be minimized. With X'_i and Y'_i denoting the horizontal and vertical normalized coordinate of the ith landmark of the aligned original image, we used Equation (4) to quantify the asymmetry associated with the ith landmark. Hereafter, these asymmetry measures will be referred to as landmark superimposition asymmetry distances (LSADs). The sum of LSAD is also proposed as an asymmetry measure (Equation (5)).

$$LSAD_i = \sqrt{(A_i - X'_i)^2 + (B_i - Y'_i)^2} \quad (4)$$

$$LSAD_s = \sum_{i=1}^{29} LSAD_i \quad (5)$$

With the asymmetry measures specified, the depth coefficient c can be determined by the following steps. First, we extensively tested different values of the depth coefficient c. For each of these tested c values, we calculated all the asymmetry measures of Equations (4) and (5) for all the test subjects. With these 30 asymmetry measures logged for all test individuals, we performed an independent sample one-tailed t-test between AD and controls and counted the number of asymmetry measures with significant differences. Because the number of asymmetry measures with significant differences is the most when the depth coefficient was 0.016, the value of the depth coefficient c was chosen as 0.016 for subsequent analysis.

2.4. Statistic Analysis

Continuous variables are expressed as the mean with the standard deviation, whereas categorical variables are presented as percentages. The association between the AD and controls and demographic and clinical characteristics (age, sex, CDR, CDR-SB, MMSE, and CASI) was explored using t-tests and the chi-square test. p-values for comparisons across groups of clinical and demographic characteristics were derived from the aforementioned analyses. The independent t-test is used to determine if the mean of the LSAD of the AD patients and controls is significantly different. All reported p-values are two-sided, with a p-value < 0.05 considered to be statistically significant. Analyses were performed using SPSS Version 26.

3. Results

3.1. Demographic Characteristics of Recruited Participants

Patients' age ranged from 56 to 79 years (mean: 72.2 years; standard deviation: 4.9 years). Fifty-seven patients were male and ninety-three were female. The CDR sum of boxes score was 4.8 ± 2.9 (mean ± SD), the MMSE total score was 21.0 ± 4.4 (mean ± SD), and the CASI total score was 65.7 ± 14.2 (mean ± SD).

Healthy subjects were chosen as the control group (age: 52–93 years, mean: 71.8 years, standard deviation: 7.4 years) and included forty-six males and one hundred and four females. The CDR sum of boxes score was 1.5 ± 1.4 (mean ± SD), the MMSE total score was 24.5 ± 3.7 (mean ± SD), and the CASI total score was 83.7 ± 10.5 (mean ± SD). A summary of subjects' characteristics is reported in Table 1.

Table 1. Demographic characteristics of recruited participants.

	AD	Controls	*p*-Value
Age, years (mean ± SD)	72.2 ± 4.9	71.8 ± 7.4	0.15
Gender (patient No., (%))			0.19
Male	57 (38%)	46 (31%)	
Female	93 (62%)	104 (69%)	
CDR (%)			
0	2 (1.4%)		
0.5	49 (34.8%)		
1.0	76 (53.9%)		
2.0	14 (9.9%)		
3.0	0		
CDR-SB (mean ± SD)	4.8 ± 2.9	1.5 ± 1.4	
MMSE (mean ± SD)	21.0 ± 4.4	24.5 ± 3.7	
CASI (mean ± SD)	65.7 ± 14.2	83.7 ± 10.5	

CDR: Clinical Dementia Rating. MMSE: Mini-Mental State Examination. SD: standard deviation.

3.2. The Comparison of Landmark Superimposition Asymmetry Distances (LSADs) of AD and Controls

Figure 4 shows the 68 landmarks, including 29 hemiface landmarks for each side of the faces and 10 midface landmarks. The landmark superimposition asymmetry distances (LSADs) of AD and controls are shown in Table 2, expressed as the mean with the standard deviation. Among the 29 LSADs of the AD patients, 20 of these LSADs are significantly larger than those of the controls. In face edge pair 1, the mean distance was 0.71 ± 0.51 for AD patients and 0.63 ± 0.53 for controls (p = 0.003). In face edge pair 2, the mean distance was 0.43 ± 0.30 for AD patients and 0.40 ± 0.37 for controls (p = 0.006). In face edge pair 3, the mean distance was 0.47 ± 0.34 for AD patients and 0.39 ± 0.33 for controls (p = 0.009). In face edge pair 4, the mean distance was 0.56 ± 0.37 for AD patients and 0.46 ± 0.37 for controls (p = 0.012). In face edge pair 5, the mean distance was 0.57 ± 0.39 for AD patients and 0.48 ± 0.37 for controls (p = 0.010). In face edge pair 6, the mean distance was 0.51 ± 0.33 for AD patients and 0.44 ± 0.32 for controls (p = 0.003). In face edge pair 7, the mean distance was 0.41 ± 0.31 for AD patients and 0.37 ± 0.31 for controls (p = 0.041). In face edge pair 8, the mean distance was 0.34 ± 0.35 for AD patients and 0.25 ± 0.24 for controls (p = 0.007). In eyebrows pair 9, the mean distance was 0.25 ± 0.19 for AD patients and 0.22 ± 0.15 for controls (p = 0.005). In eyebrows pair 10, the mean distance was 0.17 ± 0.12 for AD patients and 0.16 ± 0.12 for controls (p = 0.004). In eyebrows pair 13, the mean distance was 0.29 ± 0.20 for AD patients and 0.25 ± 0.18 for controls (p = 0.001). In nostrils pair 14, the mean distance was 0.37 ± 0.23 for AD patients and 0.31 ± 0.22 for controls (p = 0.013). In nostrils pair 15, the mean distance was 0.44 ± 0.25 for AD patients and 0.39 ± 0.26 for controls (p = 0.016). In eyes pair 16, the mean distance was 0.12 ± 0.10 for AD patients and 0.09 ± 0.06 for controls (p = 0.024). In eyes pair 17, the mean distance was 0.15 ± 0.12 for AD patients and 0.11 ± 0.09 for controls (p = 0.001). In eyes pair 18, the mean distance was 0.13 ± 0.10 for AD patients and 0.11 ± 0.09 for controls (p = 0.0004). In eyes pair 19, the mean distance was 0.12 ± 0.07 for AD patients and 0.10 ± 0.07 for controls (p = 0.0009). In mouth pair 22, the mean distance was 0.13 ± 0.09 for AD patients and 0.11 ± 0.08 for controls (p = 0.023). In mouth pair 24, the mean distance was 0.43 ± 0.23 for AD patients and 0.37 ± 0.23 for controls (p = 0.035). In mouth pair 26, the mean distance was 0.25 ± 0.16 for AD patients and 0.21 ± 0.15 for controls (p = 0.042). The sum of LSAD was 10.33 ± 4.39 for AD patients and 9.14 ± 4.45 for controls (p = 0.003). Other LSADs of the AD patients were also larger than those of the controls but did not show statistical significance.

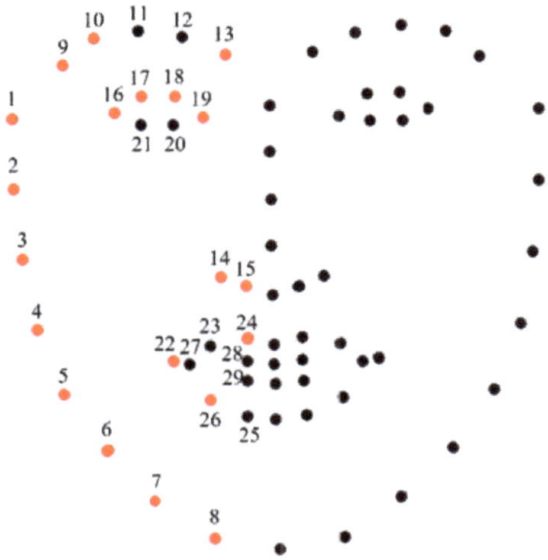

Figure 4. Facial feature point pairs of LSADs with a significant difference between AD patients and controls are marked as red.

Table 2. The facial feature point pairs of LSADs, calculated with *t*-test between AD and controls.

Face Part	Pair	AD	Controls	*p*-Value
Face edge	1	0.71 ± 0.51	0.63 ± 0.53	0.003 *
	2	0.43 ± 0.30	0.40 ± 0.37	0.006 *
	3	0.47 ± 0.34	0.39 ± 0.33	0.009 *
	4	0.56 ± 0.37	0.46 ± 0.37	0.012 *
	5	0.57 ± 0.39	0.48 ± 0.37	0.010 *
	6	0.51 ± 0.33	0.44 ± 0.32	0.003 *
	7	0.41 ± 0.31	0.37 ± 0.31	0.041 *
	8	0.34 ± 0.35	0.25 ± 0.24	0.007 *
Eyebrows	9	0.25 ± 0.19	0.22 ± 0.15	0.005 *
	10	0.17 ± 0.12	0.16 ± 0.12	0.004 *
	11	0.24 ± 0.18	0.22 ± 0.18	0.059
	12	0.30 ± 0.22	0.27 ± 0.20	0.053
	13	0.29 ± 0.20	0.25 ± 0.18	0.001 *
Nostrils	14	0.37 ± 0.23	0.31 ± 0.22	0.013 *
	15	0.44 ± 0.25	0.39 ± 0.26	0.016 *
Eyes	16	0.12 ± 0.10	0.09 ± 0.06	0.024 *
	17	0.15 ± 0.12	0.11 ± 0.09	0.001 *
	18	0.13 ± 0.10	0.11 ± 0.09	0.0004 *
	19	0.12 ± 0.07	0.10 ± 0.07	0.0009 *
	20	0.32 ± 0.11	0.32 ± 0.09	0.209
	21	0.29 ± 0.11	0.28 ± 0.08	0.747
Mouth	22	0.13 ± 0.09	0.11 ± 0.08	0.023 *
	23	0.31 ± 0.17	0.27 ± 0.17	0.054
	24	0.43 ± 0.23	0.37 ± 0.23	0.035 *
	25	0.33 ± 0.19	0.27 ± 0.17	0.083
	26	0.25 ± 0.16	0.21 ± 0.15	0.042 *
	27	0.82 ± 0.27	0.79 ± 0.25	0.936
	28	0.52 ± 0.15	0.55 ± 0.13	0.645
	29	0.36 ± 0.20	0.31 ± 0.19	0.069
Sum of LSAD		10.33 ± 4.39	9.14 ± 4.45	0.003 *

* $p < 0.05$.

4. Discussion

4.1. Key Findings

In this work, we aimed to develop a facial asymmetry assessment system to differentiate Alzheimer's patients from non-dementia people. Our study showed, among the 29 tested landmark pairs, 20 pairs of LSADs of the AD patients are significantly larger than those of the controls, including all face edge landmarks, 3 eyebrow landmarks, all landmarks of the nostrils, 4 landmarks of the eyes, and 3 mouth landmarks.

4.2. Facial Differences in Ethnic Skin

Taiwan is located in East Asia and its population is primarily composed of Han Chinese and indigenous peoples. Also, there are subtle differences in the facial features of northeast Asian and southeast Asian ethnic groups, often reflecting mixed phenotypic characteristics influenced by their proximity to neighboring populations. Farkas et al. found that the most significant differences among different racial groups were observed in the eye socket area, nose height, and nose width. Middle Eastern and Asian populations had narrower intercanthal distances with less eye corner width, whereas Caucasians exhibited a narrower nasal base with a more pronounced nasal tip [38,39]. Facial aging processes are similar across races, but differences in skeletal support and soft tissue tendencies result in slower facial aging in Asians compared to Caucasians. Asians often have dense fat and fiber connections in the mid-face, reducing sagging and resulting in fewer superficial wrinkles [40]. Although our assessment method is not influenced by skin color, wrinkles, or nasal bridge height, it is important to acknowledge that racial differences have a significant impact on morphological variations related to facial asymmetry [41]. This could limit the comparability of facial asymmetry measurements across different ethnic groups, representing a limitation in our study.

4.3. Possible Biological and Neural Mechanisms of Facial Asymmetry in AD

Facial development begins in the early fourth week of embryonic development when the frontonasal process emerges. By the fifth week, the nasal processes and maxillary/mandibular processes appear. They grow and fuse, forming the foundation of facial development. This process is typically completed by the eighth week, defining three primary facial regions: the frontal, maxillary, and mandibular parts [42,43].

In human facial development, genetic factors and growth factors play crucial roles. Key pathways include Fibroblast Growth Factor (FGF), Hedgehog (HH), and Bone Morphogenetic Protein (BMP). FGFs are involved in precise regulation, with mutations linked to syndromes like Crouzon and Apert. The HH pathway influences neural crest cells and jaw development, and mutations in the Sonic Hedgehog (SHH) gene can cause midline defects and eye issues. BMP signaling is essential for craniofacial bone development and disruptions can lead to various anomalies, including a cleft palate and facial defects [7,8,16]. However, there is currently no direct evidence showing that these signaling molecules are physiologically relevant to the pathogenesis of AD.

AD causes cortical atrophy and brain function decline. Abbate et al. proposed a pathophysiological hypothesis for AD, suggesting shared spatial information in cortical arealization during development and AD [44,45]. Some AD subtypes affect specific brain regions, potentially leading to lateralization. However, limited literature explores this. Compared to other vertebrates, AD processes, like amyloid deposition due to metabolism and tau pathogenesis from adult neurogenesis/migration, are emphasized in the complex human cortex. The human longevity revolution likely contributes to these extremes.

The two most substantiated risk factors for AD are genetics and aging. Mutations in genes like PSEN1, PSEN2, and APP lead to early-onset familial AD, while late-onset sporadic AD results from a combination of factors, including aging, lifestyle, environment, and genetics [46]. APOE4 is the most significant genetic risk factor for late-onset AD, associated with earlier accumulation of amyloid plaques and neurofibrillary tangles. APOE gene variants directly impact brain development [47]. In a study with 1187 healthy children,

APOE4 carriers had a thinner temporal cortex, smaller hippocampus, and weaker executive function correlations [48].

In normal aging, neuron loss is minimal, but there are changes in dendrite characteristics. These alterations vary across brain regions, with the most significant volume reduction occurring in specific areas like the frontal and temporal cortex [49]. Facial aging involves changes in bone structure, soft tissues, and skin, with interrelated effects. Bone resorption occurs with aging, affecting support, leading to soft tissue contraction and shifting. External factors like sun exposure and smoking impact skin aging, while collagen degradation accelerates and synthesis decreases with age, resulting in dermal atrophy [50–52].

Similar to our study, the BrainAGE algorithm via MRI has shown accelerated brain aging patterns in AD patients [10]. Dysfunctional DNA repair is also implicated in AD risk. While DNA methylation patterns generally decrease with age, specific gene regions may experience excessive methylation, resulting in increased variability. Epigenetic clocks, based on DNA methylation at specific sites, serve as reliable aging markers [53,54]. The difference between actual age and biological age is referred to as accelerated or decelerated epigenetic aging. Studies on dementia and mild cognitive impairment have yielded inconclusive results, with some suggesting a link between epigenetic age and dementia risk while others find no significant association [53,54].

Unlike our study, Naqvi et al. provided genetic and MRI evidence supporting the link between human facial and brain shape. They explored changes in various facial quadrants using GWAS but found no significant associations in AD [55]. This lack of association may be due to the complex etiology of AD, which involves a combination of genes and factors related to late-life plaque accumulation and neurodegeneration.

4.4. Method Comparisons

Recent studies used deep learning for age estimation from facial images [17–19] and showed promise. However, the connection between facial images and AD detection remains intriguing due to natural facial asymmetry variation. Quantifying facial asymmetry lacks a universally accepted standard [38]. This study introduces a landmark-based measure to address this issue.

Previous research has employed various methods to assess facial asymmetry, such as using the asymmetry distance calculated by root-mean-squared-error (RMSE) [56,57]. For instance, Ferrario et al. [58] utilized a camera-automatic three-dimensional landmark detection system, employing 16 landmarks, including 6 median points and 10 points representing the eyes, nose, mouth, and face edges. They applied Euclidean distance matrix analysis to compare the left and right hemifaces. Xiong et al. [59] analyzed 21 automatic facial landmarks, encompassing 7 medial points and 7 pairs of landmarks for the eyes, nose, and mouth. Ekrami et al. [60] examined 19 manual facial landmarks, consisting of 7 medial points and 6 pairs of landmarks for the eyes, nose, and mouth. In addition to biological landmarks, some studies incorporated nevi and wrinkles to enhance sensitivity. Many studies attempted to establish a reference frame for quantifying asymmetry, but determining the accurate midline frames posed another challenge [36,37,56]. To reduce errors, some studies employed multiple validation methods.

Regarding the assessment of facial asymmetry for facial palsy, there are various methods available. Gaber et al. employed Kinect V2 for automated recognition of facial features and created their own database. To address the issue of small sample sizes, they utilized undersampling and data augmentation for compensation [61]. Abayomi-Alli et al. introduced a deep learning-based method for facial paralysis detection and classification. They employed a novel image enhancement technique that extended random erasure enhancement using Voronoi subdivision structures. Subsequently, they used the SqueezeNet deep neural network for extracting deep features and employed a multi-class classifier for classification [62]. Wei et al. proposed a set of new facial features and augmented reality tools to assist users in interactively assessing facial symmetry. The development process involved four different datasets and focused on extracting features suitable for application on a smartphone program with lower computational costs [63].

After reviewing the previous literature, this study utilized a camera-automatic three-dimensional landmark detection system with OpenFace and analyzed facial asymmetry using the Procrustes method, which appeared to be the most effective and intuitive approach. The LSADs in our study indicated increased facial asymmetry in AD patients, particularly in regions such as the face edge, eyebrows, eyes, nostrils, and mouth. This method has been applied in other studies, albeit with different landmarks. Concerning age, Linden et al. demonstrated increased facial asymmetry in the lower two-thirds compared to the upper one-third in older age groups, while in younger age groups, more asymmetries were found in the upper third of the face [15]. Recently, Umeda et al. employed deep learning models to distinguish between the faces of dementia patients and non-dementia patients, with the lower face epochs providing better sensitivity and specificity. However, their results may have been influenced by the significantly older age of their AD group [23]. Greater normal variability in the global population was observed in the location of facial landmarks, including tragion, gonion, and zygion [64]. Zygion is close to our face edge landmark pair 2, and gonion is near our face edge landmark pair 5. Vertical eye movement differences have been found in AD patients compared to normal individuals [65], and abnormal oculomotor movement has been noted in several neurodegenerative diseases [66]. However, direct associations between eye shape or location and AD have not been identified in previous studies, nor have such associations been found for the rest of the facial landmarks.

4.5. Strengths

Facial asymmetry assessment is our initial step in evaluating facial features. While some conditions like stroke exhibit obvious facial asymmetry, its impact in chronic degenerative diseases is less discernible and is compounded by age-related effects. Thus, we employed a state-of-the-art machine learning algorithm to automatically and effectively identify facial landmarks, reducing human labor and enhancing the reproducibility of facial asymmetry measurements.

Compared to previous research, our study possesses several strengths. Firstly, by utilizing a 3D camera for facial capture, our study introduced a systematic approach to calibrate the relative orientation between the human head and the camera, leading to more accurate facial asymmetry computation. Secondly, to our knowledge, this is the first study to distinguish AD patients from non-dementia individuals through the objective evaluation of facial asymmetry. Thirdly, our study incorporated more reference points than other studies, allowing for the assessment of more subtle and precise features. Lastly, the included AD patients were primarily in the mild severity range (CDR: 0.5–1.0), indicating that our results may be applicable for early disease detection.

4.6. Limitations

The limitations include the automatic machine learning system used to differentiate AD patients from healthy subjects, which is still developing, and the fact that our participants consisted of only Taiwanese people; therefore, an extensive application still needs to be further evaluated. Our study includes a small participant number and is a cross-sectional study, thus a larger, longitudinal study may provide more information on the issue of AD patients' facial characteristics.

OpenFace uses Conditional Local Neural Fields (CLNFs) for facial landmark detection and tracking. A CLNF's performance depends on dataset diversity. Diverse datasets enhance adaptability, while small or biased datasets may hinder performance. Fine-tuning, data augmentation, and context-specific evaluation are often needed. In our study, we controlled image quality, facial pose, and expression. However, our dataset was limited in diversity and scale.

Additionally, overstating the connection between facial appearance and diseases can lead to biases. The current diagnostic criteria continue to be the basis for AD diagnosis. The early and accurate detection of AD remains an unmet need, and we propose that facial asymmetry could potentially serve as a supplementary tool in the future, alongside emerging early diagnostic methods for AD.

5. Conclusions

AD patients exhibited increased facial asymmetry compared to age- and gender-matched individuals without dementia. Our analysis encompassed a total of 29 facial landmarks, revealing that 20 pairs of LSADs in AD patients were significantly larger than those in the control group. Asymmetry in facial features, including face edges, eyebrows, eyes, nostrils, and mouth, contributed to distinguishing AD from non-dementia controls. Specifically, differences in face edge pairs 1 through 8, as well as eyebrows pairs 9, 10, and 13, nostrils pairs 14 and 15, eye pairs 16 through 19, and mouth pairs 22, 24, and 26, were statistically significant, with p-values ranging from 0.001 to 0.041. Furthermore, the total LSAD was notably higher in AD patients compared to controls, with a p-value of 0.003. Facial asymmetry may potentially serve as a tool for early AD detection in the future. However, it is essential to validate these findings in larger and more diverse cohorts.

Author Contributions: Conceptualization, Y.-H.Y.; methodology, Y.-H.Y. and C.-W.Y.; investigation, J.-L.S. and C.-P.W.; software, J.-L.S.; data curation, C.-P.W. and C.-W.Y.; writing—draft preparation, C.-F.C.; writing—review and editing C.-W.Y. and Y.-H.Y. All authors have read and agreed to the published version of the manuscript.

Funding: This study was supported by NSYSU-KMU joint research project (NSYSUKMU 108-I003), Kaohsiung Medical University Research Center Grant (KMU-TC112B02), Department of Neurology, Kaohsiung Municipal Ta-Tung Hospital, Kaohsiung, Taiwan (KMTTH-DK(C)112003).

Institutional Review Board Statement: This study was conducted according to the guidelines of the Declaration of Helsinki and approved by the Institutional Review Board of the of the Kaohsiung Medical University Chung-Ho Memorial Hospital (KMUHIRB-SV(I)-20210067).

Informed Consent Statement: Informed consent was obtained from all subjects involved in this study.

Data Availability Statement: Third party data: Restrictions apply to the availability of these data. The data were obtained from Department of Mechanical and Electromechanical Engineering, National Sun Yat-Sen University, Kaohsiung, Taiwan and are available from Chen-Wen Yen and Yuan-Han Yang with the permission of Department of Mechanical and Electromechanical Engineering, National Sun Yat-Sen University, Kaohsiung, Taiwan.

Conflicts of Interest: The authors declare no conflict of interest.

References

1. Jellinger, K.A. Neuropathological assessment of the Alzheimer spectrum. *J. Neural Transm.* **2020**, *127*, 1229–1256. [CrossRef]
2. Pelucchi, S.; Gardoni, F.; Di Luca, M.; Marcello, E. Synaptic dysfunction in early phases of Alzheimer's Disease. *Handb. Clin. Neurol.* **2022**, *184*, 417–438. [CrossRef]
3. Bairamian, D.; Sha, S.; Rolhion, N.; Sokol, H.; Dorothee, G.; Lemere, C.A.; Krantic, S. Microbiota in neuroinflammation and synaptic dysfunction: A focus on Alzheimer's disease. *Mol. Neurodegener.* **2022**, *17*, 19. [CrossRef]
4. Gonzalez, H.; Elgueta, D.; Montoya, A.; Pacheco, R. Neuroimmune regulation of microglial activity involved in neuroinflammation and neurodegenerative diseases. *J. Neuroimmunol.* **2014**, *274*, 1–13. [CrossRef]
5. Kalaria, R. Similarities between Alzheimer's disease and vascular dementia. *J. Neurol. Sci.* **2002**, *203–204*, 29–34. [CrossRef]
6. Kalaria, R.N.; Ballard, C. Overlap between pathology of Alzheimer disease and vascular dementia. *Alzheimer Dis. Assoc. Disord.* **1999**, *13*, S115–S123. [CrossRef] [PubMed]
7. Roth, D.M.; Bayona, F.; Baddam, P.; Graf, D. Craniofacial Development: Neural Crest in Molecular Embryology. *Head Neck Pathol.* **2021**, *15*, 1–15. [CrossRef] [PubMed]
8. Marcucio, R.; Hallgrimsson, B.; Young, N.M. Facial Morphogenesis: Physical and Molecular Interactions Between the Brain and the Face. *Curr. Top. Dev. Biol.* **2015**, *115*, 299–320. [CrossRef]
9. Smeriglio, P.; Zalc, A. Cranial Neural Crest Cells Contribution to Craniofacial Bone Development and Regeneration. *Curr. Osteoporos. Rep.* **2023**, *21*, 624–631. [CrossRef] [PubMed]

10. Franke, K.; Gaser, C. Ten Years of BrainAGE as a Neuroimaging Biomarker of Brain Aging: What Insights Have We Gained? *Front. Neurol.* **2019**, *10*, 789. [CrossRef]
11. Cole, J.H.; Franke, K. Predicting Age Using Neuroimaging: Innovative Brain Ageing Biomarkers. *Trends Neurosci.* **2017**, *40*, 681–690. [CrossRef] [PubMed]
12. Franke, K.; Ziegler, G.; Kloppel, S.; Gaser, C. Alzheimer's Disease Neuroimaging I. Estimating the age of healthy subjects from T1-weighted MRI scans using kernel methods: Exploring the influence of various parameters. *Neuroimage* **2010**, *50*, 883–892. [CrossRef] [PubMed]
13. Lin, L.; Min, X.; Yue, J.; Wenjie, K.; Shuicai, W.; Shen, S.; Zhenrong, F. Quantifying Brain and Cognitive Maintenance as Key Indicators for Sustainable Cognitive Aging: Insights from the UK Biobank. *Sustainability* **2023**, *15*, 9620. [CrossRef]
14. Huang, W.; Li, X.; Li, H.; Wang, W.; Chen, K.; Xu, K.; Zhang, J.; Chen, Y.; Wei, D.; Shu, N.; et al. Accelerated Brain Aging in Amnestic Mild Cognitive Impairment: Relationships with Individual Cognitive Decline, Risk Factors for Alzheimer Disease, and Clinical Progression. *Radiol. Artif. Intell.* **2021**, *3*, e200171. [CrossRef]
15. Linden, O.E.; He, J.K.; Morrison, C.S.; Sullivan, S.R.; Taylor, H.O.B. The Relationship between Age and Facial Asymmetry. *Plast. Reconstr. Surg.* **2018**, *142*, 1145–1152. [CrossRef] [PubMed]
16. Marcucio, R.S.; Young, N.M.; Hu, D.; Hallgrimsson, B. Mechanisms that underlie co-variation of the brain and face. *Genesis* **2011**, *49*, 177–189. [CrossRef]
17. Adameyko, I.; Fried, K. The Nervous System Orchestrates and Integrates Craniofacial Development: A Review. *Front. Physiol.* **2016**, *7*, 49. [CrossRef] [PubMed]
18. Demyer, W.; Zeman, W.; Palmer, C.G. The Face Predicts the Brain: Diagnostic Significance of Median Facial Anomalies for Holoprosencephaly (Arhinencephaly). *Pediatrics* **1964**, *34*, 256–263. [CrossRef]
19. Hammond, P.; Forster-Gibson, C.; Chudley, A.E.; Allanson, J.E.; Hutton, T.J.; Farrell, S.A.; McKenzie, J.; Holden, J.J.; Lewis, M.E. Face-brain asymmetry in autism spectrum disorders. *Mol. Psychiatry* **2008**, *13*, 614–623. [CrossRef]
20. Balestrini, S.; Lopez, S.M.; Chinthapalli, K.; Sargsyan, N.; Demurtas, R.; Vos, S.; Altmann, A.; Suttie, M.; Hammond, P.; Sisodiya, S.M. Increased facial asymmetry in focal epilepsies associated with unilateral lesions. *Brain Commun.* **2021**, *3*, fcab068. [CrossRef]
21. Elliott, M.L.; Belsky, D.W.; Knodt, A.R.; Ireland, D.; Melzer, T.R.; Poulton, R.; Ramrakha, S.; Caspi, A.; Moffitt, T.E.; Hariri, A.R. Brain-age in midlife is associated with accelerated biological aging and cognitive decline in a longitudinal birth cohort. *Mol. Psychiatry* **2021**, *26*, 3829–3838. [CrossRef] [PubMed]
22. Penke, L.; Bates, T.C.; Gow, A.J.; Pattie, A.; Starr, J.M.; Jones, B.C.; Perrett, D.I.; Deary, I.J. Symmetric faces are a sign of successful cognitive aging. *Evol. Hum. Behav.* **2009**, *30*, 429–437. [CrossRef]
23. Umeda-Kameyama, Y.; Kameyama, M.; Tanaka, T.; Son, B.K.; Kojima, T.; Fukasawa, M.; Iizuka, T.; Ogawa, S.; Iijima, K.; Akishita, M. Screening of Alzheimer's disease by facial complexion using artificial intelligence. *Aging* **2021**, *13*, 1765–1772. [CrossRef] [PubMed]
24. Yang, Y.H.; Lee, Y.H.; Yen, C.W.; Huang, L.C.; Chang, Y.P.; Chien, C.F. Association between Cerebral Coordination Functions and Clinical Outcomes of Alzheimer's Dementia. *Brain Sci.* **2022**, *12*, 1370. [CrossRef]
25. Vrahatis, A.G.; Skolariki, K.; Krokidis, M.G.; Lazaros, K.; Exarchos, T.P.; Vlamos, P. Revolutionizing the Early Detection of Alzheimer's Disease through Non-Invasive Biomarkers: The Role of Artificial Intelligence and Deep Learning. *Sensors* **2023**, *23*, 4184. [CrossRef]
26. Atallah, R.; Kamsin, A.; Ismail, M.A.; Abdelrahman, S.; Zerdoumi, S. Face Recognition and Age Estimation Implications of Changes in Facial Features: A Critical Review Study. *IEEE Access* **2018**, *6*, 28290–28304. [CrossRef]
27. Osman, O.F.; Yap, M.H. Computational Intelligence in Automatic Face Age Estimation: A Survey. *IEEE Trans. Emerg. Top. Comput. Intell.* **2019**, *3*, 271–285. [CrossRef]
28. Punyani, P.; Gupta, R.; Kumar, A. Neural networks for facial age estimation: A survey on recent advances. *Artif. Intell. Rev.* **2020**, *53*, 3299–3347. [CrossRef]
29. Dubois, B.; Feldman, H.H.; Jacova, C.; DeKosky, S.T.; Barberger-Gateau, P.; Cummings, J.; Delacourte, A.; Galasko, D.; Gauthier, S.; Jicha, G.; et al. Research criteria for the diagnosis of Alzheimer's disease: Revising the NINCDS-ADRDA criteria. *Lancet Neurol.* **2007**, *6*, 734–746. [CrossRef]
30. Folstein, M.F.; Folstein, S.E.; McHugh, P.R. "Mini-mental state". A practical method for grading the cognitive state of patients for the clinician. *J. Psychiatr. Res.* **1975**, *12*, 189–198. [CrossRef]
31. McCurry, S.M.; Edland, S.D.; Teri, L.; Kukull, W.A.; Bowen, J.D.; McCormick, W.C.; Larson, E.B. The cognitive abilities screening instrument (CASI): Data from a cohort of 2524 cognitively intact elderly. *Int. J. Geriatr. Psychiatry* **1999**, *14*, 882–888. [CrossRef]
32. Cummings, J.L.; Mega, M.; Gray, K.; Rosenberg-Thompson, S.; Carusi, D.A.; Gornbein, J. The Neuropsychiatric Inventory: Comprehensive assessment of psychopathology in dementia. *Neurology* **1994**, *44*, 2308–2314. [CrossRef] [PubMed]
33. Morris, J.C. The Clinical Dementia Rating (CDR): Current version and scoring rules. *Neurology* **1993**, *43*, 2412–2414. [CrossRef] [PubMed]
34. Baltrušaitis, T.; Robinson, P.; Morency, L.-P. OpenFace: An open source facial behavior analysis toolkit. In Proceedings of the IEEE Winter Conference on Applications of Computer Vision (WACV), Lake Placid, NY, USA, 7–10 March 2016.
35. Tzortzis, G.F.; Likas, A.C. The global kernel k-means algorithm for clustering in feature space. *IEEE Trans. Neural Netw.* **2009**, *20*, 1181–1194. [CrossRef] [PubMed]

36. Slice, D.E. Landmark coordinates aligned by procrustes analysis do not lie in Kendall's shape space. *Syst. Biol.* **2001**, *50*, 141–149. [CrossRef]
37. Damstra, J.; Fourie, Z.; De Wit, M.; Ren, Y. A three-dimensional comparison of a morphometric and conventional cephalometric midsagittal planes for craniofacial asymmetry. *Clin. Oral Investig.* **2012**, *16*, 285–294. [CrossRef]
38. Farkas, L.G.; Katic, M.J.; Forrest, C.R.; Alt, K.W.; Bagic, I.; Baltadjiev, G.; Cunha, E.; Cvicelová, M.; Davies, S.; Erasmus, I.; et al. International anthropometric study of facial morphology in various ethnic groups/races. *J. Craniofac. Surg.* **2005**, *16*, 615–646. [CrossRef]
39. Vashi, N.A.; de Castro Maymone, M.B.; Kundu, R.V. Aging Differences in Ethnic Skin. *J. Clin. Aesthetic Dermatol.* **2016**, *9*, 31–38.
40. Liew, S.; Wu, W.T.; Chan, H.H.; Ho, W.W.; Kim, H.J.; Goodman, G.J.; Peng, P.H.; Rogers, J.D. Consensus on Changing Trends, Attitudes, and Concepts of Asian Beauty. *Aesthetic Plast. Surg.* **2016**, *40*, 193–201. [CrossRef]
41. Monteiro, L.C.P.; Ripardo, R.C.; Torro-Alves, N.; Souza, G.S. Facial morphometric differences across face databases: Influence of ethnicities and sex. *Front. Neurosci.* **2023**, *19*, 1130867. [CrossRef]
42. Som, P.M.; Naidich, T.P. Illustrated review of the embryology and development of the facial region, part 1: Early face and lateral nasal cavities. *Am. J. Neuroradiol.* **2013**, *34*, 2233–2240. [CrossRef]
43. Som, P.M.; Naidich, T.P. Illustrated review of the embryology and development of the facial region, part 2: Late development of the fetal face and changes in the face from the newborn to adulthood. *Am. J. Neuroradiol.* **2014**, *35*, 10–18. [CrossRef]
44. Abbate, C. Topographic Markers Drive Proteinopathies to Selection of Target Brain Areas at Onset in Neurodegenerative Dementias. *Front. Aging Neurosci.* **2018**, *10*, 308. [CrossRef]
45. Abbate, C. The Adult Neurogenesis Theory of Alzheimer's Disease. *J. Alzheimer's Dis.* **2023**, *93*, 1237–1276. [CrossRef] [PubMed]
46. Isaev, N.K.; Stelmashook, E.V.; Genrikhs, E.E. Neurogenesis and brain aging. *Rev. Neurosci.* **2019**, *30*, 573–580. [CrossRef] [PubMed]
47. Yassine, H.N.; Finch, C.E. APOE Alleles and Diet in Brain Aging and Alzheimer's Disease. *Front. Aging Neurosci.* **2020**, *12*, 150. [CrossRef] [PubMed]
48. Chang, L.; Douet, V.; Bloss, C.; Lee, K.; Pritchett, A.; Jernigan, T.L.; Akshoomoff, N.; Murray, S.S.; Frazier, J.; Kennedy, D.N.; et al. Pediatric Imaging, Neurocognition, and Genetics (PING) Study Consortium. Gray matter maturation and cognition in children with different APOE ε genotypes. *Neurology* **2016**, *87*, 585–594. [CrossRef]
49. Wang, H.; Lautrup, S.; Caponio, D.; Zhang, J.; Fang, E.F. DNA Damage-Induced Neurodegeneration in Accelerated Ageing and Alzheimer's Disease. *Int. J. Mol. Sci.* **2021**, *22*, 6748. [CrossRef] [PubMed]
50. Liang, W.S.; Goetz, L.H.; Schork, N.J. Assessing brain and biological aging trajectories associated with Alzheimer's disease. *Front. Neurosci.* **2022**, *16*, 1036102. [CrossRef]
51. Swift, A.; Liew, S.; Weinkle, S.; Garcia, J.K.; Silberberg, M.B. The Facial Aging Process From the "Inside Out". *Aesthetic Surg. J.* **2021**, *41*, 1107–1119. [CrossRef]
52. Farkas, J.P.; Pessa, J.E.; Hubbard, B.; Rohrich, R.J. The Science and Theory behind Facial Aging. *Plast. Reconstr. Surg. Glob. Open* **2013**, *1*, e8–e15. [CrossRef]
53. Zhou, A.; Wu, Z.; Zaw Phyo, A.Z.; Torres, D.; Vishwanath, S.; Ryan, J. Epigenetic aging as a biomarker of dementia and related outcomes: A systematic review. *Epigenomics* **2022**, *14*, 1125–1138. [CrossRef] [PubMed]
54. Sugden, K.; Caspi, A.; Elliott, M.L.; Bourassa, K.J.; Chamarti, K.; Corcoran, D.L.; Hariri, A.R.; Houts, R.M.; Kothari, M.; Kritchevsky, S.; et al. Association of Pace of Aging Measured by Blood-Based DNA Methylation with Age-Related Cognitive Impairment and Dementia. *Neurology* **2022**, *99*, e1402–e1413. [CrossRef] [PubMed]
55. Naqvi, S.; Sleyp, Y.; Hoskens, H.; Indencleef, K.; Spence, J.P.; Bruffaerts, R.; Radwan, A.; Eller, R.J.; Richmond, S.; Shriver, M.D.; et al. Shared heritability of human face and brain shape. *Nat. Genet.* **2021**, *53*, 830–839. [CrossRef]
56. Claes, P.; Walters, M.; Vandermeulen, D.; Clement, J.G. Spatially-dense 3D facial asymmetry assessment in both typical and disordered growth. *J. Anat.* **2011**, *219*, 444–455. [CrossRef] [PubMed]
57. Taylor, H.O.; Morrison, C.S.; Linden, O.; Phillips, B.; Chang, J.; Byrne, M.E.; Sullivan, S.R.; Forrest, C.R. Quantitative facial asymmetry: Using three-dimensional photogrammetry to measure baseline facial surface symmetry. *J. Craniofac. Surg.* **2014**, *25*, 124–128. [CrossRef]
58. Ferrario, V.F.; Sforza, C.; Miani, A., Jr.; Serrao, G. A three-dimensional evaluation of human facial asymmetry. *J. Anat.* **1995**, *186*, 103–110.
59. Xiong, Y.; Zhao, Y.; Yang, H.; Sun, Y.; Wang, Y. Comparison Between Interactive Closest Point and Procrustes Analysis for Determining the Median Sagittal Plane of Three-Dimensional Facial Data. *J. Craniofac. Surg.* **2016**, *27*, 441–444. [CrossRef]
60. Ekrami, O.; Claes, P.; White, J.D.; Zaidi, A.A.; Shriver, M.D.; Van Dongen, S. Measuring asymmetry from high-density 3D surface scans: An application to human faces. *PLoS ONE* **2018**, *13*, e0207895. [CrossRef]
61. Gaber, A.; Taher, M.F.; Wahed, M.A.; Shalaby, N.M.; Gaber, S. Classification of facial paralysis based on machine learning techniques. *Biomed. Eng. Online* **2022**, *21*, 65. [CrossRef]
62. Abayomi-Alli, O.O.; Damaševičius, R.; Maskeliūnas, R.; Misra, S. Few-Shot Learning with a Novel Voronoi Tessellation-Based Image Augmentation Method for Facial Palsy Detection. *Electronics* **2021**, *10*, 978. [CrossRef]
63. Wei, W.; Ho, E.S.L.; McCay, K.D.; Damaševičius, R.; Maskeliūnas, R.; Esposito, A. Assessing Facial Symmetry and Attractiveness using Augmented Reality. *Pattern Anal. Appl.* **2022**, *25*, 635–651. [CrossRef]

64. Ferrario, V.F.; Sforza, C.; Ciusa, V.; Dellavia, C.; Tartaglia, G.M. The effect of sex and age on facial asymmetry in healthy subjects: A cross-sectional study from adolescence to mid-adulthood. *J. Oral Maxillofac. Surg.* **2001**, *59*, 382–388. [CrossRef] [PubMed]
65. Nam, U.; Lee, K.; Ko, H.; Lee, J.Y.; Lee, E.C. Analyzing Facial and Eye Movements to Screen for Alzheimer's Disease. *Sensors* **2020**, *20*, 5349. [CrossRef] [PubMed]
66. Antoniades, C.A.; Kennard, C. Ocular motor abnormalities in neurodegenerative disorders. *Eye* **2015**, *29*, 200–207. [CrossRef] [PubMed]

biomedicines

MDPI

Article

Epileptic Patient Activity Recognition System Using Extreme Learning Machine Method

Ummara Ayman [1], Muhammad Sultan Zia [2], Ofonime Dominic Okon [3], Najam-ur Rehman [4], Talha Meraj [5], Adham E. Ragab [6] and Hafiz Tayyab Rauf [7,*]

1 Department of Computer Science, The University of Lahore, Chenab Campus, Gujrat 50700, Pakistan
2 Department of Computer Science, The University of Chenab, Gujrat 50700, Pakistan
3 Department Of Electrical/Electronics & Computer Engineering, Faculty of Engineering, University of Uyo, Uyo 520103, Nigeria
4 Department of Human Resource Section, Hafiz Hayat Campus, University of Gujrat, Gujrat 50700, Pakistan
5 Department of Computer Science, COMSATS University Islamabad—Wah Campus, Wah Cantt 47040, Pakistan
6 Industrial Engineering Department, College of Engineering, King Saud University, P.O. Box 800, Riyadh 11421, Saudi Arabia
7 Centre for Smart Systems, AI and Cybersecurity, Staffordshire University, Stoke-on-Trent ST4 2DE, UK
* Correspondence: hafiztayyabrauf093@gmail.com

Abstract: The Human Activity Recognition (HAR) system is the hottest research area in clinical research. The HAR plays a vital role in learning about a patient's abnormal activities; based upon this information, the patient's psychological state can be estimated. An epileptic seizure is a neurological disorder of the human brain and affects millions of people worldwide. If epilepsy is diagnosed correctly and in an early stage, then up to 70% of people can be seizure-free. There is a need for intelligent automatic HAR systems that help clinicians diagnose neurological disorders accurately. In this research, we proposed a Deep Learning (DL) model that enables the detection of epileptic seizures in an automated way, addressing a need in clinical research. To recognize epileptic seizures from brain activities, EEG is a raw but good source of information. In previous studies, many techniques used raw data from EEG to help recognize epileptic patient activities; however, the applied method of extracting features required much intensive expertise from clinical aspects such as radiology and clinical methods. The image data are also used to diagnose epileptic seizures, but applying Machine Learning (ML) methods could address the overfitting problem. In this research, we mainly focused on classifying epilepsy through physical epileptic activities instead of feature engineering and performed the detection of epileptic seizures in three steps. In the first step, we used the open-source numerical dataset of epilepsy of Bonn university from the UCI Machine Learning repository. In the second step, data were fed to the proposed ELM model for training in different training and testing ratios with a little bit of rescaling because the dataset was already pre-processed, normalized, and restructured. In the third step, epileptic and non-epileptic activity was recognized, and in this step, EEG signal feature extraction was automatically performed by a DL model named ELM; features were selected by a Feature Selection (FS) algorithm based on ELM and the final classification was performed using the ELM classifier. In our presented research, seven different ML algorithms were applied for the binary classification of epileptic activities, including K-Nearest Neighbor (KNN), Naïve Bayes (NB), Logistic Regression (LR), Stochastic Gradient Boosting Classifier (SGDC), Gradient Boosting Classifier (GB), Decision Trees (DT), and three deep learning models named Extreme Learning Machine (ELM), Long Short-Term Memory (LSTM), and Artificial Neural Network (ANN). After deep analysis, it is observed that the best results were obtained by our proposed DL model, Extreme Learning Machine (ELM), with an accuracy of 100% accuracy and a 0.99 AUC. Such high performance has not attained in previous research. The proposed model's performance was checked with other models in terms of performance parameters, namely confusion matrix, accuracy, precision, recall, F1-score, specificity, sensitivity, and the ROC curve.

Citation: Ayman, U.; Zia, M.S.; Okon, O.D.; Rehman, N.-u.; Meraj, T.; Ragab, A.E.; Rauf, H.T. Epileptic Patient Activity Recognition System Using Extreme Learning Machine Method. *Biomedicines* **2023**, *11*, 816. https://doi.org/10.3390/biomedicines11030816

Academic Editors: Hulin Kuang and Wu Qiu

Received: 2 February 2023
Revised: 16 February 2023
Accepted: 2 March 2023
Published: 7 March 2023

Keywords: electroencephalography; deep learning; machine learning; epileptic seizure detection; human activity recognition; extreme learning machine

1. Introduction

Human Activity Recognition (HAR) is a widely studied and targeted research area focusing on human beings' average daily activity recognition. Even though activity recognition has attracted many researchers and has been studied for a long time, researchers did not just stop at HAR; they further targeted the subtype of activity recognition which is aimed at the recognition of abnormal activity in patients. Furthermore, researchers are moving toward abnormal activity detection of patients or physically impaired people [1]. Abnormal activities are activities that are rarely performed and vary in their characteristics from other regular activities. These abnormal activities can be hand flapping, vomiting, fainting, headaches, epileptic activities, chest pain, abnormal heartbeat, falling backward, falling forward, etc. [2]. According to medical professionals, the best way to detect these activities is to look toward the emerging change in daily life activities before becoming more critical. In recent research, different methods have been used to detect abnormal activities, including wearable, sensor-based, and ambient device methods. The triggered alarm checks the status of activity detection. The detection accuracy of these activities depends upon analyzing and learning the patterns of exact features [3].

Although they solved this challenging problem by detecting abnormal activities of different diseases, they did not target the detection of epileptic disorders through epileptic activities. Many abnormal activities are mentioned above, but this study focuses on those observed during epileptic seizures. Very little work has been done on epileptic activity using a deep learning approach, and what has been published has not been in-depth. This study focuses on epilepsy detection through an epileptic activity using a deep learning approach. However, most of the work is conducted using medical imaging techniques that use images and not numerical data. Therefore, before digging deeper into previous detection methods, machine learning, or deep learning, we should have an idea about epilepsy.

Epilepsy is derived from the well-known Greek word "Epilepsia". In ancient times when there was no well-known knowledge available about epilepsy, it was considered to be a curse from the gods. Furthermore, with time awareness about epilepsy grew and a method called Electroencephalography (EEG) was discovered. It is now understood that epilepsy is a strenuous, non-communicable, chronic, and uncontrolled activity in the brain of a patient and is associated with abrupt attacks that affect millions of people's lives, be they adults, the elderly, or newborn babies. Epilepsy can occur at any age in both sexes, either male or female, but usually it is observed in people of a young or advanced age.

In the automated detection of epilepsy in previous research, the main focus is to differentiate between EEG and non-seizure EEG. Epileptic seizures are usually periods where the brain's regular activity becomes abnormally increased and synchronized. Seizures are expeditious, and premature abnormalities in the brain due to anomalous electrical activity affect the person's whole body. However, not all people who have seizures also have epilepsy because sometimes seizures can be caused by some psychological tissue stress in the brain; these are called non-epileptic seizures. As these non-epileptic seizures resemble actual seizures, this can make the diagnosis of the disease more complex [4].

Current epilepsy detection procedures assess the tissues of the brain that are generating epileptic seizure activity. There are many manual approaches as well as automated diagnostic methods that can be employed for detecting epilepsy. The most widely used traditional and manual method for epilepsy detection is through EEG. EEG represents a chaotic detection method because it produces blurred images as well as fails to represent the state and sites of the tissues of the brain [5]. The medical diagnosis of epilepsy is usually performed manually using EEG signals, which is very complex and requires highly skilled professional neurologists [6]. EEG signals are categorized into two types: (i) scalp EEG and (ii) iEEG. In scalp EEG, electrodes are placed on the scalp of the patient to capture seizure periods, but in the case of iEEG, the electrodes are directly placed on the surface of the brain to directly detect brain seizure activity from the cerebral part of the brain. As in the case of scalp EEG, it is very complex and time-consuming to capture brain activity from the scalp of a patient, Therefore, it is called a traditional or manual method of detecting epileptic seizure activity. Although EEG is a very common method, it still has some limitations in detecting epilepsy signals due to epilepsy's chaotic behavior, and although highly skilled professional neurologists have extensive experience in visually detecting seizure activity from EEG data, such analysis still requires a lot of time.

EEG signals in nature are neither linear nor stationary; therefore, they cause difficulties in the manual monitoring and detection of normal and abnormal activities. Although it is not an efficient method [7], EEG is an effective tool for the evaluation as well as treatment of epileptic seizures. However, the drawback of EEG is that it requires highly skilled and professional neurologists to detect epilepsy correctly due to its complexity, and even for an experienced professional it is very time-consuming. Therefore, there is a need for a computer-based system, or Computer-Aided Diagnosis (CAD) tools, for the automatic detection and interpretation of epilepsy to overcome the drawbacks associated with the traditional EEG method [8].

Computer-Aided Diagnosis (CAD) tools are automated methods to detect epilepsy. These are a combination of image processing, artificial intelligence, and computer vision. These are the best systems and are designed to be cost-effective, fast, as well as effective at detecting abnormalities [9]. CAD tools are proposed to be the best way to detect epileptic seizure activity and to perform feature extraction and classification from images to monitor the abnormal brain activity in a short period. In the field of medical imaging, CADe and CADx are helpful for medical professionals to make quick decisions. CAD tools use Magnetic Source Imaging (MSI), Magnetic Resonance Imaging (MRI), Magnetoencephalography (MEG), CT scans, etc. For the evaluation of epilepsy, the required data for these methods are scanned images. These are neuroimaging techniques for the evaluation of epilepsy that map brain electrical activities with detailed images produced using magnetic fields, radio waves, and electrical currents by interacting and recording seizures that are naturally present in the brain. These combined graphical, electrical, and structural data play an important role in the final selection of tools chosen for the evaluation of epilepsy, which further influences the final decision on treatment [10].

Furthermore, there are many signal- and image-processing-based procedures used for the evaluation of epilepsy with some spatial as well as temporal features. These tools can be used if there is a need for high-quality images for the evaluation of epileptic seizure activity, but these imaging techniques are very high energy and can thus harm the human body. Hence, these images are taken with less energy, due to which they are of bad quality, and later, the image quality is cost-effectively improved through CAD tools. This process helps to efficiently interpret the image with better accuracy and highlight conspicuous parts of the brain to detect epileptic seizure activity [11]. EEG is a necessary step for detecting epileptic seizures and it assists medical professionals in speeding up the detection process. For this purpose, along with CAD tools, many signal processing and classification techniques have been used in manual procedures but they still have some complexity, performance, classification, and speed issues [12]. Therefore, to overcome these problems, there is a need to use efficient machine learning algorithms for the proper classification of multi-class seizure activities. ML algorithms help to pre-process the images as well as to extract features. ML algorithms help to account for the state of the brain as well as predict epileptic seizures [7].

Recent research has shown that many ML algorithms assist neurologists in detecting epileptic seizures and classifying epileptic seizure activities. These include Support Vector Machine (SVM), K-Nearest Neighbors (KNN), Random Forest (RF), Neural Networks (NN), Naïve Bayes (NB), Logistic Regression (LR), Decision Trees (DT), Probabilistic Neural

Networks (PNN), and Multilayer Perceptron (MLP) [13,14]. Although many of these machine learning algorithms are very successful in detecting epileptic seizure activities, they are still not as successful as Deep Learning algorithms. EEG signal analysis is very complex and requires a lot of human skill and expertise. Human work can be prone to errors in epilepsy detection. To overcome this issue, ML algorithms are used.

Although ML algorithms are helpful in overcoming human error, this problem is more tricky and complex than it looks; hence, somewhat more robust algorithms such as Deep Learning methods are required for epileptic seizure activity detection [15]. To automatically detect epilepsy, Deep Neural Networks are used that are based on the processing techniques of signals (EEG) as well as pattern recognition. They use the data of EEG for the detection of locations as well as durations of spikes and seizures. Recent advances in DL algorithms have paved the way for epileptic seizure detection. These include Artificial Neural Networks (ANNs), Convolutional Neural Networks (CNN), Long Short-Term Memory (LSTM), Hopified Networks (HN), Restricted Boltzmann Machine (RBN), and the Wavelet-Based approach. In our presented research, we applied an Extreme Learning Machine (ELM) for this purpose and also applied some ML techniques including KNN, NB, LR, DT, RF, GB, and SGDC, as well as the DL LSTM technique. A further review of recent studies is continued below.

There have been many types of research carried out in the field of HAR that combine different techniques which could be used for recognizing human activities. Recent research has shown that the recognition of activities is usually addressed by machine learning techniques including decision trees, Support Vector Machines, Bayesian Methods, Neural networks, fuzzy logic, Markov Models, Hidden Markov Models, and Regression models. Different authors have proposed different machine learning techniques for the recognition of normal and abnormal human activities. Normal activities include walking, standing up, sitting down, jumping, and eating. One author applied state-of-the-art techniques by using 2D AbHAR and 3D AbHAR datasets along with Hidden Markov Models (HMM) and KNN to recognize abnormal human activities such as chest pain, headaches, and fainting [1]. This author also applied Decision Trees, Support Vector Machine, and Hidden Markov Models to recognize abnormal activities such as walking to a chair, crouching, falling to the right or left, and falling forward and backward. This process was completed in two stages, namely data input through sensors and data processing, and recognized activities with 98% accuracy [16].

Although there are many kinds of research on normal human activity recognition, in recent years, there a lot of research is also being carried out on the recognition of activities of people who are physically impaired or injured ambulatory patients at home or who have psychological or neurological disorders. For security reasons, the recognition of abnormal activities has become an important and challenging task. The activities of such patients deviate from normal behavior and are usually referred to as abnormalities. Abnormal patient activities are those that require medical help immediately. The current research aims to effectively create new techniques as well as solutions for further research. To recognize abnormal patient activities and to monitor patient care either in the hospital or at home, different authors have proposed different machine learning techniques.

1.1. Machine Learning Techniques

One author used different machine learning techniques, namely K-Nearest Neighbors (KNN), Support Vector Machine (SVM), Decision Tree (DT), Artificial Neural Network (ANN), and Principal Component Analysis (PCA), to perform classification on an epileptic seizure dataset using 9200 normal activities named Partial epilepsy without seizures and 2300 abnormal epileptic activities named General epilepsy with seizures. The accuracy of the classifiers in the prediction of epilepsy using PCA and without using PCA was observed. Findings showed that RF without using PCA with low computational time and with 97% accuracy produced the best result. Without using PCA, KNN and RF achieved 99% accuracy as compared to other ML classifiers [17].

Another author used different ML algorithms, namely KNN, SVM, PCA, and ANN, for the recognition of the epileptic seizure dataset. This research had two principal methods. In the first method, features were extracted and then classified into binary classes labeled as Epileptic and Non-Epileptic seizures. In the second method, the performance of the feature extraction method was improved by using the Principal Component Analysis (PCA) method, and a 96% accuracy was achieved [18].

Another author used the SVM and its twin variant and then embedded these with univeram data to classify the EEG Signals. The author used Principal Component Analysis (PCA), Independent Component Analysis (ICA), and wavelet analysis. The author used 30 EEG datasets, one of which was the Bonn university EEG dataset which showed that accuracy was 100% [19].

Another author used different classifiers of machine learning to perform the classification of normal activities, named Tumor, Hstumor, Eyec, Eyeo, and abnormal activities, named Es, using the epileptic seizure dataset. The ML classifiers used for the classification were KNN, Logistic Regression, Naïve Bayes, Decision Tree, Stochastic Gradient Descent, J48, Random Tree, and Random Forest. Compared to the other ML classifiers, Random Forest greatly outperformed all of these classifiers and achieved a 97.08% maximum accuracy with an ROC = 0.996. In this research, to analyze the performance of different classifiers, a sensitivity analysis was performed by changing different parameters and using different attributes chosen as feature selection in prediction [20].

Another author proposed a model which used wavelet transform as well as common spatial pattern filtering for the pre-processing. For the purpose of feature extraction, the technique Principal Component Analysis (PCA) was used and for the Pre_ictal stage classifier, Support Vector Machine (SVM) was used, achieving an average sensitivity of 93.1% observed across 84 seizures in 23 subjects. The normal activities used in this paper were Pre_ictal, Inter_ictal, Eyes open, and Eyes Close, and the abnormal activity was Ictal [21].

Another author performed classification on the Epileptic Seizure dataset. The classifier which was used for classification was SVM, and the Bayesian optimization algorithm was used by the SVM classifier for the optimization of the hyperparameter. In this research paper, to perform the comparison, Linear Discriminant Analysis (LDA) and Quadratic Linear Discriminant Analysis (QLDA) were used, and the accuracy achieved by the SVM classifier was 97.05% [22].

Another author applied the Discrete Wavelet Transform (DWT) technique for feature extraction and then used the Radiant Basis Kernal function (RBF) to train the SVM classifier. For better EEG classification, an optimizer named the Grey Wolf Optimizer (GWO) was used for the selection of the important subset of features and parameters of the SVM with 99% accuracy [23].

Another author used the DWT technique to retrieve statistical features from the decomposition of EEG data into bands and the classifier was trained to learn these statistical features. To predict whether signals were epileptic or not, two classifiers named Naïve Bayes and KNN were used for the classification of the epileptic seizure dataset with normal epileptic activities named Eyes open, Eyes close, Inter_ictal, and Pre_ictal and abnormal activity named Epileptic seizure. In this research paper, 14 successful results of a different combination of two classes of epilepsy detection were obtained. A Naive Bayes classifier with less computing time and 100% accuracy was used for the classification of an epileptic dataset [24].

Another author used a classifier named dual-tree wavelet complex transform (DTCWT) for signal decomposition as well as for the calculation of statistical measurement. Then, for the training of the statistical environment, a classifier named General Regression Neural Network was used and achieved 95.24% maximum accuracy in less than 0.028 s [25].

Another author in his paper proposed a new method for epileptic and non-epileptic seizure detection. The transformation of the multiresolution decomposition was performed on the base of the wavelet and was then used in combination with an Artificial Neural

Network (ANN) for the classification of the EEG signal regarding whether a seizure is present or not. The achieved accuracy was 97.77% using normal epileptic activities named Normal, Non-seizure, Non-seizure with eyes closed, and Non-seizure with eyes open and the abnormal activity named Seizure [26].

Another author used the technique of permutation entropy to extract the features from the signals of the EEG. For the classification purpose, the Support Vector Machine (SVM) classifier achieved the maximum accuracy of 93.55% for the selected case of A-E and the accuracy achieved for other datasets was 86.1% using normal activity named Tumor, Non-epileptic, Eyes close, Eyes Open, and abnormal activity named Seizure Activity [27].

Another author used DWT for the extraction of energy features, standard deviation, and entropy from the signals of the EEG. The maximum accuracy, i.e., 95.44%, was achieved by using the classifier Probabilistic Neural Network (PNN) and Support Vector Machine (SVM) and using normal activities named Tumor, Non-epileptic, Eyes close, and Eyes Open and abnormal activity named Seizure Activity [28].

Another author applied a patient-specific methodology and for classification applied an SVM classifier to distinguish between epileptic or non-epileptic activities of a patient. A maximum accuracy of 96% was achieved using normal epileptic activities named Eyes open, Eyes close, Inter_ictal, and Pre_ictal and abnormal activity named ictal [29].

Another author used Linear Discriminate Analysis (LDA) to classifying seizures using the data of 65 seizures across five patients and achieved 91.8% accuracy by using binary case classes in which the normal activity class was named Non-Epileptic Seizure and the abnormal activity class was named Epileptic-seizure [30].

Another author performed the detection and analysis of EEG data using entropies as well as seven different classifiers. The classifier which performed the best was the Fuzzy Sugeno classifier with an overall accuracy of 98.1%, a 100% specificity, and a 99.4% sensitivity. The classifier which performed the worst was Naïve Bayes, which achieved an accuracy of 88.1% using the normal activity classes named Normal and Pre-ictal and the abnormal activity class named Epileptic [31].

1.2. *Deep Learning Techniques*

Machine learning is very successful in the recognition of abnormal activities of patients. Therefore, there is a need for the automatic recognition of abnormal activities. For this purpose, different authors have proposed different deep learning algorithms that greatly help with automated detection. All the above-mentioned machine learning techniques did not use the automated method to extract features; instead, they used hand-crafted methods. Therefore, to avoid the extra effort of extracting features through the handcrafted method, deep learning techniques need to be used and DL models need a lot of data to train the DL models. In this section, we list a few researchers who used deep learning techniques to classify whether the activity is epileptic or non-epileptic. For example, one author proposed a deep learning model named the pyramidal One-Dimensional Convolutional Neural Network. This CNN model uses refined and less trainable parameters as compared to the traditional convolutional neural network. Compared to the state-of-the-art techniques, this model achieved an accuracy of 99.1% with normal activities named Eyes Close, Eyes Open, and Pre-ictal and abnormal activities named Inter-ictal and ictal [32].

In this research, the author performed epileptic seizure recognition through binary classification using classes labeled as Epileptic Seizure and Non-Epileptic Seizure. For the classification of monitored data, a two-layer Recurrent Neural Network (RNN) was used, and for the first layer and the dropout layer, Long Short-Term Memory (LSTM) and the Horse Optimization Algorithm (HOA) were used, respectively [33].

Another author used a one-dimensional, sequential Convolutional Neural Network (CNN). The architecture used for the classification of time series data of EEG comprised a one-dimensional module and a one-dimensional ResNet module to check whether there was epilepsy or not, achieving an AUC of 0.98 [34].

Another author proposed a deep learning model named Long Short-Term Memory (LSTM) for the training, detection, as well as prediction of epileptic seizures with state change as well as EEG seizures of a chaotic nature. The purpose of this research was to launch a small and low-cost gadget that can be wearable. Normal activities named Tumor, Hstumor, Eyec, and Eyeo and abnormal activities named Es on the Epileptic seizure dataset were used in this paper, achieving an accuracy of 99% [35].

Similarly, another author proposed a novel deep-learning-based model named Deep Canonical Sparse Autoencoder Epileptic Seizure Detection for the classification of EEG signals, which involved two steps, namely, feature selection and classification. This research involved a coyote algorithm for the selection of features and a novel derived classifier named DCSAE, based on an epileptic seizure detection model, for the classification of epileptic and non-epileptic seizures. The DSCAE was tuned by an algorithm named the krill herd algorithm (KHA). The maximum accuracy achieved in this research for binary classification was 98.67% and was 98.73% for multi-classification. Binary classification involved labelling abnormal activity (that is, EEG signals showing seizure activity) as 0 based on 2300 instances to train the model and labelling normal activity (that is, EEG signals having no seizure activity as 1 based on 9200 instances to train the model. Multi-classification involved labelling normal classes from EEG signals showing seizure activity, tumor regions, a healthy brain, eyes closed, and eyes open as 0, 1, 2, 3, and 4, respectively, with each class having 200 instances to train the model [36].

Another author proposed a DL-based model named EESC, abbreviated for Epileptic EEG signal classification. For the extraction of features, a DCNN, abbreviation for Deep Convolutional Neural Network, and the Transfer Learning method were used. In the end, four classes of normal activities were categorized as seizure and classes of abnormal activities were categorized as Inter-ictal and pre-ictal duration. An accuracy of 90% [37].

Many diseases such as Parkinson's, Alzheimer's, and epilepsy are the causes of stress or mental disorders. Hence, to monitor the activity of such types of diseases, different authors have proposed different deep learning techniques. For example, for monitoring patient activities, on author proposed a DL model for the detection of epileptic seizures on the basis of inter-ictal recordings, and on that data, filtration as well as segmentation was performed. In this research, Long Short-Term Memory (LSTM) as well as a Convolutional Neural Network (CNN) were used for the classification of the epileptic and non-epileptic data, and an accuracy of 94.74% was achieved [38].

Another author proposed an Artificial Neural Network (ANN) based on a deep learning model to solve the complex problem of detecting epileptic seizures. The deep learning CNN provided excellent accuracy on the EEG dataset. While many other ML techniques have been applied in combination to reduce and pre-process the data, CNN does not require pre-processing and achieved an accuracy of 95.24% using the normal activities named Pre_ictal, Inter_ictal, Eyes open, and Eyes Close and Ictal used as the abnormal activity [39].

Although this literature review has briefly described many types of research along with their benefits, there is still some room to improve the efficiency of classifying epileptic activity. Due to the incessant deepening of DL models, there has been a rapid increase in the number of parameters, which may in consequence lead to the problems of overfitting and generalization; therefore, there is a need to tune these parameters. Hence, to tune the parameters, there are also some hyperparameters available that affect the operation and efficiency of the Convolutional Neural Network (CNN). Usually, the hyperparameters that are effective and beneficial are batch size, learning rate, and the number of epochs. The trial-and-error method is the state-of-the-art method for checking every model's performance, but it is an erroneous as well as very tedious process. Hence, to avoid this hectic and time-consuming process, metaheuristic algorithms can be used. Therefore, in our research, we used the DL technique named Extreme Learning Machine (ELM). Previous authors compared the results with the traditional method of EEG. However, in this paper, we detect epileptic seizures through patient activities observed during epileptic seizures.

1.3. Contribution

The main contribution of this research is that it does not use imaging data to train the classifier, and this is help to use less memory because of using numerical datasets and proposed model does not require backpropagation and calls for less user intervention.

We also tried to overcome the pressing problems of generalization and overfitting previous researchers faced by using the ELM classifier.

An efficient system with less training and testing time as compared to previous models is developed. It show improvements in terms of faster convergence and higher accuracy.

2. Proposed Methodology

The proposed methodology consists of three steps: (i) Data Acquisition (ii) Data Preparation, and (iii) Activity Recognition. These three steps are described below, and the methodology is shown in Figure 1.

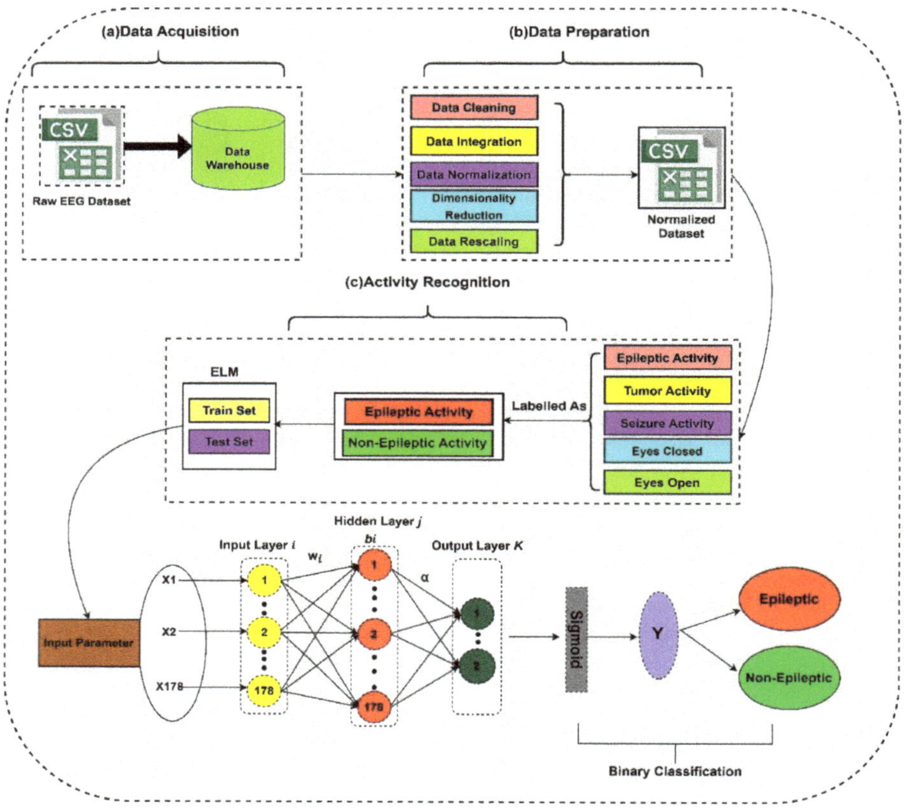

Figure 1. Proposed Methodology.

2.1. Data Acquisition

Data acquisition is a process to gather and store digital or numerical data to input into our model either in raw or pre-processed form, depending on the availability of data. Therefore, before data acquisition, it is very necessary to have an understanding of the dataset used.

- Dataset Understanding

We used a numerical database named Epileptic Seizures Recognition Dataset, which is a pre-processed and well-organized dataset commonly used for the recognition of epileptic seizures provided by the UCI Machine Learning Repository. For epilepsy analysis and diagnosis, there are a lot of EEG datasets available on the Internet; some of these datasets are private due to a lack of ethical clearance, but some of these are made openly available by medical analysts for research purposes. The concerned dataset is openly and freely available from the UCI Machine Learning Repository provided by Bonn University [40]. As the current authors did not perform experiments on humans, animals, or plants to collect the data and instead made use of a freely and openly available dataset, this research does not require any ethical clearance. Based on this dataset's description, this is the original dataset and it consists of 5 different folders. Each folder consists of 100 files, and each file represents an individual person's information. In each of these files, brain activity was recorded for 23.6 s. The recorded brain activity is further sampled into 4097 different data points. Each recorded EEG value represents a data point at different points in time. Therefore, we have data from 500 individuals in total and each individual has 4097 data points over 23.5 s. All 4097 data points are further subdivided and shuffled into 23 different chunks. Each chunk further consists of 178 data points lasting 1 s. Each of these data points is the recorded value of the EEG at different points in time. Therefore, in total, we have $500 \times 23 = 11{,}500$ rows (instance) as a piece of recorded information. The random sample view of the Epileptic Seizure Recognition Dataset is shown in Figure 2.

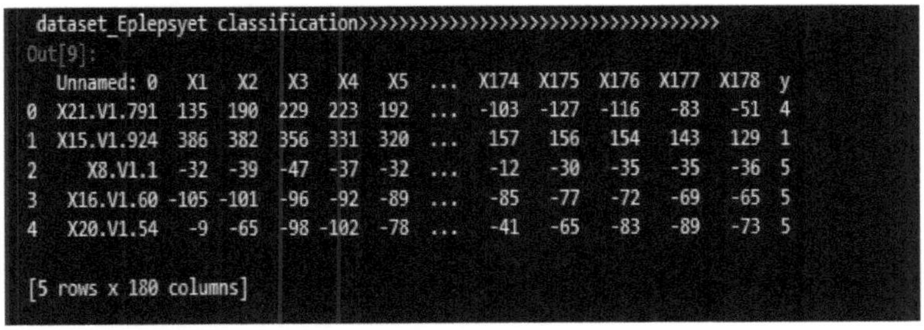

```
dataset_Eplepsyet classification>>>>>>>>>>>>>>>>>>>>>>>>>>>>>>>>>>
Out[9]:
   Unnamed: 0   X1   X2  X3   X4   X5  ...  X174  X175  X176  X177  X178  y
0  X21.V1.791  135  190  229  223  192  ...  -103  -127  -116   -83   -51  4
1  X15.V1.924  386  382  356  331  320  ...   157   156   154   143   129  1
2     X8.V1.1  -32  -39  -47  -37  -32  ...   -12   -30   -35   -35   -36  5
3   X16.V1.60 -105 -101  -96  -92  -89  ...   -85   -77   -72   -69   -65  5
4   X20.V1.54   -9  -65  -98 -102  -78  ...   -41   -65   -83   -89   -73  5

[5 rows x 180 columns]
```

Figure 2. Randomly Sample View of Epileptic Recognition Dataset.

In this dataset, 178 columns are used as a numerical input parameter and the last one, column 179, is used to label the data as output 1, 2, 3, 4, or 5. These five classes in the epileptic dataset are the five mentioned health conditions of epileptic patients in which one is the epileptic patient condition and the other four mentioned are normal conditions in which the concerned data point does not show epileptic activity. The details of all five classes and their samples are listed in the following Table 1.

The raw EEG signal data of all five of the above-mentioned health conditions are shown as waveforms in Figure 3. This is the initial raw form of the data, but these data are not directly fed into the model. Although this dataset is a normalized, structured, and reshaped version of the data, the dataset needed to be rescaled into unit variance and the five classes needed to transform into binary form. Hence, data in their initial forms will not show the same result, which is not as promising as it requires pre-processing. These results will definitely change once the initial signal samples undergo pre-processing and preliminary transformation or if signal samples other than initial data are used. Hence, in this first stage of data acquisition, numerical recorded data are stored in an Excel spreadsheet used as a database from where data are read from columns X1 to X178 as input parameters to train the model, and the last column, named as Y, is used as an output column of labeled data. After reading the data from the database, the data are passed on to the next phase of data preparation according to the proposed model.

Table 1. Details of the Epileptic Dataset Classes.

Classes Name	No of Samples	Output Classes Labels (Medically)	Description of Classes
1	2300	ictal	Signals recorded during seizures
2	2300	Pre_ictal	Signals recorded before the occurrence of one-site seizure
3	2300	Inter_ictal	Signals recorded during the occurrence of consecutive seizures
4	2300	healthy (close eye)	A healthy subject having closed eyes
5	2300	healthy (open eye)	A healthy subject having open eyes

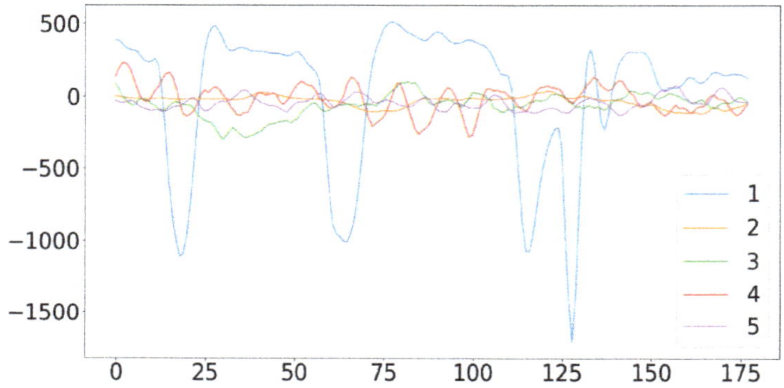

Figure 3. EEG Waveform of four normal conditions vs. one epileptic condition.

2.2. Data Preparation

Data preparation is a very complex phase of data mining in a project. The performance and results of the selected algorithm and model are highly impacted by the dirty and noisy dataset selected. A noisy dataset consists of data in which some significant values are missing as well as some outliers are present which may adversely result in low-quality and inconsistent data. Inconsistent data lead to unimpressive and invaluable results in the results evaluation phase. Therefore, data preparation plays an important role in the case of creating quality data; it is the phase in which data are manipulated and cleaned for the rest of the project phases. The principal tasks of data cleaning include data cleaning, data integration, data normalization, dimensionality reduction, and data splitting. However, since the UCI epileptic dataset is a normalized, pre-processed, structured, and reshaped version of the data. This dataset does not have any missing values or repetitive values.

2.3. Activity Recognition

Activity recognition is a process of recognizing the performed activities read from the database after data preparation. These activities are represented in the form of different classes. There are 5 classes, and each class represents different activities: Seizure activity, Tumor activity, EEG activity, Eyes closed, and Eyes open. Although there are a lot of techniques of deep learning that can be applied to this complex recognition task, here we will use the Extreme Learning Machine (ELM) to train our model on these 5 epileptic activities by using the ratio of 80% training data and 20% testing data since ELM has a simple and straight-forward architecture and does not need any gradient-based propagation to work. The architecture of ELM is displayed in Figure 4.

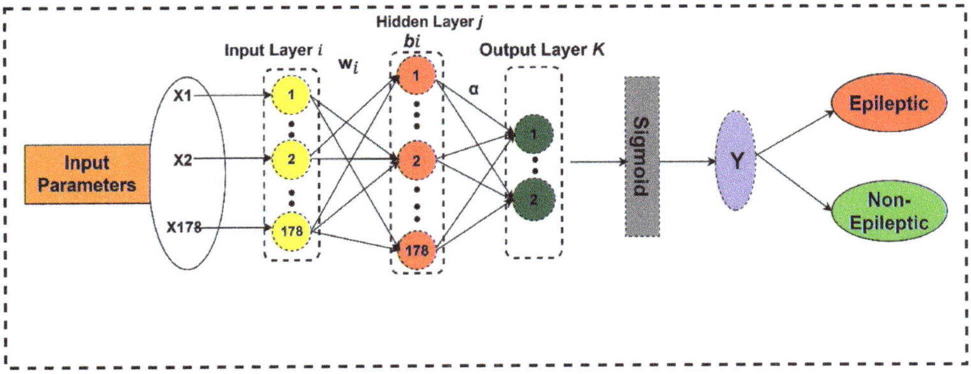

Figure 4. Extreme Learning Machine.

Here, the ELM classifier is presented. ELM is a feedforward neural network and has one input layer i, a single hidden layer j, bias b, input weights w, and a single output layer k which is used at the end for the classification and activity recognition process.

The classifier used in this step is ELM and before digging deeper into the detail of the activity recognition process we will discuss the working of the ELM algorithm described below:

2.3.1. Extreme Learning Machine (ELM):

According to the architecture of ELM shown in Figure 4, ELM is a feedforward neural network with a single hidden layer that selects the inputs and weights randomly and analytically determines the output weights of single hidden-layer feedforward networks (SLFNs) [41,42]. The most important key principle of ELM is that one can randomly choose or fix the hidden parameters of the node. After randomly selecting the hidden node parameters, the weights of outputs can be determined analytically by using hidden layer matrices for output by using generalized inverse operation when SLFN becomes the linear system [43]. In the hidden observation layer, the activation function Q is a sigmoid function and the N is the number of nodes of the data set; the extreme learning model can be expressed as:

$$f(x) = \sum_{i=1}^{N} \alpha_i Q(w_i, b_i, x_i) = \alpha \cdot h(x), \tag{1}$$

In the above equation, α_i is the weight of the output neuron of the ith hidden layer node, whereas w_i is the input weight of the input neurons of the ith hidden layer node; b_i is the offset, usually called the bias, of the ith hidden layer node; and $h(x) = [Q(w_1, b_1, x_1), \ldots Q(w_N, b_N, x_N)]$ represents the hidden layer output matrix. Before training the algorithm, w_i and b_i are selected randomly and remain frozen during all training procedures. By solving the least-square solutions of the following linear equation, the output of weight α_i can be obtained:

$$min \sum_{i=1}^{N} ||\alpha_i \cdot h(x_i) - y_i|| \tag{2}$$

The least-square solution of the above equation is:

$$\alpha = H^+ Y, \tag{3}$$

In the above equation, H^+ is called the Moore–Penrose generalized inverse of the hidden layer output matrix H.

After analyzing the workings of the ELM, we will recognize the epileptic and non-epileptic activities through ELM. The principal steps to perform signal classification for the activity recognition process are discussed in the following sections.

2.3.2. Feature Extraction

Before performing deep classification, first we need to extract the features to train the model. Keenly observing the previous research before the rise of DL shows us that manual feature extraction was performed by the conventional ML algorithms, and this use of ML algorithm was the reason the performance of the model's ability was limited using handcrafted features. After the advent of DL, the process of feature extraction performed by the model became automated. In our proposed model, we just list all the features from X1 to X178 as the input feature data and Y as the target label data and then ELM will automatically reveal the correlations between the samples of successive data and will extract high-level representations of non-epileptic and epileptic signal features, resulting in a feature matrix. The learning of the extracted features by the model is performed through training by fitting the model using processed, extracted training input data at a ratio of 80% training data to 20% testing data.

2.3.3. Feature Selection

The extracted features are then selected by the Feature Selection (FS) algorithm based on ELM. The working of the FS algorithm is described below:

- ELM-based Feature Selection Algorithm:

The neuron of the input layer's contribution to the neuron of the output layer is reflected to some extent by the magnitude of the input weight. After the training of the ELM model is completed, the input weight's and output weight's information reflect the input feature's importance. The ELM-based selection algorithm's steps are described below:

Step No 1: In this step, we will calculate the significant coefficient correlation:

$$c_{ij} = \sum_{i=1}^{q} \alpha_{jk} \left(1 - e^{-w_{ij}}\right) / 1 + e^{-w_{ij}}\Big) \tag{4}$$

Step No 2: In this step, we will calculate the index correlation:

$$c_{ij} = \left| \left(1 - e^{-c_{ij}}\right) / 1 + e^{-c_{ij}}\right) \right| \tag{5}$$

where w_{ij} is the input weight used to connect the ith input layer nodes to jth hidden layer nodes and α_{jk} is the output weight used to connect the jth hidden layer node to the kth output layer node.

Step No 3: In this step, we will calculate the coefficient of absolute influence:

$$S_{ij} = c_{ij} / \sum_{i=1}^{m} C_{ij} \tag{6}$$

Step No 4: In this step, we will calculate the feature weight:

$$W_{ij} = \sum_{i=1}^{m} C_{ij} / m \tag{7}$$

By using this algorithm, the features selected are the features that have high weights; features which have low weights are not important and should be removed.

2.3.4. Classification

Here, the classification of activities is based on the ELM classifier and works as shown in Figure 4. The model parameters' input size is 178 neurons, and the hidden layer size of the neuron depends upon the input layer and is selected randomly. Therefore, firstly, the bias and weight matrix for the input layer of the model are created randomly. In the next step, the output matrix for the hidden layer is calculated by multiplying the training data (X) with the transposed weight matrix from the input layer. Here, the activation function used is Sigmoid because it yields better nonlinear transformations and feature mapping. In addition, it is easy to implement and its outcome has the best accuracy compared to other activation functions. In the next step, the Moore–Penrose pseudo-inverse is calculated. After that output weight matrix is calculated. After that, the result matrix is calculated, which is the epileptic activity as an output. We will use a trial-and-error strategy here to identify the best tuning parameters and optimize the model. We perform the classification and recognition of activities of epileptic disorders. By using binary classification, testing data will be further used for evaluating whether the 5 activities that are further binary labeled are accurately recognized or not. Here, prediction is performed by Predict(X), which is further used to give the target output (Y) when an unlabeled observation (X) is given as an input to the model.

3. Results and Discussion

3.1. Running Environment

The pipeline of our proposed methodology model is carried out with advanced and modern computer software tools and libraries. All working experiments are conducted on a system with an Intel Corei7 with 8 GB Ram and the Windows 10 operating system installed on it. The platform tool used for the experimentation and analysis of the results is Anaconda with python language version 3.8.6 installed. The Interactive Development Environment (IDE) used by Anaconda for the whole process of execution is Spyder.

3.2. Dataset Specification

The proposed model is applied to the UCI machine learning dataset consisting of five classes, which are later labeled as y = {0, 1}.

0—Not Recorded Seizure;

1—Recorded Seizure.

The specifications for this dataset is briefly described in Table 2.

Table 2. Details of the Epileptic Seizure Dataset.

Output Classes	Total No of Records	Normal Records	Abnormal Records	Attributes	Description
5	11,500	9200	2300	X1 to X178	These columns consist of the EEG data of epileptic patients ranging from −1415 to 2047; these variables are called explanatory variables
				X179	In this column, variable y comprises the response variable, and if its value is 0 values, then no seizure is occurring; if the value is 1, then an epileptic seizure is occurring.

The epileptic seizure dataset is divided into the following training and testing ratios to train the model for the best accuracy:

80% training, 20% testing;

70% training, 30% testing;

60% training, 40% testing.

3.3. Parameter Tuning

Parameter tuning is the procedure in which different parameters are set to tune the model to increase its performance. There are different parameters shown in Table 3, and their values increase the ELM model's performance. The results of the model vary as the values of these parameters change.

Table 3. Tuning Parameters of the ELM model.

Parameters	Values
Bias	[0, 1]
Hidden Layers	1
Input Weight Range	[−1, 1]
Output Weight Range	[0, 1]
Input Nodes Size	Arbitrarily Chosen
Activation Function	Sigmoid

To adequately evaluate the performance of the proposed model, the proposed deep learning model was trained using the three different dataset ratios and its performance measured in terms of F1-score, accuracy, specificity, sensitivity, precision, the area under the curve, and the ROC with some sufficient feature details. The experiments and the results of our proposed model are discussed in the remainder of this section.

3.4. Experiment 1

The Extreme Learning Machine (ELM) model was trained the best on 80% of data chosen randomly and the remaining 20% of data set aside for later use, i.e., for the evaluation of model accuracy, called testing, and for validation. The training accuracy of our model for this dataset ratio is 99.9% and the accuracy of testing is 100%, which is higher than the other dataset division ratios. Details of the ELM experiment are shown in Table 4.

Table 4. ELM Performance Parameters of Experiment # 1.

ELM Model	Accuracy %	Dataset Division%	Samples	Prevalence	Precision	Recall	F1-Score	Specificity	Sensitivity	AUC
Training	99.9	80	9200	0.500	0.996	0.998	0.996	0.99	0.998	0.999
Testing	100	20	1150	0.19	0.95	0.99	0.969	1.0	0.999	0.999

As can be seen from Table 4, the Extreme Learning Machine yields promising results at this dataset ratio with 920 random hidden neurons, as further shown in Figure 5.

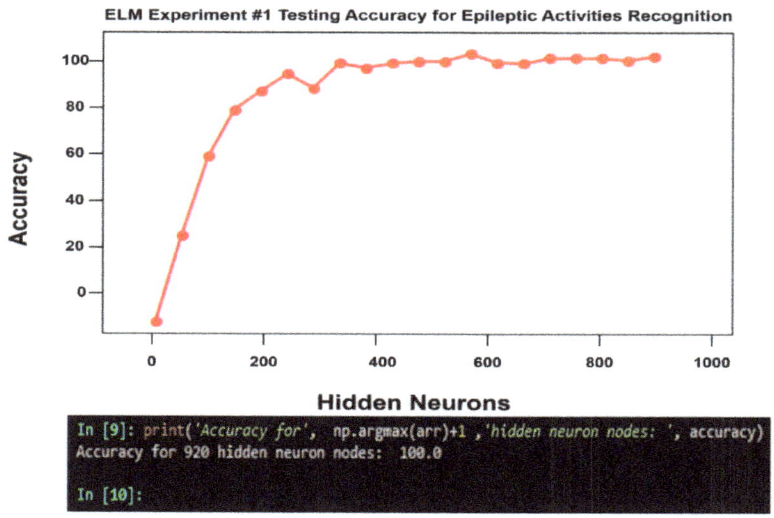

Figure 5. ELM Model Accuracy of Experiment #1.

Meanwhile, the random selection of neurons here promises universal approximation, less intervention, global optimal solution, and much faster convergence with less training and testing time. As Figure 5 illustrates, the accuracy of the ELM model increases as the hidden neurons increase in the start, but it gives 100% accuracy at 920 hidden neurons. It is not the case that it always gives the best accuracy just by increasing hidden neurons. The best accuracy is obtained by arbitrarily incremental and random predictions of the given hidden neurons to train itself according to the size of the dataset, following which unimportant hidden neurons are pruned by the model to make it optimal; otherwise, just by increasing the number of hidden neurons in the model, the accuracy will go down due to overfitting.

Another performance evaluation parameter is the ROC curve, which is shown in combined ROC curves in Figure 8, where the best training and testing accuracy of the model is shown for the false positive rate of 1.0 and the true positive rate of 1.0.

As in Figure 9, the confusion matrix chart is shown for and 80% and 20% data partition, where the diagonal matrix shows the correct prediction of positive classes while wrong predictions are shown outside of the diagonal matrix. Here the classifier shows promising results for the ideal prediction of correct classes with no wrong predictions.

3.5. Experiment 2

In Experiment 2, epileptic and non-epileptic seizure data are divided into 70% chosen randomly for training and 30% set aside for testing. This ratio achieved 96% accuracy at 805 hidden neuron nodes; other performance parameters are shown in Table 5.

Table 5. ELM Performance Parameters for Experiment # 2.

ELM Model	Accuracy %	Dataset Division%	Samples	Prevalence	Precision	Recall	F1-Score	Specificity	Sensitivity	AUC
Training	99	70	8050	0.500	0.995	0.999	0.996	0.995	0.999	0.999
Testing	96	30	1725	0.206	0.860	0.972	0.912	0.959	0.972	0.970

From Table 5, it can be seen that the Extreme Learning Machine in experiment 2 with 805 random hidden neurons does not yield as promising results as experiment 1, as shown in Figure 6.

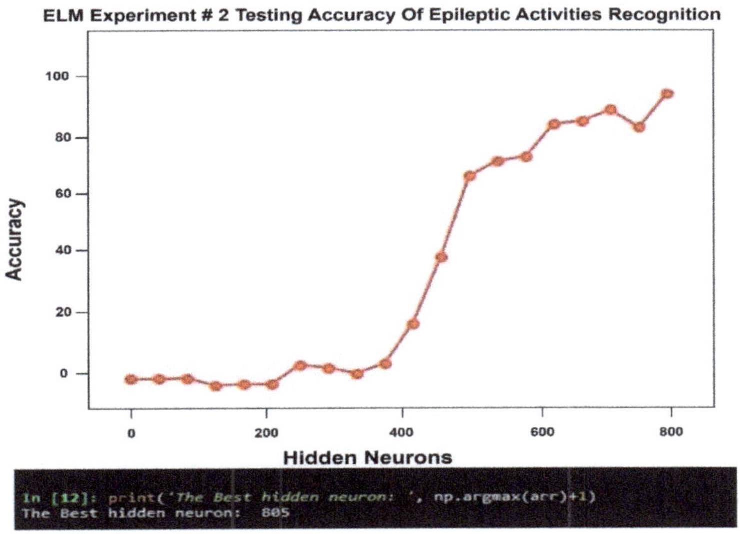

Figure 6. ELM Model Accuracy of Experiment #2.

From Figure 6, it can be seen that in the start, accuracy is uniform, but as the number of hidden neurons increases, the accuracy is gradually increased, reaching 96% accuracy at best using 805 hidden neuron nodes arbitrarily chosen by the model. Although experiment 2 showed good results, it is not competitive as compared to experiment 1 because the model may become underfit due to the smaller size of the trained dataset and the deep learning model demands huge training datasets for good features training understanding.

As can be seen from Table 5, the ELM at this dataset ratio does not give results as promising as experiment 1. Other performance parameters such as the confusion matrix and ROC curve are shown in Figures 8 and 9, respectively, illustrating that these results are less competitive as compared to experiment 1's results.

3.6. Experiment 3

In experiment 3, the epileptic seizure recognition dataset was randomly divided into 60% for training and 40% for testing purposes, and the maximum accuracy achieved in this partition is 95%. Detailed performance parameters are listed in Table 6.

Table 6. ELM Performance Parameters for Experiment # 3.

ELM Model	Accuracy %	Dataset Division%	Samples	Prevalence	Precision	Recall	F1-Score	Specificity	Sensitivity	AUC
Training	99	60	6900	0.500	0.997	0.999	0.997	0.957	0.999	0.998
Testing	95	40	2300	0.213	0.859	0.965	0.908	1.0	0.965	0.957

As seen in Table 6 and Figure 7, the Extreme Learning Machine in experiment 3 with 690 random hidden neurons does not yield as promising results as experiment 1. Experiment 3 also shows much lower values in accuracy and other performance parameters compared to experiment 2. The reason for this is that the same model may become underfit due to lower dataset training ratios.

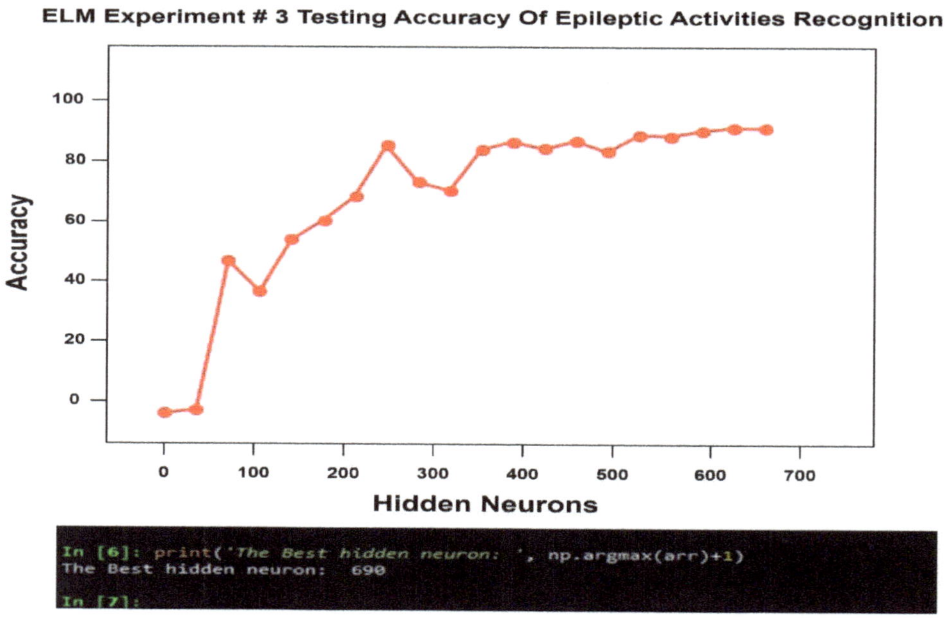

Figure 7. ELM Model Accuracy of Experiment #3.

It can be seen from Figure 7 that accuracy initially uniformly increases as the number of hidden neurons increases, giving the best accuracy of 95% at 690 hidden neuron nodes arbitrarily chosen by the model. Other performance parameters are the confusion matrix chart and ROC curve shown in Figures 8 and 9. Respectively illustrating that these results are less competitive as compared to experiment #1.

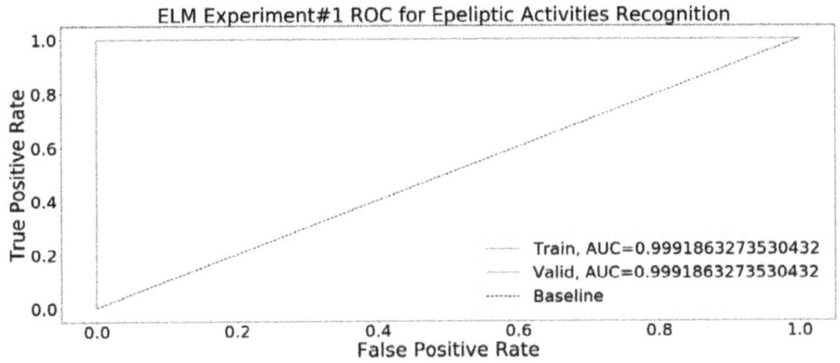

(**a**) **Experiment #1**

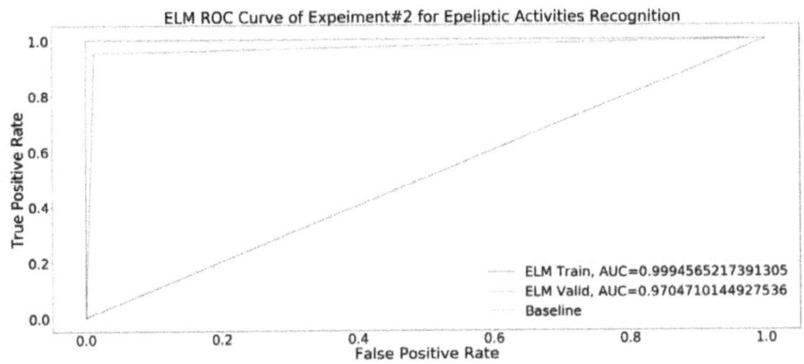

(**b**) **Experiment #2**

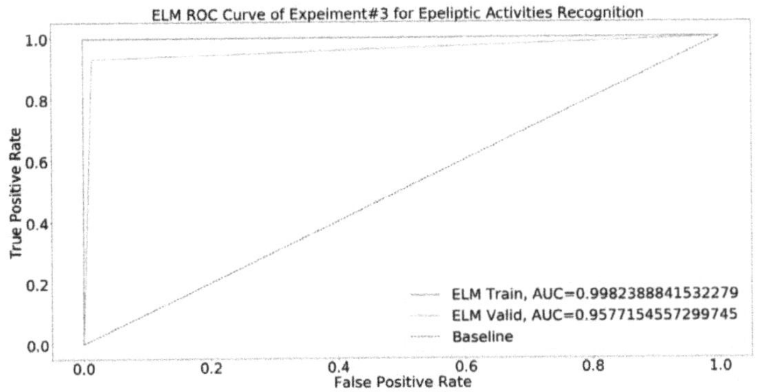

(**c**) **Experiment #3**

Figure 8. ROC Curves of (**a**) Experiment #1; (**b**) Experiment #2; (**c**) Experiment #3.

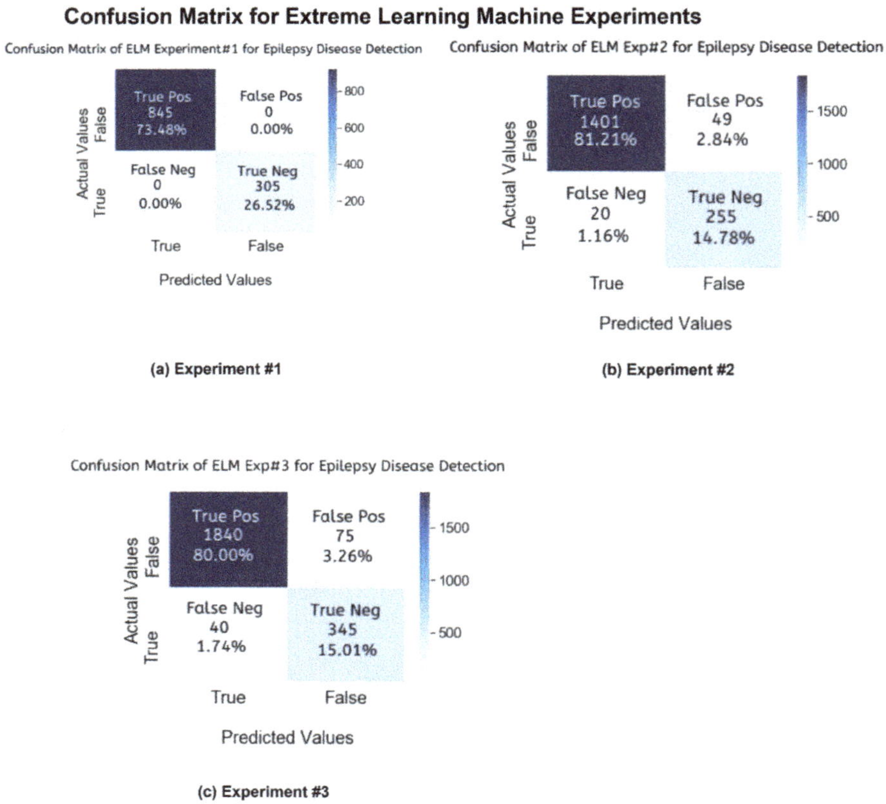

Figure 9. Confusion Matrices of (**a**) Experiment #1; (**b**) Experiment #2; (**c**) Experiment #3.

4. Performance Parameters Comparison of ML and DL Models

In this section, we will report the outcomes of the classifier, named Extreme Learning Machine (ELM), used for the classification of an epilepsy dataset at a ratio of 80% training data with 9200 samples and a 0.500 prevalence of positive classes and 20% testing data with 2300 samples a 0.206 prevalence of positive classes. From this dataset, 10% of the data is set aside for validation and the remaining 10% is used for testing consisting of 1150 samples with a 0.197 prevalence of positive classes for each.

Now it is time to select the classifiers to be compared with the proposed classifier. From previous research results, it is clear that feedforward classifiers are very slow in terms of speed of processing big data, and this issue was the major bottleneck observed in previous research. The reason for this slow speed is the algorithm and classifiers used are low-gradient based, and by using these algorithms, all the required parameters are tuned by the algorithm iteratively. So, keeping in view these reasons, we need a feedforward classifier that can solve these problems. So, the purpose of choosing ELM as a classifier is that it randomly chooses the hidden nodes of its SLFN, and its output weights are determined analytically. The ELM results are enriched in sparsity, stability, and accuracy in general conditions. ELM converges and learns at a very fast speed with good generalization performance when processing big data and does not require user intervention as compared to conventional feedforward algorithms [41].

After keenly observing the previous research we chose the most widely used and competitive machine learning and deep learning models, namely KNN, NB, LR, RF, DT, SGDC, ANN, and LSTM, for comparing with our proposed ELM model using different performance evaluation parameters, namely confusion matrix, accuracy, precision, recall, sensitivity, specificity, F1-score, and AUC.

In this study, after conducting experiments, we will compare the results of our proposed ELM model and other state-of-the-art machine learning and deep learning techniques. First, we will discuss the first performance parameter, the confusion matrix. In Figures 10 and 11, the confusion matrix charts of ML and DL classifiers are represented for epileptic seizure activity recognition, and the column represents the actual label instances of the classes while the rows represent the predicted instances of the actual classes. The correct class count predicted by the model matrix is shown in a diagonal position while the wrong prediction counts of the model are shown outside of the diagonal matrix. Our proposed model, the Extreme Learning Machine (ELM), predicts the wrong predictions and correct predictions with 100% accuracy, as shown in Figure 11.

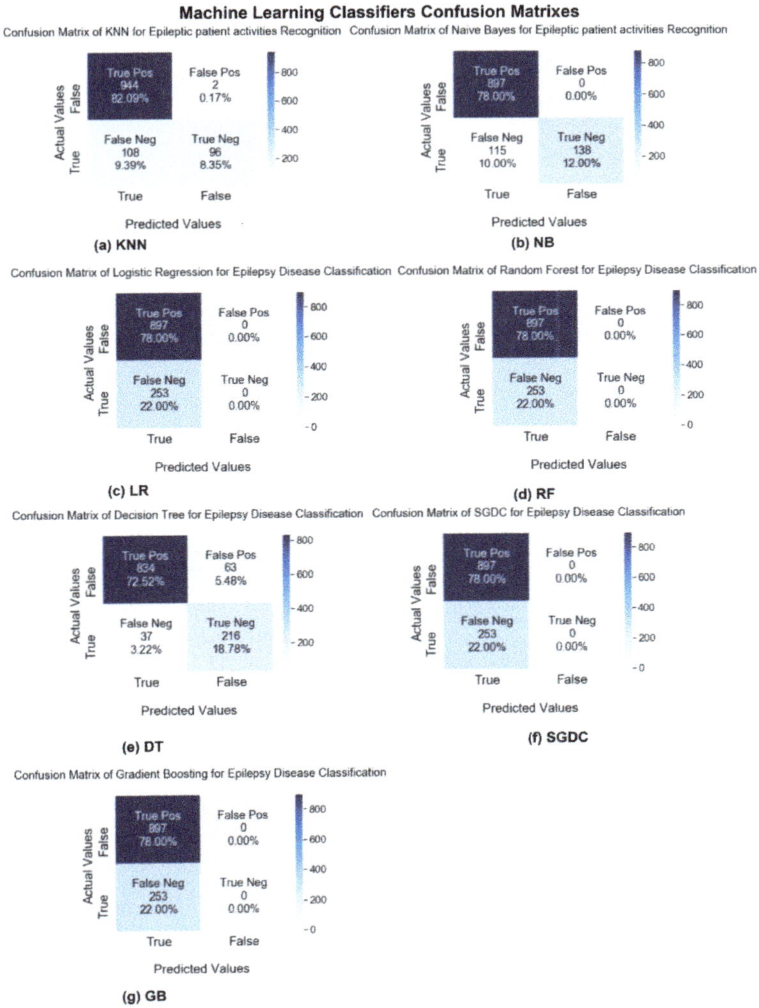

Figure 10. Confusion Matrix of (**a**) KNN, (**b**) NB, (**c**) LR, (**d**) RF, (**e**) DT, (**f**) SGDC, and (**g**) GB.

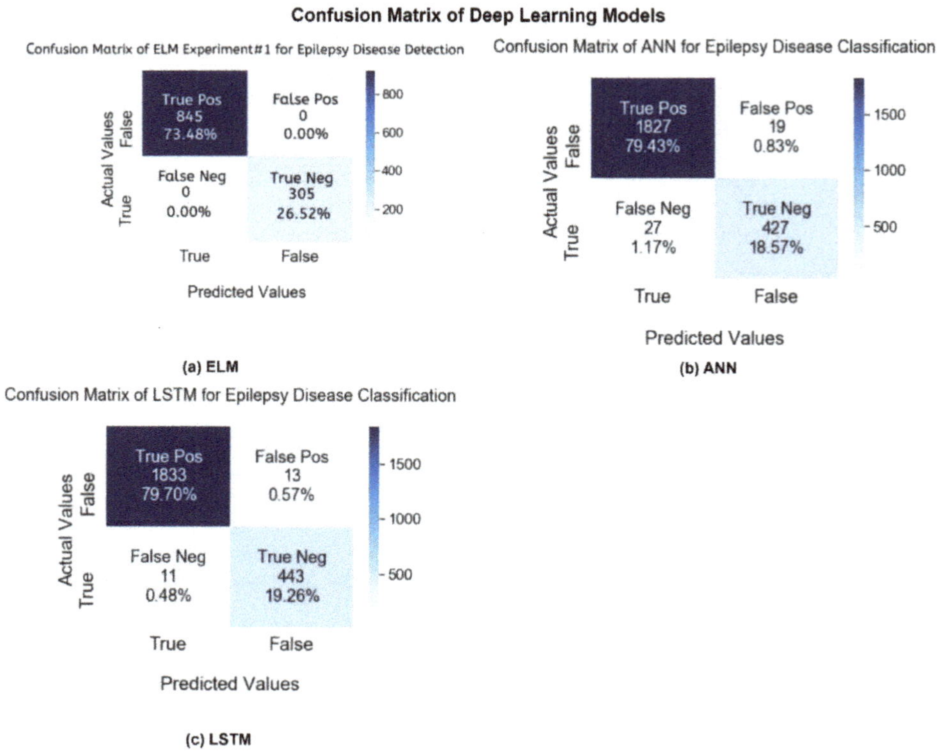

Figure 11. Confusion Matrices of (**a**) ELM #1; (**b**) ANN; (**c**) LSTM.

Figure 12 shows the comparison of yielded accuracies of different ML and DL models with our proposed model. Blue bars represent the training accuracies and orange bars represent the testing accuracies of different ML and DL models.

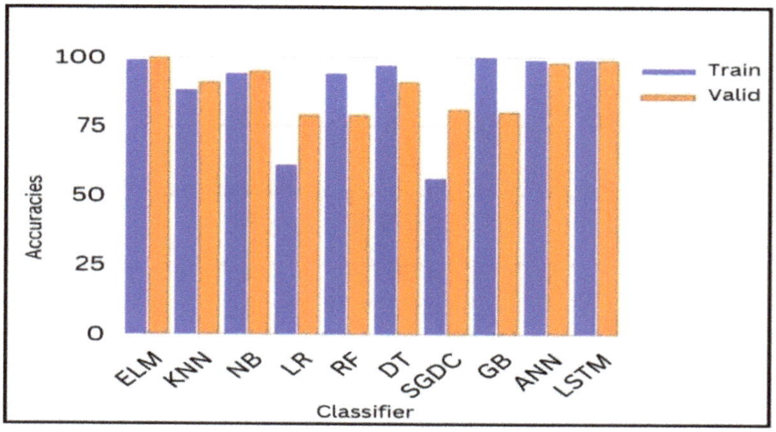

Figure 12. Training and Testing Accuracies of ML and DL Models.

After experiments, we dig deeper into detail to analyze and investigate the result of binary classification by ML and DL classifiers. As can be seen, except for two linear classifiers, logistic regression (LR) and Random Forest (RF), all eight remaining configured classifiers' results give an accuracy of over 80%, and most of these classifiers show a competitive accuracy of over 90%. In Table 7 our proposed ELM, highlighted in bold, yields the most competitive results as to other models with a low computational time for training and testing.

Table 7. The performance comparison of different models.

	Training/Testing Results	Accuracy %	Precision	Recall	F1-Score	Specificity	Sensitivity	AUC	Time (s)
				ML Techniques					
KNN	Training	95.5	0.992	0.756	0.858	0.994	0.756	0.997	0.015
	Testing	91	0.9927	0.5596	0.7157	0.9988	0.5596	0.7573	0.29
NB	Training	93.7	0.974	0.898	0.933	0.976	0.898	0.982	2.23
	Testing	95	0.9004	0.8559	0.8776	0.9746	0.8559	0.9195	0.42
LR	Training	83.7	0.761	0.532	0.624	0.832	0.532	0.610	0.97
	Testing	79	0.9004	0.8559	0.8776	1.0	0.01	0.5123	0.07
RF	Training	83.7	0.981	0.907	0.941	0.982	0.907	0.9926	0.92
	Testing	79	0.8661	0.895	0.8423	1.0	0.0	0.5122	0.06
DT	Training	98.1	0.988	0.907	0.892	0.988	0.907	0.97	0.057
	Testing	91	0.7415	0.8389	0.7872	0.9245	0.8389	0.8664	0.0008
SGDC	Training	90	0.90	0.907	0.903	0.996	0.907	0.56	0.97
	Testing	81	0.246	0.506	0.225	0.593	0.506	0.5121	0.77
GB	Training	100	1.0	1.0	1.0	1.0	1.0	0.999	0.014
	Testing	80	0.6666	0.0095	0.0188	0.9987	0.0095	0.5111	0.73
				DL Techniques					
ELM	**Training**	**99.9**	**0.996**	**0.998**	**0.996**	**0.99**	**0.998**	**0.1**	**0.96**
	Testing	**100**	**0.95**	**0.99**	**0.969**	**1.0**	**0.999**	**0.998**	**0.0009**
ANN	Training	99	0.996	0vb.998	0.996	0.99	0.998	0.992	6.71
	Testing	98	0.9411	0.9515	0.9463	0.9853	0.9515	0.9965	0.005
LSTM	Training	99	0.996	0.998	0.996	0.99	0.998	0.999	7.52
	Testing	99	0.9799	0.9691	0.9745	0.9951	0.9691	0.9941	0.003

It is shown that among the ML algorithms, only the Naïve Bayes classifier performed well with a 95% achieved accuracy. A sensitivity analysis was also performed to test the performance of KNN, RF, and SGDC with different parameters, e.g., the training/testing ratio is changed. When the value of K for KNN is changed to above 5, SGDC classifier is used as the regularization parameter, and the loss function is changed then the performance of the classifiers changes accordingly.

After a thorough analysis, it can be seen from Table 7 that among all the classifiers, ELM proved to be high-performing model based on the binary classification technique with a 100% accuracy, 0.99 AUC, 0.95 precision, 0.99 sensitivity and recall, 1.0 specificity, and 0.96 F1-score. The ELM model outperformed other state-of-the-art ML and DL models in the prediction of epileptic and non-epileptic seizures.

This ideal performance of the ELM indicates that it is the best fit for the recognition of epileptic activities; on the other hand, linear models such as LR and RF are not the most suitable classifiers for epileptic seizure activity recognition because the large data requirement (e.g., 11,500 feature) deep learning need for learning and understanding training features effectively will result in overfitting, and these classifiers usually become underfit when using lower training dataset ratios. That is also why our proposed model yields less promising results in experiments 2 and 3 than in our first experiment dataset ratio, i.e., the model is not trained well on low dataset ratios. The ANN and LSTM DL models achieve the nearest accuracies to our model: 98% and 99%, respectively, at the dataset division ratio of 80% and 20%. These models have a low computational testing time but are more time-consuming classifiers for training because they use backpropagation to tune the weights, requiring repetitive iterations and thus more time to train the model. These models also become overfit compared to our proposed model, which has no backpropagation and no iterations to tune the weights. The lack of backpropagation is why a feedforward models converge faster and take less time to train. Due to the absence of backpropagation, our model solves the problem of overfitting experience by other deep learning models. It is worth mentioning here that the power of the best computer workstation is related to the computational time, and it is indirectly indicated that the best workstation has a low computational time. So, it is admitted by our observation that although our model's results are biased due to the more time-consuming training computational time, the current observed results show that only deep models are fit for epileptic activity recognition tasks as compared to traditional machine learning classifiers.

Figure 13 represents the combined training ROC curve of our proposed model in comparison with other state-of-the-art classifiers for epileptic seizure activity recognition. In the training curve, the blue line represents the baseline for the curve. If a model curved at the top left corner of the blue dotted baseline and off to the 45 degree triangle to the top left corner, then it is the best performing model. The curve shows that only two models, namely Logistic Regression (LR) and Stochastic Gradient Descent (SGDC), do not show better performance for the training model, approaching AUC values of 0.61 and 0.57, respectively, because the training line's accuracy increase at the start and then suddenly starts decreasing and diverges from the baseline and on to the 45 degree triangle. Except for these two models, all other models yield an AUC over 0.90, and the maximum AUC approaches 0.99, yielded by DL models. In the training curve, it can be easily observed that, for training, the model's true positive rates are higher as compared to the true positive rates for testing. If the figure is closely observed, then it can be concluded that the AUC values of the DL models are higher than those of the ML models for training.

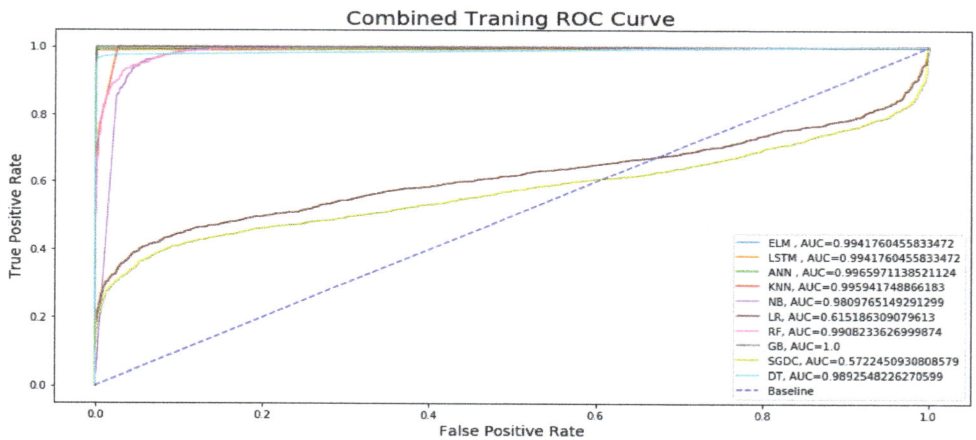

Figure 13. ROC Curve for Training Comparison of Epileptic Activities.

Similarly, Figure 14 presents the testing ROC curve of our proposed ELM model with other state-of-the-art ML and DL models. After keenly analyzing the results, it is concluded that only four Machine Learning (ML) models, namely Logistic Regression (LR), Random Forest (RF), Gradient Boosting (GB), and Stochastic Gradient Descent (SGDC), are approaching an AUC of 0.5, and the testing accuracy line following the blue dotted baseline and on to the 45 degree which is not a representation of best-performing models because best performing models are curved at the top of the left corner and off to the 45 degree triangle. All six remaining models are approaching an AUC over 0.70, and the maximum testing AUC of 0.99 is approached by DL models. From the figure, it can be easily observed that the True Positive Rate for the ELM is higher than the other state-of-the-art ML and DL classification techniques. If the testing ROC is closely observed in comparison with the ROC curve of training, then it can be seen that the rate of the training dataset is slightly higher than the testing rates.

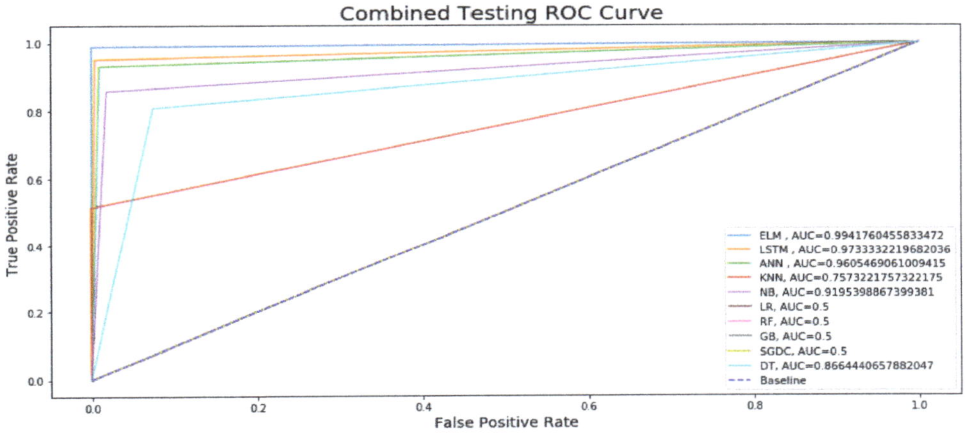

Figure 14. ROC Curve for Testing Comparison of Epileptic Activities Recognition.

5. Conclusions

In this research, a deep learning-based technique is applied named Extreme Learning Machine. Some deficiencies in the previous research are overcome in the presented research. Although many machine learning and deep learning techniques have been applied in previous research, there is still more room to improve these models' accuracy in detecting epilepsy through epileptic activities, and the overfitting problem also needed to be resolved. We improved these imperfections in the presented research. In this research, different Machine Learning algorithms, namely K-Nearest Neighbors (KNN), Logistic Regression (LR), Random Forest (RF), Naïve Bayes (NB), Support Vector Machine (SVM), Stochastic Gradient Descent (SGDC), and Gradient Boosting Classifier (GB), Decision Tree (DT), and Deep Learning (DL) algorithms, namely Long Short-Term Memory (LSTM) and Artificial Neural Network (ANN), are applied. We obtained robust results with the 80% to 20% training to testing ratios. We found that among the ML algorithms, only the Naïve Bayes classifier performed well with a 95% accuracy. Although this ML classifier performed well, the Deep Learning (DL) models are preferred over ML classifiers because of their automated feature extraction and the higher accuracy achieved. The ELM, LSTM, and ANN DL models were used and achieved accuracies of 100%, 99%, and 98%, respectively. Although LSTM and ANN performed well, the accuracy of the ELM is the highest achieved accuracy out of all the models proposed in the current and previous research. This research did not use imaging data to train the classifier, which reduced memory usage compared to using numerical datasets. The model used also does not require backpropagation and thus needs less user intervention. We also tried to overcome the problem of generalization and overfitting faced by the different models by using the ELM classifier. Therefore, it is concluded that the results of this research can be effectively implemented by the community working on the research of epilepsy. We did not check this proposed model for other problems diagnosed using EEG signals from this dataset, but if they lie within the parameters constraints of the model, with a little bit of modification according to the problem's domain, it should be able to its promising performance for the detection of the problem. The occurrence of epilepsy can be predicted through the detection of epileptic and non-epileptic physical activities instead of through EEG signals collected from the scalp directly or via brain MRI. This research will help neurologists in epilepsy detection and other problems using EEG data by reducing examination time and promising high efficiency and effectiveness.

Author Contributions: Conceptualization, U.A., M.S.Z., O.D.O., N.-u.R., T.M., A.E.R. and H.T.R.; methodology, U.A., M.S.Z., O.D.O. and N.-u.R.; software, N.-u.R., T.M., A.E.R. and H.T.R.; formal analysis, T.M., A.E.R. and H.T.R.; resources, M.S.Z. and H.T.R.; data curation, U.A.; writing—original draft preparation, U.A., M.S.Z., O.D.O., N.-u.R., T.M., A.E.R. and H.T.R.; writing—review and editing, U.A., M.S.Z., O.D.O., N.-u.R., T.M., A.E.R. and H.T.R.; supervision, M.S.Z. and H.T.R.; funding acquisition, A.E.R. All authors have read and agreed to the published version of the manuscript.

Funding: The authors extend their appreciation to King Saud University for funding this work through Re-searchers Supporting Project number (RSPD2023R711), King Saud University, Riyadh, Saudi Arabia.

Institutional Review Board Statement: Not applicable.

Informed Consent Statement: Not applicable.

Data Availability Statement: Not applicable.

Acknowledgments: Not applicable.

Conflicts of Interest: The authors declare no conflict of interest.

References

1. Dhiman, C.; Vishwakarma, D.K. A review of state-of-the-art techniques for abnormal human activity recognition. *Eng. Appl. Artif. Intell.* **2019**, *77*, 21–45. [CrossRef]
2. Wang, C.; Zheng, Q.; Peng, Y.; De, D.; Song, W.-Z. Distributed abnormal activity detection in smart environments. *Int. J. Distrib. Sens. Netw.* **2014**, *10*, 283197. [CrossRef]
3. Shoeibi, A.; Khodatars, M.; Ghassemi, N.; Jafari, M.; Moridian, P.; Alizadehsani, R.; Panahiazar, M.; Khozeimeh, F.; Zare, A.; Hosseini-Nejad, H.; et al. Epileptic seizures detection using deep learning techniques: A review. *Int. J. Environ. Res. Public Health* **2021**, *18*, 5780. [CrossRef] [PubMed]
4. Fisher, R.S.; van Emde Boas, W.; Blume, W.; Elger, C.; Genton, P.; Lee, P.; Engel, J., Jr. Epileptic seizures and epilepsy: Definitions proposed by the International League Against Epilepsy (ILAE) and the International Bureau for Epilepsy (IBE). *Epilepsia* **2005**, *46*, 470–472. [CrossRef]
5. Paul, Y. Various epileptic seizure detection techniques using biomedical signals: A review. *Brain Inform.* **2018**, *5*, 6. [CrossRef] [PubMed]
6. Saminu, S.; Xu, G.; Zhang, S.; Isselmou, A.E.K.; Jabire, A.H.; Karaye, I.A.; Ahmad, I.S. Hybrid feature extraction technique for multi-classification of ictal and non-ictal EEG epilepsy signals. *ELEKTRIKA-J. Electr. Eng.* **2020**, *19*, 1–11. [CrossRef]
7. Sridhar, C.; Lih, O.S.; Jahmunah, V.; Koh, J.E.W.; Ciaccio, E.J.; San, T.R.; Arunkumar, N.; Kadry, S.; Acharya, U.R. Accurate detection of myocardial infarction using non linear features with ECG signals. *J. Ambient. Intell. Humaniz. Comput.* **2021**, *12*, 3227–3244. [CrossRef]
8. Halalli, B.; Makandar, A. Computer aided diagnosis-medical image analysis techniques. *Breast Imaging* **2018**, *85*, 85–109.
9. Atal, D.K.; Singh, M. A hybrid feature extraction and machine learning approaches for epileptic seizure detection. *Multidimens. Syst. Signal Process.* **2020**, *31*, 503–525. [CrossRef]
10. Sharaf, A.I.; Abu El-Soud, M.; El-Henawy, I.M. An automated approach for epilepsy detection based on tunable Q-wavelet and firefly feature selection algorithm. *Int. J. Biomed. Imaging* **2018**, *2018*, 5812872. [CrossRef] [PubMed]
11. Elghamry, H.; Ghoneim, M.; Haggag, A.A.; Darweesh, M.S.; Ismail, T. Comparative Analysis of Various Machine Learning Techniques for Epileptic Seizures Detection and Prediction Using EEG Data. In Proceedings of the 2020 2nd Novel Intelligent and Leading Emerging Sciences Conference (NILES), Giza, Egypt, 24–26 October 2020; IEEE: New York, NY, USA, 2020; pp. 175–180.
12. Torse, D.A.; Khanai, R.; Desai, V.V. Classification of epileptic seizures using recurrence plots and machine learning techniques. In Proceedings of the 2019 International Conference on Communication and Signal Processing (ICCSP), Chennai, India, 4–6 April 2019; IEEE: New York, NY, USA, 2019; pp. 0611–0615.
13. Akut, R. Wavelet based deep learning approach for epilepsy detection. *Health Inf. Sci. Syst.* **2019**, *7*, 8. [CrossRef] [PubMed]

14. Kaziha, O.; Jarndal, A.; Bonny, T. Genetic Algorithm Augmented Convolutional Neural Network for Image Recognition Applications. In Proceedings of the 2020 International Conference on Communications, Computing, Cybersecurity, and Informatics (CCCI), Sharjah, United Arab Emirates, 3–5 November 2020; IEEE: New York, NY, USA, 2020; pp. 1–5.
15. Hossain, M.S.; Amin, S.U.; Alsulaiman, M.; Muhammad, G. Applying deep learning for epilepsy seizure detection and brain mapping visualization. *ACM Trans. Multimed. Comput. Commun. Appl. (TOMM)* **2019**, *15*, 1–17. [CrossRef]
16. Lentzas, A.; Vrakas, D. Non-intrusive human activity recognition and abnormal behavior detection on elderly people: A review. *Artif. Intell. Rev.* **2020**, *53*, 1975–2021. [CrossRef]
17. Nahzat, S.; Yağanoğlu, M. Classification of Epileptic Seizure Dataset Using Different Machine Learning Algorithms and PCA Feature Reduction Technique. *J. Investig. Eng. Technol.* **2021**, *4*, 47–60.
18. Rajendran, P.; Ganapathy, K. Neural network based seizure detection system using statistical package analysis. *Bull. Electr. Eng. Inform.* **2022**, *11*, 2547–2554. [CrossRef]
19. Hazarika, B.B.; Gupta, D.; Kumar, B. EEG Signal Classification Using a Novel Universum-Based Twin Parametric-Margin Support Vector Machine. *Cogn. Comput.* **2023**, 1–16. [CrossRef]
20. Almustafa, K.M. Classification of epileptic seizure dataset using different machine learning algorithms. *Inform. Med. Unlocked* **2020**, *21*, 100444. [CrossRef]
21. Usman, S.M.; Latif, S.; Beg, A. Principle components analysis for seizures prediction using wavelet transform. *arXiv* **2020**, arXiv:2004.07937.
22. Nandy, A.; Alahe, M.A.; Nasim Uddin, S.M.; Alam, S.; Nahid, A.; Awal, M.A. Feature extraction and classification of EEG signals for seizure detection. In Proceedings of the 2019 International Conference on Robotics, Electrical and Signal Processing Techniques (ICREST), Dhaka, Bangladesh, 10–12 January 2019; IEEE: New York, NY, USA, 2019; pp. 480–485.
23. Hamad, A.; Houssein, E.H.; Hassanien, A.E.; Fahmy, A.A. A hybrid EEG signals classification approach based on grey wolf optimizer enhanced SVMs for epileptic detection. In Proceedings of the International Conference on Advanced Intelligent Systems and Informatics 2017, Cairo, Egypt, 9–11 September 2017; Springer: Cham, Switzerland, 2018; pp. 108–117.
24. Sharmila, A.; Geethanjali, P. DWT based detection of epileptic seizure from EEG signals using naive Bayes and k-NN classifiers. *IEEE Access* **2016**, *4*, 7716–7727. [CrossRef]
25. Swami, P.; Gandhi, T.K.; Panigrahi, B.K.; Tripathi, M.; Anand, S. A novel robust diagnostic model to detect seizures in electroencephalography. *Expert Syst. Appl.* **2016**, *56*, 116–130. [CrossRef]
26. Guo, L.; Rivero, D.; Dorado, J.; Rabuñal, J.R.; Pazos, A. Automatic epileptic seizure detection in EEGs based on line length feature and artificial neural networks. *J. Neurosci. Methods* **2010**, *191*, 101–109. [CrossRef] [PubMed]
27. Nicolaou, N.; Georgiou, J. Detection of epileptic electroencephalogram based on permutation entropy and support vector machines. *Expert Syst. Appl.* **2012**, *39*, 202–209. [CrossRef]
28. Gandhi, T.; Panigrahi, B.K.; Anand, S. A comparative study of wavelet families for EEG signal classification. *Neurocomputing* **2011**, *74*, 3051–3057. [CrossRef]
29. Shoeb, A.H. Application of Machine Learning to Epileptic Seizure Onset Detection and Treatment. Ph.D. Thesis, Massachusetts Institute of Technology, Cambridge, MA, USA, 2009.
30. Khan, Y.U.; Rafiuddin, N.; Farooq, O. Automated seizure detection in scalp EEG using multiple wavelet scales. In Proceedings of the 2012 IEEE International Conference on Signal Processing, Computing and Control, Solan, India, 15–17 March 2012; IEEE: New York, NY, USA, 2012; pp. 1–5.
31. Acharya, U.R.; Molinari, F.; Sree, S.V.; Chattopadhyay, S.; Ng, K.-H.; Suri, J.S. Automated diagnosis of epileptic EEG using entropies. *Biomed. Signal Process. Control.* **2012**, *7*, 401–408. [CrossRef]
32. Ullah, I.; Hussain, M.; Qazi, E.-U.; Aboalsamh, H. An automated system for epilepsy detection using EEG brain signals based on deep learning approach. *Expert Syst. Appl.* **2018**, *107*, 61–71. [CrossRef]
33. Moldovan, D. Horse Optimization Algorithm Based Recurrent Neural Network Method for Epileptic Seizures Classification. In Proceedings of the 7th International Conference on Advancements of Medicine and Health Care through Technology: MEDITECH-2020, Cluj-Napoca, Romania, 13–15 October 2020; Springer: Cham, Switzerland, 2022; pp. 183–190.
34. Manocha, G.; Rustagi, H.; Singh, S.P.; Jain, R.; Nagrath, P. Epilepsy Seizure Classification Using One-Dimensional Convolutional Neural Networks. In *Data Management, Analytics and Innovation: Proceedings of ICDMAI 2021*; Springer: Singapore, 2022; Volume 2, pp. 155–168.
35. Nanthini, K.; Tamilarasi, A.; Pyingkodi, M.; Dishanthi, M.; Kaviya, S.M.; Mohideen, P.A. Epileptic Seizure Detection and Prediction Using Deep Learning Technique. In Proceedings of the 2022 International Conference on Computer Communication and Informatics (ICCCI), Coimbatore, India, 25–27 January 2022; IEEE: New York, NY, USA, 2022; pp. 1–7.
36. AHilal, A.M.; Albraikan, A.A.; Dhahbi, S.; Nour, M.K.; Mohamed, A.; Motwakel, A.; Zamani, A.S.; Rizwanullah, M. Intelligent Epileptic Seizure Detection and Classification Model Using Optimal Deep Canonical Sparse Autoencoder. *Biology* **2022**, *11*, 1220.
37. Gao, Y.; Gao, B.; Chen, Q.; Liu, J.; Zhang, Y. Deep convolutional neural network-based epileptic electroencephalogram (EEG) signal classification. *Front. Neurol.* **2020**, *11*, 375. [CrossRef]
38. Singh, K.; Malhotra, J. Prediction of epileptic seizures from spectral features of intracranial eeg recordings using deep learning approach. *Multimed. Tools Appl.* **2022**, *81*, 28875–28898. [CrossRef]

39. Yuvaraj, R.; Thomas, J.; Kluge, T.; Dauwels, J. A deep learning scheme for automatic seizure detection from long-term scalp EEG. In Proceedings of the 2018 52nd Asilomar Conference on Signals, Systems, and Computers, Pacific Grove, CA, USA, 28–31 October 2018; IEEE: New York, NY, USA, 2019; pp. 368–372.
40. Andrzejak, R.G.; Lehnertz, K.; Mormann, F.; Rieke, C.; David, P.; Elger, C.E. Indications of nonlinear deterministic and finite-dimensional structures in time series of brain electrical activity: Dependence on recording region and brain state. *Phys. Rev. E* **2001**, *64*, 061907. [CrossRef] [PubMed]
41. Huang, G.-B.; Zhu, Q.-Y.; Siew, C.-K. Extreme learning machine: Theory and applications. *Neurocomputing* **2006**, *70*, 489–501. [CrossRef]
42. Liang, N.-Y.; Huang, G.-B.; Saratchandran, P.; Sundararajan, N. A fast and accurate online sequential learning algorithm for feedforward networks. *IEEE Trans. Neural Netw.* **2006**, *17*, 1411–1423. [CrossRef] [PubMed]
43. Lu, C.-J.; Shao, Y.E. Forecasting computer products sales by integrating ensemble empirical mode decomposition and extreme learning machine. *Math. Probl. Eng.* **2012**, *2012*, 831201. [CrossRef]

biomedicines

MDPI

Article

Early Prediction of Dementia Using Feature Extraction Battery (FEB) and Optimized Support Vector Machine (SVM) for Classification

Ashir Javeed [1,2], Ana Luiza Dallora [2], Johan Sanmartin Berglund [2], Alper Idrisoglu [2], Liaqat Ali [3], Hafiz Tayyab Rauf [4] and Peter Anderberg [2,5,*]

1 Aging Research Center, Karolinska Institutet, 171 65 Stockholm, Sweden
2 Department of Health, Blekinge Institute of Technology, 371 79 Karlskrona, Sweden
3 Department of Electrical Engineering, University of Science and Technology Bannu, Bannu 28100, Pakistan
4 Centre for Smart Systems, AI and Cybersecurity, Staffordshire University, Stoke-on-Trent ST4 2DE, UK
5 School of Health Sciences, University of Skövde, 541 28 Skövde, Sweden
* Correspondence: peter.anderberg@bth.se

Abstract: Dementia is a cognitive disorder that mainly targets older adults. At present, dementia has no cure or prevention available. Scientists found that dementia symptoms might emerge as early as ten years before the onset of real disease. As a result, machine learning (ML) scientists developed various techniques for the early prediction of dementia using dementia symptoms. However, these methods have fundamental limitations, such as low accuracy and bias in machine learning (ML) models. To resolve the issue of bias in the proposed ML model, we deployed the adaptive synthetic sampling (ADASYN) technique, and to improve accuracy, we have proposed novel feature extraction techniques, namely, feature extraction battery (FEB) and optimized support vector machine (SVM) using radical basis function (rbf) for the classification of the disease. The hyperparameters of SVM are calibrated by employing the grid search approach. It is evident from the experimental results that the newly pr oposed model (FEB-SVM) improves the dementia prediction accuracy of the conventional SVM by 6%. The proposed model (FEB-SVM) obtained 98.28% accuracy on training data and a testing accuracy of 93.92%. Along with accuracy, the proposed model obtained a precision of 91.80%, recall of 86.59, F1-score of 89.12%, and Matthew's correlation coefficient (MCC) of 0.4987. Moreover, the newly proposed model (FEB-SVM) outperforms the 12 state-of-the-art ML models that the researchers have recently presented for dementia prediction.

Keywords: dementia; feature fusion; machine learning; imbalance classes

Citation: Javeed, A.; Dallora, A.L.; Berglund, J.S.; Idrisoglu, A.; Ali, L.; Rauf, H.T.; Anderberg, P. Early Prediction of Dementia Using Feature Extraction Battery (FEB) and Optimized Support Vector Machine (SVM) for Classification. *Biomedicines* **2023**, *11*, 439. https://doi.org/10.3390/biomedicines11020439

Academic Editors: Wu Qiu and Hulin Kuang

Received: 15 January 2023
Revised: 30 January 2023
Accepted: 31 January 2023
Published: 2 February 2023

1. Introduction

Dementia is a mental disorder marked by a progressive decline in cognitive functions that interferes with daily living skills such as visual perception, problem-solving, memory, and the ability to focus on a single topic. Dementia is more common in older adults, yet many consider it an inevitable outcome of aging. This impression of aging might be incorrect. A wide range of illnesses and injuries to the brain are the primary causes of dementia development [1]. The number of people with dementia is swiftly growing globally, and statistical forecasts indicate that 135 million individuals might have dementia by 2050 [2]. According to the World Health Organization, dementia is the sixth leading cause of death globally, and it is the leading cause of disability and dependency among the aged worldwide [3].

Current early-stage dementia diagnosis relies on pathology features or cognitive diagnostic procedures. Pathology features can be detected via neuroimaging. Magnetic resonance imaging (MRI) is employed to investigate the changes in neuron structure [4]. Electroencephalography (EEG) is utilized to assess event-related possibilities to determine the early stages of dementia [5]. However, such techniques are ineffective in identifying dementia. These prediction tests are relatively inexpensive and time-consuming. In addition, a recent study proposes employing computed tomography (CT) or electromagnetic resonance imaging (MRI) to rule out structural causes of the clinical phenotype [6]. It is estimated that primary-care physicians overlook between 29% and 76% of dementia patients or suspected dementia patients [7]. The use of cognitive tests to assess the early stages of dementia also has some disadvantages. It is difficult for paramedics to engage patients and urge them to participate in testing procedures because older individuals often fear visiting clinics. On the other hand, dementia tests performed at home are usually conducted by inexperienced relatives unfamiliar with the scales; as a result, many test findings are incorrect. ML algorithms provide a novel approach to this challenge. Because of developments in information technology, paramedics now have better access to patients' lives and can detect decreased cognitive function at an earlier stage. ML algorithms may also provide expert medical knowledge. ML-based tools can provide excellent accuracy and a user-friendly approach to the early prediction of dementia. Scientists have built multiple automated diagnostic systems for various ailments using ML methods, such as heart failure [8–10], Parkinson's [11], hepatitis [12], and clinical decision support systems [13].

Different automated diagnostic methods based on ML methodologies have been presented in the past for early diagnosis of dementia. F. A. Salem et al. developed an ML algorithm for dementia prediction using a regression model. They also studied ML techniques for unbalanced classes in the dataset. They utilized oversampling and undersampling to eliminate the bias in the ML model. The balanced random forest (RF) model was the most resilient probabilistic model using only 20 variables from the dataset. Their proposed model reported an F1-score of 0.82%, G-Mean of 0.88%, and AUC of 0.88% [14]. Dallora et al. [15] employed decision trees (DT) to evaluate predictive factors for the ten-year prediction of dementia. In their proposed technique, they employed a recursive feature elimination (RFE) feature selection method to determine the most important variables from a dataset for dementia classification. Their proposed approach, based on RFE and DT, had an AUC of 74.50%. Through feature engineering and genetic algorithms, F.G. Gutierrez et al. devised an ML approach for diagnosing AD and FTD. Their suggested method had an accuracy of 84% [16]. G. Mirzaei and H. Adeli investigated cutting-edge ML approaches for identifying and categorizing AD [17]. H. Hsiu et al. investigated ML techniques for the early detection of cognitive deterioration using a threefold cross-validation approach, and their suggested model achieved an accuracy of 70.32% [18]. A. Shahzad et al. proposed an ML model for pre-screening MCI using an inertial sensor-derived gait biomarker with a 71.67% accuracy rate [19].

Aim of Study

The previously proposed ML models suffer from lower accuracy and bias in ML models. Motivated by these factors, we proposed a novel feature extraction method to extract useful features from the dataset. Moreover, we optimized an SVM using a grid search algorithm. The proposed hybrid model uses two components: the feature extraction battery (FEB) and support vector machine (SVM), leading to the newly proposed model, namely, (FEB-SVM). To address the issue of bias in the ML model, we deployed the adaptive synthetic sampling (ADASYN) scheme to balance the classes in the dataset. To validate the effectiveness of the proposed model (FEB-SVM), we used different evaluation metrics, e.g., accuracy, precision, recall, PR curve, area under the curve (AUC), F1 score, and Matthew's correlation coefficient (MCC). Moreover, we conducted three different experiments to evaluate the performance of the newly proposed model.

It is essential to understand that dementia is classified into various subtypes, the most frequent being AD and Vascular dementia, among others. Mixed comorbidities are uncommon, and AD commonly comports with Vascular or Lewy Bodies dementia. Furthermore, unusual forms of AD are sometimes misdiagnosed, according to [20]. The study mentioned here makes no difference between subtypes of dementia, and the word dementia refers to all kinds of dementia.

2. Materials and Methods

This research collected data from the Swedish National Study on Aging and Care (SNAC) for the experimental purpose of the proposed model (FEB-SVM). The SNAC is a longitudinal consortium that has been collecting multimodal data from the Swedish senior population to "create trustworthy, comparable, durable datasets" to be used for aging research and aged care [21]. The SNAC was developed as a multifunctional program to explore healthcare quality for the aging population. It comprises a database containing details regarding physical assessment, metacognition, social variables, lifestyle factors, medical records, and so on. Blekinge, Skåne, Nordanstig, and Kungsholmen are the sites from which the SNAC database is collected. They consider a couple of Swedish counties—municipal and borough. This research adopted the SNAC-Blekinge baseline examination, with data gathered from 2000 to 2003. In the literature, there is substantial evidence that environmental factors may impact dementia development [22,23]. This research is based on standard criteria and uses data from urban areas (Blekinge). The inclusion methodology used to eliminate individuals from this investigation is given as follows:

1. Individuals who presented a dementia diagnosis at the beginning of the study or before the ten-year mark.
2. Individuals with missing data in the outcome column.
3. Individuals with more than 10% incomplete data.
4. Individuals who expired (died) well before the ten-year study period.

From the 1402 participants in the SNAC-Blekinge baseline, after the application of the selection criteria, 726 participants (313 males and 413 females) were included, 91 (12.5%) of whom had dementia in the 10 years, and 635 (87.5%) who were free of dementia. The demographics of the sample population in the collected dataset are shown in Table 1. The factors chosen from the SNAC-Blekinge database were based on published research [24,25]. The collected dataset (SNAC-Blekinge) consists of 13 physical measurement parameters such as body mass index (BMI), pain in the last four weeks, heart rate sitting, heart rate lying, blood pressure on the right arm, hand strength in the right arm, hand strength in the left arm, feeling of safety when rising from a chair, assessment of rising from a chair, single-leg standing with right leg, single-leg standing with left leg, dental prosthesis, and several teeth.

Table 1. Demographic overview of the data samples.

Age_Group	Male	Female	Healthy_Subject	Dementia_Cases
60	82	82	164	02
66	75	95	170	06
72	50	74	124	10
78	41	50	91	17
81	35	46	81	19
84	26	42	68	22
87	04	19	23	14
90+	00	05	05	01
Total	313	413	726	91

It is important to remember that all of the features used in the SNAC were picked based on the evidence relevant to the aging process [21]. At the commencement of the study (2000–2003), 75 variables were identified from the seven categories: demographics, lifestyle, social, psychological, medical history, physical examination, blood tests, and the assessment of various health instruments connected to dementia examination. Medical practitioners provide the target variable employed by the proposed model to predict dementia 10 years after the SNAC baseline. The dementia diagnosis was made using the International Statistical Classification of Diseases and Related Health Problems-10th Revision (ICD-10) and the Diagnostic and Statistical Manual of Mental Disorders (DSM-IV). Table 2 provides a feature category and name from the selected dataset (SNAC-Blekinge).

Table 2. Overview of features in the dataset.

Feature_Class	Feature_Names	Total
Demographic	Age, Gender	02
Lifestyle	Light Exercise, Alcohol Consumption, Alcohol Quantity, Work Status, Physical Workload, Present Smoker, Past Smoker, Number of Cigarettes a Day, Social Activities, Physically Demanding Activities, Leisure Activities	11
Social	Education, Religious Belief, Religious Activities, Voluntary Association, Social Network, Support Network, Loneliness	07
Physical Examination	Body Mass Index (BMI), Pain in the last 4 weeks, Heart Rate Sitting, Heart Rate Lying, Blood Pressure on the Right Arm, Hand Strength in Right Arm in a 10 s Interval, Hand Strength in Left Arm in a 10 s Interval, Feeling of Safety from Rising from a Chair, Assessment of Rising from a Chair, Single-Leg Standing with Right Leg, Single-Leg Standing with Left Leg, Dental Prosthesis, Number of Teeth	13
Psychological	Memory Loss, Memory Decline, Memory Decline 2, Abstract Thinking, Personality Change, Sense of Identity	06
Health Instruments	Sense of Coherence, Digit Span Test, Backwards Digit Span Test, Livingston Index, EQ5D Test, Activities of Daily Living, Instrumental Activities of Daily Living, Mini-Mental State Examination, Clock Drawing Test, Mental Composite Score of the SF-12 Health Survey, Physical Composite Score of the SF-12 Health Survey, Comprehensive Psychopathological Rating Scale	12
Medical History	Number of Medications, Family History of Importance, Myocardial Infarction, Arrhythmia, Heart Failure, Stroke, TIA/RIND, Diabetes Type 1, Diabetes Type 2, Thyroid Disease, Cancer, Epilepsy, Atrial Fibrillation, Cardiovascular Ischemia, Parkinson's Disease, Depression, Other Psychiatric Diseases, Snoring, Sleep Apnea, Hip Fracture, Head Trauma, Developmental Disabilities, High Blood Pressure	22
Biochemical Test	Hemoglobin Analysis, C-Reactive Protein Analysis	02

Proposed Work

In this work, we designed an automated diagnostic technique for the early prediction of dementia using machine learning and data mining approaches. The suggested diagnostic system is divided into two modules: the first module extracts valuable features from datasets to avoid the problem of model overfitting and the second module works as a classifier to predict dementia. We developed a novel feature extraction method based on linear discriminate analysis (LDA), independent component analysis (ICA), principal component analysis (PCA), locally linear embedding (LLE), and t-distributed Stochastic Neighbor Embedding (t-SNE). The aforementioned feature extraction methods have been cascaded into a single component, which we named a "feature extraction battery" (FEB). Feature extraction begins with an initial set of measured data. It creates derived values (features) that are meant to be useful and non-redundant, allowing future learning and generalization phases and, in some situations, leading to improved human interpretations. Feature extraction helps reduce the dimensionality of the dataset, which eventually reduces the computational complexity of the machine-learning models. The extracted features from FEB are fed into the predictive module of the proposed diagnostic system for the prediction of dementia. We employed a support vector machine (SVM) as a predictive module, and the working of the proposed diagnostic system (Figure 1).

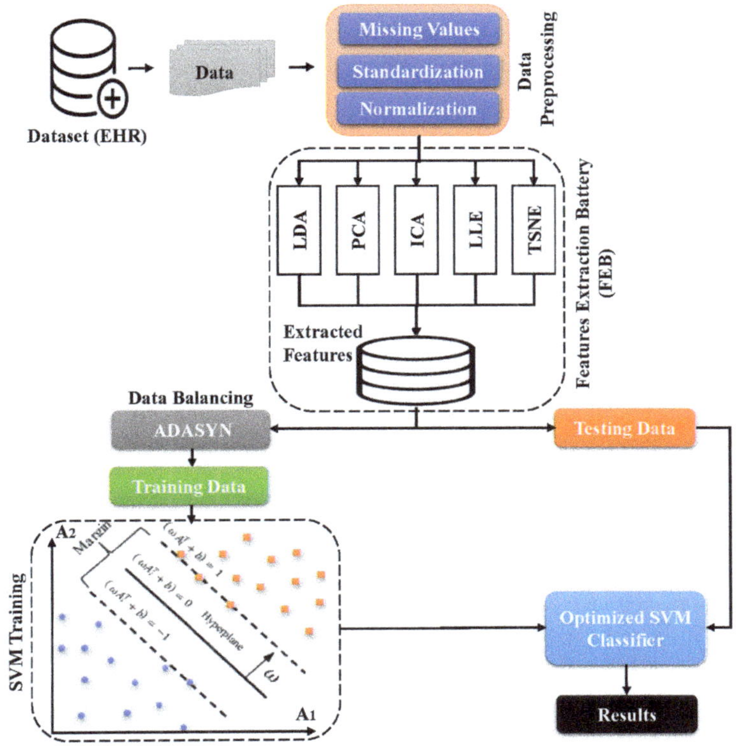

Figure 1. Schematic overview of the proposed model SVM-FEB.

The first stage of the proposed diagnostic system is data preprocessing because data play a vital role in predictive ML models. The dataset is refined, standardized, and normalized. We deal with the missing values in the data preprocessing stage by employing K-nearest neighbors (KNN) imputation [26]. This technique finds the K-items comparable (near) to the missing data. The KNN replaces the mean or most common value of K in the missing data with the most comparable neighbors. The selected dataset for the experiments portrays highly imbalanced classes. Hence, KNN imputation is employed independently on missing data from the majority and minority classes. Through this technique, the chance of infecting the minority class with data from the dominant class was reduced. Following the resolution of missing values, we performed the StandardScaler function on the selected dataset. The StandardScaler function helps to standardize a dataset by eliminating the mean and scaling to unit variance. A sample's average score λ is computed as follows:

$$\mathbb{Z} = \frac{(\lambda - \upsilon)}{\gamma} \tag{1}$$

where υ denotes the mean of training samples and γ is the standard deviation of the training samples. By calculating the relevant statistics on the training set samples, standardizing and scaling are performed independently on each feature. The mean and standard deviation are then saved for further use to transform on additional data.

When ML models are trained using all the feature space of a dataset, they tend to overfit, which means that ML models display improved performance on training data but poor performance on testing data [27,28]. This might be because the classifier learned superfluous or noisy features in the training data, or it could be due to a weak classifier with too many parameters. As a result, we should extract a subset of features from the dataset and a properly constructed classifier. In feature extraction methods, new features are constructed from the given dataset. Feature extraction decreases the resources necessary to explain a vast dataset. One of the primary issues with analyzing complex data is the number of variables involved. Analysis with many variables often necessitates a substantial memory and computing capacity. It may also lead a classification method to overfit training examples and generalize poorly to new samples. Feature extraction is a broad term encompassing ways of building variable combinations to avoid these issues while accurately summarizing the data. Many machine learning practitioners feel that well-optimized feature extraction is the key to good model design [29]. Therefore, we proposed a novel feature extraction method (FEB) to avoid the problem of model overfitting while simultaneously reducing data dimensionality. Reduced data dimensionality increases the performance of the proposed SVM-FEB in terms of time complexity. In FEB, we cascaded different feature extraction methods (LDA, PCA, ICA, LLE, TSNE) into a single module. The four feature extraction methods (PCA, ICA, LLE, TSN) construct a couple of new features, while LDA constructs only one new feature. The newly extracted FEB features are combined to generate an optimum dataset with low dimensionality. The proposed FEB constructs nine new features from the original dataset, which consists of 75 features.

After the feature extraction stage, we divided the dataset into two parts; one for training and the other for the testing purposes of the proposed SVM-FEB model. The classes in the dataset for the experiments are highly imbalanced, which means that the model would be biased toward the majority class. To address this issue, we used the ADASYN approach to tackle the imbalanced class issue [30]. The ADASYN approach uses a density distribution δ_i as a criterion to automatically compute the number of synthetic samples necessary for minority data samples. δ_i is a physical evaluation of the weight distribution of unique minority class instances depending on their level of learning difficulty. Following ADASYN, the final dataset will not only provide a balanced structure of classes in the data distribution (as defined by the coefficient) but also compels the learning algorithm to concentrate on complicated cases. As a consequence, the proposed system (FEB-SVM) is trained on balanced data, mitigating the risk of bias in the ML model. It is worth noting that the ADASYN approach is applied to training data following the data split. Suppose the ADASYN technique is used for the entire dataset (i.e., before data partitioning). In that case, the performance of the ML model will be skewed because samples from the testing dataset will also be included in the training dataset. Using ADASYN to balance the training dataset, we employed SVM for the classification task.

SVM is a powerful tool for classification and regression problems [31]. SVM attempts to construct a hyperplane with the greatest possible margin. In the case of a classification problem, the hyperplane $h(x) = (\sigma^T * x) + \gamma$, where γ denotes the bias and σ represents a weight vector that is built using training data and serves as a decision boundary for determining the class of a data point (a multidimensional feature vector). In the case of binary classification, SVM employs two support vectors and identifies the nearest vectors (data points) of two classes to create a margin. These vectors are referred to as support vectors. Margin is computed by taking the perpendicular distance between the lines going through the support vectors and multiplying by $\frac{2}{||\sigma||_2^2}$. The primary objective is to develop an optimized SVM predictive model to provide an ideal hyperplane with the highest margin. SVM employs a set of slack variables known as ν_i, i = 1, 2, ..., $\mho$, as well as a penalty parameter known as β, and attempts to maximize $||\sigma||_2^2$ while minimizing misclassification errors. This fact is mathematically expressed as follows:

$$\underbrace{\min_{\sigma,\gamma,\nu} \frac{1}{2}||\sigma||_2^2}_{Regularized} + \gamma \underbrace{\sum_{i=1}^{\mho} \nu_i}_{Error} \tag{2}$$

$$S.t\begin{cases} y_i(\sigma x_i + \gamma) \geq 1 - \nu_i \\ \nu_i \geq 0, i = 1, 2, \ldots, \mho \end{cases} \quad (3)$$

where ν is the slack variable that is used to calibrate the degree of misdiagnosis and penalized factor is the Euclidean norm, also known as the L2-norm.

The major difficulty is that a linear hyperplane cannot correctly partition the binary classes' data points (i.e., with the lowest classification error). For this reason, the SVM employs a kernel technique in which the SVM model converts local data points into hyperdimensional points to convert non-separable data points into separable data points. Different kernels are used, including the radial basis function (RBF) kernel, linear kernel, sigmoid kernel, and polynomial kernel. These kernels are SVM model hyperparameters that must be adjusted for each task. To design the SVM model that works best on a dementia prediction challenge, we must carefully update or optimize its hyperparameters. Grid search is the main way to reach this purpose. As a result, we employed the grid search approach to tweak the SVM hyperparameters. Consequently, in this paper, we suggest an FEB decrease in the data dimensionality. The suggested SVM-FEB approach dynamically optimizes the SVM model's hyperparameters using the grid search method.

3. Validation and Evaluation

The holdout validation technique has been extensively used in the literature as a benchmark for assessing the effectiveness of ML-based diagnostic systems [10,12,13]. In a holdout validation procedure, a dataset is partitioned into a couple of segments where one half is utilized for training while the remaining half is utilized for testing purposes of the proposed ML model. The dataset is split with a ratio of 70% for training the ML model and 30% used for testing. Thus, in our tests, we employed the data mentioned above partition criteria for the training and testing of the proposed SVM-FEB model. Following the data partition, we select evaluation measures to compare the performance of the proposed model with existing state-of-the-art ML models for dementia prediction. The assessment criteria used for evaluating the SVM-FEB model are accuracy, precision, recall, F1-score, Matthew's correlation coefficient (MCC), and area under the curve (AUC) using PR plot. The evaluation metrics are presented mathematically as

$$Accuracy = \frac{T^+ + T^-}{T^+ + T^- + F^+ + F^-} \quad (4)$$

where T^+ stands for the No. of true positive, F^+ represents the No. of false positives, T^- denotes the number of true negatives, and F^- represents the No. of false negatives.

$$Precision = \frac{T^+}{T^+ + F^+} \quad (5)$$

$$Recall = \frac{T^+}{T^+ + F^-} \quad (6)$$

$$F1\_score = \frac{2T^+}{2T^+ + F^+ + F^-} \quad (7)$$

$$MCC = \frac{T^+ \times T^- - F^+ \times F^-}{\sqrt{(T^+ + F^+)(T^+ + F^-)(T^- + F^+)(T^- + F^-)}} \quad (8)$$

A binary classification problem is statistically examined. The F1-score is defined as the F-measure. The F1-score gives a score between 0 and 1, with 1 representing excellent predictions and 0 representing the worst. MCC is used to determine whether or not a test is correct. The value range for MCC is between 1 and −1, with 1 being the best prognosis and −1 representing the worst prediction.

4. Experimental Results

Three kinds of experiments were conducted on the dementia dataset to examine the efficacy of the newly developed model (FEB-SVM). The first experiment used the grid search algorithm to construct and optimize traditional ML models using all the dataset's features (75). The proposed SVM-FEB approach is built in the second experiment. At the same time, additional state-of-the-art ML models are constructed in the third experiment while utilizing the same dementia data and a novel, suggested feature extraction module (FEB). All computation tasks were carried out on an Intel (R) Core (TM) i5-8250U CPU running at 1.60 GHz using Windows 10 64bit. The Python software package is employed to carry out all of the experiments.

4.1. Experiment No.1: Performance of ML Models Using All Features

In this experiment, we set up multiple ML models, i.e., naive Bayes (NB), logistic regression (LR), decision tree (DT), random forest (RF), k-nearest neighbors (KNN), and support vector machine (SVM) with various kernels (rbf, linear, polynomial, sigmoid), which are implemented in Python. The efficiency of the constructed ML models was assessed using all the dataset's features (75). It is noteworthy that the classes in the dataset are balanced through the ADASYN technique. Table 3 shows the accuracy, precision, recall, and MCC of dementia prediction. The SVM with a polynomial kernel obtained the best dementia diagnosis accuracy of 88.59 percent. However, the SVM training accuracy is lower than the test accuracy, indicating that the ML model overfits. Therefore, we constructed a feature extraction battery (FEB) to prevent the problem of model overfitting.

Table 3. Performance of ML models on balance data using all features.

Model	Acc._train	Acc._test	Precision	Recall	F1_score	MCC	95% CI [1]
NB	66.78	40.36	56.00	63.00	40.00	0.1695	0.77, 0.87
LR	90.65	77.25	55.00	57.00	77.00	0.1124	0.82, 0.91
DT	100	77.98	49.00	49.00	78.00	0.1157	0.78, 0.88
RF	100	88.07	55.00	51.00	88.00	0.4058	0.85, 0.93
KNN	89.17	86.69	51.00	50.00	87.00	0.3851	0.82, 0.92
Adaboost	95.15	80.27	66.00	51.00	80.00	0.1834	0.83, 0.91
SVM_rbf	99.30	85.78	88.00	56.00	86.00	0.2131	0.84, 0.93
SVM_sigmoid	78.54	74.28	56.00	63.00	74.00	0.1986	0.83, 0.92
SVM_linear	93.54	80.75	58.00	61.00	81.00	0.2042	0.82, 0.91
SVM_poly	73.24	88.59	45.00	50.00	89.00	0.2331	0.83, 0.92

[1] CI = Confidence Intervals.

4.2. Experiment No.2: Performance of Proposed Model SVM-FEB

In the proposed model (FEB-SVM), features are extracted from the dataset using a novel feature extraction battery (FEB). From FEB, we obtained the nine features that were extracted from the whole dataset. The classes were found to be highly unbalanced; so, we deployed the adaptive synthetic (ADASYN) oversampling method. After balancing the classes in the dataset, we optimized the hyperparameters of the SVM with the rbf kernel. We employed a grid research algorithm for the optimization of SVM hyperparameters. The optimal values of the hyperparameters of SVM are set by exploiting an exhaustive grid search algorithm. Table 4 shows that the proposed model SVM-FEB achieved the best dementia prediction accuracy, 93.92%, where C = 10 and G = 0.1 (C = Cost, G = Gamma) are the values of hyperparameters that are searched through using the grid research technique. The comparison of Tables 3 and 4 shows that the proposed model SVM-FEB improves the performance of traditional SVM by 8%. Furthermore, traditional SVM with rbf used all the features of the dataset (see Table 3), while in the proposed model SVM-FEB, only 9 features are used for the prediction of dementia (see Table 4).

Table 4. Performance of ML models on balance data while utilizing FEB.

Model	Hyper.	Acc._train	Acc._test	Precision	Recall	F1_score	MCC
SVM_rbf	C:100, G:0.1	99.77	90.88	92.39	87.62	89.50	0.4178
SVM_rbf	C:10, G:0.1	97.48	91.16	92.81	86.59	90.00	0.4216
SVM_rbf	C:100, G:0.1	99.88	91.79	92.22	85.56	91.00	0.4487
SVM_rbf	C:10, G:1	98.28	91.83	91.80	86.59	89.12	0.4387
SVM_rbf	C:10, G:1	98.50	92.46	89.67	85.05	90.00	0.4725
SVM_rbf	C:300, G:0.01	95.46	92.02	93.88	87.11	92.00	0.4747
SVM_rbf	C:10, G:1	100	92.70	89.37	95.36	92.00	0.4852
SVM_rbf	C:10, G:0.01	98.74	92.95	93.82	86.08	92.50	0.4810
SVM_rbf	C:100, G:0.1	98.41	93.31	92.34	87.11	93.00	0.4853
SVM_rbf	C:10, G:0.1	98.28	93.92	91.80	86.59	89.12	0.4987
SVM_linear	C: 0.1, G: 01	84.54	82.99	96.15	77.31	85.71	0.3630
SVM_sigmoid	C: 10, G: 0.001	83.23	82.97	96.52	71.64	82.00	0.3359
SVM_poly	C:01, G:01	88.23	84.57	95.75	90.28	84.00	0.3732

To validate the efficiency of the proposed model (FEB-SVM), we also used a precision–recall (PR) curve. In total, two types of experiments were conducted. In the first experiment, a simple SVM with an rbf kernel is tested against the PR-curve; in contrast, in the second experiment, the proposed SVM-FEB is tested. The important parameter in the PR plot is the area under the curve (AUC), in which a model having more area under the curve is considered better. Figure 2b shows the PR curve plot of the traditional SVM model with an AUC of 88% while Figure 2a presents the PR plot of the proposed SVM-FEB model with an AUC of 93%. Hence, the proposed model has better dementia prediction accuracy in comparison to the simple SVM model.

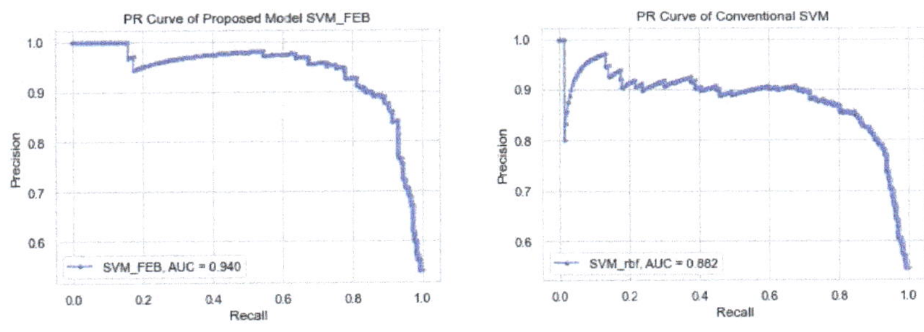

(a) (b)

Figure 2. Performance comparison based on AUC. (**a**) PR curve of proposed model; (**b**) PR curve of the conventional SVM.

Furthermore, we analyzed the training and testing accuracy of the proposed model (SVM-FEB) with other ML models. From Figure 3, it can be observed that the proposed (SVM-FEB) model achieved the highest testing accuracy compared with the rest of the ML models.

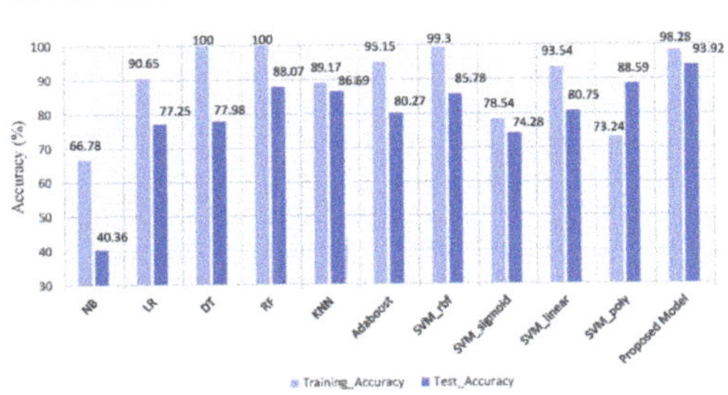

Figure 3. Performance comparison of proposed model with other ML models.

4.3. Experiment No.3: Performance of ML Models Based on FEB

In this experiment, we compared the newly developed model (SVM-FEB) performance with other ML models using a novel feature extraction model (FEB). We selected the following ML models, i.e., Naive Bayes (NB), K-Nearest Neighbors (KNN), Random Forest (RF), Decision Tree (DT), Logistic Regression (LR), and Support Vector Machine (SVM) with different kernels (linear, sigmoid, ref, linear). The selected ML models' hyperparameters were optimized using a grid search algorithm. For a fair comparison, we used balanced classes in the dataset, which were obtained through the ADASYN technique. Table 5 presents the results of each ML model along with the values of tuned hyperparameters, i.e., D—depth, E—edge, Ne—number of estimators, G—gamma, and K—number of neighbors. The performance of each model is assessed across different evaluation metrics such as accuracy on training data (ACC._train), accuracy on test data (ACC._test), precision, recall, f1_score, and Matthew's correlation coefficient (MCC). The proposed model (SVM-FEB) has achieved the highest accuracy of 93.92% in comparison with other ML models using the same feature extraction module (FEB), as shown in Table 5. Furthermore, we can also compare the results of Table 5 with Table 3 where the same ML models are used using all dataset features. From the comparative analysis of both tables, it can be seen that the novel proposed feature extraction method (FEB) has significantly improved the performance of ML models. Thus, the proposed feature extraction model reduced the complexity of the ML models because ML models used only 9 features compared with all the available feature space of 75 features. The proposed feature extraction module (FEB) and optimized SVM with an rbf kernel obtained improved accuracy results compared with conventional SVM.

Table 5. Performance of ML models on balance data using FEB.

Model	Hyper.	Acc._train	Acc._test	Precision	Recall	F1_score	MCC
NB	Var:0.006	79.40	75.22	62.00	77.00	75.00	0.3642
LR	C:100, S: newton, p:l2	84.46	78.36	64.00	79.00	78.00	0.3954
DT	D: 03, E:04	87.80	86.00	96.02	74.74	85.00	0.3374
RF	D:10, Ne:100. E:01	97.95	90.15	94.79	84.53	89.00	0.4286
KNN	Lf:01, K:01, P:02	100	90.54	92.98	81.95	87.00	0.4324
Adaboost	Lr:01, Ne: 10	86.77	85.63	79.38	86.76	86.00	0.3567
SVM_Linear	C: 0.1, G: 01	84.54	84.99	96.15	77.31	85.71	0.3630
SVM_Sigmoid	C: 10, G: 0.001	83.23	82.97	96.52	71.64	82.00	0.3359
SVM_Poly	C:01, G:01	88.23	84.57	95.75	90.28	84.00	0.3732
SVM_rbf	C:10, G:0.1	98.28	93.92	91.80	86.59	89.12	0.4987

4.4. Comparison of Dementia Prediction Methods

We evaluated the performance of numerous ML-based automated diagnostic systems that were proposed by researchers in the literature for dementia prediction. Table 6 summarizes the performance of previously proposed ML-based approaches for dementia prediction along with our proposed model. Compared with the recently proposed models such as F. A. Salem et al. [14], F. G. Gutierrez et al. [16], G. Mirzaei and H. Adeli [18], and A. Shahzad et al. [19] and A. Javeed et al. (2022) [32], our newly developed model (FEB-SVM) performed considerably better.

Table 6. Comparison of classification accuracies with previously proposed methods for dementia prediction.

Study (Year)	Method	Accuracy (%)	Balancing
P. C. Cho and W. H. Chen (2012) [33]	PNNs	83.00	No
P. Gurevich et al. (2017) [34]	SVM	89.00	Yes
D. Stamate et al. (2018) [35]	Gradient Boosting	88.00	Yes
Visser et al. (2019) [36]	XGBoost+ RF	88.00	No
Dallora et al. (2020) [15]	DT	74.50	Yes
M. Karaglani et al. (2020) [37]	RF	84.60	No
E. Ryzhikova et al. (2021) [38]	ANN + SVM	84.00	No
F. A. Salem et al. (2021) [14]	RF	88.00	Yes
F. G. Gutierrez et al. (2022) [16]	GA	84.00	No
G. Mirzaei and H. Adeli (2022) [18]	MLP	70.32	No
A. Shahzad et al. (2022) [19]	SVM	71.67	No
A. Javeed et al. (2022) [32]	Autoencoder + Adaboost	90.23	Yes
Proposed Model (2023)	FEB + SVM	93.92	Yes

5. Conclusions

In this study, we addressed the problems of low accuracy and bias in ML models for dementia prediction, which researchers in the recent past have raised. Unfortunately, dementia is a rare, occurring disease, so classes in the dementia datasets are significantly imbalanced, causing bias in ML models. Therefore, we deployed the adaptive synthetic sampling (ADASYN) technique to resolve this issue. For improved accuracy, we proposed a novel feature extraction (FEB) method that extracts the valuable features from the dataset so that the proposed model would not learn the noisy features from the dataset and avoid model overfitting problems. The feature extraction (FEB) module extracts 9 features from the dataset, comprising 75 features. The FEB helps to improve the accuracy and reduce the computational complexity of the proposed model. For classification purposes, SVM is deployed with different kernel functions, and hyperparameters of the SVM are fine-tuned using a grid research algorithm. From the experimental results, it is evident that the proposed model (FEB-SVM) improved the performance of conventional SVM by 6% for dementia prediction. Moreover, the proposed model outperformed the 12 recently proposed models based on ML for dementia prediction, which the researchers presented. However, the proposed method (SVM-FEB) has significant shortcomings that the researchers must overcome. The newly proposed FEB's constructed features cannot help identify the features causing dementia in older persons because the newly generated FEB is based on feature extraction techniques. Therefore, new methods should be proposed in the future for identifying the features that cause dementia problems based on feature selection algorithms [39]. Furthermore, a machine learning model based on meta-heuristics and deep learning should be built to improve dementia prediction accuracy.

Supplementary Materials: The following are available online at https://www.mdpi.com/article/10.3390/biomedicines11020439/s1, Table S1: List of the input variables with description, possible values and number of missing values. References [40–49] are cited in the Supplementary Materials.

Author Contributions: Conceptualization and validated by P.A.; data curation and formal analysis by A.L.D.; methodology and write up by A.J.; supervised by J.S.B. A.I. has validated the results, L.A. has provided the technical support and co-supervision, and the manuscript writing and proofreading are done by H.T.R. All authors have read and agreed to the published version of the manuscript.

Funding: This research received no external funding.

Institutional Review Board Statement: This study was carried out in accordance with the Declaration of Helsinki and was approved by the Research Ethics Committee at Blekinge Institute of Technology (BTH).

Informed Consent Statement: Written informed consent has been obtained from the patient(s) to publish this paper.

Data Availability Statement: Data can be available in Supplementary Materials.

Acknowledgments: The first author's learning process was supported by the National E-Infrastructure for Aging Research (NEAR), Sweden. NEAR is working on improving the health condition of older adults in Sweden.

Conflicts of Interest: The authors declare no conflict of interest.

References

1. Lo, R.Y. The borderland between normal aging and dementia. *Tzu-Chi Med. J.* **2017**, *29*, 65. [CrossRef] [PubMed]
2. Vrijsen, J.; Matulessij, T.; Joxhorst, T.; de Rooij, S.E.; Smidt, N. Knowledge, health beliefs and attitudes towards dementia and dementia risk reduction among the Dutch general population: A cross-sectional study. *BMC Public Health* **2021**, *21*, 857. [CrossRef] [PubMed]
3. Who. Dementia. Available online: https://www.who.int/news-room/fact-sheets/detail/dementia (accessed on 21 December 2022).
4. Duchesne, S.; Caroli, A.; Geroldi, C.; Barillot, C.; Frisoni, G.B.; Collins, D.L. MRI-based automated computer classification of probable AD versus normal controls. *IEEE Trans. Med. Imaging* **2008**, *27*, 509–520. [CrossRef] [PubMed]
5. Lai, C.L.; Lin, R.T.; Liou, L.M.; Liu, C.K. The role of event-related potentials in cognitive decline in Alzheimer's disease. *Clin. Neurophysiol.* **2010**, *121*, 194–199. [CrossRef]
6. Patel, T.; Polikar, R.; Davatzikos, C.; Clark, C.M. EEG and MRI data fusion for early diagnosis of Alzheimer's disease. In Proceedings of the 2008 30th Annual International Conference of the IEEE Engineering in Medicine and Biology Society, Vancouver, BC, Canada, 20–25 August 2008; pp. 1757–1760.
7. Patnode, C.D.; Perdue, L.A.; Rossom, R.C.; Rushkin, M.C.; Redmond, N.; Thomas, R.G.; Lin, J.S. Screening for cognitive impairment in older adults: Updated evidence report and systematic review for the US Preventive Services Task Force. *JAMA* **2020**, *323*, 764–785. [CrossRef]
8. Javeed, A.; Rizvi, S.S.; Zhou, S.; Riaz, R.; Khan, S.U.; Kwon, S.J. Heart risk failure prediction using a novel feature selection method for feature refinement and neural network for classification. *Mob. Inf. Syst.* **2020**, *2020*, 884315. [CrossRef]
9. Javeed, A.; Zhou, S.; Yongjian, L.; Qasim, I.; Noor, A.; Nour, R. An intelligent learning system based on random search algorithm and optimized random forest model for improved heart disease detection. *IEEE Access* **2019**, *7*, 180235–180243. [CrossRef]
10. Javeed, A.; Khan, S.U.; Ali, L.; Ali, S.; Imrana, Y.; Rahman, A. Machine learning-based automated diagnostic systems developed for heart failure prediction using different types of data modalities: A systematic review and future directions. *Comput. Math. Methods Med.* **2022**, *2022*, 9288452. [CrossRef]
11. Ali, L.; Zhu, C.; Golilarz, N.A.; Javeed, A.; Zhou, M.; Liu, Y. Reliable Parkinson's disease detection by analyzing handwritten drawings: Construction of an unbiased cascaded learning system based on feature selection and adaptive boosting model. *IEEE Access* **2019**, *7*, 116480–116489. [CrossRef]
12. Akbar, W.; Wu, W.-p.; Saleem, S.; Farhan, M.; Saleem, M.A.; Javeed, A.; Ali, L. Development of Hepatitis Disease Detection System by Exploiting Sparsity in Linear Support Vector Machine to Improve Strength of AdaBoost Ensemble Model. *Mob. Inf. Syst.* **2020**, *2020*, 8870240. [CrossRef]
13. Javeed, A.; Ali, L.; Mohammed Seid, A.; Ali, A.; Khan, D.; Imrana, Y. A Clinical Decision Support System (CDSS) for Unbiased Prediction of Caesarean Section Based on Features Extraction and Optimized Classification. *Comput. Intell. Neurosci.* **2022**, *2022*, 1901735. [CrossRef] [PubMed]
14. Salem, F.A.; Chaaya, M.; Ghannam, H.; Al Feel, R.E.; El Asmar, K. Regression based machine learning model for dementia diagnosis in a community setting. *Alzheimers Dement.* **2021**, *17*, e053839. [CrossRef]
15. Dallora, A.L.; Minku, L.; Mendes, E.; Rennemark, M.; Anderberg, P.; Sanmartin Berglund, J. Multifactorial 10-year prior diagnosis prediction model of dementia. *Int. J. Environ. Res. Public Health* **2020**, *17*, 6674. [CrossRef] [PubMed]
16. Garcia-Gutierrez, F.; Delgado-Alvarez, A.; Delgado-Alonso, C.; Díaz-Álvarez, J.; Pytel, V.; Valles-Salgado, M.; Gil, M.J.; Hernández-Lorenzo, L.; Matías-Guiu, J.; Ayala, J.L.; et al. Diagnosis of Alzheimer's disease and behavioural variant frontotemporal dementia with machine learning-aided neuropsychological assessment using feature engineering and genetic algorithms. *Int. J. Geriatr. Psychiatry* **2022**, *5667*. [CrossRef]
17. Mirzaei, G.; Adeli, H. Machine learning techniques for diagnosis of alzheimer disease, mild cognitive disorder, and other types of dementia. *Biomed. Signal Process. Control* **2022**, *72*, 103293. [CrossRef]
18. Hsiu, H.; Lin, S.K.; Weng, W.L.; Hung, C.M.; Chang, C.K.; Lee, C.C.; Chen, C.T. Discrimination of the Cognitive Function of Community Subjects Using the Arterial Pulse Spectrum and Machine-Learning Analysis. *Sensors* **2022**, *22*, 806. [CrossRef]
19. Shahzad, A.; Dadlani, A.; Lee, H.; Kim, K. Automated Prescreening of Mild Cognitive Impairment Using Shank-Mounted Inertial Sensors Based Gait Biomarkers. *IEEE Access* **2022**, *10*, 15835. [CrossRef]
20. World Health Organization *Dementia: A Public Health Priority*; World Health Organization: Geneva, Switzerland, 2012.
21. Lagergren, M.; Fratiglioni, L.; Hallberg, I.R.; Berglund, J.; Elmstahl, S.; Hagberg, B.; Holst, G.; Rennemark, M.; Sjolund, B.M.; Thorslund, M.; et al. A longitudinal study integrating population, care and social services data. The Swedish National study on Aging and Care (SNAC). *Aging Clin. Exp. Res.* **2004**, *16*, 158–168. [CrossRef]
22. Nunes, B.; Silva, R.D.; Cruz, V.T.; Roriz, J.M.; Pais, J.; Silva, M.C. Prevalence and pattern of cognitive impairment in rural and urban populations from Northern Portugal. *BMC Neurol.* **2010**, *10*, 42. [CrossRef]

23. Killin, L.O.; Starr, J.M.; Shiue, I.J.; Russ, T.C. Environmental risk factors for dementia: A systematic review. *BMC Geriatr.* **2016**, *16*, 175. [CrossRef]
24. Yu, J.T.; Xu, W.; Tan, C.C.; Andrieu, S.; Suckling, J.; Evangelou, E.; Pan, A.; Zhang, C.; Jia, J.; Feng, L.; et al. Evidence-based prevention of Alzheimer's disease: Systematic review and meta-analysis of 243 observational prospective studies and 153 randomised controlled trials. *J. Neurol. Neurosurg. Psychiatry* **2020**, *91*, 1201–1209. [CrossRef] [PubMed]
25. Arvanitakis, Z.; Shah, R.C.; Bennett, D.A. Diagnosis and management of dementia. *JAMA* **2019**, *322*, 1589–1599. [CrossRef] [PubMed]
26. Zhang, S. Nearest neighbor selection for iteratively kNN imputation. *J. Syst. Softw.* **2012**, *85*, 2541–2552. [CrossRef]
27. Loughrey, J.; Cunningham, P. Overfitting in wrapper-based feature subset selection: The harder you try the worse it gets. In Proceedings of the International Conference on Innovative Techniques and Applications of Artificial Intelligence, 13 December 2004; Springer: Cambridge, UK, 2004; pp. 33–43.
28. Pourtaheri, Z.K.; Zahiri, S.H. Ensemble classifiers with improved overfitting. In Proceedings of the 2016 1st Conference on Swarm Intelligence and Evolutionary Computation (CSIEC), Bam, Iran, 9–11 March 2016; pp. 93–97.
29. Alpaydin, E. *Introduction to Machine Learning*; MIT Press: Cambridge, MA, USA, 2020.
30. He, H.; Bai, Y.; Garcia, E.A.; Li, S. ADASYN: Adaptive synthetic sampling approach for imbalanced learning. In Proceedings of the 2008 IEEE International Joint Conference on Neural Networks (IEEE World Congress on computational Intelligence), Hong Kong, China, 1–8 June 2008; pp. 1322–1328.
31. Cortes, C.; Vapnik, V. Support-vector networks. *Mach. Learn.* **1995**, *20*, 273–297. [CrossRef]
32. Javeed, A.; Dallora, A.L.; Berglund, J.S.; Anderberg, P. An Intelligent Learning System for Unbiased Prediction of Dementia Based on Autoencoder and Adaboost Ensemble Learning. *Life* **2022**, *12*, 1097. [CrossRef] [PubMed]
33. Cho, P.C.; Chen, W.H. A double layer dementia diagnosis system using machine learning techniques. In Proceedings of the International Conference on Engineering Applications of Neural Networks, London, UK, 20–23 September 2012; pp. 402–412.
34. Gurevich, P.; Stuke, H.; Kastrup, A.; Stuke, H.; Hildebrandt, H. Neuropsychological testing and machine learning distinguish Alzheimer's disease from other causes for cognitive impairment. *Front. Aging Neurosci.* **2017**, *9*, 114. [CrossRef] [PubMed]
35. Stamate, D.; Alghamdi, W.; Ogg, J.; Hoile, R.; Murtagh, F. A machine learning framework for predicting dementia and mild cognitive impairment. In Proceedings of the 2018 17th IEEE International Conference on Machine Learning and Applications (ICMLA), Orlando, FL, USA, 17–20 December 2018; pp. 671–678.
36. Visser, P.J.; Lovestone, S.; Legido-Quigley, C. *A metabolite-Based Machine Learning Approach to Diagnose Alzheimer-Type Dementia in Blood: Results from the European Medical Information Framework for Alzheimer Disease Biomarker Discovery Cohort*; Wiley Online Library: Hoboken, NJ, USA, 2019.
37. Karaglani, M.; Gourlia, K.; Tsamardinos, I.; Chatzaki, E. Accurate blood-based diagnostic biosignatures for Alzheimer's disease via automated machine learning. *J. Clin. Med.* **2020**, *9*, 3016. [CrossRef]
38. Ryzhikova, E.; Ralbovsky, N.M.; Sikirzhytski, V.; Kazakov, O.; Halamkova, L.; Quinn, J.; Zimmerman, E.A.; Lednev, I.K. Raman spectroscopy and machine learning for biomedical applications: Alzheimer's disease diagnosis based on the analysis of cerebrospinal fluid. *Spectrochim. Acta Part A Mol. Biomol. Spectrosc.* **2021**, *248*, 119188. [CrossRef]
39. Javeed, A.; Dallora, A.L.; Berglund, J.S; Arif, A.A; Liaqata, L.; Anderberg, P. Machine Learning for Dementia Prediction: A Systematic Review and Future Research Directions. *J Med Syst.* **2023**, *47*, 1573. [CrossRef]
40. Antonovsky, A. The structure and properties of the sense of coherence scale. *Soc. Sci. Med.* **1993**, *36*, 725–733. [CrossRef]
41. Wechsler, D. *WAIS-III Administration and Scoring Manual*; The Psychological Corporation: San Antonio, TX, USA, 1997.
42. Livingston, G.; Blizard, B.; Mann, A. Does sleep disturbance predict depression in elderly people? A study in inner London. *Br. J. Gen. Pract.* **1993**, *43*, 445–448. [PubMed]
43. Brooks, R.; Group, E. EuroQol: The current state of play. *Health Policy* **1996**, *37*, 53–72. [CrossRef] [PubMed]
44. Katz, S. Assessing Self-maintenance: Activities of Daily Living, Mobility, and Instrumental Activities of Daily Living. *J. Am. Geriatr. Soc.* **1983**, *31*, 721–727. [CrossRef] [PubMed]
45. Lawton, M.P.; Brody, E.M. Assessment of Older People: Self-Maintaining and Instrumental Activities of Daily Living. *Gerontologist* **1969**, *9*, 179–186._Part_1.179. [CrossRef] [PubMed]
46. Folstein, M.F.; Folstein, S.E.; McHugh, P.R. "Mini-Mental State". A Practical Method for Grading the Cognitive State of Patients for the Clinician. *J. Psychiatr. Res.* **1975**, *12*, 189–198. [CrossRef] [PubMed]
47. Agrell, B.; Dehlin, O. The clock-drawing test. *Age Ageing* **1998**, *27*, 399–403. [CrossRef]
48. Jenkinson, C.; Layte R. Development and testing of the UK SF-12 (short form health survey). *J. Health Serv. Res. Policy* **1997**, *2*, 14–18. [CrossRef] [PubMed]
49. Montgomery, S.A.; Åsberg, M. A New Depression Scale Designed to be Sensitive to Change. *Br. J. Psychiatry* **1979**, *134*, 382–389. [CrossRef]

biomedicines MDPI

Article

Computer-Aided Early Melanoma Brain-Tumor Detection Using Deep-Learning Approach

Rimsha Asad [1,2,†], Saif ur Rehman [2], Azhar Imran [3,†], Jianqiang Li [1], Abdullah Almuhaimeed [4,*] and Abdulkareem Alzahrani [5]

[1] School of Software Engineering, Beijing University of Technology, Beijing 100124, China
[2] University Institute of Information Technology, PMAS-Arid Agriculture University, Rawalpindi 46000, Pakistan
[3] Department of Creative Technologies, Air University, Islamabad 42000, Pakistan
[4] Digital Health Institute, King Abdulaziz City for Science and Technology, Riyadh 11442, Saudi Arabia
[5] Faculty of Computer Science and Information Technology, Al Baha University, Al Baha 65779, Saudi Arabia
* Correspondence: muhaimed@kacst.edu.sa
† These authors contributed equally to this work.

Abstract: Brain tumors affect the normal functioning of the brain and if not treated in time these cancerous cells may affect the other tissues, blood vessels, and nerves surrounding these cells. Today, a large population worldwide is affected by the precarious disease of the brain tumor. Healthy tissues of the brain are suspected to be damaged because of tumors that become the most significant reason for a large number of deaths nowadays. Therefore, their early detection is necessary to prevent patients from unfortunate mishaps resulting in loss of lives. The manual detection of brain tumors is a challenging task due to discrepancies in appearance in terms of shape, size, nucleus, etc. As a result, an automatic system is required for the early detection of brain tumors. In this paper, the detection of tumors in brain cells is carried out using a deep convolutional neural network with stochastic gradient descent (SGD) optimization algorithm. The multi-classification of brain tumors is performed using the ResNet-50 model and evaluated on the public Kaggle brain-tumor dataset. The method achieved 99.82% and 99.5% training and testing accuracy, respectively. The experimental result indicates that the proposed model outperformed baseline methods, and provides a compelling reason to be applied to other diseases.

Keywords: medical imagery; brain tumor; convolutional neural network; deep learning; feature extraction

Citation: Asad, R.; Rehman, S.u.; Imran, A.; Li, J.; Almuhaimeed, A.; Alzahrani, A. Computer-Aided Early Melanoma Brain-Tumor Detection Using Deep-Learning Approach. *Biomedicines* **2023**, *11*, 184. https://doi.org/10.3390/biomedicines11010184

Academic Editors: Wu Qiu, Hulin Kuang and Alejandro Speck-Planche

Received: 26 October 2022
Revised: 6 January 2023
Accepted: 9 January 2023
Published: 11 January 2023

1. Introduction

In any living organism, cells are the main ingredient that makes up life. Cells are comprised of a cell membrane, a nucleus, and the third component, cytoplasm [1], which is the most complex organism in human beings. It is fabricated of a significant number of cells, and each of them differs in morphology. In the human body, cells continuously grow and divide in tissues. On reaching the stage of maturity, cells stop growing further and start performing their functions properly. They kill themselves when cells become damaged or their life span is completed. Due to metabolic disorders, cellular anxiety, and pathogenic incursion, cells may die during the span of development. Tissues contain natural killer cells [2], which perform such activities. These events are performed through a well-defined process known as programmed cell death (PCD) [3]. Mainly, three routes are considered under PCD for carrying out the tasks of the disposal of cells that are at risk. These paths include: pyroptosis, apoptosis, and necroptosis. The very first programmed cell death is apoptosis [4]. All of these processes are capable of sensing irritation and responding to inflammatory responses against the immune system by discharging immunostimulatory particles. Each of them is deployed with different consequences because all of them include discrete molecular processes. Those brain cells that are not proficient enough to perform phases of their life cycle in a normal fashion, form a brain tumor. Figure 1 depicts the structure of a cell. A core part of the cell is the nucleus surrounded by fluid. The exterior boundary of cells is covered by a protective sheet known as a membrane. An inside cell contains different micro-organelles including mitochondria, ribosomes, cytoplasm, DNA, etc.

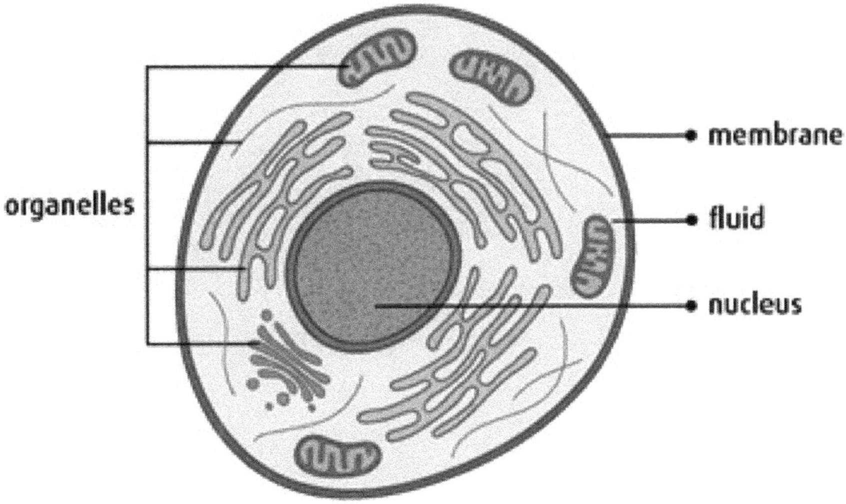

Figure 1. The cell.

The most complex organ of the human body is the brain. It controls the whole body, including our sentiments, opinions, moods, temperature, motor action, starvation, etc. It helps all the organs of the body to coordinate [5] appropriately in order to execute their functions. At the central end of the human body, the brain is composed of a significant number of of nerve tissues. The weight of the human brain is around 3 pounds. Approximately 60% of the brain is fat and the remaining 40% is a blend of protein, salts, water, and glucose. The brain is the main part of the central nervous system. The structure of the brain includes the brainstem, cerebellum, and forehead [6]. The brain is comprised of grey and white matter, as shown in Figure 2. The cerebrum, cerebellum, and medulla oblongata are parts of the brain. The largest fragment is the cerebrum, the cerebellum is the next largest fragment, and then the medulla.

The exterior portion, which is dark in colour and is comprised of neurons, is denoted as grey matter. White matter refers to the innermost light portion, which mainly contains axons. Sometimes, this grey matter is also denoted as the cerebral cortex. The purposeful hiearcrhy of the brain extends straight from the "uni-modal sensory cortex" into the "trans-modal association cortex" [7]. Different parts of the brain are involved in the process of memorization. Three phases are included in memorization. First is encoding, where memory is built up for any event. The second is storing a particular event in the short-term memory. Third is recalling, during which a certain event is moved from short to long-term memory. There are trillions of cells in the brain. Brain cells are known as neurons. Neurons are the chief module of the nervous system. Neurons are comprised of: sensory neurons, motor, and interneurons. They accept and transmute information from and to the brain from all parts of the body in the form of signals, as shown in Figure 3. Information from sensory receptor cells is carried from the body to the brain by sensory neurons. Then, brain information is carried to the muscles by motor neurons. Meanwhile, information between the remaining neurons of the body is transmuted through interneurons. Only one axon of a neuron, with an extensive tail-like structure, carries the nerve impulse in the form of electric signals from the body. Dendrites can be of more than one type, and accepts signals from axons.

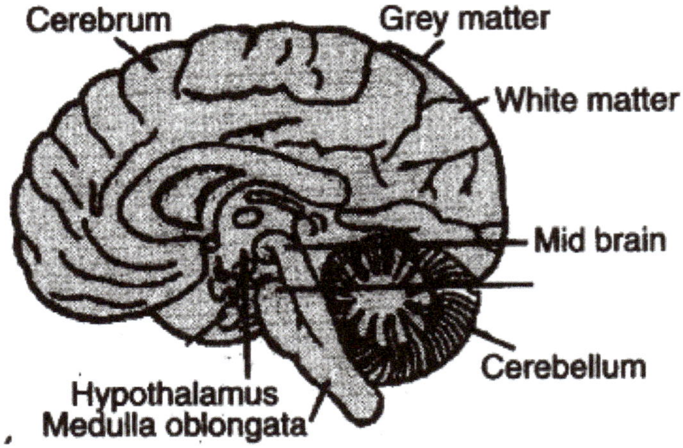

Figure 2. Structure of brain.

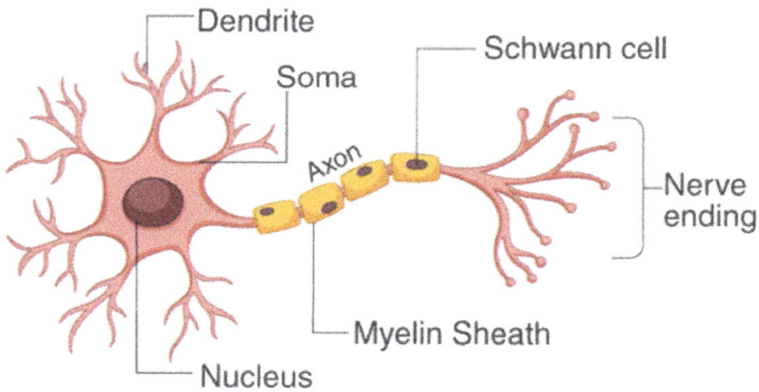

Figure 3. Structure of neuron.

The frame of abnormal tissues, when grouped, forms into tumor. Skin, muscles, secretory organs and different body parts have the chance to be affected by a tumor. These tumors are classified into two main types, as depicted in Figure 4. One is malignant, which is cancerous. Another is benign, noncancerous [8]. Each of these tumors varies in its treatment. Therefore, before preliminary action, first of all, it is necessry to recognize the type.

Benign tumors remain at one location. They grow at these sites without changing their positions. They do not harm cells that reside near them. They are not dangerous. Once this type of tumor is disposed of, they have no chance of returning. On the other hand, malignant tumors do not reside in one location. They tend to continuously change their position along with their growth. These cells are dangerous, as they are cancerous. They harm other cells near them by invading. Therefore, they need to be treated to control them. They are treated through immunotherapy or chemotherapy [9].

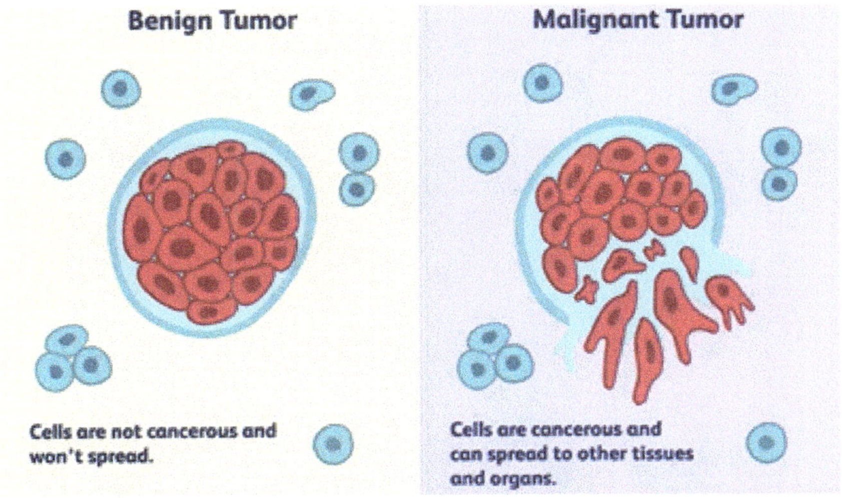

Figure 4. Types of tumor.

When cells abnormally grow in the brain, they form a brain tumor. Symptoms of these tumors vary according to their size and location. Sites for the occurrence of tumors in brains include cranial nerves, meninges (membranes), pineal secretory organs, and pituitary secretors. Risk factors for brain tumors may vary. When tumors from skin cells spread to the brain, this is known as a melanoma brain tumor. Studies have revealed that some environmental reasons may pave the way for triggering tumors in the brain. Out of these, air pollution is one reason [10]. People who are exposed to radiation at their jobs have higher chances of suffering from a brain tumor. Genetic variation is another reason for its occurrence. About 5–10 percent of people with this disease are those who have a family history of brain tumors. The most important categories of tumor include: the skin, lungs, and breast, which may spread to the brain, triggering a tumor there. In 2021, around 84,000 individuals were detected to have a primary brain tumor. About 120 variants of this primary brain tumor exist. Out of them, one-third of tumors are cancerous (malignant). Tumors can be detected at any age group. In the US, more than 28,000 children are detected as having this hazardous disease. Due to primary brain tumors, approximately 18,000 persons died [11]. Figure 5 illustrate the shape and size of a tumor and how they start growing on a mass of tissues.

The field of artificial intelligence which enables machines to see is known as computer vision (CV). CV enables machines to distinguish visual stimuli clearly [12]. These machines then process and interpret digital multimedia images and videos. After interpreting images, information is extracted to make certain decisions. Components of CV are: machines for the interpretation of scenes, a camera for capturing images, and lighting effects for illumination to better recognize objects. This CV trains machines to perform object detection through image processing. Training such a machine requires a lot of data because computer machines work consistently and make objective decisions only. CV has flourished in every field, from medical to digital marketing. The list of the various applications of CV includes road-traffic administration and self-propelled driver aid, industrial robotics and scrutiny in semiconductor unit engineering, simultaneous visualization for medical applications, and eye and head tracking for purchaser investigation [13]. Much work on CV in the field of medical science has been carried out using deep-learning techniques [11]. Some tasks that come under CV are the classification of images, detection of objects, tracking objects, and retrieving content-based images. CV uses certain algorithms to train machines on a large set of data. After training, digital images are passed on. Machines train themselves to learn by extracting information from images. Later the objects are classified on the basis of feature extraction. Figure 6 demonstrates the tasks of the classification, detection, and segmentation of images. It shows how the trained model has worked by passing images of cats and dogs to it. Digital images are processed successfully by classifying and detecting these objects by extracting their features.

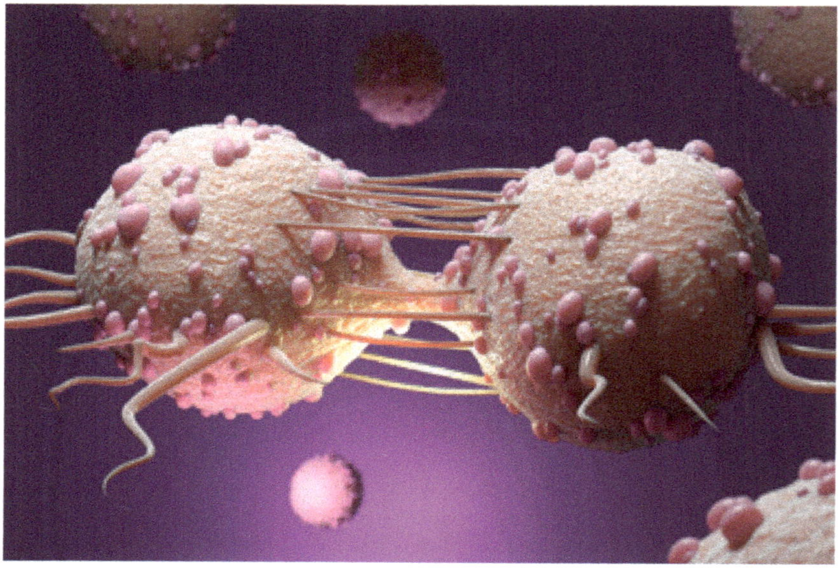

Figure 5. Shape of tumor.

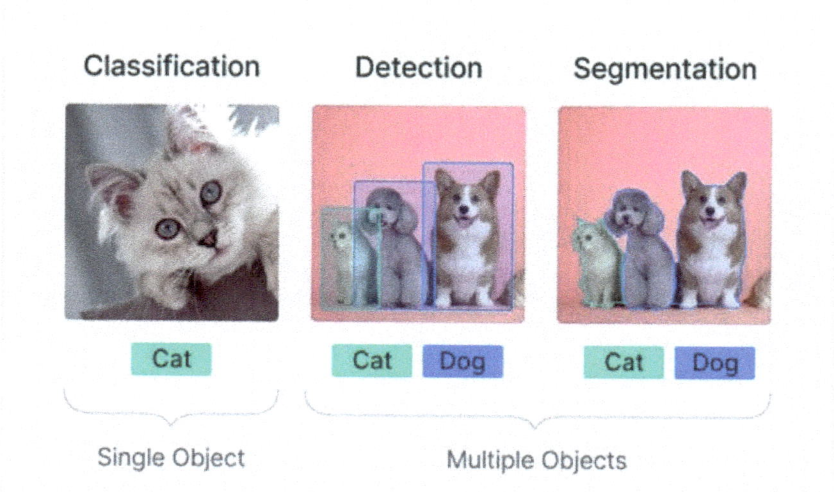

Figure 6. Tasks of computer vision.

Deep learning (DL) is a sub-field of artificial intelligence. It enables computational models to acquire knowledge and expand their ability to work like humans. It has multiple layers for providing abstraction and retrieving information [8]. DL is a central component of data science, including analytical modelling with facts and figures. It helps data scientists who need to carry out the tasks of collecting useful insights from huge datasets. Utilizing a huge number of datasets, deep learning achieves the best performance and accuracy [5]. It also makes the procedure of examining data effective and easier. A predominantly convolutional neural network (CNN) is implemented for the acknowledgement of patterns [14]. CNN assists in the understanding of digital images. CNN breaks down images into picture elements and allocates tabs and markers to them. Then, it classifies objects by training models based on these markers. Figure 7 shows the working of machine learning (ML) vs deep learning (DL). Utilizing ML techniques for recognizing tumors in the brain accurately is a complicated job [15,16]. For identifying features, ML techniques are deployed [17].

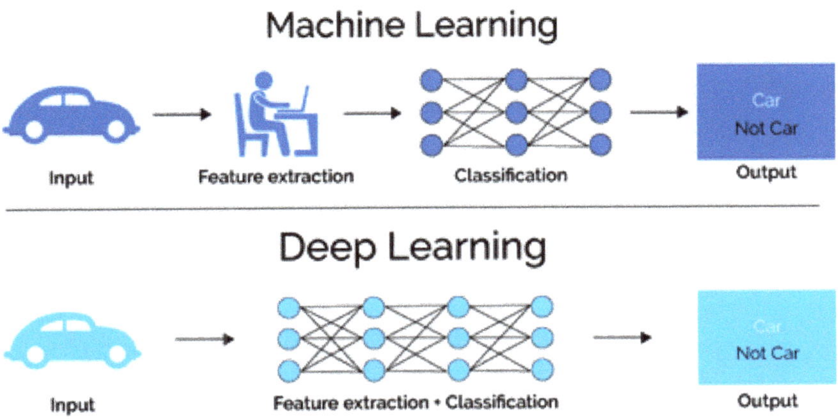

Figure 7. Working on deep-learning model.

The physical sorting of brain-tumor MR images with similar structures or presences is a problematic and challenging task [18]. Using different imagery procedures, irregular changes in tissues of brain cells are identified at an early stage from "computed tomography (CT)" scans and "magnetic resonance imaging (MRI)" [9]. Along with the CT scan, the X-ray technique also helps in the examination [19]. MRI images are classified into grey and white matter after detection [7].

The main contribution of this study includes the detection and classification of brain tumors using a deep-learning-based convolutional neural network with an SGD optimization algorithm. Most of the previous studies have implemented CNN on a smaller dataset; while the proposed method is evaluated on a larger public dataset comprising three datasets (figshare, SARTAJ, and Br35H). The transfer-learning-based ResNet-50 is employed to extract features from MRI scan images. The detection and classification of these images are performed efficiently with better accuracy and performance using the SGD classifier with CNN. This combination of classifiers has made it possible to achieve 99.82% training accuracy and 99.5% testing accuracy using a deep convolutional neural network with stochastic gradient descent (SGD) optimization algorithm.

The rest of this paper is organized as follows. Section 2 contains the literature review on brain-tumor detection and a comprehensive analysis of other related work. Section 3 includes the proposed methodology, process for the detection and classification of tumors, as well as the proposed framework. Section 4 presents experiments and results which will contain the experimental analysis and discussion, followed by a conclusion and future work in Section 5.

2. Literature Review

This section highlights that detecting tumors of the brain with the help of machine-learning and deep-learning algorithms is an ongoing research area. A lot of work has already been carried out and researchers are continuously completing studies to improve this progress. The segmentation of the brain constitutes [10] a crucial part in medical training and exploration setting. A 3D deep neural algorithm based on networks was proposed for finding infected cells in the brain. Segmentation within the cells of tumors was achieved together with edema, mortification, non-magnified, and magnified tumors using MRI images. A collection of cascaded U-Nets was designed for the recognition of tumors. Along with this, Deep-CNN was made for patch-based segmentation within tumor cells. This model was used to learn the position of tumors in the brain before segmentation. The proposed model used the "BraTS-2017" challenge database as a dataset, which consisted of 285 trained subjects, 146 subjects for testing, and 46 subjects for validation. Four sequences of MRI images were made which were used by each of these subjects. These sequences include T1, T2, T1C, and FLAIR. The resolution of all the MRI data images used was set to comprehensible. Before detection, a ground-truth table was pre-processed. Using segmentation, four classes of intra-tumours were identified through the ground-truth table. depicts how the two different scales of cascaded U-Nets were used to perform the proposed work. Datasets consisted of three up-sampled and two down-sampled blocks. Using the proposed algorithm on the data set of BraTS 2017, a Dice-similarity coefficient of 0.81, 0.69 and 0.55 was achieved. The limitation of the proposed algorithm is that the machine-learning algorithm used encountered generation difficulties when they were encountered by a new dataset. Problems with deep models cause decreased performance on validation and test datasets. The class imbalance used in the dataset was another problem faced by deep models.

Sharif et al.'s recent work [20] was carried out using many procedures for classifying brain tumors using different computer-aided methods. However, the low accuracy produced by these applied methods was a significant concern. For the classification of a multi-brain tumor, a new computerized deep-learning model was proposed. That model deals with major issues encountered during classification, which include: the resemblance between different types of tumor, a highly dimensional dataset, and using a smaller number of attributes for feature extraction. The deep-learning model was applied without any pre-processing of data. The already-trained deep-learning model "Densenet201" was used and later trained for the proposed work using "deep-transfer learning". An imbalanced dataset was used for directing training. An approach known as "Entropy–Kurtosis-based High Feature Values" was used for extracting features and the KNN was applied to hand pick the best feature out of them. Using standard deviation, the "Modified Genetic Algorithm (MGA)" was also used for picking the best features. That was carried out by finding the Euclidean distance of each attribute in the dataset. Mutation and cross-over were applied, in case the best-fit criteria was not met. Redundancy was detached from the dataset later on. After feature extraction, at the final stage, support vector machine (SVM) was utilized to research the classification of multi-class brain tumors. To reduce the computational cost of the entire work and take out information from the images in the dataset, a convolutional neural network (CNN) was utilized. From the CNN, two layers were removed and a new fully connected layer was introduced which consisted of four major kinds of brain tumor. BRATS 2018 and BRATS 2019 were two datasets used for directing this research because they are most useful for this field and are, additionally, projective. Both of them were reduced to the ratio of 50/50 for training and testing, respectively. The accuracy of BRATS 2018 was observed to be 99.7% and 98.8%, and for BRATS 2019 98.8% and 98.2% were noted. The accuracy of both of the datasets was improved as compared to their past performance. Still, some features can be considered to improve accuracy further.

Another work focused on the recognition of brain tumors in a transferable electromagnetic (EM) mental imagery system through a newly made "YOLOv3" model of the deep neural network [3]. Most often, the YOLOv3 model is utilized in recognizing objects with the best accuracy and with better quality speediness in computation. Using deep learning, the position of tumors in the head was perceived. For creating high-quality pixel imageries, a 3D portable, unidirectional, and compact imagery system with high bandwidth was cast-off. A deep neural network-based algorithm of YOLOv3 with a darknet-53 was utilized for programmed recognition of tumors in the brain with their position and bounding boxes in produced EM imageries. The Python program writing language with TensorFlow

API was used for employing the algorithm of YOLOv3. An improved algorithm of the "delay-multiply-and-sum" image processing system was used to create EM images of the head. Every single image in the dataset created had a pixel power of 416 × 416. Almost 50 sampled images from diverse situations were composed. Additionally, for creating the final dataset, an image-augmentation technique was utilized. This created a set of data that was used for the purpose of testing, training, and validation later on. The total number of sample images in the dataset was 1000, out of which 800 were utilized for training, 100 for validation, and the remaining one hundred for the purpose of testing. After considering diverse datasets, the performance of tumor detection was inspected. The observed F1-Score and accuracy that were achieved by the trained dataset were 94% and 95%, respectively. For experimenting with "Non-Maximum Suppression (NMS)," a well-known technique was applied to identify the bounding boxes of target objects in an image. The YOLOv3 model was passed out with training data for about 200 epochs with a learning rate of 0.001. Improved accuracy with reduced validation loss was detected with the alteration in learning rate during the experiment. Thus, the applied model proved effective in recognizing diverse brain tumors which were dissimilar in their form and dimensions.

In another research work, the technique of deep learning was used to find a well-known kind of tumor known as a "Glioma" [21]. When comparing "low-grade glioma (LGG)" and "high-grade glioma (HGG)" the most serious and dangerous is HGG. MRIs proved beneficial for recognizing such forms of tumor in the brain region. Recent work performed was patch-based. Its limitation was that it takes more computational cost and also there is the chance of loss of information from the images. In this work, the segmentation and recognition of tumors in the head section were carried out using the feature-based extraction technique of deep learning. For enhancing the image quality taken for identifying tumor sections "Pixel Increase along with Limit (PIaL)" was used. The extraction of features from the images for segmentation was performed via a novel "Standard Balanced Digital Link (SBDL)". After feature extraction, the best and finest attributes were found by applying the "Particle Swarm Optimization (PSO)" algorithm. After finding the optimal set of features, classification was performed. For the experiment inception, the V3 pre-trained model of deep learning was modified. Improvement in imageries in the dataset was achieved using the contrast-stretching technique. It was carried out to enhance the visibility of the target area in images, so that tumors could be recognized. The dataset used for the experiment was divided into two phases. In the first phase, segmentation was performed using the SBDL approach on the dataset of BRATS 2017 and BRATS 2018. Meanwhile, in the second phase, the classification technique was applied to BRATS 2013–2014 and BRATS 2017–2018. Both phases resulted in diverse accuracies and performances on the dataset used for validation. An experiment was conducted on the toolbox Matconvnet environment of deep learning using MATLAB 2018. The error rate for both datasets was different for selected optimal features. The accuracy achieved was more than 92% for classification. The inclusive consequences demonstrate that the presented approach is state of the art for both the arrangement and subdivision of brain tumors.

Recently, a lot of work has been carried out on the discovery of brain tumors. These works range from single-based analyses up to the techniques for image processing for finding the solution to eradicating the propagation of this disease. A vigorous technique known as image processing [22] was applied for the recognition and segmentation of tumors in the brain. The applied methodology used was to first segment past images of brain tumors and then to detect them. MRI images are used to obtain the final outcome. In phase one, these MRI imageries are first pre-processed. Then, those images are passed through a further algorithm to complete the task. The technique applied for classifying the picture element of an image is image segmentation. After obtaining pixel information, feature extraction was performed to obtain the optimal attributes of the images. For that purpose, "Discrete Wavelet Transform (DWT)" was applied. Later, to identify the performance of the algorithm, "Support Vector Machine (SVM)" was utilized. Pre-processing was performed so that each image in the dataset had the same dimension. During this, the processed image was first converted to grayscale. It becomes easier to fetch the characteristics from such images, as in RGB images, pixel color can act as noise. Resized grayscale images are converted into a binary representation. Later on, the technique of image segmentation was performed so that each image had its own unique attributes. An unsupervised technique known as K-means clustering was applied to segment the target objects in images into regions. Next, feature extraction was performed on the used dataset of MRI images. Seven key attributes that were fetched include energy, kurtosis, skewness, contrast, smoothness and RMS. Based on these features, SVM was applied to classify the tumors into benign and non-cancerous tumors. The study successfully showed that SVM is robust in the classification of tumors in the brain. Through it, the calculated performance comes out with an accuracy of 94.6%.

Özyurt et al. focused on finding brain tumors through super-resolution (SR) [23], which has been a challenging problem recently for too many years. Image pixel quality is enhanced through super-resolution. Using it for MRI images made it helpful for extracting useful information from images by making them more observable and vibrant. Therefore, through their borders, tumors in images will become more visible so that a tumor can be easily recognized by further passing through an algorithmic process. They proposed the use of super-resolution with the fuzzy C-means clustering technique and using machine-learning algorithms for the identification of brain tumors. The proposed work was carried out using the "DICOT format MRI images". These images were transformed from having a lower pixel value into high-quality images through super-resolution. These images were then passed through image-processing techniques. Firstly, images were pre-processed. Later, for the extraction of features, the "SqueezeNet architecture" related to CNN was deployed. Segmented images coming out with the finest features after extraction were actually greyscaled images, which were converted from the RGB format during pre-processing. The dataset used included 50 malignant and 50 benign tumor images. These segmented images were then passed through an "extreme learning machine (ELM)" for classification. The "Cancer Genome Atlas Glioblastoma Multiform (TCGA-GBM) database" was used, which includes around 500 sampled images of diverse kinds of cancers collected worldwide. The performance and accuracy rate of the ELM model used for classification was based on the number of neurons that were present in its hidden layer. Along with the learning rate and activation function: "tribes", "sin", "sig", "radbas", "hardline", and "lin" was also considered. The most suitable activation function out of them in brain tumor identification was "sigmoid" and the total number of neurons was around 1500. The proposed model proved helpful in the identification and removal of a segmented tumor in the brain through the FCM-SR algorithm. The study also showed that the performance of the model with FCM-SR was 10% more than the previous work involving the detection of the same tumor with (FCM) only. The performance of the model was higher, with an achieved accuracy of 98.33%.

Some other work was carried out to detect asymmetrical tumors [24] in the brain, which is a difficult task. The proposed model was based on four phases, which include: fetching features, selecting the finest attribute for classification, positioning, and subdivision. MRI images, if used without pre-processing, can be noisy in different forms such as instability in compelling pitch loops and image procurement. For reducing such noisiness from images and improving pixel quality, a "homomorphic wavelet filter" was applied. After the phase of pre-processing, suitable attributes were fetched through a "non-dominated sorted genetic algorithm (NSGA)" using a pre-trained model, "Inception V3". These selected best attributes were, later on, passed on for classification. After that, slices of classified tumors weer passed to the YOLVO-V2 model to identify the position of the tumor area in the head section. After localization, images were passed on for segmentation of real tumor sections through the "McCulloch's Kapur" selective information approach. The applied technique was conducted using three dataset databases. The proposed technique was evaluated on datasets from BRATS 2018 to BRATS 2020. Each dataset included a diverse number of confined images. Utilizing these images, four experiments were performed.

Each came out with a different outcome. The second experiment achieved the result that the SVM classifier was the best in performance of all the used algorithms. After conducting the whole proposed research, it was found that ACC is the overall best classifier. Therefore, it was proved that, through this work, tumors were classified correctly. Prediction scores for all four phases were greater than 0.90. Tumor classification and segmentation were perfomred effectively. In the future, research conducted for the identification of tumors can be carried out through quantum-computation algorithms.

On the critical disease of brain tumors, Sharif et al. proposed a framework [25] for the identification of tumors at an early stage. According to him, if brain tumors are not treated early, the tumor may progress to a cancerous stage. Therefore, in this proposed research, at the initial phase, the "brain surface extraction (BSE)" approach was utilized to eliminate the skull. The imagery of that eliminated skull is then processed for the segmentation of tumors through the "particle swarm optimization (PSO)" technique. Pre-processed grayscale binary images are fed into the genetic algorithm (GA) for extracting optimal features for selection. Later, for classification, algorithms such as ANN, and SVM are used. Easily available databases of BRATS 2018 and RIDER were utilized for experimenting. The outcome was 99% performance with the proposed model. Another work that contributed to brain-tumor recognition used computer-vision techniques [26] along with machine-learning algorithms. The author proposed the computational framework because manually performing this task may be subject to human error during identification. The convolutional neural network deep-learning technique was used for this case, to obtain the best results. Two labels were used for the classification of the final result. One was "Tumor Detected" and another was "Tumor Not Detected". The dataset of MRI images was downloaded and unzipped to pass through the CNN model with three layered architectures. Keras and the library of TensorFlow were used to train the model for up to 35 epochs. Before finishing with the dataset, computer-vision techniques such as pre-processing, and extracting features were performed. After experimenting, the model worked accurately with a performance of 96.08%. Further, while identifying tumors in the brain, along with CNN, a neutrosophic set of rules can be used.

Visual interface systems [27] can easily classify images into the category of tumor or not tumor by visualizing brain waves efficiently. However, practically, it is a difficult task to deploy. Therefoer, the author proposed a novel framework to perform this task more precisely with higher performance. Motor images are used for this study utilizing "electroencephalography (EEG)" motion to make it work more practically and more accurately. A well-known predictor, "OPTICAL", was used with the long short-term memory (LSTM) algorithm of machine learning to obtain improved and enhanced images. To achieve a better performance, a regression-based approach is used along with an SVM classifier. The dataset used for performing the research was taken from two well-known databases. "BCI Competition IV" and "GigaDB" were the datasets. Through these, the OPTICAL predictor classified the motor images efficiently with better accuracy. The error rate observed during the experiment for both datasets was: 2.07 percent for the GigaDB database and 3.09% for the BCI Competition IV database.

In another work, it was mentioned that recent work focused on using surgical techniques for the treatment of tumors found in the brain. Therefore, they proposed a computational framework model of deep learning [15]. A newly proposed model of CNN known as "BrainMRNet" was utilized. The framework was built based on attention segments and a hypercolumn approach. BrainMRNet was utilized for pre-processing at an initial stage. Later on, the method of image augmentation was performed by an attention segment for each pre-processed image. Through this, important features from the image were fetched and then pass on to layers of the convolutional network. A hypercolumn approach of the BrainMRNet model fetched the important attributes from each layer of the network and maintained an array to store information. From the array, the finest and most optimal features were later selected. The dataset used for carrying out research was made up of easily available MRI imageries. These images were regarded as two labels. One is a normal image and the other included a tumor. Images were transformed into JPEG images. The conducted research depicts the comparison between the proposed model and old CNN models, which includes: VGG-16, GoogleNet, and AlexNet.

BrainMRNet model proved more effective in identifying tumors and came out with a performed accuracy of 96.05%.

Windisch et al. [28] focused on the advancement of previous methods used for brain-tumor recognition in a well-organized manner. They proposed a new approach known as the "correlation learning mechanism (CLM)". CLM, along with a convolution deep-learning network, trained the model for identification. CT-scanned images wee rused as the dataset. CNN was trained through a thresholding approach and an algorithm known as an artificial neural network (ANN). Around 64 squared fragments of CT brain images were used as input data. This dataset was taken from the Kaggle repository specially designed for carrying out experiments on brain-tumor identification. It includes images of CT scans for both healthy and normal patients. After the pre-processing of images, they were passed to the model. The tumor was detected successfully with the CLM model. Observed accuracy was 96 and with 95% recall and precision. For the detection of tumors in GLIOMAS, a newly created deep-learning framework is known as "DeepSeg" [29]. The BRATS 2019 dataset was used for segmentation and effectively proved the relative performance of applying a variety of deep-learning models.

A "hybrid manta ray foraging optimization" approach was proposed for selecting optimal features. CNN was deployed for the identification of tumors. The dataset consisted of (a) normal Images, (b) benign tumors, and (c) malignant tumors. A study was conducted to compare between existed models of machine learning and proved helpful in the recognition of tumors in the brain with better efficiency and accuracy. Another work used CNN, DNN, and KNN [30] for identifying tumors in the brain with high accuracy and with less computational cost. The same was carried out for predicting the accuracy of SVM in [31] and the model of a neural network in [32].

Table 1 summarizes the different research work suggested recently in the area of recognizing tumors in the brain. Each study depicts different results using different techniques, approaches, and their own created proposed model for carrying out their research. Diverse databases with MRI images as a dataset were utilized to conduct experiments. The most used database was found to be "BRATS". In addition, most of the classifiers observed for performing research were: SVM, ANN, CNN and PSO. Each algorithm came with different performances and accuracies. The final observation is to use a CNN deep-machine-learning classifier for identifying tumors, as it performs well in most of the studies giving fruitful results.

Table 1. Prediction algorithm as applied in EDM.

Ref.	Algorithm	Dataset	Results
[32]	3D deep neural network	BraTS 2017	Detected and segmented brain tumor into the core, whole, and magnified tumor with a coefficient of 0.69,0.81 & 0.55, respectively.
[33]	Modified genetic algorithm, support vector machine	BRATS 2018 & BRATS 2019	Classified the tumor with accuracy of 99.7% and 98.8% for BRATS 2018 and 99.8% and 99.3% for 2019.
[34]	Darknet-53 YOLOv3 algorithm (deep neural network-based)	MSCOCO (Microsoft Common Objects in Context) data set and final image data set	The position of the tumor in the head was detected effectively with amplified accuracy and diminished validation loss.
[20]	Standard balanced digital link (SBDL) and particle swarm optimization (PSO)	MRI imagres dataset	At classifying brain tumors, achieved more than 92% accuracy.
[35]	Discrete wavelet transform (DWT), support vector machine (SVM)	Brain MRI images	SVM proves to be a robust algorithm for the recognition of brain tumors, with 94.6% accuracy.
[36]	Fuzzy C-means clustering with super-resolution (FCM-SR) & CNN	Cancer Genome Atlas Glioblastoma Multiform (TCGA-GBM) database	FCM-SR recognized brain tumor with a magnificent accuracy of 98.33%

Table 1. *Cont.*

Ref.	Algorithm	Dataset	Results
[4]	Non-dominated sorted genetic algorithm (NSGA)	BRATS 2018–2020	Brain tumors were classified and segmented accurately with final score accuracy of more than 0.90.
[24]	PSO algorithm, ANN	RIDER and BRATS 2018	99% accuracy was achieved with the proposed model for tumor identification in the brain.
[14]	Convolutional neural network (CNN)	MRI brain imageries	96.08% accuracy for three-layer CNN-trained model.
[22]	Support vector machine (SVM), Long-Short Term Memory (LSTM)	GigaDB and BCI Competition IV	OPTICAL predictor along with SVM classified motor images accurately.
[15]	Convolutional neural network (CNN)	Free Accessible MRI images	BrainMRNet model effectively identified tumor with an accuracy of 96.05 and proved better than the previously existing models.
[21]	Artificial neural network (ANN), Convolutional Neural Network (CNN)	Brain MRI Images	CLM came out with 96% accuracy while identifying the tumors.

3. Proposed Methodology

This section introduces the proposed framework for predicting brain tumors from the imagery data of patients with a tumor and those without. It utilizes the dataset of brain tumors taken from Kaggle. Firstly, the data is gathered. Data pre-processing is performed next, to clean the data through noise reduction, and the image pixels are converted to floating point/decimal type. Later, the pixel values of images are reduced. After that, feature extraction is performed. The working of the proposed model is shown in Figure 8.

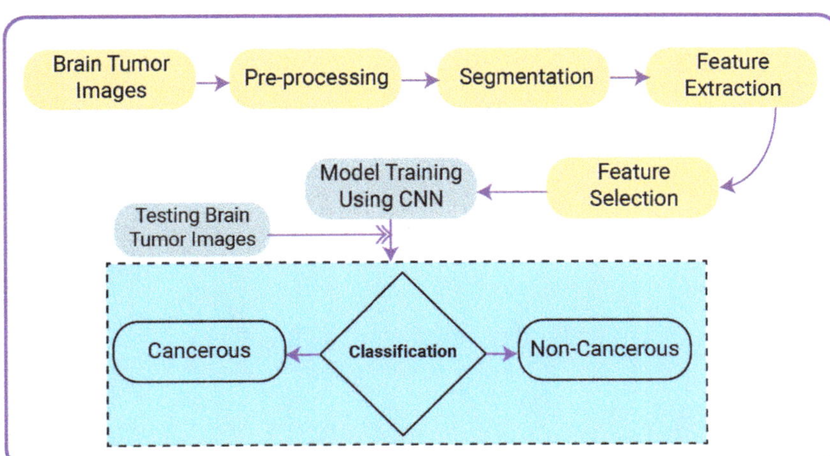

Figure 8. Proposed model for classification.

To conduct this proposed research work, a model is trained through a supervised machine-learning algorithm known as a "Convolutional Neural Network (CNN)". The model is trained on provided training data of brain tumors. Model, after training, classifies the provided tested brain-tumor images into cancerous and non-cancerous labels. The algorithm of the proposed framework is given below:

Recently, very little work has been carried out using MRI brain-tumor dataset of Kaggle and optimization algorithms used were ADAS, PSO, ADAM, etc. Along with the Kaggle dataset, this work will use SGD optimization algorithm. Firstly, CNN will be applied, and then an optimization algorithm (see, Algorithm 1) to gain effective results.

Algorithm 1: Proposed methodology algorithm

Algorithm brain-tumor detection
INPUT: MRI scanned brain tumor Image
OUTPUT: Detection (Cancerous/Non-Cancerous)

1. **Begin:**
2. Collection of brain-tumor imagery data.
3. Combine data.
4. Apply pre-processing techniques
   a. Noise removal
   b. Segmentation
5. Apply image-processing techniques
   a. Feature extraction
   b. Feature selection
6. Train the model using CNN algorithm
   a. Apply model
   b. Apply optimizer and loss function
7. Analyze result after classification
8. **End**

4. Materials and Methods

4.1. Supervised Learning

A subordinate category of artificial intelligence is known as supervised machine learning. Supervised learning makes use of a labelled set of data for training machines [30]. It uses the training data to train a model to achieve the expected outcome. Training data is comprised of input and accurate outputs, which the model uses to learn with the passage of time. The accuracy of the algorithm is calculated through the loss function and is continuously adjusted until the error is minimalized, as given in Equation (1) [32].

$$Y = f(x) \tag{1}$$

An algorithm is used to map the function from input to output values, where 'Y' is the output variable, 'X' is the input variable and 'f' is the mapping function. The mapping function is adjusted in such a way that when new input values (X) are entered for the data, it gives out the desired predicted outcome (Y). Supervised learning is classified into algorithms of "classification" and "regression". With the help of past experience, it optimizes the performance of the model.

4.2. CNN Architecture

The very common deep neural network [11] and a type of feed-forward artificial neural network are CNN. It has four layers which include: "Convolution", "ReLU Layer", "Pooling" and "Fully Connected", as shown in Figure 9.

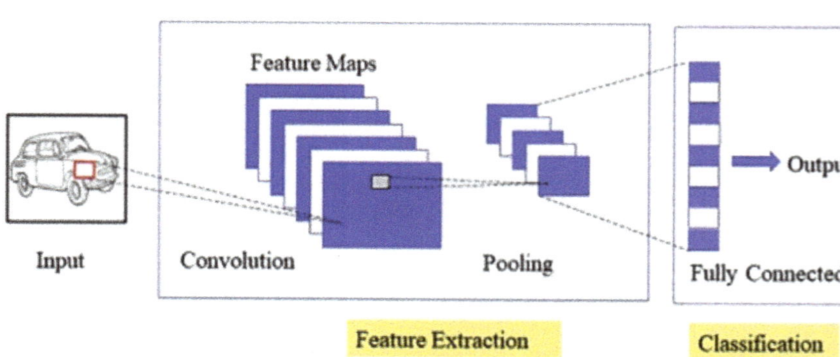

Figure 9. CNN architecture.

When applying CNN, within an image, a filter is moved to every possible position in the convolutional layer which consists of several kernels (see, Algorithm 2). Then, "Rectified Linear Unit (ReLU)" performs its work by removing the negative values from the filtered images. Each negative value is replaced with zero. Then, pooling helps to diminish complexity by shrinking down an image. The number of filters is not affected by pooling. Actual classification takes place at the fully connected layer. The input images are passed through a trained model of CNN which are classified into some predicted outcomes. CNN shows the best accuracy in resolving classification problems with its excellent performance. It is considered a powerful tool for executing tasks related to the classification of images, image processing, and segmentation through the use of computer-vision techniques.

Algorithm 2: Proposed CNN architecture

Input: An input signal is given to CNN in form of an image or pattern.
Output: Classified resultant output.

```
For (i=0; i<L; i++) {
For (m=0; m<M; m++) {
For (n=0; n<N; n++) {
Sum =bias[i];
For (k=0; k<K; k++) {
For (s1=0; s1<S1; s2++) {
Sum+-weight[k][i] [s1] [s2] *input[k][m+s1] [n+s2];
}}}
Output [i][m][n] =activation_func(sum);
}}}
```

5. Experiment and Results

This section describes the process of experiments alongside the results of the proposed methodology. Once the data is cleaned, it is ready to use for classification purposes. The deep convolutional neural network is used to generate a classification model.

5.1. Dataset

The dataset of brain tumors used for this research was taken from Kaggle. About "3762" MRI imageries were used for the classification of brain tumors. This dataset is divided into training and testing data. The dataset used for learning is termed training data and the dataset used for testing is known as testing data. Training and testing data are divided into 80 and 20 ratios, respectively. The dataset holds 2079 non-tumor images and 1683 tumor images. Here is given (Figure 10) a small glimpse of data used for experimentation purposes.

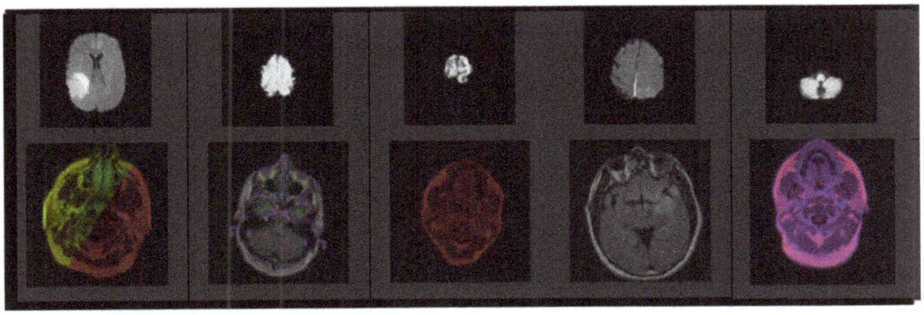

Figure 10. Sample images of Kaggle brain tumor dataset.

5.2. Prepossessing of Dataset

After the assemblage of data, it is refined through the procedure known as "preprocessing". It is a complex and difficult task and, occasionally, this segment can take more than half of the time that is required to resolve the whole problem. It is mandatory to clean the data before employing it for training the model because most of the data gathered are not in the usable format at the time. Therefore, it needs to refine the data by preprocessing it and filtering out the data intended to be useful for classification purposes.

Data sometimes is not in a comprehensive form; to manage this issue, data is made complete through the attributes of interest that are necessary to carry out certain tasks for resolving the problem. Old traditional techniques previously used to filter data had some problems [24], including feature engineering. Before passing the dataset to any algorithm, it is cleaned by eradicating the attributes and terms that are not related to the process of classification [1]. Through this stage, data that is missing is occupied and made free of redundancy and data also comes in a suitable format.

5.3. Tools and Techniques

For conducting experiments, the model was created on a platform known as "Google Collaboratory". Through it, a model was built using CNN known as "ResNet-50". It is one of the best-known models of deep learning utilized for classifying images effectively. The residual neural network of CNN is 50 layers deep and is utilized to construct an effective model by calling the sequence model. Different libraries from Python used in model construction were TensorFlow, Keras, etc. The loss function used for the supporting model was "Binary Cross Entropy". The optimizer algorithm used for optimizing the model's performance was "Stochastic Gradient Descent (SGD)".

5.4. Performance Matrix

Table 2, below, shows the performance metrics used to evaluate the performance of the proposed methodology. It is the confusion matrix of 2 × 2 used for plotting the diversity between the proposed values of datasets and the predicted values estimated by the models for making different assessments. The schematic of the confusion matrix is shown in Table 3.

Table 2. Hyperparameter configuration after performing the optimization for brain-tumor detection.

Hyperparameter	Configuration
Optimizer	SGD
Number of Epochs	50
Learning Rate	0.001
Momentum	0.9
No. of Layers	7
Filter Size	5×5
Batch Size	32
Activation Function	Relu

Table 3. Confusion matrix.

		Predicted	
		Positive	**Negative**
Actual	Positive	*TP*	*FN*
	Negative	*FP*	*TN*

- *Accuracy*: It is the number of correct predictions in the dataset to the total number of given inputs and is collected by Equation (2).

$$Accuracy = \frac{TP + TN}{TP + FP + TN + FN} \quad (2)$$

- *Precision*: It can be defined as the number of correct predictions to the total number of inputs. The *precision* can be calculated using the following Equation (3).

$$Precision = \frac{TP}{TP + FP} \tag{3}$$

- *Recall*: It can be defined as the correct prediction of class to the total number of inputs of that class. *Recall* can be calculated with the help of Equation (4).

$$Recall = \frac{TP}{TP + FN} \tag{4}$$

- *F1-Score* It is difficult to decide whether high precision or low recall is better when comparing different models. *F1-Score* combines both the precision and recall to calculate results. Equation (5). shows the *F1-Score*:

$$F1\text{-}Score = \frac{Precision * Recall}{Precision + Recall} \tag{5}$$

According to the proposed methodology mentioned in Section 5 and the experiment conducted on the data, the performance of the system is evaluated in terms of *accuracy*, *precision*, *recall*, and *F1-Score*.

5.5. Optimal Algorithms

Optimization classifiers are the main core for constructing a model through a neural network. The model learns from the input data, initializes weights, and makes an optimal prediction. The most commonly used optimization algorithms include: SGD-Stochastic Gradient Descent, GD-Gradient Descent, ADAM-Adaptive Moment Estimation, Momentum, RMSProp, AdaGrad-Adaptive Subgradient, and ADAS-Adaptive Scheduling of Stochastic Gradients. The schematic of an optimizer algorithm is shown in Figure 11.

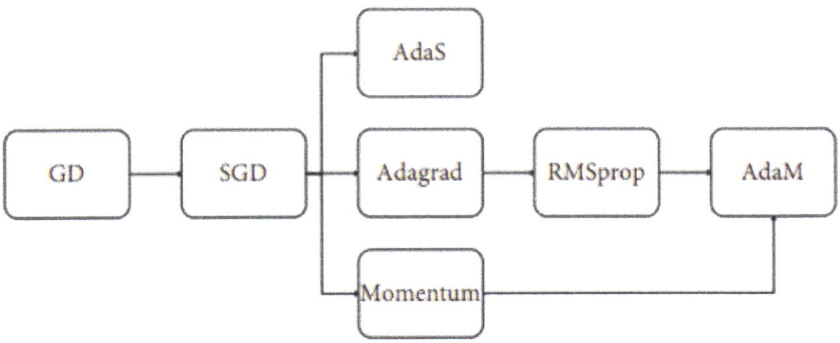

Figure 11. Optimization classifier.

Figure 11 shows all the optimization algorithms. SGD was picked for conducting this research because it is better than all the other classifiers in terms of having: "high generalization ability", "quick convergence" and "high accuracy".

5.6. Experimentation

All the images were resized to 244 × 244 pixels from an original size of 1440 × 1440 to be used further for training and testing purposes. The model was trained with the help of an SGD optimizer along with a learning rate of 0.01 and binary cross entropy loss function. The learning rate helps sort out convergence problems. The model was trained for up to 50 epochs with a batch size of 10 and imagenet weights. The model was successfully trained on the given dataset with a training accuracy of 99.82%. A total of "753" images was used for the testing model and the accuracy achieved during the testing phase was 99.5%. The model summary of the proposed model is given in Figure 12. The graphical representation of accuracy and loss during model training is shown in Figure 13 and Figure 14, respectively.

Layer (type)	Output Shape	Param #
conv2d (Conv2D)	(None, 112, 112, 16)	448
conv2d_1 (Conv2D)	(None, 56, 56, 16)	2320
max_pooling2d (MaxPooling2D)	(None, 28, 28, 16)	0
conv2d_2 (Conv2D)	(None, 14, 14, 32)	4640
conv2d_3 (Conv2D)	(None, 7, 7, 32)	9248
max_pooling2d_1 (MaxPooling2D)	(None, 4, 4, 32)	0
conv2d_4 (Conv2D)	(None, 2, 2, 64)	18496
conv2d_5 (Conv2D)	(None, 1, 1, 64)	36928
max_pooling2d_2 (MaxPooling2D)	(None, 1, 1, 64)	0
flatten (Flatten)	(None, 64)	0
dense (Dense)	(None, 256)	16640
dense_1 (Dense)	(None, 128)	32896
dense_2 (Dense)	(None, 1)	129

Figure 12. Model summary of the proposed model.

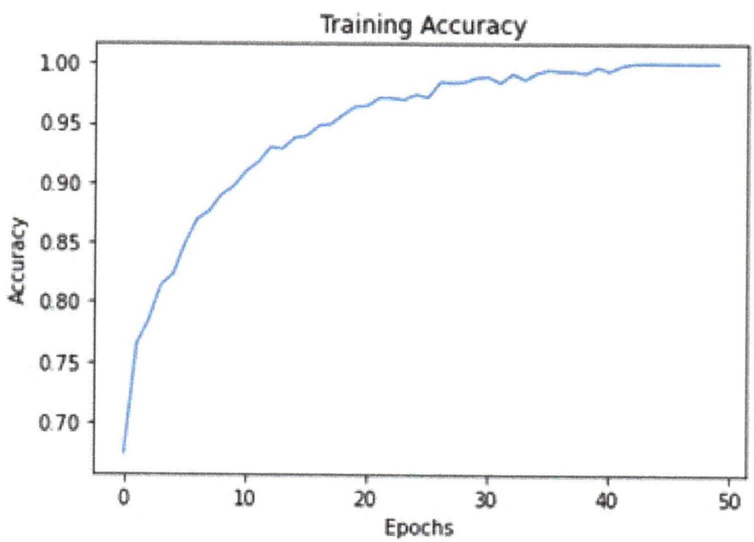

Figure 13. Training accuracy per epoch.

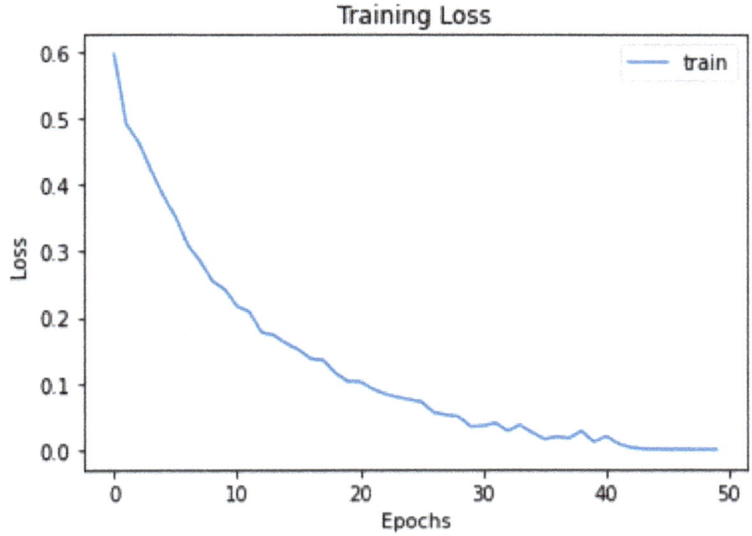

Figure 14. Training loss per epoch.

We presented a basic CNN architecture comprised of seven layers with various hyperparameter tunings for brain-tumor detection and retained the batch size of 32 which showed optimal performance. The convolution layer has a 5 × 5 filter size followed by a pooling layer with a 2 × 2 filter size and stride of 2. The penultimate layer is fully connected and we applied a dropout of 0.3 to only this layer. In the final layer, we opted for a softmax output layer with 'n' classes. After the entire optimization process, we present the hyperparameter configurations in Table 2, which show the best possible results for brain-tumor detection.

There are various machine-learning and deep-learning models and their variations were tested in order to achieve better performance for brain-tumor detection, as depicted in Table 4. It can be evident from the results that the proposed method with the SGD optimizer outperformed the baseline method in terms of various performance metrics, i.e., F1-Score, precision, recall, and accuracy

Table 4. Performance measure for various techniques for brain-tumor detection.

Method	F1-Score	Precision	Recall	Accuracy
SVM	90.80%	90.12%	89.67%	91.63%
CNN	92.75%	92.90%	91.13%	93.53%
AlexNet	92.60%	93.30%	91.05%	94.50%
ResNet-18	93.33%	94.55%	90.65%	95.06%
ResNet-34	94.22%	94.64%	93.22%	96%
ResNet-50	95.05%	94.65%	91.25%	96.75%
VGG-16	95.35%	95.10%	92.95%	97.80%
Proposed Method	96.10%	96.50%	95.62%	99%

Figure 15 shows the pictorial view of the whole dataset, in which 2079 images had no tumor and 1683 images included tumors. These numbers represent how correctly the model predicted the tumor and normal images.

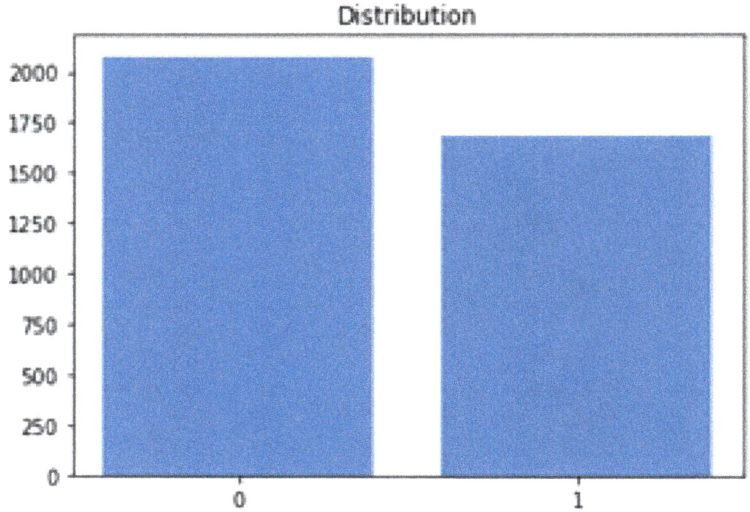

Figure 15. Data classification.

Figure 16 shows the confusion matrix for the result predicted by the model. A total of 111 images weer misclassified out of 753 images used for the testing phase. For the No-tumor label, the achieved F1-Score, precision and recall were 96.1%, 96.5% and 95.62%, respectively. For the tumor label, F1-Score was 96.68%, precision 96.50% and recall 95.73%.

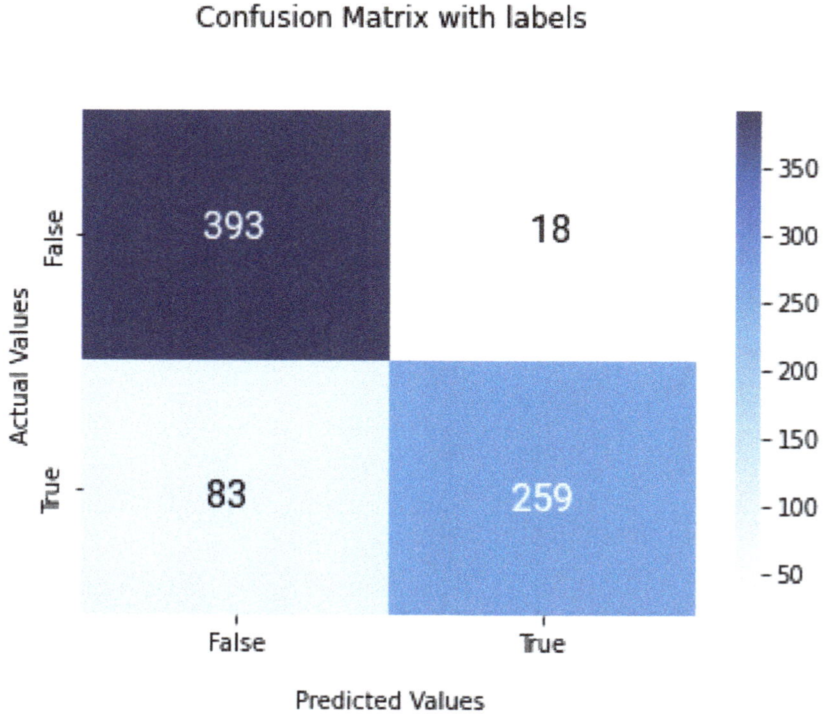

Figure 16. Proposed-model confusion matrix.

The model was trained efficiently through the use of ResNet-50 and a 2-D convolutional layered network. The brain tumor dataset used was divided between training and testing data. Achieved accuracy for training and testing was 99.82% and 99.5%, respectively. Data preprocessing, pixel reduction, loss function, and optimizer are some of the techniques used for facilitating the experimentation phase. The performance achieved using the SGD optimizer is highly generalized and accurate. The uniqueness of this model is that it has been trained upon a large number of datasets which was previously not performed. In addition, the accuracy achieved with a combination of CNN and SGD made it a more preferable approach to adopt for the prediction of brain tumors.The limitation of using CNN with SGD is that the model is trained using a very small learning rate. To further enhance the efficiency of the model and make it more generalized, the proposed model should be trained with stochastic gradient classifiers other than SGD.

The results of the proposed method were also compared with some state-of-the-art methods in terms of accuracy and F1-Score. It is evident that the proposed method outperformed the baseline methods. The significance of the diagnosis provided by the doctor increased the accuracy of their assistance in identifying the tumour and treating the patient. The comparative results are presented in Table 5.

Table 5. Comparative result analysis.

Method	Dataset (No. of Images)	Accuracy	F1-Score
VGG-19 with ADAS Optimizer	Brain MRI Dataset (1307 Images)	94.56%	94.90%
Discrete Wavelet Transform (DWT) and support vector machine (SVM)	DICOM dataset (750 samples)	94.6%	93.56%
AlexNet with Shallow CNN and ADAM optimizer	Brain MRI Images (253 Images)	96.05%	94.12%
Fuzzy C-means with super-resolution and CNN with ADAM	The Cancer Imaging Archive (500 samples)	98.33%	-
Modified genetic algorithm and support vector machine	BRATS-2018	98.67%	93.67%
Proposed Method	Kaggle Br35H Dataset (804 Images)	99%	96.1%

6. Conclusions

This paper focused on developing a general model that works best for the detection of tumors in brain cells. The major objective behind conducting this research was to help doctors identify one of most precarious diseases found in humans. The dataset used for this research was taken from the Kaggle repository. In total, there are 3762 images in the dataset. This study used the CNN deep-learning algorithm to classify tumors. ResNet-50 and a 2D layered network of CNN were utilized to train the model. SGD optimizer algorithm was deployed to enhance the performance of the model. The accuracy observed during the training phase came out to be 99.82% and the accuracy achieved during the model testing phase was 99.5%. Techniques of computer vision (CV) such as image processing and image segmentation were used to facilitate the research work. The performance of the model achieved using the SGD optimizer is highly generalized and precise. In the future, the accuracy and some other performance-measure values can be improved using a large number of datasets with some other deep-learning approaches utilizing an SGD optimizer or using CNN with gradient-boosting algorithms other than SGD. Besides using more datasets for achieving more improved accuracy from the system, the research can also progress by developing approaches to specifically classify tumors on the basis of their characteristics or by their disease type, i.e., malignant or benign.

Author Contributions: Conceptualization, R.A. and A.I.; methodology, R.A. and S.u.R.; validation, A.A. (Abdulkareem Alzahrani); formal analysis, A.A. (Abdulkareem Alzahrani); resources, A.A. (Abdullah Almuhaimeed); data curation, A.A. (Abdullah Almuhaimeed); writing—original draft preparation, R.A.; writing—review and editing, J.L.; supervision, A.A. (Abdullah Almuhaimeed); funding acquisition, J.L. All authors have read and agreed to the published version of the the manuscript.

Funding: This research received no external funding.

Institutional Review Board Statement: Not applicable.

Informed Consent Statement: Not applicable.

Data Availability Statement: Not applicable.

Conflicts of Interest: The authors declare no conflict of interest.

References

1. Cory, S.; Huang, D.; Adams, J.M. The Bcl2 family: Regulators of the cellular life-or-death switch. *Nat. Rev. Cancer* **2002**, *2*, 647–656. [CrossRef] [PubMed]
2. Bedoui, S.; Herold, M.J.; Strasser, A. Emerging connectivity of programmed cell death pathways and its physiological implications. *Nat. Rev. Mol. Cell Biol.* **2020**, *21*, 678–695. [CrossRef] [PubMed]
3. Frank, D.; Vince, J.E. Pyroptosis versus necroptosis: Similarities, differences, and crosstalk. *Cell Death Differ.* **2019**, *26*, 99–114. [CrossRef] [PubMed]
4. Melaiu, O.; Lucarini, V.; Cifaldi, L.; Fruci, D. Influence of the tumor microenvironment on NK cell function in solid tumors. *Front. Immunol.* **2019**, *10*, 3038. [CrossRef]
5. Vanderah, T.; Gould, D. *Nolte's The Human Brain E-Book: An Introduction to its Functional Anatomy*; Elsevier Health Sciences: Amsterdam, The Netherland, 2020.
6. Baum, G.L.; Cui, Z.; Roalf, D.R.; Ciric, R.; Betzel, R.F.; Larsen, B.; Cieslak, M.; Cook, P.A.; Xia, C.H.; Moore, T.M.; et al. Development of structure–function coupling in human brain networks during youth. *Proc. Natl. Acad. Sci. USA* **2020**, *117*, 771–778. [CrossRef]
7. Patel, A. Benign vs malignant tumors. *JAMA Oncol.* **2020**, *6*, 1488. [CrossRef]
8. Wu, A.H.; Wu, J.; Tseng, C.; Yang, J.; Shariff-Marco, S.; Fruin, S.; Larson, T.; Setiawan, V.W.; Masri, S.; Porcel, J.; et al. Association between outdoor air pollution and risk of malignant and benign brain tumors: The multiethnic cohort study. *JNCI Cancer Spectr.* **2020**, *4*, pkz107. [CrossRef]
9. Sharif, M.; Amin, J.; Raza, M.; Anjum, M.A.; Afzal, H.; Shad, S.A. Brain tumor detection based on extreme learning. *Neural Comput. Appl.* **2020**, *32*, 15975–15987. [CrossRef]
10. Ostrom, Q.T.; Patil, N.; Cioffi, G.; Waite, K.; Kruchko, C.; Barnholtz-Sloan, J.S. CBTRUS statistical report: Primary brain and other central nervous system tumors diagnosed in the United States in 2013–2017. *Neuro-Oncology* **2020**, *22*, iv1–iv96. [CrossRef] [PubMed]
11. Xu, S.; Wang, J.; Shou, W.; Ngo, T.; Sadick, A.M.; Wang, X. Computer vision techniques in construction: A critical review. *Arch. Comput. Methods Eng.* **2021**, *28*, 3383–3397. [CrossRef]
12. Esteva, A.; Chou, K.; Yeung, S.; Naik, N.; Madani, A.; Mottaghi, A.; Liu, Y.; Topol, E.; Dean, J.; Socher, R. Deep learning-enabled medical computer vision. *NPJ Digit. Med.* **2021**, *4*, 5. [CrossRef] [PubMed]
13. Amin, J.; Sharif, M.; Gul, N.; Raza, M.; Anjum, M.A.; Nisar, M.W.; Bukhari, S.A.C. Brain tumor detection by using stacked autoencoders in deep learning. *J. Med. Syst.* **2020**, *44*, 32. [CrossRef] [PubMed]
14. Voulodimos, A.; Doulamis, N.; Doulamis, A.; Protopapadakis, E. Deep learning for computer vision: A brief review. *Comput. Intell. Neurosci.* **2018**, *2018*, 7068349. [CrossRef] [PubMed]
15. Toğaçar, M.; Ergen, B.; Cömert, Z. BrainMRNet: Brain tumor detection using magnetic resonance images with a novel convolutional neural network model. *Med. Hypotheses* **2020**, *134*, 109531. [CrossRef] [PubMed]
16. Bober, P.; Alexovič, M.; Tomková, Z.; Kilík, R.; Sabo, J. RHOA and mDia1 promotes apoptosis of breast cancer cells via a high dose of doxorubicin treatment. *Open Life Sci.* **2019**, *14*, 619–627. [CrossRef]
17. Swati, Z.N.K.; Zhao, Q.; Kabir, M.; Ali, F.; Ali, Z.; Ahmed, S.; Lu, J. Brain tumor classification for MR images using transfer learning and fine-tuning. *Comput. Med. Imaging Graph.* **2019**, *75*, 34–46. [CrossRef]
18. Siar, M.; Teshnehlab, M. Brain tumor detection using deep neural network and machine learning algorithm. In Proceedings of the 2019 9th International Conference on Computer and Knowledge Engineering (ICCKE), Mashhad, Iran, 24–25 October 2019; IEEE: Mashhad, Iran, 2019; pp. 363–368.
19. Saba, T.; Mohamed, A.S.; El-Affendi, M.; Amin, J.; Sharif, M. Brain tumor detection using fusion of hand crafted and deep learning features. *Cogn. Syst. Res.* **2020**, *59*, 221–230. [CrossRef]
20. Han-Trong, T.; Nguyen Van, H.; Nguyen Thi Thanh, H.; Tran Anh, V.; Nguyen Tuan, D.; Vu Dang, L. An Efficient Method for Diagnosing Brain Tumors Based on MRI Images Using Deep Convolutional Neural Networks. *Appl. Comput. Intell. Soft Comput.* **2022**, *2022*, 2092985. [CrossRef]
21. Hossain, A.; Islam, M.T.; Islam, M.S.; Chowdhury, M.E.; Almutairi, A.F.; Razouqi, Q.A.; Misran, N. A YOLOv3 deep neural network model to detect brain tumor in portable electromagnetic imaging system. *IEEE Access* **2021**, *9*, 82647–82660. [CrossRef]
22. Sharif, M.I.; Khan, M.A.; Alhussein, M.; Aurangzeb, K.; Raza, M. A decision support system for multimodal brain tumor classification using deep learning. *Complex Intell. Syst.* **2022**, *8*, 3007–3020. [CrossRef]
23. Sharif, M.I.; Li, J.P.; Khan, M.A.; Saleem, M.A. Active deep neural network features selection for segmentation and recognition of brain tumors using MRI images. *Pattern Recognit. Lett.* **2020**, *129*, 181–189. [CrossRef]

24. Hu, Y.; Xia, Y. 3D deep neural network-based brain tumor segmentation using multimodality magnetic resonance sequences. In Proceedings of the International MICCAI Brainlesion Workshop, Quebec City, QC, Canada, 14 September 2017; Springer: Quebec City, QC, Canada, 2017; pp. 423–434.
25. Deb, D.; Roy, S. Brain tumor detection based on hybrid deep neural network in MRI by adaptive squirrel search optimization. *Multimed. Tools Appl.* **2021**, *80*, 2621–2645. [CrossRef]
26. Razzaq, S.; Mubeen, N.; Kiran, U.; Asghar, M.A.; Fawad, F. Brain Tumor Detection From MRI Images Using Bag Of Features And Deep Neural Network. In Proceedings of the 2020 International Symposium on Recent Advances in Electrical Engineering & Computer Sciences (RAEE & CS), Islamabad, Pakistan, 20–22 October 2020; IEEE: Piscatawaty, NJ, USA, 2020; Volume 5, pp. 1–6.
27. Liu, T.; Yuan, Z.; Wu, L.; Badami, B. An optimal brain tumor detection by convolutional neural network and enhanced sparrow search algorithm. *Proc. Inst. Mech. Eng. Part H J. Eng. Med.* **2021**, *235*, 459–469. [CrossRef] [PubMed]
28. Kumar, S.; Sharma, A.; Tsunoda, T. Brain wave classification using long short-term memory network based OPTICAL predictor. *Sci. Rep.* **2019**, *9*, 9153. [CrossRef]
29. Manjunath, S.; Sanjay Pande, M.; Raveesh, B.; Madhusudhan, G. Brain tumor detection and classification using convolution neural network. *Int. J. Recent Technol. Eng. (IJRTE)* **2019**, *8*, 2277–3878.
30. Sharif, M.; Amin, J.; Raza, M.; Yasmin, M.; Satapathy, S.C. An integrated design of particle swarm optimization (PSO) with fusion of features for detection of brain tumor. *Pattern Recognit. Lett.* **2020**, *129*, 150–157. [CrossRef]
31. Sharif, M.I.; Li, J.P.; Amin, J.; Sharif, A. An improved framework for brain tumor analysis using MRI based on YOLOv2 and convolutional neural network. *Complex Intell. Syst.* **2021**, *7*, 2023–2036. [CrossRef]
32. Chaudhary, A.; Bhattacharjee, V. An efficient method for brain tumor detection and categorization using MRI images by K-means clustering & DWT. *Int. J. Inf. Technol.* **2020**, *12*, 141–148.
33. Sukumaran, A.; Glan, D.G.; Kumar, S. An improved tumor segmentation algorithm from T2 and FLAIR multimodality MRI brain images by support vector machine and genetic algorithm. *Cogent Eng.* **2018**, *5*, 1470915. [CrossRef]
34. Deepak, S.; Ameer, P. Brain tumor classification using deep CNN features via transfer learning. *Comput. Biol. Med.* **2019**, *111*, 103345. [CrossRef]
35. Wasson, V.; Kaur, B. Meta-analysis of distortions effects on quality of digital images using standard IQA datasets. *J. Discret. Math. Sci. Cryptogr.* **2021**, *24*, 1545–1558. [CrossRef]
36. Özyurt, F.; Sert, E.; Avcı, D. An expert system for brain tumor detection: Fuzzy C-means with super resolution and convolutional neural network with extreme learning machine. *Med. Hypotheses* **2020**, *134*, 109433. [CrossRef] [PubMed]

biomedicines

MDPI

Article

Investigation of Cerebral Autoregulation Using Time-Frequency Transformations

Vladimir Semenyutin [1], Valery Antonov [2], Galina Malykhina [3,*] and Vyacheslav Salnikov [3]

1 Almazov National Medical Research Center, Ministry of Health of Russia, Polenov Neurosurgical Research Institute, 12 Mayakovsky Street, Saint-Petersburg 191014, Russia

2 Department of Higher Mathematics, Peter the Great St. Petersburg Polytechnic University, Saint-Petersburg 195251, Russia

3 Higher School of Cyber-Physical Systems and Control, Institute of Computer Science and Control, Peter the Great St. Petersburg Polytechnic University, Saint-Petersburg 195251, Russia

* Correspondence: g_f_malykhina@mail.ru; Tel.: +8-921-43-15-114

Abstract: The authors carried out the study of the state of systemic and cerebral hemodynamics in normal conditions and in various neurosurgical pathologies using modern signal processing methods. The results characterize the condition for the mechanisms of cerebral circulation Institute of Computer Science and Control, Higher School of Cyber-Physical Systems and Control regulation, which allows for finding a solution to fundamental and specific clinical problems for the effective treatment of patients with various pathologies. The proposed method is based on the continuous wavelet transform of systemic arterial pressure and blood flow velocity signals in the middle cerebral artery recorded by non-invasive methods of photoplethysmography and transcranial doppler ultrasonography. The study of these signals in real-time in the frequency range of Mayer waves makes it possible to determine the cerebral autoregulation state in certain diseases before and after surgical interventions. The proposed method uses a cross-wavelet spectrum, which helps obtain wavelet coherence and a phase shift between the wavelet coefficients of systemic arterial pressure signals and blood flow velocity in the Mayer wave range. The obtained results enable comparing the proposed method with that based on the short-time Fourier transform. The comparison showed that the proposed method has higher sensitivity to changes in cerebral autoregulation and better localization of changes in time and frequency.

Keywords: cerebral autoregulation; transcranial doppler; Mayer waves; wavelet transform; wavelet coherence; phase shift

Citation: Semenyutin, V.; Antonov, V.; Malykhina, G.; Salnikov, V. Investigation of Cerebral Autoregulation Using Time-Frequency Transformations. *Biomedicines* **2022**, *10*, 3057. https://doi.org/10.3390/biomedicines10123057

Academic Editors: Wu Qiu and Tommaso Bocci

Received: 4 September 2022
Accepted: 20 November 2022
Published: 28 November 2022

1. Introduction

The future development of personalized medicine is determined by the synergy of knowledge and efforts of scientists from several fields of medicine, physiology, mathematics, and computer science. Approaches based on signal processing, computer modeling, and machine learning complement the main instrumental methods for studying biological processes and allow a deeper understanding of the mechanisms of human disease and personalized treatment strategies. Despite the increased popularity of artificial intelligence, machine learning, and signal processing approaches, a lot of effort still needs to be put into preparing them for clinical implementation. The use of modern methods of signal processing and neural networks allows for increasing the possibilities of non-invasive methods to measure and control regulation processes. Features of integrating general and personalized heterogeneous data is a complex task, the solution of which should comply with accepted ethical and legal standards.

Cerebral autoregulation (CA) maintains relatively constant cerebral blood flow despite perfusion pressure change. The study of the CA phenomenon was difficult when using invasive methods for assessing changes in cerebral blood flow and perfusion pressure, which are not applicable in clinical practice [1]. The introduction of transcranial Doppler ultrasound into practice and the development of non-invasive methods for assessing systemic blood pressure (BP) and dynamic CA made it possible to conduct studies directly at the patient's bedside [2–5].

CA functions through myogenic, metabolic, and neurogenic mechanisms. Usually, there is a distinction between static and dynamic CA. Static CA characterizes changes in cerebral blood flow with long-term changes in perfusion pressure, whereas dynamic CA is associated with relatively rapid fluctuations in BP. The CA system dampens these fluctuations, which manifests itself in the presence of consistency and phase shift between fluctuations in BP and blood flow velocity (BFV) in the arteries at the base of the brain. Early diagnosis of CA violations and their res allows for the prevention of a number of ischemic and hemorrhagic complications.

The rapid development of digitalization in medicine, the use of computers, and modern software packages make it possible to develop and apply methods of mathematical statistics, digital signal processing, and machine learning in medical research to study the processes of CA [6–10].

The spectral analysis of BFV and BP showed the presence of four relatively stable fluctuations: heart rate (0.65–1.4 Hz), respiratory excursions (0.15–0.65 Hz), Mayer systemic waves (0.08–0.12 Hz), and intracranial B-waves (less than 0.05 Hz) [11,12]. The slow arterial pressure oscillations originally described by S. Mayer [13] had in anesthetized rabbits a frequency of 6 to 9 cycles/min, i.e., 0.1 to 0.15 Hz, which is slower than the frequency of spontaneous sympathetically mediated arterial pressure oscillations in conscious rabbits (~0.3 Hz). The term Mayer waves are widely used now.

For continuous assessment of the CA state in real-time, some authors use several methods of digital signal processing [14–16]. They select the M-waves of the BFV and BP signals using an ideal filter and calculate the coherence value, the phase shift (PS) in the coherence intervals for the received signals. The violation of CA leads to an increase in the bandwidth of the autoregulatory filter in the range of M-waves and, as a result, to an increase in coherence and a decrease in the PS between the BFV and BP oscillations. This protective mechanism plays a significant role in the functioning of the brain. The disadvantage of the real-time implementation of this method is the insufficiently good localization of the coherence intervals.

Other authors apply the method of assessing the CA by calculating the cross-correlation coefficient between the BFV and BP signals in the M-wave range. In-phase slow fluctuations of these signals with low efficiency of the CA lead to an increase in the transmission of M-waves, whereas the cross-correlation between BFV and BP is close to unity. While in the normal state of the CA, the cross-correlation decreases. The disadvantage of this method is the dependence of the CA estimation results on the shape of the cross-correlation function and on the phase shift angle between BFV and BP, which can vary from 0.8 to 1.4 radians, affecting the cross-correlation coefficient [17–19].

A number of publications show the possibility of using the wavelet transform of the BFV and BP signals to estimate the coherence and phase shift in the wavelet decomposition spaces that correspond to the M-wave range [20,21].

Further development of this approach seems promising. Therefore, the goal of our study is to develop an algorithm for diagnosing disorders of the regulation of cerebral circulation, using the functions of wavelet coherence and phase shift of the BFV and BP signals in the wavelet decomposition spaces corresponding to the range of M-waves, and to implement this algorithm in the measuring information system in real-time.

The paper aims to develop a method for determining the current state of the patient's cerebrovascular autoregulation system in real-time, including "at the patient's bedside". Real-time CA monitoring, along with conventional monitoring, seems to be a promising method for improving individualized patient care. Early diagnosis of impaired cerebral autoregulation and its restoration allows the prevention of a number of ischemic and hemorrhagic complications.

Evidently, this method reflects our knowledge of the autoregulation process, having higher sensitivity and lower delay. The method based on the cross-correlation function, which is being developed by scientists [22,23], indirectly determines the state of autoregulation, but it is not sensitive enough. The result of this method depends on the form of the cross-correlation function. Transcranial Doppler sonography (TCD) is the main non-invasive method for the continuous recording of cerebral blood flow, which makes it possible to assess the rate of CA in real-time with a simultaneous non-invasive recording of BP [24]. TCD is implemented as a portable, bedside, non-invasive diagnostic tool used to assess cerebral hemodynamics in real-time [25].

Assessment of CA using NIRS-only methodology seems feasible in critically ill sedated/coma patients after incorporating methodological improvements. As the authors of the article [26] state, the NIRS-only methodology has the advantage that it is non-invasive and does not require monitoring of arterial blood pressure. However, the method has not yet entered into practice and requires further validation. R. Panerai et al. [27] use an approach to measuring CA based on transfer function analysis. They showed that although the TCD is only capable of measuring blood flow index and not true blood flow, the measurement results are representative and widely used to assess dynamic CA [28,29].

A new assessment of dynamic CA using magnetic resonance imaging technology makes it possible to evaluate both global and spatially differentiated values of the autoregulation index [27]. Big data in intensive care units expand the opportunities for neurocritical care and helps prevent secondary brain damage [30].

2. Materials and Methods

2.1. Patients and Healthy Volunteers

We examined 6 patients aged 41 to 63 with arteriovenous malformations of the brain, 6 patients aged 52–72 with stenosis of the brachiocephalic arteries, and 9 healthy volunteers, including four women and five men, aged 19 to 35 from students and staff of the Almazov National Medical Research Center (ANMC), Saint Petersburg, Russia, who did not have any cardiovascular, pulmonary, and cerebrovascular pathology in accordance with the Protocol of 5 April 2010, approved by the Ethics Committee of the ANMC and Carnet-consensus. At the same time, we performed non-invasive monitoring of BP using digital photoplethysmography (CNAP, Graz, Austria) and BFV in both middle cerebral arteries using transcranial doppler ultrasonography (MultiDop X, DWL, Singen, Germany,) in the supine position under the control of end-tidal CO_2.

We performed hypercapnic (breathing with a 5% mixture of CO_2 with air for two minutes) and hypocapnic (hyperventilation, providing a significant decrease in BFV, which characterizes an increase in the tone of the distal arteries and arterioles) tests. The tests were used to evaluate changes in the state of the CA.

All studies were approved by the Ethics Committee of ANMC.

2.2. Time-Frequency Analysis of Signals Characterizing CA

The numerical method for assessing the CA state is determined by the presence of consistency between the fluctuations of BP and BFV in the range of M-waves. In our survey, we used the range of M-waves, in which fluctuations are primary, and the phase shift between BP and BFV characterizes the state of CA. The analysis of other frequency ranges is not the subject of this article. The state of the target audience should be diagnosed both offline and online. When working in real-time, the signal analysis is performed within a frame sliding along the signals. In both cases, it is required to isolate the coherent components of the signal in the given frequency range to determine the coherence coefficient of the signals and the phase shift between them. The offline method allows us to analyze the signal after the end of the measurements.

2.2.1. Short-Time Fourier Transform

The traditional mathematical method that allows exploring the signal in the frequency domain, which is based on the classical Fourier transform, implicitly assumes that the signals are stationary in time. For non-stationary signals, the windowed Fourier transform is usually used, which in the case of the Gaussian window is called the Gabor transform [31].

The short-time Fourier transform (STFT) is performed within the frame sliding along the BP and BFV signals, which we denote as $x(n), y(n), n = 1, \ldots, N_{frame}$, where N_{frame} is the frame length. Signals $x(n)$ and $y(n)$ are mixed with other physiological signals and noise. Therefore, when calculating the signal coherence characteristics and the phase angle, the signals are smoothed within the frame. For smoothing, the frame is divided into L windows $x(n), y(n), n = 1, \ldots, N_{win}$, of length N_{win}, and the signal characteristics averaged over all windows within each frame are calculated. The Hann window is used for processing. The window is shifted within the frame by the amount equal to half the length of the window $N_{shift} = \frac{1}{2}N_{win}$.

For the centered signals in the windows, the N_{win}–point Fourier transform $X(k)$, $Y(k)$, is calculated, where k are discrete frequencies. The mutual spectral density $S_{x,y}(k) = X^*(k)Y(k)/N_{win}$, its modulus $|S_{x,y}(k)|$, and the phase $\Theta_{x,y}$ are related by: $S_{x,y}(k) = |S_{x,y}(k)|exp(-j\Theta_{x,y})$.

The spectral densities of signals $x(n)$ and $y(n)$ are the following:

$$S_{x,x}(k) = \frac{X(k)X^*(k)}{N_{win}}; \tag{1}$$

$$S_{y,y}(k) = \frac{Y(k)Y^*(k)}{N_{win}}. \tag{2}$$

The calculations are repeated for each shifted position of the window; as a result, we obtain k values of the mutual and intrinsic spectral densities. The frame is characterized by the smoothed averaged spectral densities obtained for each window within the frame:

$$\hat{S}_{x,x}(k) = \frac{1}{L}\sum_{l=1}^{L} S_{x,x}(k), \hat{S}_{y,y}(k) = \frac{1}{L}\sum_{l=1}^{L} S_{y,y}(k), \hat{S}_{x,y}(k) = \frac{1}{L}\sum_{l=1}^{L} S_{x,y}(k), \tag{3}$$

The coherence function is calculated from the smoothed spectral densities for each frame using the formula:

$$\gamma_{x,y}(k) = \sqrt{\frac{|\hat{S}_{x,y}(k)|^2}{\hat{S}_{x,x}(k)\hat{S}_{y,y}(k)}} \tag{4}$$

The average phase shift $\hat{\Theta}_{x,y}$ between the signals is obtained from the relation $\hat{S}_{x,y}(k) = |\hat{S}_{x,y}(k)|exp(-j\hat{\Theta}_{x,y})$.

The signals are represented as a mixture with other physiological signals and with noise. Therefore, when calculating their spectra, averaging is proposed to suppress the noise. For this purpose, the data frame is divided into windows, and the Fourier spectrum is calculated for each window. The resulting spectra are averaged within the frame boundaries. The offset of a window within the frame depends on the type of window. The frame offset is set equal to the window offset. This allows us to speed up the calculations.

After calculating the coherence function and the phase shift of the signals for all L windows of the current frame, the frame is shifted by the number of samples $N_{shift} = \frac{N_{win}}{2}$, then the number of windows in every frame equals to $L = \frac{N_{frame}}{N_{shift}}$.

The coherence function and the phase shift for each next frame are obtained from the corresponding values of the previous frame by removing the characteristics of the first window and adding the characteristics of the last window within the new frame. Then for each m-th frame, the coherence function $\gamma_{x,y}(k, m)$ and the phase shift function $\hat{\Theta}_{x,y}(k, m)$ are obtained, where k is the frequency sample number and m is the sample number by time. The discreteness of time is counted by $N_{shift} = \frac{N_{win}}{2}$. Therefore, the result of the preprocessing algorithm is a two-dimensional time-frequency function of the signal coherence $\gamma_{x,y}(k,m)$ and a two-dimensional time-frequency function of the phase shift $\hat{\Theta}_{x,y}(k,m)$.

When analyzing the state of cerebral autoregulation in real-time, time resolution, which is determined by the N_{shift} frame shift in time, becomes important. Frequency resolution matters when fine-tuning Mayer's frequency to determine the signal coherence. The STFT-based method has a constant resolution in time and frequency over the entire frequency range of the BP and BFV signals, which does not always ensure the best analysis results. The wavelet transform of the signal makes it possible to detect localized discontinuous periodicity associated with certain disorders of the CA [32].

2.2.2. Continuous Wavelet Transform

The disadvantage of the windowed Fourier transform is the fact that the window size is chosen once and remains constant; it does not adjust to the spectral properties of the signal. To eliminate this shortcoming, we have replaced the traditional STFT-based approach with the wavelet transform-based approach. A continuous wavelet can be interpreted as a set of harmonic functions with a window that changes its size depending on the frequency band of the signal under study.

Continuous Wavelet Transform (CWT), using a harmonic wavelet basis, is better applied for detecting the harmonic components of the BP and BFV signals [33]. Wavelets of this type include the complex Morlet wavelet, the complex Pole wavelet, and the real wavelet representing the difference between Gaussians.

The idea behind the CWT is to use the wavelet as a band-pass filter. The CWT of the signal $x(t)$ is defined as the convolution with the scaled and normalized wavelet.

$$\hat{X}(a,b) = \frac{1}{\sqrt{a}} \int_{-\infty}^{\infty} x(t)\psi^*\left(\frac{t-b}{a}\right)dt; \quad (5)$$

where $\psi^*(.)$ denotes the complex conjugation, $\frac{1}{\sqrt{a}}\psi\left(\frac{t-b}{a}\right)$ is the normalized wavelet function whose parameter b corresponds to the time shift, and the parameter $a > 0$ specifies the scaling.

After replacing the integral with the sum for discrete calculations $n = \frac{t}{\delta t}$, the relation for the CWT coefficients becomes:

$$\hat{X}(s,n) = \sum_{n'=0}^{N-1} x(n)\psi^*\left(\frac{(n-n')\delta t}{s}\right) \quad (6)$$

By the convolution theorem, the wavelet coefficients can be calculated more efficiently as the inverse discrete Fourier transform (DFT) of the product of the Fourier transforms of the signal and the wavelet coefficients in accordance with the formula:

$$\hat{X}(s,n) = x(n) * \psi(n) = F^{-1}[F(x(n))\cdot F(\psi(n,s))] \quad (7)$$

where F^{-1} is the operator of the inverse discrete Fourier transform and s is the scale number.

To analyze the BP and BFV signals, we choose the Morlet wavelet, which is used in medicine for cardiogram and encephalogram analyses more often than other wavelet bases since it ensures the rapid determination of changes in non-stationary signals.

Continuous non-orthogonal wavelets are effective for the analysis of time series and aperiodic shifts: the Morlet complex wavelet, the Pole complex wavelet, and the real Gaussian difference wavelet. The Morlet wavelet is determined by the formula:

$$\psi(t) = \pi^{-\frac{1}{4}}e^{-i\omega_0 t}e^{-\frac{t^2}{2}} \quad (8)$$

with parameter $\omega_0 = 6$. The Morlet wavelet in the frequency domain has the form $\hat{\psi}(s\omega) = \pi^{-\frac{1}{4}} e^{-\frac{(s\omega-\omega_0)^2}{2}}$.

2.3. Wavelet Transform of Signals Characterizing CA

The state of the CA is characterized by a phase shift between the BP and BFV separately for the right and left hemispheres of the brain in the presence of signal coherence in the decomposition space corresponding to the M-wave range, where the coherence is maximum. When describing the algorithm, we use the designation ξ_n for the sequence of readings of the BP signal and ζ_n for the BFV.

The algorithm for calculating the coherence and phase shift of signals by CWT, which is applied to two discrete centered signals $x_n = \xi_n - \frac{1}{N}\sum_{n=0}^{N-1} \xi_n$ and $y_n = \zeta_n - \frac{1}{N}\sum_{n=0}^{N-1} \zeta_n$, is measured with the use of optical sensors. The calculation is applied to data frames of length: $= N = 2^{floor(\log_2(N'))+1}$, where N' is the initial length of the signal frame to be analyzed.

For each signal frame x_n and y_n, we calculated the DFT:

$$\hat{x}_k = \sum_{n=0}^{N-1} x_n e^{-i2\pi kn}, \; \hat{y}_k = \sum_{n=0}^{N-1} y_n e^{-i2\pi kn} \tag{9}$$

where $k = 0, 1, 2 \ldots N-1$ denotes the frequency index.

The wavelet decomposition parameters, such as the minimum scale s_0, the maximum decomposition level J, specific decomposition levels $j = 0.1 \ldots J$ and the scale vector s_j are determined by the formulas: $s_0 = 2\delta t$, $J = \delta j^{-1} \log_2(\frac{Nx\delta t}{s_0})$, $s_j = s_0 2^{j\delta j}$.

The localization of wavelets in time and frequency makes it possible to associate the pseudo-frequencies f_j with the scale s_j: $f_j = \frac{\omega_0}{2\pi s_j}$ with allowance for the Fourier factor $\eta_0 = \frac{\omega_0}{2\pi}$.

The circular frequency at each expansion scale is determined by the formula:

$$\omega_k = \begin{cases} \frac{2\pi k}{N\delta t}, & k \leq \frac{N}{2} \\ -\frac{2\pi k}{N\delta t}, & k > \frac{N}{2} \end{cases} \tag{10}$$

The parameter ω_0 affects the resolution in time and frequency. The temporal resolution decreases as the frequency resolution increases. To analyze the signals, the Morlet wavelet parameter $\omega_0 = 6$ is chosen, which approximately corresponds to the respiratory rate.

DFT of the analytical Morlet wavelet defined by the formula:

$$\hat{\psi}(s\omega_k) = \pi^{-\frac{1}{4}} e^{-\frac{(s\omega-\omega_0)^2}{2}} H(\omega), \tag{11}$$

contains the Heaviside function $H(\omega_k) = \begin{cases} 1, & \omega_k > 0 \\ 0, & \omega_k \leq 0 \end{cases}$. On each expansion scale, the wavelet coefficients are normalized according to the formula:

$$\hat{\psi}(s\omega_k) = \sqrt{\frac{2\pi s}{\delta t}} \hat{\psi}_0(s\omega_k). \tag{12}$$

Element-by-element multiplication of the Fourier image of the analyzed signal and the Fourier images of wavelets at each decomposition level and the subsequent inverse DFT transformation allows us to obtain the coefficients of the wavelet decomposition of the signals x_n and y_n in the following form:

$$c_x(n,s) = \sum_{n=0}^{N-1} \hat{x}_k \hat{\psi}^*(s\omega_k) e^{i\omega_k n\delta t}, \tag{13}$$

$$c_y(n,s) = \sum_{n=0}^{N-1} \hat{y}_k \hat{\psi}^*(s\omega_k) e^{i\omega_k n\delta t}. \tag{14}$$

The calculation of the wavelet coefficients of the Fourier domain enables reducing the complexity of the calculations.

2.3.1. Smoothing

The signals $x(n)$ and $y(n)$ are mixed with other physiological signals and noise; it is necessary to perform smoothing when calculating the wavelet transform of the signals.

Time smoothing is conveniently performed in the frequency domain using the Gaussian window. To do this, on each scale, $s = 1 : N_s$, we multiply the Fourier transform of the wavelet coefficients $F(c_x(n,s))$, $s = 1 : N_s$ by the filter impulse response $h(n,s) = e^{-\frac{1}{4}s^2\omega(s)^2}$ and perform the inverse Fourier transform of the results:

$$\tilde{c}_x(n,s) = F^{-1}[h(n,s) \cdot F(c_x(n,s))], \tag{15}$$

where F^{-1} is the inverse DFT operator, $\tilde{c}_w(n,s)$ are the smoothed wavelet coefficients.

Scale smoothing was performed by averaging for a rectangular window:

$$\tilde{\tilde{c}}_x(n,s) = \sum_{l=0}^{L_s-1} \tilde{c}_x(n,s+l)\frac{1}{L_s}, \tag{16}$$

$$\tilde{\tilde{c}}_y(n,s) = \sum_{l=0}^{L_s-1} \tilde{c}_y(n,s+l)\frac{1}{L_s}. \tag{17}$$

where L_s is the length of the window.

Consequently, we obtained the wavelet coefficients of two signals $x(n)$ and $y(n)$ smoothed in time and scales $\tilde{\tilde{c}}_x(n,s)$ и $\tilde{\tilde{c}}_y(n,s)$.

The distribution of the wavelet coefficients in the area of Mayer waves is more peaked than the Gaussian distribution. This fact should be taken into account, when smoothing the coefficients in order to obtain more accurate results of the coherence analysis.

2.3.2. Cross-Wavelet Transform

The wavelet cross-spectrum characterizes the total energy of two signals, which is non-zero if the two signals correlate with each other and disappear if the two signals are independent:

$$\tilde{\tilde{c}}_{x,y}(n,s) = \tilde{\tilde{c}}_x^*(n,s)\tilde{\tilde{c}}_y(n,s). \tag{18}$$

In the general case, the wavelet cross-spectrum is a complex function, which is represented as an amplitude and a phase:

$$\tilde{\tilde{c}}_{x,y}(n,s) = \lfloor \tilde{\tilde{c}}_{x,y}(n,s) \rfloor exp\left(arctg\frac{Im\left(\tilde{\tilde{c}}_{x,y}(n,s)\right)}{Re\left(\tilde{\tilde{c}}_{x,y}(n,s)\right)} \right). \tag{19}$$

The coherence or consistency of two signals can be defined as the modulus of the normalized cross-spectrum. Coherence defines a linear relationship between two signals. The value of coherence varies from zero to one. The square of the normalized coherence value is determined by the formula:

$$H_{x,y}^2(n,s) = \frac{\left\lfloor \tilde{\tilde{c}}_x^*(n,s)\tilde{\tilde{c}}_y(n,s) \right\rfloor^2}{\left\lfloor \tilde{\tilde{c}}_x^*(n,s) \right\rfloor^2 \left\lfloor \tilde{\tilde{c}}_y(n,s) \right\rfloor^2}. \tag{20}$$

In the presence of the signal coherence specified by the condition $H^2_{x,y}(n,s) \geq 0.6$, the local phase shift of the signals can be obtained by the following formula:

$$\theta_{x,y}(n,s) = arctg\frac{Im\left(\tilde{\tilde{c}}^*_{x,y}(n,s)\right)}{Re\left(\tilde{\tilde{c}}_{x,y}(n,s)\right)}. \quad (21)$$

The coefficient, 0.6, corresponds to the scale decorrelation length for the Morlet wavelet [33,34]. A. Kulaichev [35] empirically showed in the analysis of encephalograms that the value of the coherence coefficient should be greater than 0.6.

The value of the phase shift allows us to define the delay between two coherent signals. Statistical data processing and calculations were carried out using the Matlab computer program. The significance of differences in values was assessed using the Student's t-test.

The sensitivity of phase shift changes during the tests was determined by the formula: $\eta = \frac{|\theta_{ext-} - \overline{\theta}|}{\overline{\theta}}$, where θ_{ext-} is the extreme value of PS when it affects on autoregulation, $\overline{\theta}$ is the average value of PS when there is no effect on autoregulation.

3. Results

3.1. Results of the Wavelet Analysis of the BP and BFV Signals

BP and BFV measurements were obtained synchronously with a time interval of 0.01 s after analog-to-digital conversion. The received BP and BFV formed into frames were processed using the continuous wavelet transform. For each frame, CWT was performed using the Morlet wavelets. As a result, the coherence values (20) were obtained for the sequence of frames. The phase shifts (21) were calculated for those samples for which the coherence values met the condition $H^2_{x,y}(n,s) \geq 0.6$.

The results obtained for one frame are shown in Figure 1 The arrows show the phase angles between the BP and BFV signals in the left middle cerebral artery against the background of the magnitude-squared coherence between these signals. The magnitude-squared coherence value is shown in color according to the color bar. High coherence is observed in the area of pseudo-frequencies that correspond to the heart rate, respiratory rate, and M-waves. It is typical for a healthy volunteer (Figure 1a) to obtain a stable value of the coherence and shear angle. For a patient with an arteriovenous malformation in the basin of the left middle cerebral artery (Figure 1b), the shift angle was significantly smaller (0.5 rad). These plots were obtained using the Matlab coherence function wcoherence().

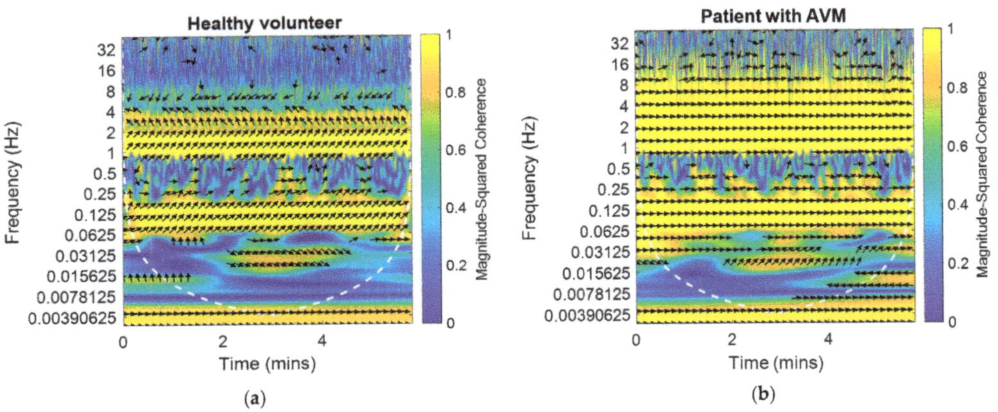

Figure 1. The example of the dependences of the phase shift between the BP and BFV signals in the left and right middle cerebral arteries against the background of the magnitude-squared coherence between the signals on time and pseudo-frequency: (**a**) For a healthy volunteer on one side; (**b**) For a patient with an arteriovenous malformation in the left middle cerebral artery on the AVM side.

Figure 2 shows the values of the average phase angle between the BP and BFV obtained during the observation time (6 min) for both study groups. For each subject, the average values of the phase shift angle on both sides and the confidence limits at the level of two standard deviations ($\theta_{x,y} \pm 3\sigma$) are shown. Healthy volunteers are characterized by more stable and symmetrical values of the angles. In patients with arteriovenous malformation (AVM) in the region of the left middle cerebral artery, the values of the shear angles are almost half of that on the right, and their values are more variable, with increased standard deviation and wider confidence intervals.

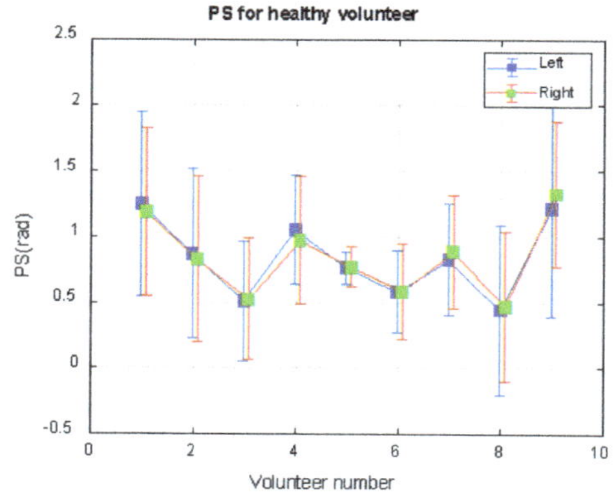

(a)

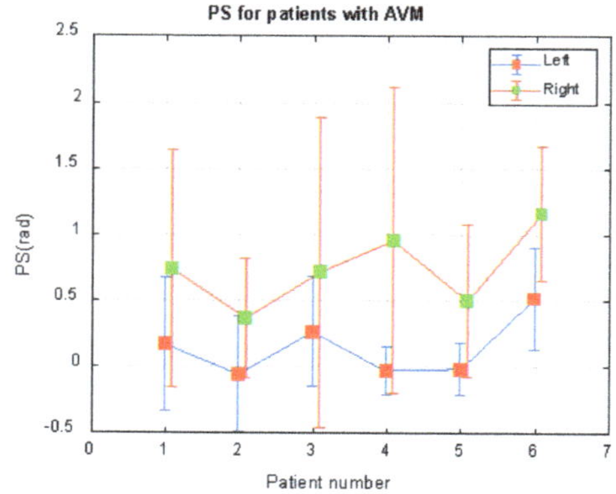

(b)

Figure 2. Average phase shift (PS) between the BP and BFV signals in the Mayer waveband: (**a**) For nine healthy volunteers; (**b**) For six patients with an AVM in the area of the left middle cerebral artery.

3.2. *System of Neuro Care Monitoring*

The system of Neuro Care Monitoring (NCM), designed to assess the state of the CA in real-time, implements the algorithm presented here for the frame-by-frame determination of the phase angle between the BP and BFV in the Mayer wave range in areas of coherence.

Figure 3 shows a block diagram of the NCM system applying transducers of the multichannel system (1) Multi Dop X (DWL, Singen, Germany) for continuous non-invasive assessment of BFV in the arteries of the brain base with the use of transcranial Doppler ultrasonography and the Instrument (2) CNAP (Austria, Graz), for measuring systemic blood pressure by photo-plethysmography. The measurement results after the analog-to-digital conversion and the formation of frames in Data Input Device (3) are fed to the input of the Computing Unit (4), which implements the developed algorithm in real-time, sequentially processing data frames using the wavelet transform. Parameter Input Interface (5) allows us to set a number of algorithm parameters: frame size and offset, coherence threshold value, frequency from the Mayer range, etc. To document the results of the study, you can enter the date and time of the study, patient or volunteer data, preliminary diagnosis, etc. The results of patients' examinations can be displayed (6), printed as a document (7), saved in a data file, and sent to the database (8). The software interface is designed to set calculation parameters and view results in real time.

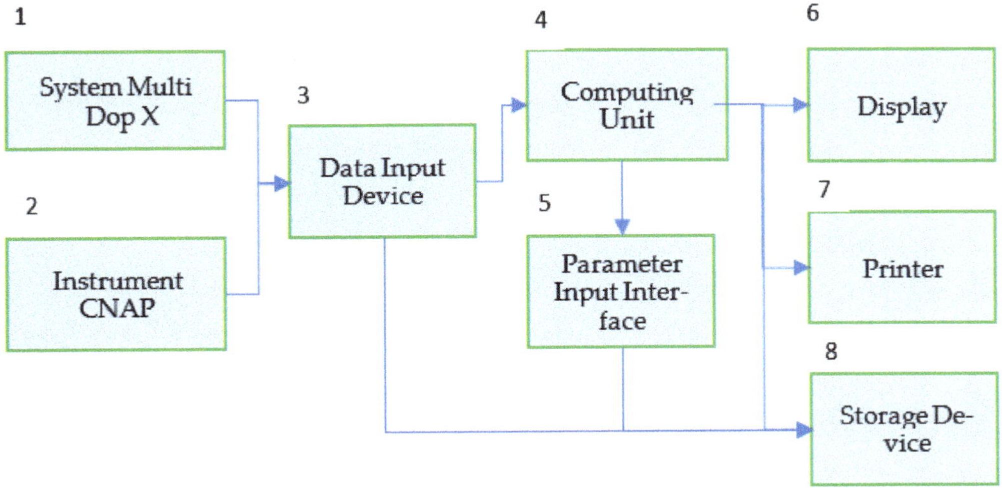

Figure 3. Block diagram of the NCM system for monitoring the state of the target audience in real time.

The standalone application (software) was written in the C programming language to acquire a reasonable calculation result in real-time. To get a better user-friendly interface, we used the National Instruments Labwindows/CVI software developing environment [https://ni.com/cvi]. (accessed on 20 August 2022). Its run-time library has a wide range of control and representation features we utilized in our application. Moreover, it has a set of data analysis functions that we also use in our software. The screenshots in Figures 5 and 6 were taken by our application.

The sensors were always placed standardly bilaterally for registration of BFV in the initial segments of the middle cerebral arteries. The frame size for STFT was 214 = 16,384 samples with an interval of 0.01 s, and the frame duration was 163.84 s. Inside the frame, the sliding Hamming window was used, the size of which was 1024 samples, and the offset was 512. Accordingly, the number of windows inside the frame was 32.

The frame size for the CWT transform was 214 = 16,384 samples with an interval of 0.01 s, and the frame duration was 163.84 s. The duration of the study was 35 min. The frequency range of M-waves approximately corresponds to the frequency range of 0.08–0.12 Hz. The study of signals in the range of M-waves shows that a more accurate frequency setting within the M-range allows for increased sensitivity of the algorithm. The higher frequency resolution of the wavelet transform makes it possible to determine the phase shift in a specific space with maximum signal coherence.

Figure 4 shows the displayed results of examining a healthy volunteer during standardized exercise. The hypercapnic test was based on breathing for 2 min with a carbogen—5% mixture of CO_2 with air, and the hypocapnic test was based on rapid, deep breathing for 1 min, leading to a significant decrease in CO_2 in exhaled air.

The graphs results of measuring the BP and BFV in the left middle cerebral artery (MCA) and the right MCA are shown in red, blue, and dark green, respectively. The scale of these parameters is shown on the left. Graphs of the phase shift between the BP and the left BFV and between the BP and the right BFV, calculated on the basis of wavelets, are shown by the yellow and red lines, respectively. These plots can be compared with similar plots derived from the FFT, as shown by the blue and green lines. Curves on the graphs show that the CWT-based algorithm is more sensitive to PS changes during hypercapnic (1) and hypocapnic (2) trials, and it has better time localization. The arrow pointing up indicates the beginning of the hypercapnic test (1), while the arrow pointing down indicates its end. Similarly directed arrows indicate the beginning and end of the hypocapnic test (2).

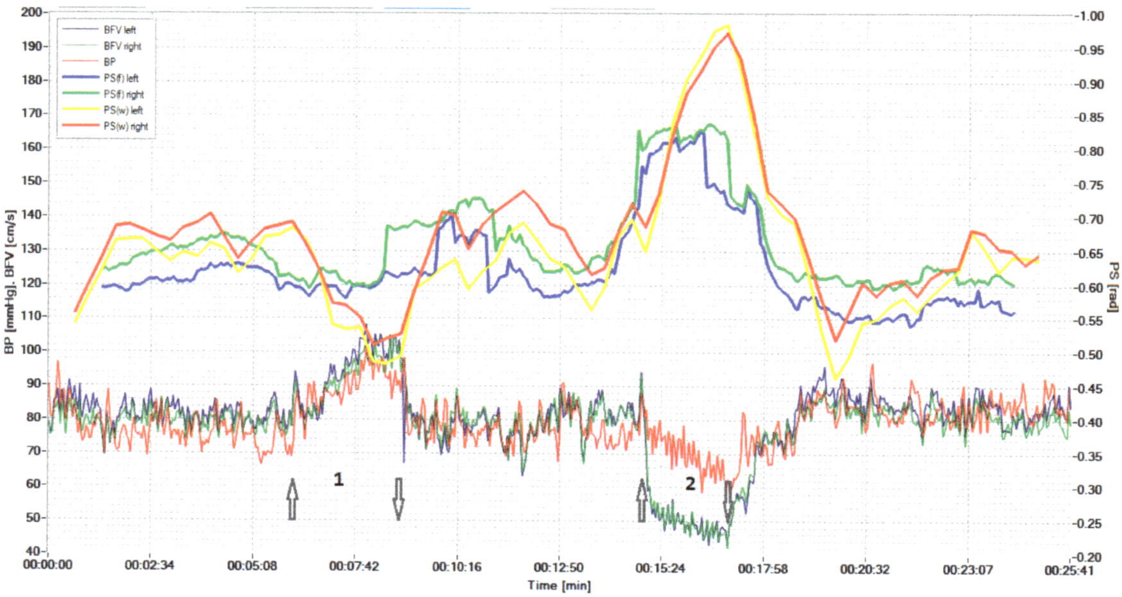

Figure 4. Simultaneous monitoring of parameters of the cerebral, systemic hemodynamics, and the cerebral autoregulation state in a 19-year-old healthy volunteer. The arrow pointing up indicates the beginning of the hypercapnic test (1), while the arrow pointing down indicates its end. Similarly directed arrows indicate the beginning and end of the hypocapnic test (2).

Sensitivity analysis of phase shift changes showed that the CWT-based method is more sensitive. The sensitivity to the hypercapnic test using STFT for the left and right hemispheres averaged 0.065 and 0.060, and for the CWT method—0.11 and 0.10, respectively. The sensitivity to the hypocapnic test of the STFT method averaged 0.33 and 0.31, and the sensitivity of the CWT method was 0.46 and 0.47, respectively.

For smaller samples of examined persons, we determined the reliability of the difference between the methods based on CWT and STFT using the t-test.

As a result of testing, we obtained the following:

- The hypercapnic test led to a greater relative decrease in PS on both sides for the CWT method than for the STFT method; the magnitude of the decrease was 14.6 $\pm$ 6.6% for CWT and 8.2 $\pm$ 4.5% on the left ($p = 0.022$), and for STFT—14.4 $\pm$ 5.8% and 8.2 $\pm$ 4.2% on the right ($p = 0.014$).
- The hypocapnic test led to a greater relative increase in PS on both sides for the CWT method than for the STFT method; the magnitude of the increase was 44.4 $\pm$ 22.7% for CWT and 28.8 $\pm$ 17.3% for STFT on the left ($p = 0.035$), 45.9 $\pm$ 24.8% and 28.2 $\pm$ 17.9% on the right ($p = 0.041$).

Figure 5 shows the results of the survey of a patient with a unilateral CA disorder in the region of the stenotic artery, detected in real-time during the hypercapnic test (1) at time intervals indicated by the number (2). The arrow pointing up indicates the beginning of the hypercapnic test (1), while the arrow pointing down indicates its end. Similarly directed arrows indicate the beginning and end of the hypocapnic test (2). Figures 4 and 5 adopted the same designation as the dependency graphs.

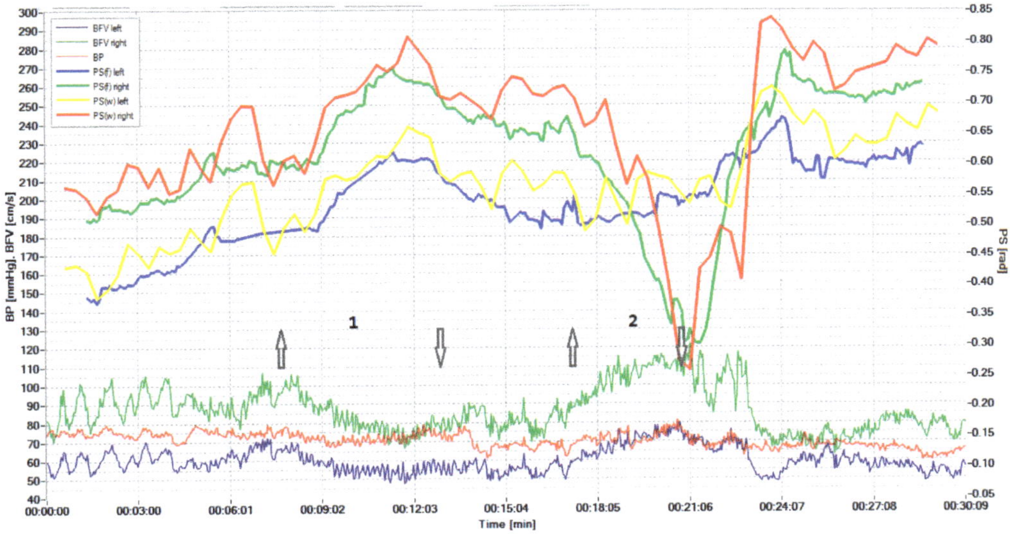

Figure 5. Simultaneous monitoring of the cerebral, systemic hemodynamics, and the state of the CA in a 73-year-old patient with critical stenosis of the internal carotid artery. The arrow pointing up indicates the beginning of the hypercapnic test (1), while the arrow pointing down indicates its end. Similarly directed arrows indicate the beginning and end of the hypocapnic test (2).

Hypercapnic and hypocapnic tests are not always attractive for patients with pathology. Therefore, such tests were carried out for one patient. The sensitivity of the CWT-based method was also slightly better than that of the STFT method.

To validate the CWT-based method, we obtained BP and BFV measurements from volunteers and patients within 8–10 min. These data were used to evaluate wavelet coherence and PS for 11 healthy volunteers, six patients with malformation, four patients with stenosis, and 10 patients with thrombosis (six patients before surgery). Reliable determination of the left or right affected part of the artery was a criterion for the quality of the algorithm. The PS between the BP and BFV signals in the wavelet domain of the Mayer waveband for AVM patients is shown in Figure 2b.

Figure 6 presents the average values of PS for patients with carotid stenosis.

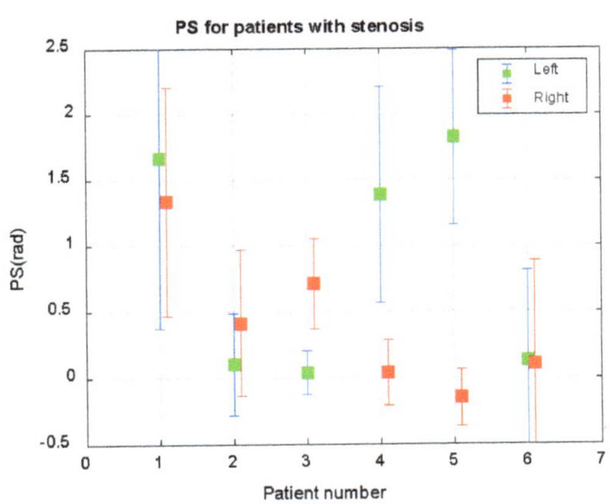

Figure 6. Average phase shift (PS) between the BP and BFV signals in the Mayer waveband in 6 patients with carotid stenosis.

The analysis of the results of the PS assessment for patients with stenosis, shown in Figure 6, allows us to conclude that Patient 1 has normal CA, Patients 2 and 6 have a very low PS value, indicating a violation of CA, Patients 2 and 3 have stenosis of the left, and in Patients 4 and 5—stenosis of the right internal carotid artery. The asymmetry of CA for Patients 2–5 is determined with a reliability greater than 0.999.

Tests on healthy volunteers and patients were performed with a data frame length of 16,384 samples, obtained in 2.7 min. The number of scales of the wavelet transform is 16 with a 12 voices number. Taking into account the Fourier factor 0.9549, it turned out that in the Mayer wavelength range, we had nine frequencies f = [0.124, 0.117, 0.110, 0.104, 0.098, 0.093, 0.088, 0.083, 0.078] Hz. This number of frequency gradations allowed us to fine-tune the algorithm. The frequency resolution varied along the M-wave range. At the beginning of the range at the frequency of 0.12 Hz, it was 0.007 Hz, and at the end of the range at the frequency of 0.08 Hz, it was 0.005 Hz. The time resolution was 0.01.

The algorithm based on the short-time Fourier cross-spectrum had the worst frequency resolution, which was the same over the entire range, equal to 0.04 Hz for our example.

4. Discussion

When monitoring CA in humans under various pathological conditions or in normal conditions, it is advisable to use non-invasive assessment methods based on retrospective cross-spectral and cross-correlation analysis of slow fluctuations in systemic and cerebral hemodynamics. When conducting functional tests and diagnosing emergency conditions in intensive care, it is necessary to apply a method that would provide prompt information about the state of the CA in real time, with the best resolutions in time and frequency. In our previous study [36,37], we proposed an algorithm based on the short-time cross-Fourier spectrum and the coherence spectrum, which makes it possible to obtain the estimated characteristics with constant scale resolution in time and frequency. The results received under standardized loads on the cerebral circulatory systems showed the possibility of assessing the state of cerebral autoregulation in real-time, and it first established the advantages of the wavelet analysis to collect reliable data on the phase shift between M-waves of BFV and BP.

The present study is different, as it allows monitoring with both higher sensitivity and better resolution in the time-frequency domain due to the use of continuous wavelet transform of the signals. In order to prove this, the authors carried out special tests that affect CA.

At certain time slots, the condition $H^2_{x,y}(n,s) < 0.6$ may not be satisfied, there is no coherence, and the phase shift cannot be calculated. In such cases, the graphs (Figures 5 and 6) may have gaps, the number of which should be reduced. To do this, we propose the use of a more accurate Mayer frequency fit. In our case, the wavelet transform using 12 voices allows us to search at 14 pseudo-frequencies in the Mayer waveband. The subrange selection criterion may be the largest proportion of values suitable for calculating the phase shift. When scanning subranges of Mayer waves, it turned out that the relative proportion of coherence intervals varies from 0.35 to 0.82 for the BP and BFV in the left hemisphere and from 0.50 to 0.88 for the BP and BFV in the right hemisphere. Thus, increasing the resolution in frequency improved the result of the study.

The proposed method was implemented as an algorithm for the operation of the analytical NCM. Studies of healthy volunteers and patients with CA disorders carried out with the NCM indicated the reliability of the results of a non-invasive assessment of the CA rate in real time. By simultaneously monitoring indicators of systemic and cerebral hemodynamics and CA rate, the developed analytical measuring system allowed in real-time enhancing non-invasiveness, the efficiency of an objective assessment of a person's state in the norm, and the identification of a group of patients with CA disorders and a high risk of complications. All this can determine tactics and continuous monitoring of treatment results.

Accumulation and centralization of the digitized research data of many patients and the combination and formation of the knowledge base in the field of medicine and physiology can serve as a prerequisite for further research. The observations related to one patient contribute to a deeper understanding of the disease mechanisms and personalization of treatment. The integration of general and personalized data can make it possible to generate big data for the analysis of hidden patterns, where it is possible to use machine learning methods.

One of the trends for the development of methods for studying CA characteristics is to supplement the traditional methods of spectral, correlation, and wavelet analysis of signals with fractal analysis algorithms since the width of the multifractal spectrum and the correlation dimension of the BP and BFV signals are informative since they can correctly show the relationship between these signals having different scaling behavior.

5. Conclusions

Ultimately, the application of time-frequency transformations makes it possible to optimize the timing of obtaining the necessary information about the state of CA in order to study the mechanisms of the regulation of cerebral blood flow and make therapeutic and tactical decisions in real time, including in intensive care.

The results of our studies reflect the reliability of the data obtained from the non-invasive assessment of the CA rate in real-time and allow us to identify a group of patients with impaired CA and a high risk of complications and to determine the tactics and continuous monitoring of treatment results.

The comparative analyses of the Fourier and wavelet transform show certain advantages of the latter when carrying out standardized loads and allow us to recommend using the wavelet transform to build algorithms for processing indicators from systemic and cerebral hemodynamics.

Author Contributions: Conceptualization, V.S. (Vladimir Semenyutin) and G.M.; methodology, G.M.; software, V.S. (Vyacheslav Salnikov) and G.M.; validation, V.S. (Vladimir Semenyutin), V.A.(Valery Antonov) and G.M.; formal analysis, V.A.; investigation, V.S. (Vladimir Semenyutin); resources, V.S. (Vladimir Semenyutin); data curation, V.S. (Vladimir Semenyutin); writing—original draft preparation, G.M.; writing—review and editing, V.S. (Vladimir Semenyutin), V.A. and G.M.; visualization, V.S. (Vyacheslav Salnikov); supervision, V.S. (Vladimir Semenyutin); project administration, V.S. (Vladimir Semenyutin); funding acquisition, V.S. (Vladimir Semenyutin). All authors have read and agreed to the published version of the manuscript.

Funding: This research work was supported by project No. 19-29-01190/19 on the topic development and application of methods of mathematical analysis of physiological parameters for the operational diagnosis of pathological conditions of patients with an assessment of the risks of their transition to critical conditions in a real-time proposal by the Russian Foundation for Basic Research.

Institutional Review Board Statement: The study was conducted in accordance with the Declaration of Helsinki and approved by the Ethics Committee of the Russian Polenov Neurosurgical Institute (protocols of investigation volunteers and neurosurgical patients dated 16 July 2010).

Informed Consent Statement: Informed consent was obtained from all subjects involved in the study. Written informed consent has been obtained from the patients to publish this paper.

Data Availability Statement: Not applicable here.

Acknowledgments: The Laboratory of Brain Circulation Pathology staff for technical support during the examination of patients and healthy volunteers.

Conflicts of Interest: The authors declare no conflict of interest. The funders had no role in the design of the study; in the collection, analyses, or interpretation of data; in the writing of the manuscript; or in the decision to publish the results.

References

1. Olesen, J. Quantitative evaluation of normal and pathologic cerebral blood regulation to perfusion pressure: Changes in man. *Arch. Neurol.* **1973**, *28*, 143–149. [CrossRef] [PubMed]
2. Aaslid, R.; Markwalder, T.M.; Nornes, H. Noninvasive transcranial Doppler ultrasound recording of flow velocity in basal cerebral arteries. *J. Neurosurg.* **1982**, *57*, 769–774. [CrossRef] [PubMed]
3. Kontos, H. Validity of cerebral arterial blood flow calculations from velocity measurements. *Stroke* **1989**, *20*, 1–3. [CrossRef]
4. Newell, D.; Wim, H. Transcranial Doppler in cerebral vasospasm. *Neurosurg. Clin. N. Am.* **1990**, *1*, 319–328. [CrossRef] [PubMed]
5. Lewis, S.B.; Wong, M.L.; Bannan, P.E.; Piper, I.R.; Reilly, P.L. Transcranial Doppler identification of changing autoregulatory threshold after autoregulatory impartment. *Neurosurgery* **2001**, *48*, 369–375.
6. Kuo, T.C.; Chern, C.C.; Yang Hsu, H.-Y.; Wong, W.-J.; Sheng, W.Y.; Hu, H.-H. Mechanisms underlying phase lag between systemic arterial blood pressure and cerebral blood flow velocity. *Cerebrovasc. Dis.* **2003**, *16*, 402–409. [CrossRef]
7. Soehle, M.; Czosnyka, M.; Pickard, J.D.; Kirkpatrick, P.J. Continuous assessment of cerebral autoregulation in subarachnoid hemorrhage. *Anedth. Amalg.* **2004**, *98*, 1133–1139. [CrossRef] [PubMed]
8. Van Beek, A.H.; Claassen, J.; Rikkert, M.; Jansen, R. Cerebral autoregulation on overview of current concepts and methodology with special focus on the elderly. *J. Cereb. Blood Flow Metab.* **2008**, *28*, 1071–1085. [CrossRef] [PubMed]
9. Panerai, R. Transcranial Doppler for evaluation of cerebral autoregulation. Cerebral autoregulation dynamics in premature newborns. *Clin. Auton Res.* **2009**, *19*, 197–211. [CrossRef] [PubMed]
10. Porras, S.; Santos, E.; Czosnyka, M.; Zheng, Z.; Unterberg, A.W.; Sakowitz, O.W. Long pressure reactivity index (L-PRx) as a measure of autoregulation correlates with outcomes in traumatic brain injury patients. *Acta Neurochir.* **2012**, *154*, 1575–1581. [CrossRef] [PubMed]
11. Hlatky, R.; Valadka, A.B.; Robertson, C.S. Analisis of dynamic autoregulation assessed by the cuff deflation method. *Neurocrit. Care* **2006**, *4*, 127–132. [CrossRef]
12. Julien, C. The enigma of Mayer waves: Facts and models. *Cardiovasc. Res.* **2006**, *70*, 12–21. [CrossRef]
13. Mayer, S. Studien zur physiologie des herzens und der blutgefässe. *Sitz. Kais. Akad. Wiss.* **1876**, *74*, 281–307.
14. Reinhard, M.; Roth, M.; Müller, T.; Guschlbauer, B.; Timmer, J.; Czosnyka, M.; Hetzel, A. Effect of carotid Endarterectomy or Stenting on improvement of dynamic cerebral autoregulation. *Stroke* **2004**, *35*, 1381–1387. [CrossRef]
15. Czosnyka, M.; Brady, K.; Reinhard, M.; Smielewski, P.; Steiner, L.A. Monitoring of cerebrovascular autoregulation: Facts, myths, and missing links. *Naurocrit. Care* **2009**, *10*, 373–386. [CrossRef]
16. Payne, S. *Cerebral Autoregulation Control of Blood Flow in the Brain*; Springer: Berlin, Germany, 2016; Volume XV, p. 125.
17. Smielewski, P.; Czosnyka, M.; Zabolotny, W.; Kirkpatrick, P. A computing system for the clinical and experimental investigation of cerebrovascular reactivity. *Int. J. Clin. Monit. Comput.* **1997**, *14*, 185–198. [CrossRef]
18. Budohoski, K.; Czosnyka, M.; de Riva, N.; Smielewski, P.; Pickard, J.D.; Menon, D.K.; Kirkpatrick, P.J.; Lavinio, A. The relationship between cerebral blood flow autoregulation and cerebrovascular pressure reactivity after traumatic brain injury. *Neurosurgery* **2012**, *71*, 652–660. [CrossRef]
19. Xiuyun, L.; Czosnyka, M.; Donnelly, J.; Smielewski, P. Comparison of Frequency and Time Domain Methods of Assessment of Cerebral Autoregulation in Traumatic Brain Injury. *J. Cereb. Blood Flow Metab.* **2014**, *35*, 192.
20. Liu, X.; Hu, X.; Brady, K.M. Comparison of wavelet and correlation indices of cerebral autoregulation in a pediatric swine model of cardiac arrest. *Sci. Rep.* **2020**, *10*, 5926. [CrossRef]
21. Tian, F.; Tarumi, T.; Liu, H.; Zhang, R.; Chalak, L. Wavelet coherence analysis of dynamic cerebral autoregulation in neonatal hypoxic–ischemic encephalopathy. *NeuroImage Clin.* **2016**, *11*, 124–132. [CrossRef]
22. Smielewski, P.; Czosnyka, M.; Kirkpatrick, P.; McEroy, H.; Rutkowska, H.; Pickard, J.D. Assessment of cerebral autoregulation using carotid artery compression. *Stroke* **1996**, *27*, 2197–2203. [CrossRef]
23. Lewis, P.M.; Smielewski, P.; Rosenfeld, J.V.; Pickard, J.D.; Czosnyka, M. Assessment of cerebral autoregulation from respiratory oscillations in ventilated patients after traumatic brain injury. *Acta Neurochir. Suppl.* **2012**, *114*, 141–146.
24. Pan, Y.; Wan, W.; Xiang, M.; Guan, Y. Transcranial Doppler Ultrasonography as a Diagnostic Tool for Cerebrovascular Disorders. *Front. Hum. Neurosci.* **2022**, *16*, 841809. [CrossRef]
25. D'Andrea, A.; Conte, M.; Cavallaro, M.; Scarafile, R.; Riegler, L.; Cocchia, R.; Pezzullo, E.; Carbone, A.; Natale, F.; Santoro, G.; et al. Transcranial Doppler ultrasonography: From methodology to major clinical applications. *World J. Cardiol.* **2016**, *8*, 383–400. [CrossRef]
26. Tas, J.; Eleveld, N.; Borg, M.; Bos, K.D.J.; Langermans, A.P.; van Kuijk, S.M.J.; van der Horst, I.C.C.; Elting, J.W.J.; Aries, M.J.H. Cerebral Autoregulation Assessment Using the Near Infrared Spectroscopy 'NIRS-Only' High Frequency Methodology in Critically Ill Patients: A Prospective Cross-Sectional Study. *Cells* **2022**, *11*, 2254. [CrossRef]
27. Panerai, R.B.; Jara, J.L.; Saeed, N.P.; Horsfield, M.A.; Robinson, T.G. Dynamic cerebral autoregulation following acute ischaemic stroke: Comparison of transcranial Doppler and magnetic resonance imaging techniques. *J. Cereb. Blood Flow Metab.* **2016**, *36*, 2194–2202. [CrossRef]
28. Watanabe, H.; Washio, T.; Saito, S.; Hirasawa, A.; Suzuki, R.; Shibata, S.; Brothers, R.M.; Ogoh, S. Validity of transcranial Doppler ultrasonography-determined dynamic cerebral autoregulation estimated using transfer function analysis. *J. Clin. Monit. Comput.* **2022**, *36*, 1711–1721. [CrossRef]

29. d Classen, J.; Abeelen, A.M.; Simpson, D.M. Transfer function analysis of dynamic cerebral autoregulation research network. *J. Cereb. Blood Flow Metab.* **2016**, *1*, 1–16.
30. Alkhachroum, A.; Kromm, J.; De Georgia, M.A. Big data and predictive analytics in neurocritical care. *Curr. Neurol. Neurosci. Rep.* **2022**, *22*, 19–32. [CrossRef]
31. Malykhina, G.F.; Merkusheva, A.V. Classes of transformations of a non-stationary signal in information-measuring systems. VI. Correspondence of the form of covariance and the type of time-frequency transformation. *Sci. Instrum.* **2007**, *17*, 75–87.
32. Merkusheva, A.V.; Malykhina, G.F. The generalized Fourier transform method for time-frequency transformations, multiplexing and filtering of non-stationary signals in information systems. *Sci. Instrum.* **2006**, *16*, 85–96.
33. Torrence, C.; Compo, G.P. Program in Atmospheric and Oceanic Sciences, University of Colorado, Boulder, Colorado. *Bull. Am. Meteorol. Soc.* **1998**, *79*, 61–78. [CrossRef]
34. Grinsted, A.; Moore, J.C.; Jevrejeva, S. Application of the cross wavelet transform and wavelet coherence to geophysical time series. Nonlinear Processes in Geophysics. *Eur. Geosci. Union (EGU)* **2004**, *11*, 561–566.
35. Kulaichev, A.P. The Informativeness of Coherence Analysis in EEG Studies. *Neurosci. Behav. Phys.* **2011**, *41*, 321–328. [CrossRef]
36. Malykhina, G.; Salnikov, V.; Semenyutin, V.; Tarkhov, D. Digitalization of medical services for detecting violations of cerebrovascular regulation based on a neural network signal analysis algorithm. *ACM Int. Conf. Proc. Ser.* **2020**, *61*, 1–11.
37. Malykhina, G.F.; Salnikov, V.Y.; Semenyutin, V.B. Neural network algorithm for the diagnosis of impaired cerebral autoregulation. In *Neuralinformatics*; Publishing House of the Moscow Engineering Physics Institute: Moscow, Russia, 2020.

biomedicines

Article

Electroencephalography Signatures for Hepatic Encephalopathy in Cirrhosis Patients Treated with Proton Pump Inhibitors: An Exploratory Pilot Study

Pan Zhang [1,†], Lizhi Zhou [1,2,†], Li Chen [3], Zhen Zhang [3], Rui Han [3], Gangwen Guo [3,*] and Haocheng Zhou [3,4,*]

1 Department of Infectious Diseases, Third Xiangya Hospital, Central South University, Changsha 410013, China
2 Department of Infectious Diseases, Xiangtan Central Hospital, Xiangtan 411100, China
3 Department of Pain, Third Xiangya Hospital and Institute of Pain Medicine, Central South University, Changsha 410013, China
4 Hunan Key Laboratory of Brain Homeostasis, Central South University, Changsha 410013, China
* Correspondence: gangwen.guo@outlook.com (G.G.); haocheng.zhou@csu.edu.cn (H.Z.)
† These authors contributed equally to this paper.

Citation: Zhang, P.; Zhou, L.; Chen, L.; Zhang, Z.; Han, R.; Guo, G.; Zhou, H. Electroencephalography Signatures for Hepatic Encephalopathy in Cirrhosis Patients Treated with Proton Pump Inhibitors: An Exploratory Pilot Study. *Biomedicines* **2022**, *10*, 3040. https://doi.org/10.3390/biomedicines10123040

Academic Editors: Wolfgang Kreisel and Michele Morari

Received: 19 October 2022
Accepted: 23 November 2022
Published: 24 November 2022

Abstract: (1) Background: Hepatic encephalopathy (HE) is a common complication in cirrhosis patients, and recently, clinical evidence indicates that a higher risk of HE is associated with the usage of proton pump inhibitors. However, the cortical mechanism underlying this neurological disorder of HE remains unknown. (2) Methods: We review the medical recordings of 260 patients diagnosed with liver cirrhosis between January 2021 and March 2022 in one tertiary hospital. Logistic regression analyses were performed to identify the risk factor of HE development. To examine the relationship between cortical dynamics and the administration of proton pump inhibitors, resting-state electroencephalograms (EEGs) were conducted in cirrhosis patients who were treated with proton pump inhibitors. (3) Results: About 28.5% (74 out of 260) of participants developed secondary HE in this study. The logistics regression model indicated that multiple risk factors were associated with the incidence of secondary HE, including proton pump inhibitors usage, white blood cell and neutrophil counts, hemoglobin, prothrombin time activity, and blood urea nitrogen. A total of twelve cirrhosis patients who were scheduled to use proton pump inhibitors consented to performing electroencephalogram recordings upon admission, and eight of twelve participants were diagnosed with HE. Spectral analysis revealed that the decrease in alpha oscillation activities was potentially associated with the development of HE. (4) Conclusions: Our data support the susceptibility of secondary HE in cirrhosis patients treated by proton pump inhibitors. One potential cortical mechanism underlying the neurological disease is the suppression of alpha oscillations in the brain.

Keywords: hepatic encephalopathy; cirrhosis; proton pump inhibitor; risk factor; EEG; cortical; neural oscillation

1. Introduction

It has been estimated that the aged-standardized prevalence of cirrhosis was about 0.7% in China, with the leading cause being the hepatitis B virus [1]. Multiple complications of cirrhosis significantly reduced the quality of life and accounted for the increasing mortality, including ascites, varices, hepatocellular carcinoma, hepatic encephalopathy (HE), hepatopulmonary syndrome, and coagulation disorders [2]. The featured neurological dysfunction was the most devastating complication of cirrhosis; namely, the HE is frequently reported to be associated with the medical usage of benzodiazepines, opiates, and proton pump inhibitors (PPIs) [3]. PPIs remains one of the most commonly used medication in cirrhosis populations despite its abuse in clinical practice [4,5]. Emerging evidence suggested the potential link between PPI applications and HE development [4,6–8]. Thus, it is essential to identify the susceptibility of HE in patients with advanced liver disease during PPI treatments.

Functional magnetic resonance imaging may provide morphological evidence as one potential bio-marker for exploring the neural correlates of cognitive deficits [9]. However, the great cost and complicated data processing may hinder clinical applications. Alternatively, the electroencephalogram is relatively easy to perform for the diagnosis of the neurological disease, including epilepsy, autism spectrum disorder, and Alzheimer's disease [10,11]. Furthermore, emerging evidence has supported the diagnostic value of quantitative EEGs in terms of survival and the risk of developing overt HE [12,13]. However, the relationship between the cortical dynamics and HE development during PPIs management remains uncertain. In this study, we initially reviewed the medical data of 260 cirrhosis patients to confirm the role of PPIs in the development of secondary HE in hospitalized patients. Next, we aimed to investigate the potential cortical signature of HE candidates who received PPI treatment.

2. Materials and Methods

2.1. Patients and Study Design

This study was conducted in accordance with the guidance of the Helsinki Declaration and approved by the Ethics Committee of The Third Xiangya Hospital, Central South University, China (NO. 222128). The study was registered at chictr.org.cn accessed on 29 June 2022 (ChiCTR2200061590).

In the first experiment, we retrospectively reviewed the medical recordings of 260 patients who were diagnosed with liver cirrhosis using ICD-9-CM codes at The Department of Infectious Diseases, Third Xiangya Hospital. The participants were then grouped into HE and non-HE sub-groups according to the development of secondary HE during hospitalization. HE is characterized by personality changes, intellectual impairment, and a depressed level of consciousness, which was classified into five degrees based on the severity of disease [14]. The initial search of HE incidences was performed by scanning the home page of electrical medical recording systems with the ICD-9-CM code (K72.903), which was followed by the manual verification of the medical records provided by one independent researcher (L.Z.). The classification of HE is provided in Table 1. We did not obtain information on disease severities for the first experiment due to the retrospective design of the study. However, we assessed the severity of HE in the prospective EEG study. The flow chart for patient selection and inclusion and exclusion criteria are shown in Figure 1A.

Table 1. Classification of hepatic encephalopathy (HE) in patient with cirrhosis.

Revised HE Grading Criteria	Neuropsychiatric Symptoms	Nervous System Signs
Non-HE	Normal	Normal nervous system signs, normal neuropsychological test results
Minimal HE	Potential HE, no noticeable personality or behavioral changes	Normal nervous system signs, but abnormal neuropsychological test results
HE Grade One	Trivial and mild clinical signs, such as mild cognitive impairment, decreased attention, sleep disorders (insomnia and sleep inversion), euphoria, or depression	Asterixis can be elicited and neuropsychological tests are abnormal
HE Grade Two	Marked personality or behavioral changes, lethargy or apathy, slight orientation abnormality (time and orientation), decreased mathematical ability, dyskinesia, or unclear speech	Asterixis is easily elicited, and neurophysiological testing is unnecessary
HE Grade Three	Marked dysfunction (time and spatial orientation), abnormal behavior, semi-coma to coma, but responsive	Asterixis usually cannot be elicited. There is ankle clonus, increased muscle tone, and hyperreflexia. Neurophysiological testing is unnecessary
HE Grade Four	Coma (no response to speech and external stimuli)	Increased muscle tone or positive signs of the central nervous system. Neurophysiological testing is unnecessary

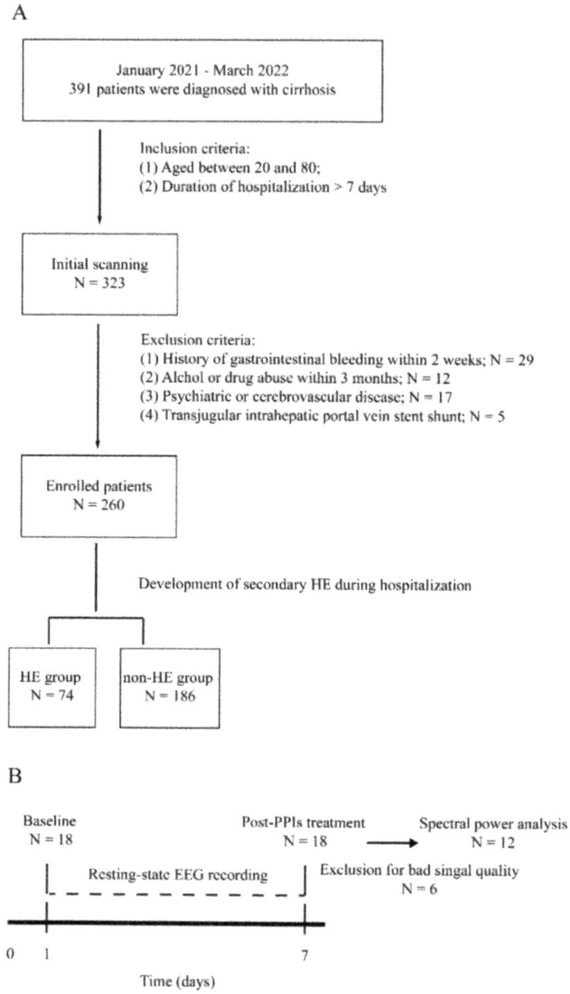

Figure 1. Study protocol for the Experiment One and Two. (**A**) Flow chart of patient selection for the first part of the study. (**B**) Schematic of EEG recording protocol for the second experiment.

In the second experiment, eighteen cirrhosis patients who were scheduled to take PPI therapy during hospitalization were enrolled and consented to performing the EEG recording. The first session of EEG recordings was conducted upon admission, and the second session was accomplished one week after PPIs treatment. Six participants were excluded for poor quality EEG signals. The schematic of experiment two is shown in Figure 1B.

2.2. Resting-State EEG Recording

To evaluate the cortical features of patient with cirrhosis, resting-state EEG recordings were conducted as previously described [15]. The EEG signal was recorded in one quiet, temperature-controlled, and electrically shielded office. Participants were required to remain salient and awake during the EEG recording with eyes closed. One 16-channel bio-sensor (Cyton & Daisy, OpenBCI, Brooklyn, NY, USA) was used for the acquisition of data, which was connected to one electrode cap. The sampling rate of the EEG collection process was 128 Hz, and the impedance of each recording channel was kept below 10 KΩ to guarantee the quality of the EEG signal. The location of recording site and its region of interest is shown in Table 2. The Cz channel was selected as the reference electrode, and the Fpz channel was selected for the ground electrode.

Table 2. Definition of recording site of the EEG.

ROI	Channel
Frontal site	FP_1, FP_2, F_3, F_4, F_7, F_8
Central site	C_3, C_4
Parietal site	P_3, P_4, P_7, P_8
Occipital site	O_1, O_2
Temporal site	T_7, T_8

ROI: Region of interest.

2.3. EEG Signal Processing

The raw EEG data were restored by the OpenBCI Graphical User Interface and then extracted for further processing with the MATLAB 2021 software (R2018b, MathWorks, Natick, MA, USA). Offline EEG data preprocessing was accomplished by using the open-source EEGLAB toolbox [16]. One independent researcher (L.Z.) manually examined EEG raw traces to reject the artifacts and malfunctioning channels. Consequently, the continuous EEG data were filtered with one band-pass filter between 1 and 45 Hz and segmented into consecutive 2 s epochs. We also rejected the epochs with amplitudes over ±80 uV. Independent component analyses were then used to identify and rule out eye movement artifacts. This was followed by the collection of fifty artifact-free segments for the generation of datasets for quantitative analyses. To capture the cortical signature of potential HE patients, fast Fourier transforms were applied to calculate the spectrogram with the "spectopo.m" function script in EEGLAB. Five physiological sub-bands were then determined, including δ (delta, 0.5–4.0 Hz), θ (theta, 4.0–8.0 Hz), α (alpha, 8.0–13.0 Hz), β (beta, 13.0–30.0 Hz), and γ (gamma, 30.0–45.0 Hz).

2.4. Statistics

Data were presented with mean ± standard deviation, and the estimated risk was provided as odds ratios (ORs) with 95% confidence intervals (CIs). To assess the normality of data, Shapiro–Wilk tests were used. The chi-squared test or Fisher's exact test were applied when comparing the categorical data, and Student's t-test or Mann–Whitney U test were considered for continuous variables. To identify the independent risk factors of secondary HE, logistic regression analyses were performed using the variables, with a p value of less than 0.05 between the HE and non-HE groups. The spectral power density of each channel was calculated by averaging the data across epochs for each patient. Statistical analyses were conducted by the SPSS software (Version 26.0, Chicago, IL, USA). A p value of less than 0.05 was considered statistically significant.

3. Results

3.1. Comparison of Clinical Data between HE and Non-HE Cohort

About 28.5% (74 out of 260) of cirrhosis patients developed the secondary HE during hospitalization in this study. In the HE subgroup, almost eighty percent of participants were males, and 69.9% for the non-HE cohort. The white cell and neutrophil counts were significantly higher in the HE sub-group. The HE population presented generalized and worsened hepatic functions, as demonstrated by the lower platelet count and albumin and increased total bilirubin. In addition, significantly lower prothrombin activities and greater international normalized ratios may reveal the worsened dysfunction of coagulation in the HE cohort. The severity of liver diseases significantly increased in the HE cohort, as assessed by the Child–Pugh and MELD scores. Less PPIs (76.3%) were administrated in the non-HE sub-group, and 95.9% were administrated for the HE group. However, we did not observe significant differences in etiologies between two cohorts. The clinical data are provided in Table 3.

Table 3. Clinical manifestations and laboratory results at admission.

	HE (n = 74)	Non-HE (n = 186)	p Value
Sex, male, n (%)	59 (79.7)	130 (69.9)	0.071
Age (years)	56.65 ± 10.94	55.13 ± 12.58	0.583
WBC ($\times 10^9$)	7.15 ± 4.82	5.04 ± 3.12	0.000 *
Hemoglobin (g/L)	103.93 ± 25.39	113.99 ± 22.64	0.002 *
Platelet ($\times 10^9$)	91.76 ± 69.55	86.07 ± 57.25	0.678
Neutrophils ($\times 10^9$)	5.31 ± 4.19	3.57 ± 2.83	0.000 *
ALT (U/L)	211.01 ± 532.61	210.55 ± 787.61	0.884
AST (U/L)	218.23 ± 456.52	242.06 ± 1138.16	0.439
TB (umol/L)	147.49 ± 145.90	100.74 ± 117.73	0.011 *
AKP (IU/L)	194.79 ± 170.60	181.28 ± 159.67	0.452
γ-GT (U/L)	111.73 ± 133.36	166.29 ± 280.14	0.557
Albumin (g/L)	26.31 ± 5.44	29.42 ± 6.18	0.000 *
BUN (mmol/L)	8.72 ± 5.44	6.26 ± 4.00	0.000 *
Creatinine(umol/L)	102.03 ± 62.74	91.22 ± 109.09	0.010 *
CRP (mg/L)	30.67 ± 43.54	20.84 ± 25.74	0.085
K^+ (mmol/L)	3.97 ± 0.65	3.80 ± 0.54	0.029 *
Na^+ (mmol/L)	136.21 ± 6.24	138.00 ± 3.83	0.080
PTA (%)	45.60 ± 17.14	57.85 ± 16.97	0.000 *
INR	1.80 ± 0.96	1.42 ± 0.32	0.000 *
Child, n (A/B/C)	0/16/58	21/113/52	0.000 *
MELD Scores	21.81 ± 7.91	16.47 ± 6.12	0.000 *
PPIs (%)	71 (95.95%)	142 (76.34%)	0.000 *
Pathogeny			0.507
Hepatitis B, n (%)	41 (55.41%)	111 (59.14%)	
Hepatitis C, n (%)	3 (4.05%)	10 (5.38%)	
Alcoholic liver, n (%)	15 (20.27%)	22 (11.83%)	
Hepatocellular carcinoma, n (%)	5 (6.76%)	18 (9.68%)	
others, n (%)	10 (13.51%)	25 (13.44%)	

WBC, white blood cell; ALT, glutamic pyruvic transaminase; AST, glutamic oxaloacetic transaminase; AKP, alkaline phosphatase; γ-GT, γ-glutamyl transpeptidase; BUN, blood urea nitrogen; CRP, C-reactive protein; TB, total bilirubin; PTA, prothrombin time activity; INR, international standard ratio; MELD, model for end stage liver disease; PPIs, proton pump inhibitors. * ($p < 0.05$) indicates that there is a statistical difference.

3.2. Risk Factor Associated with the Development of Secondary HE

In the univariate analysis, multiple variables were associated with the incidence of secondary HE in hospitalized patients, including white blood cell, hemoglobin, neutrophils, total bilirubin, albumin, blood urea nitrogen, potassium, prothrombin time activity, international standard ratio, MELD scoring, and PPIs application. This was followed by the multiple stepwise logistic regression analysis, which identified that white blood cell (OR = 1.972, 95%CIs 1.299–2.993), hemoglobin (OR = 0.978, 95%CIs 0.963–0.992), neutrophils (OR = 0.505, 95%CIs 0.317–0.805), prothrombin time activity (OR = 0.955, 95%CIs 0.936–0.975), blood urea nitrogen, (OR = 1.104, 95%CIs 1.018–1.198), and PPIs usage (OR = 7.867, 95%CIs 2.166–28.575) independently associated with the development of secondary HE (Table 4).

Table 4. Association between the development of HE and risk factors.

Covariates	Not Adjusted OR (95% CIs)	*p* Value	Adjusted OR (95% CIs)	*p* Value
WBC	1.155 (1.068–1.248)	<0.001	1.972 (1.299–2.993)	0.001
Neutrophils	1.161 (1.064–1.266)	0.001	0.505 (0.317–0.805)	0.004
Hemoglobin	0.982 (0.970–0.994)	0.003	0.978 (0.963–0.992)	0.003
PPIs	7.333 (2.201–24.438)	0.001	7.867 (2.166–28.575)	0.002
PTA	0.958 (0.941–0.975)	<0.001	0.955 (0.936–0.975)	<0.001
BUN	1.116 (1.052–1.185)	<0.001	1.104 (1.018–1.198)	0.017

WBC, white blood cell; PPIs, proton pump inhibitors; PTA, prothrombin time activity; BUN, blood urea nitrogen.

3.3. Comparison of EEG Patterns between HE and Non-HE Patients Treated with PPIs

A total of 18 cirrhosis patients who were scheduled to receive the standard PPI therapy (more than 1 week) consented to take the resting EEG recording. Six of them were excluded for further analyses for bad EEG signals. About 66.7% (8 out of 12) of these patients were diagnosed with HE after PPI treatments, and the baseline EEG data were recorded upon admission (Figure 2A,C). Infection may result in the development of HE, pneumonia was found in four HE cases and four with peritonitis, respectively. All the HE participants were classified into minimal HE according to the disease severity criteria (Table 1). In contrast, four patients who underwent baseline EEG recordings and PPI therapy (Figure 2B,D) did not present HE symptoms during hospitalization.

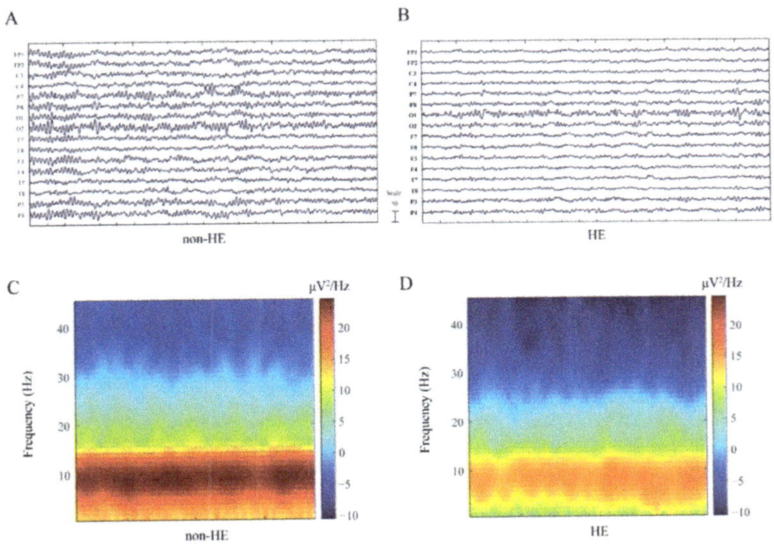

Figure 2. Comparison of EEG signal between non-HE and HE patients who received PPIs treatment. (**A**) Representative resting-state EEG traces in non-HE cohort, and (**B**) one with HE, respectively. (**C**,**D**) Comparison of spectrogram at distinct neurological condition (non-HE versus. HE).

3.4. Alpha Oscillatory Activity Decreased in HE Candidates before PPI Therapy

Spectral analyses were then performed to capture the cortical signature of patients who received PPI treatments. The grand average spectral power significantly decreased in the HE sub-group at the sub-band of the alpha rhythm (Figure 3A,B). To detect the potential source of distinct cortical oscillations, we compared the spectral power of alpha activities at different brain regions, as shown in Table.2. Likely, only alpha oscillations were significantly enhanced across the frontal, central, parietal, and occipital sites (Figure 3C–F). No statistical significance with respect to spectral power densities was found in the temporal region (Figure 3G).

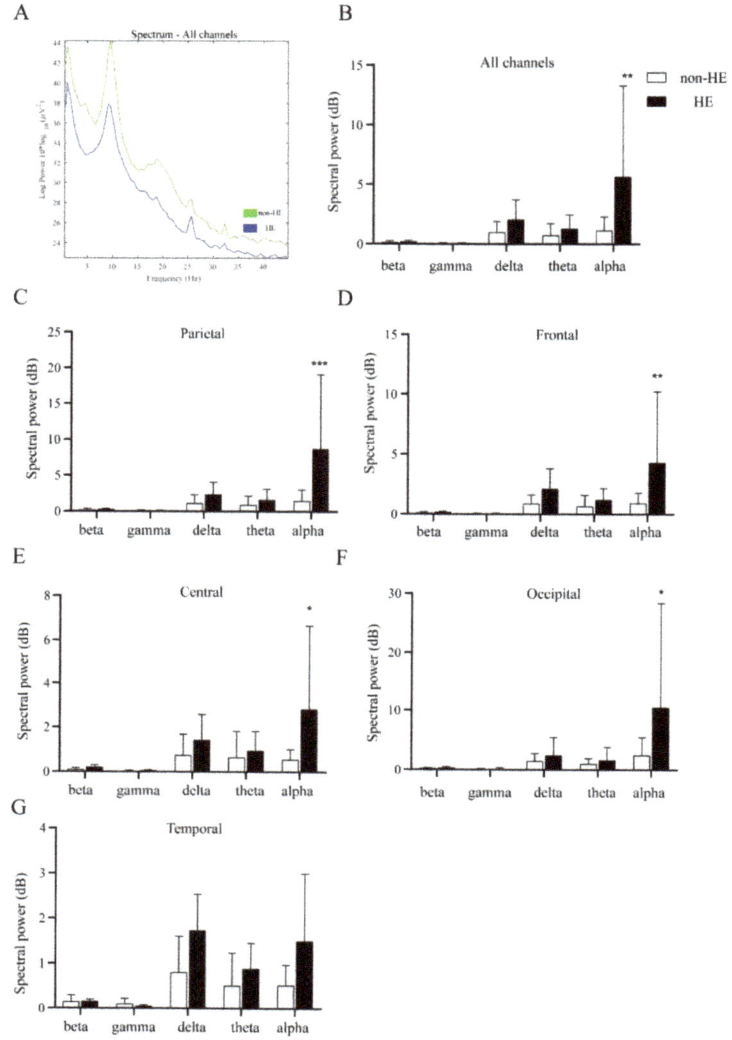

Figure 3. Reduction of alpha oscillations in the HE patients treated with PPIs. (**A**) Grand average spectral power was compared between non-HE and HE patients, (**B**) significant reduced alpha neural oscillation was associated with the HE development in cirrhosis patients under PPIs therapy. (**C–F**) Suppression of cortical alpha activity was detected in the parietal, frontal, central, and occipital, but NOT in the temporal region (**G**). A repeated-measures two-way ANOVA with post hoc Bonferroni tests. * $p < 0.05$, ** $p < 0.01$, *** $p < 0.001$.

4. Discussion

Cirrhosis is one late-stage hepatic disease caused by multiple etiologies, including viral infection, fatty liver, autoimmune, chronic biliary, and cardiovascular disease [17]. Given its increasing prevalence in recent years [18], initiatives to prevent its progress and the severe comorbidity are needed, among which the HE remains one common yet debilitating complication in the cirrhosis population. Thus, the early recognition of HE is key to improving the clinical outcomes for patients with advanced liver disease, especially for those treated with multiple medications, resulting in potential liver or neurological damage. In this study, we focused on the risk factor of secondary HE in the hospitalized population and prospectively examined the cortical signatures of susceptible HE patients with the non-invasive EEG recording method.

The estimated incidence of decompensated cirrhosis was about 34% in the newly diagnosed cirrhosis population, and more than half may suffer HE [19,20]. About 28.5% patients were diagnosed with secondary HE during hospitalization. The exclusion criteria of severe co-morbidity and trans-jugular intrahepatic portosystemic shunt cases may contribute to the relatively low rate of HE in this study [21]. In addition, the major etiology of cirrhosis was associated with hepatitis in more than half of the patients, and about 20% for alcohol-related cirrhosis in HE sub-group, which serves as a strong predictor of HE in cirrhosis patients [3].

Despite the etiologies, multiple risk factors were also considered to be related with the development of HE, including age, bilirubin, INR, creatinine, sodium, HE grading, presence of portal hypertension, minimal HE, and medications (PPIs, opiates, GABAergics, and benzodiazepines) [3,22,23]. This is consistent with our finding in this study that higher risks were associated with the usage of PPIs during hospitalization. However, the mechanism underlying the neurological dysfunction induced by PPIs remains very uncertain.

It is well known that the elevation of blood ammonia participates in the development of HE [24], of which the metabolism can be regulated by the intestinal microbiota directly or indirectly [25]. The application of PPIs can change the pH of digestive system, resulting in an unbalanced microenvironment for the intestinal microbiota [26,27]. Furthermore, the small intestinal bacterial overgrowth can also be induced directly by targeting the proton pump of the bacteria and fungi [26], which is associated with the bacterial translocation and HE development.

The early recognition of HE candidates in liver cirrhosis is essential for preventing HE and for improving clinical outcomes. However, identifying these patients at the early stages of neurological impairments remains challenging, such as minimal HE or covert HE, mainly due to the lack of clinically appreciable symptoms [28,29]. Several tools can be applied to assess the mild changes in metal conditions [30,31], which may be costly and hard to apply in clinical practices [29]. Alternatively, the non-invasive EEG recoding method has been routinely used in the diagnosis of neurological disorders, including epilepsy, autism spectrum disorders, and Alzheimer's disease [10,11]. More recently, the application of its usage in the diagnosis of overt HE may provide us with an alternative and feasible approach for distinguishing the mild cases before potentially adverse interventions, such as PPI treatments in this study.

In the EEG experiment, eight cases (66%) were diagnosed with HE after one-week of PPI therapy, and they were all classified into minimal HE. The baseline EEG was performed at admission and we found significant decreasing spectral power densities of the alpha oscillations in the HE sub-group. Our preliminary evidence may reveal one possible link between cortical oscillatory activities and the HE's development during PPI applications. Further studies with large sample sizes are needed to confirm the clinical efficiency of EEGs in the prediction of HE or minimal HE under PPI treatments. Despite PPI interventions, our data were consistent with previous findings that the disturbance of alpha oscillations is captured at the initial stage of HE [12,32].

It is well known that alpha waves play important roles in cognitive functions and dominate cortical activities during quiet wakefulness [33]. In addition, the reduction in alpha oscillations is associated with certain forms of neurological disorders, such as dementia [34]. In addition to the characteristic features of EEG patterns, the alpha oscillation may also serve as a target of neuromodulation for treating major depressive disorders and attention-deficit hyperactivity disorders [35–37]. Thus, we think that applying this index in future studies will be promising for examining its role in the identification of HE or minimal HE, or it can be a potential therapeutic target for mental dysfunctions in cirrhosis patients who take PPI treatments.

Currently, the potential mechanism underlying the abnormal rhythm of cortical oscillations caused by distinct drug usage remains unknown. For example, characteristic increasing beta frequencies were observed after the administration of benzodiazepines [38,39], which may induce EEG synchronizations and slow wave sleep to exert hypnogenic action at the level of the lower brain stem [40]. In contrast, alpha oscillatory activity has been modulated by multiple pharmacological agents via GABAergic, glutamatergic, cholinergic, and serotonergic receptors in the cortex and thalamus [41]. Recent evidence demonstrated that PPIs used against the core-cholinergic enzyme are responsible for biosynthesis of acetylcholine and contribute to the development of cognitive impairments [42]. Given the permeation kinetics via the blood–brain barrier [43], we assume that PPIs may regulate the concentration of acetylcholine and/or other neurotransmitters in the central nervous system, resulting in an altered phenotype with respect to alpha brain activities.

There were several limitations in this study. First, the main limitation of this study originates from the small sample size used in the EEG experiment, as well as the potential bias during patient selection. Thus, we may not conclude that the cortical patterns of alpha activities are generally caused by PPI treatments, but there may be one potential link between the brain function and medical therapy. Secondly, the application of PPIs may not be the only at-risk medication in cirrhosis; others such as benzodiazepines, opiates, and gamma aminobutyric acid may also contribute to the development of secondary HE. It is necessary to investigate the electrophysiological effects related with other commonly used drugs.

5. Conclusions

In this study, we evaluated the potential risk of HE development in cirrhosis patients. Multiple risk factors were independently associated with secondary HE in hospitalized patient with liver cirrhosis, including PPI usage, white blood cell and neutrophil counts, hemoglobin, prothrombin time activity, and blood urea nitrogen. Thus, our findings supported the susceptibility of secondary HE during PPI management. Furthermore, in the EEG experiment, we found one potential cortical mechanism underlying this neurological disease, is the suppression of alpha oscillations of the brain.

Author Contributions: Conceptualization, P.Z., L.Z., G.G. and H.Z.; methodology, P.Z., L.Z., G.G. and H.Z.; software, L.Z., L.C., Z.Z., R.H. and H.Z.; validation, P.Z., L.Z., L.C., Z.Z., R.H., G.G. and Z.Z.; formal analysis, L.Z.; investigation, P.Z., L.Z., G.G. and H.Z.; resources, P.Z., L.Z., G.G. and H.Z.; data curation, L.Z. and P.Z.; writing—original draft preparation, L.Z. and H.Z.; writing—review and editing, L.Z. and H.Z.; visualization, L.Z. and H.Z.; supervision, H.Z.; project administration, H.Z.; funding acquisition, P.Z. and H.Z. All authors have read and agreed to the published version of the manuscript.

Funding: This research was funded by National Natural Science Foundation of China, (81901146 and 82271259 to H.Z.), Excellent Youth Foundation of Hunan Scientific Committee (2021JJ20091), Key Laboratory of Hunan Province grants (2018TP1009 to H.Z.), and Huizhiyucai Project of the Third Xiangya Hospital, Central South University.

Institutional Review Board Statement: The study was performed under the guidance of the Helsinki Declaration. The study was approved by the Ethics Committee of The Third Xiangya Hospital, Central South University, China (NO.222128). The study was registered at chictr.org.cn (ChiCTR2200061590).

Informed Consent Statement: The informed consent is waived in the first experiment due to the respective design. Informed consent was obtained from all subjects involved in the EEG study.

Data Availability Statement: The data presented in this study are available on request from the corresponding author. The data are not publicly available due to privacy and ethical reasons.

Conflicts of Interest: The authors declare no conflict of interest.

References

1. Li, M.; Wang, Z.Q.; Zhang, L.; Zheng, H.; Liu, D.W.; Zhou, M.G. Burden of Cirrhosis and Other Chronic Liver Diseases Caused by Specific Etiologies in China, 1990–2016: Findings from the Global Burden of Disease Study 2016. *Biomed. Environ. Sci.* **2020**, *33*, 1–10. [PubMed]
2. Nusrat, S.; Khan, M.S.; Fazili, J.; Madhoun, M.F. Cirrhosis and its complications: Evidence based treatment. *World J. Gastroenterol.* **2014**, *20*, 5442–5460. [CrossRef]

3. Tapper, E.B.; Henderson, J.B.; Parikh, N.D.; Ioannou, G.N.; Lok, A.S. Incidence of and Risk Factors for Hepatic Encephalopathy in a Population-Based Cohort of Americans with Cirrhosis. *Hepatol. Commun.* **2019**, *3*, 1510–1519. [CrossRef] [PubMed]
4. Tantai, X.X.; Yang, L.B.; Wei, Z.C.; Xiao, C.L.; Chen, L.R.; Wang, J.H.; Liu, N. Association of proton pump inhibitors with risk of hepatic encephalopathy in advanced liver disease: A meta-analysis. *World J. Gastroenterol.* **2019**, *25*, 2683–2698. [CrossRef] [PubMed]
5. Kalaitzakis, E.; Björnsson, E. Inadequate use of proton-pump inhibitors in patients with liver cirrhosis. *Eur. J. Gastroenterol. Hepatol.* **2008**, *20*, 512–518. [CrossRef]
6. Nardelli, S.; Gioia, S.; Ridola, L.; Farcomeni, A.; Merli, M.; Riggio, O. Proton Pump Inhibitors Are Associated with Minimal and Overt Hepatic Encephalopathy and Increased Mortality in Patients with Cirrhosis. *Hepatology* **2019**, *70*, 640–649. [CrossRef]
7. Zhu, J.; Qi, X.; Yu, H.; Yoshida, E.M.; Mendez-Sanchez, N.; Zhang, X.; Wang, R.; Deng, H.; Li, J.; Han, D.; et al. Association of proton pump inhibitors with the risk of hepatic encephalopathy during hospitalization for liver cirrhosis. *United Eur. Gastroenterol. J.* **2018**, *6*, 1179–1187. [CrossRef]
8. Dam, G.; Vilstrup, H.; Watson, H.; Jepsen, P. Proton pump inhibitors as a risk factor for hepatic encephalopathy and spontaneous bacterial peritonitis in patients with cirrhosis with ascites. *Hepatology* **2016**, *64*, 1265–1272. [CrossRef]
9. Wu, X.; Lv, X.F.; Zhang, Y.L.; Wu, H.W.; Cai, P.Q.; Qiu, Y.W.; Zhang, X.L.; Jiang, G.H. Cortical signature of patients with HBV-related cirrhosis without overt hepatic encephalopathy: A morphometric analysis. *Front. Neuroanat.* **2015**, *9*, 82. [CrossRef]
10. Alturki, F.A.; AlSharabi, K.; Abdurraqeeb, A.M.; Aljalal, M. EEG Signal Analysis for Diagnosing Neurological Disorders Using Discrete Wavelet Transform and Intelligent Techniques. *Sensors* **2020**, *20*, 2505. [CrossRef]
11. Smith, S.J. EEG in neurological conditions other than epilepsy: When does it help, what does it add? *J. Neurol. Neurosurg. Psychiatry* **2005**, *76* (Suppl. S2), ii8–ii12. [CrossRef] [PubMed]
12. Amodio, P.; Montagnese, S. Clinical neurophysiology of hepatic encephalopathy. *J. Clin. Exp. Hepatol.* **2015**, *5* (Suppl. S1), S60–S68. [CrossRef] [PubMed]
13. Amodio, P.; Del Piccolo, F.; Petteno, E. Prevalence and prognostic value of quantified electroencephalogram (EEG) alterations in cirrhotic patients. *J. Hepatol.* **2001**, *35*, 37–45. [CrossRef] [PubMed]
14. Xu, X.Y.; Ding, H.G.; Li, W.G.; Jia, J.D.; Wei, L.; Duan, Z.P.; Liu, L.Y.; Ling-Hu, E.Q.; Zhuang, H.; Chinese Society of Hepatology. Chinese guidelines on management of hepatic encephalopathy in cirrhosis. *World J. Gastroenterol.* **2019**, *25*, 5403–5422. [CrossRef] [PubMed]
15. Zhou, H.; Han, R.; Chen, L.; Zhang, Z.; Zhang, X.; Wang, J.; Liu, Z.; Huang, D. Effect of Implantable Electrical Nerve Stimulation on Cortical Dynamics in Patients with Herpes Zoster-Related Pain: A Prospective Pilot Study. *Front. Bioeng. Biotechnol.* **2022**, *10*, 862353. [CrossRef] [PubMed]
16. Delorme, A.; Makeig, S. EEGLAB: An open source toolbox for analysis of single-trial EEG dynamics including independent component analysis. *J. Neurosci. Methods* **2004**, *134*, 9–21. [CrossRef]
17. Wiegand, J.; Berg, T. The etiology, diagnosis and prevention of liver cirrhosis: Part 1 of a series on liver cirrhosis. *Dtsch. Arztebl. Int.* **2013**, *110*, 85–91.
18. Sharma, A.; Nagalli, S. Chronic Liver Disease. In *StatPearls*; StatPearls Publishing: Treasure Island, FL, USA, 2022.
19. Orman, E.S.; Roberts, A.; Ghabril, M.; Nephew, L.; Desai, A.P.; Patidar, K.; Chalasani, N. Trends in Characteristics, Mortality, and Other Outcomes of Patients with Newly Diagnosed Cirrhosis. *JAMA Netw. Open* **2019**, *2*, e196412. [CrossRef]
20. Rahimi, R.S.; Brown, K.A.; Flamm, S.L.; Brown, R.S., Jr. Overt Hepatic Encephalopathy: Current Pharmacologic Treatments and Improving Clinical Outcomes. *Am. J. Med.* **2021**, *134*, 1330–1338. [CrossRef]
21. Poordad, F.F. Review article: The burden of hepatic encephalopathy. *Aliment. Pharmacol. Ther.* **2007**, *25* (Suppl. S1), 3–9. [CrossRef]
22. Nardelli, S.; Riggio, O.; Gioia, S.; Merli, M.; Spagnoli, A.; di Martino, M.; Pelle, G.; Ridola, L. Risk factors for hepatic encephalopathy and mortality in cirrhosis: The role of cognitive impairment, muscle alterations and shunts. *Dig. Liver. Dis.* **2022**, *54*, 1060–1065. [CrossRef] [PubMed]
23. Cordoba, J.; Ventura-Cots, M.; Simón-Talero, M.; Amorós, À.; Pavesi, M.; Vilstrup, H.; Angeli, P.; Domenicali, M.; Ginés, P.; Bernardi, M.; et al. Characteristics, risk factors, and mortality of cirrhotic patients hospitalized for hepatic encephalopathy with and without acute-on-chronic liver failure (ACLF). *J. Hepatol.* **2014**, *60*, 275–281. [CrossRef] [PubMed]
24. Dasani, B.M.; Sigal, S.H.; Lieber, C.S. Analysis of risk factors for chronic hepatic encephalopathy: The role of Helicobacter pylori infection. *Am. J. Gastroenterol.* **1998**, *93*, 726–731. [CrossRef] [PubMed]
25. Chen, Z.; Ruan, J.; Li, D.; Wang, M.; Han, Z.; Qiu, W.; Wu, G. The Role of Intestinal Bacteria and Gut-Brain Axis in Hepatic Encephalopathy. *Front. Cell Infect. Microbiol.* **2021**, *10*, 595759. [CrossRef]
26. Vesper, B.J.; Jawdi, A.; Altman, K.W.; Haines, G.K., III; Tao, L.; Radosevich, J.A. The effect of proton pump inhibitors on the human microbiota. *Curr. Drug Metab.* **2009**, *10*, 84–89. [CrossRef]
27. Tsai, C.F.; Chen, M.H.; Wang, Y.P.; Chu, C.J.; Huang, Y.H.; Lin, H.C.; Hou, M.C.; Lee, F.Y.; Su, T.P.; Lu, C.L. Proton Pump Inhibitors Increase Risk for Hepatic Encephalopathy in Patients with Cirrhosis in A Population Study. *Gastroenterology* **2017**, *152*, 134–141. [CrossRef]
28. Yanny, B.; Winters, A.; Boutros, S.; Saab, S. Hepatic Encephalopathy Challenges, Burden, and Diagnostic and Therapeutic Approach. *Clin. Liver. Dis.* **2019**, *23*, 607–623. [CrossRef]
29. Ferenci, P. Diagnosis of minimal hepatic encephalopathy: Still a challenge. *Gut* **2013**, *62*, 1394. [CrossRef]

30. Bajaj, J.S.; Schubert, C.M.; Heuman, D.M.; Wade, J.B.; Gibson, D.P.; Topaz, A.; Saeian, K.; Hafeezullah, M.; Bell, D.E.; Sterling, R.K.; et al. Persistence of cognitive impairment after resolution of overt hepatic encephalopathy. *Gastroenterology* **2010**, *138*, 2332–2340. [CrossRef]
31. Weissenborn, K.; Rückert, N.; Hecker, H.; Manns, M.P. The number connection tests A and B: Interindividual variability and use for the assessment of early hepatic encephalopathy. *J. Hepatol.* **1998**, *28*, 646–653. [CrossRef]
32. Montagnese, S.; Jackson, C.; Morgan, M.Y. Spatio-temporal decomposition of the electroencephalogram in patients with cirrhosis. *J. Hepatol.* **2007**, *46*, 447–458. [CrossRef]
33. Halgren, M.; Ulbert, I.; Bastuji, H.; Fabó, D.; Erőss, L.; Rey, M.; Devinsky, O.; Doyle, K.W.; Mak-McCully, R.; Halgren, E. The generation and propagation of the human alpha rhythm. *Proc. Natl. Acad. Sci. USA* **2019**, *116*, 23772–23782. [CrossRef]
34. Ranasinghe, K.G.; Petersen, C.; Kudo, K.; Mizuiri, D.; Rankin, K.P.; Rabinovici, G.D.; Gorno-Tempini, M.L.; Seeley, W.W.; Spina, S.; Miller, B.L.; et al. Reduced synchrony in alpha oscillations during life predicts post mortem neurofibrillary tangle density in early-onset and atypical Alzheimer's disease. *Alzheimer's Dement.* **2021**, *17*, 2009–2019. [CrossRef]
35. Alexander, M.L.; Alagapan, S.; Lugo, C.E.; Mellin, J.M.; Lustenberger, C.; Rubinow, D.R.; Fröhlich, F. Double-blind, randomized pilot clinical trial targeting alpha oscillations with transcranial alternating current stimulation (tACS) for the treatment of major depressive disorder (MDD). *Transl. Psychiatry* **2019**, *9*, 106. [CrossRef]
36. Deiber, M.P.; Hasler, R.; Colin, J.; Dayer, A.; Aubry, J.M.; Baggio, S.; Perrouda, N.; Ros, T. Linking alpha oscillations, attention and inhibitory control in adult ADHD with EEG neurofeedback. *Neuroimage Clin.* **2020**, *25*, 102145. [CrossRef]
37. Riddle, J.; Alexander, M.L.; Schiller, C.E.; Rubinow, D.R.; Frohlich, F. Reduction in Left Frontal Alpha Oscillations by Transcranial Alternating Current Stimulation in Major Depressive Disorder Is Context Dependent in a Randomized Clinical Trial. *Biol. Psychiatry Cogn. Neurosci. Neuroimaging* **2022**, *7*, 302–311. [CrossRef]
38. van Lier, H.; Drinkenburg, W.H.; van Eeten, Y.J.; Coenen, A.M. Effects of diazepam and zolpidem on EEG beta frequencies are behavior-specific in rats. *Neuropharmacology* **2004**, *47*, 163–174. [CrossRef]
39. Feinberg, I.; Maloney, T.; Campbell, I.G. Effects of hypnotics on the sleep EEG of healthy young adults: New data and psychopharmacologic implications. *J. Psychiatr. Res.* **2000**, *34*, 423–438. [CrossRef]
40. Mariotti, M.; Ongini, E. Differential effects of benzodiazepines on EEG activity and hypnogenic mechanisms of the brain stem in cats. *Arch. Int. Pharmacodyn. Ther.* **1983**, *264*, 203–219. [PubMed]
41. Lozano-Soldevilla, D. On the Physiological Modulation and Potential Mechanisms Underlying Parieto-Occipital Alpha Oscillations. *Front. Comput. Neurosci.* **2018**, *12*, 23. [CrossRef] [PubMed]
42. Kumar, R.; Kumar, A.; Nordberg, A.; Långström, B.; Darreh-Shori, T. Proton pump inhibitors act with unprecedented potencies as inhibitors of the acetylcholine biosynthesizing enzyme-A plausible missing link for their association with incidence of dementia. *Alzheimer's Dement.* **2020**, *16*, 1031–1042. [CrossRef] [PubMed]
43. Ortiz-Guerrero, G.; Amador-Muñoz, D.; Calderón-Ospina, C.A.; López-Fuentes, D.; Nava Mesa, M.O. Proton Pump Inhibitors and Dementia: Physiopathological Mechanisms and Clinical Consequences. *Neural Plast.* **2018**, *2018*, 5257285. [CrossRef]

MDPI AG
Grosspeteranlage 5
4052 Basel
Switzerland
Tel.: +41 61 683 77 34

Biomedicines Editorial Office
E-mail: biomedicines@mdpi.com
www.mdpi.com/journal/biomedicines

www.ingramcontent.com/pod-product-compliance
Lightning Source LLC
Chambersburg PA
CBHW061629210926
51850CB00009B/2479
* 9 7 8 3 7 2 5 8 1 8 1 9 8 *